Interpreting and Responding
to Classroom Behaviors

ALSO BY MICHAEL O. WEINER AND
LES PAUL GALLO-SILVER

The Complete Father: Essential Concepts and Archetypes
(McFarland, 2019)

Interpreting and Responding to Classroom Behaviors

A Guide for Early Childhood Educators

Michael O. Weiner,
Les Paul Gallo-Silver
and Tal D. Lucas

McFarland & Company, Inc., Publishers
Jefferson, North Carolina

This book has undergone peer review.

LIBRARY OF CONGRESS CATALOGUING-IN-PUBLICATION DATA

Names: Weiner, Michael O., author. | Gallo-Silver, Les Paul, author. | Lucas, Tal D., 1974– author.
Title: Interpreting and responding to classroom behaviors : a guide for early childhood educators / Michael O. Weiner, Les Paul Gallo-Silver and Tal D. Lucas.
Description: Jefferson, North Carolina : McFarland & Company, Inc., Publishers, 2021. | Includes bibliographical references and index.
Identifiers: LCCN 2021022393 | ISBN 9781476673752 (paperback : acid free paper) ∞
ISBN 9781476642734 (ebook)
Subjects: LCSH: Behavior modification. | Early childhood education. | Classroom management. | BISAC: EDUCATION / Early Childhood (incl. Preschool & Kindergarten)
Classification: LCC LB1060.2 .W46 2021 | DDC 370.15/28—dc23
LC record available at https://lccn.loc.gov/2021022393

BRITISH LIBRARY CATALOGUING DATA ARE AVAILABLE

**ISBN (print) 978-1-4766-7375-2
ISBN (ebook) 978-1-4766-4273-4**

© 2021 Michael O. Weiner, Les Paul Gallo-Silver and Tal D. Lucas. All rights reserved

No part of this book may be reproduced or transmitted in any form or by any means, electronic or mechanical, including photocopying or recording, or by any information storage and retrieval system, without permission in writing from the publisher.

Front cover photograph © 2021 Shutterstock / iofoto

Printed in the United States of America

*McFarland & Company, Inc., Publishers
Box 611, Jefferson, North Carolina 28640
www.mcfarlandpub.com*

Michael O. Weiner:
To my wife and children, Allison, Ben, Ellie and Nat,
who, as always, are my world; and
Ms. Rose, one of the first teachers who showed me
how effectively the world of child psychology could be applied
to the practice of early childhood education.

Les Paul Gallo-Silver:
To the many significant teachers in my life especially my wife,
Joan Gallo-Silver, who taught me about love and life.

Tal D. Lucas:
To Dan, Noa and Tess, who are always my guinea pigs;
Thank you for your patience.
The Editor-in-Chief who lives in my house and who has always
made sure my commas and prepositions are used correctly;
Thank you for your guidance.
J, my friend for over 30 years, whose knowledge and insight
about children and willingness to share them have made me
a better teacher and a better person.
Thank you for your friendship.
All of my amazing colleagues over the years,
who have been incredible teachers for me and
have shaped the educator I am today.
Thank you for the journey.
And the hundreds of unique children
with different personalities and behaviors
who have walked through my classroom door over the last 23 years.
I have learned the most from you: what works, what doesn't work,
and what brings out the best in you;
thank you for being you.

Acknowledgments

We would like to express our appreciation for all the early childhood educators with whom we have worked over the years. Their love for and commitment to children, combined with their openness to new ideas, instills a confidence in us that the developmental foundation of our future generations is in excellent hands. They inspired this book and we hope they will find it to be a useful companion to the indispensable work that defines our profession.

Table of Contents

Acknowledgments vi
Preface 1
Introduction 3
List of Figures and Tables 9
List of Challenging Behaviors 12

Part One
A Different View of the Children in Your Classroom

1. Children in the Round: A Holistic Approach to Understanding Children 16
2. Who Needs a Diagnosis, Anyway? Understanding Behavior as Communication 28
3. A Child's Communication Scaffolding 43

Part Two
The Children Communicating in Your Classroom

4. The Child Who Is "Troubling": Loud and Over Reactive 56
5. The Child Who Is "Testing": Loud and Under Reactive 71
6. The Child Who Is "Worrying": Quiet and Over Reactive 85
7. The Child Who Is "Hiding": Quiet and Under Reactive 103

Part Three
Pulling Back the Curtain on Specific Communicative Behaviors

8. A Week-by-Week Guide for Behavior Assessment, Prioritization, and Planning 122
9. Distractibility, Daydreaming, and Attention-Related Issues 129
10. Elopement and "Moving Away"–Related Issues 158
11. Excessive Clowning 182
12. Aggression, Bullying, Fighting, Out-of-Control Temper 196
13. "Hyperactivity" 223

14. Difficulty Observing Personal Space and Other Boundary Problems — 245
15. Not Speaking — 275
16. Toileting Accidents and Toilet-Related Issues — 299
17. Upsetting Artwork, Writings, and Play — 317

Conclusion: Keeping Your Balance — 363
Appendix A: The Troubling Child Worksheet — 371
Appendix B: The Testing Child Worksheet — 373
Appendix C: The Worrying Child Worksheet — 375
Appendix D: The Hiding Child Worksheet — 377
Appendix E: Self-Fulfilling Prophecies — 379
Bibliography — 383
Index — 389

Preface

Prior to each school year, at some point over the summer, teachers receive a list of names. These names make up our classes, the individual children that we will care for, encourage, challenge, and mold over the course of the next 9 to 10 months of the school year. At this moment, maybe we have heard about these children from other teachers, but these are other people's experiences and not our own, and so have limited use. Unless we have had some contact with these children prior to this, they are one-dimensional. Ink on paper. A series of letters that form a recognizable pattern. Interestingly, from these names, we may already start to form thoughts about these individuals: Shaniqua, Leo, Elijah, Hakeem, Billie Jo, Muhammad, or Esmeralda.

Names evoke impressions of ethnicity, race, religion, culture, and many other preconceived notions generated from our own memories and experiences (Neukrug, 2015). Names are important because they are chosen for a reason and communicate something about the individual or individuals who chose them (Alford, 1988). Is it a family name, a relative, a significant place, does it reflect one's faith, is he a junior? That said, although we can know a bit from a child's name, that name is but one small aspect of a whole child. Underneath the name is a mind, a body, a soul that is being shaped and molded by factors of nature and nurture (Ridley, 2003; West & King, 1987). Our application of this idea allows us to understand children by exploring their hidden worlds, by digging under each rock and looking behind each tree.

This book is a work of curiosity, questions, possibilities, and answers about child communication. It is about making inferences, finding clues, and resolving mysteries. It is about the empowering nature of epiphany, after one has been perplexed and puzzled. And, of course, above all, it is a book about teaching, written for teachers in a conversational style to match the interpersonal basis for early childhood education.

We believe one of the strongest aspects of this book is that it is written as a collaborative effort between two professions that take care of children in different ways and believe in the inherent growth potential of each child. We believe there is a kinship between the educators of children and child psychotherapists, in that both see children as mysteries that need to be solved in order to move children forward.

Psychotherapy and teaching require, as a foundational premise, the acute attunement to and awareness of the many ways that people communicate. For child psychotherapists, this is a conscious process. For teachers, it is most often intuitive. Where they can truly come together is in the melding of a psychotherapist's mindful empathic attunement and a deeper understanding of thoughts and feelings with an educator's ability to teach, problem solve, skills build, and critically think.

We believe that a vibrant collaboration between psychology and education is an essential part of our professional mandate to children, their parents, and those professionals who have contact with these families. In this way, we share with each other what we have learned about how young children give us information, what these communications mean, and how best to respond to them. It is for this reason that two child psychotherapists and an early-childhood educator have written this book together; and why we feel that a working bond between teachers and psychotherapists is essential. We are all partners in early education.

Introduction

This book is a mystery book, a whodunit, in the same vein as Sherlock Holmes, Nancy Drew, Peter Falk's Columbo, or Angela Lansbury's Jessica Fletcher. Instead of sifting through clues to find out the "who," this book uses clues to find out the "why." In our book, children are the mysteries—the layered nature and purpose of their feelings, the complexity and nuance of their thoughts, and the underlying symbolic meanings of their behaviors and play. To us, the "why" is intricate and contemplative. It is beyond the "why can't that child sit still?" or the "why does that child bite others?" or the "why does that child cling to me?"

This book explores what the "why" represents—the various levels, ways, and meanings of child communication. It begins with the principle that communication is the essential ingredient in human relationships. It is the material that travels back and forth between individuals and creates the links that allow for every aspect of development. To this end, communication is the essence and foundation of mutuality, empathy, trust, listening, and understanding. Without it, people are left to feel alone, misunderstood, isolated, unheard, and unloved.

Flowing from this theory is the belief that all child behavior, play, and art are communication. They are children's messages of feelings and thoughts and exist on multiple levels, the seen and the unseen, the aware and the unaware. One can observe certain aspects of a communication, the running, the disturbing, the yelling, or the ignoring, but the motivation, the purpose, and the trigger of that communication may be harder to discern. People responsible for children begin the process of interpreting these communications from the earliest moments of life. What does my infant's cry mean? Is she tired? Is he gassy? Is she hungry? It is in the process of discovering the meaning and intent that a communication becomes whole and relationships can grow.

The teacher/child relationship is a crucial element in a child's development of social, cognitive, and creative skills. It is our opinion that teachers are the most significant relationship a child has, as his or her relationship base expands beyond parents and family. Early childhood teachers open up a world of non-familial relationships, a world full of new people, thoughts, and ideas.

To this end, the National Association for the Education of Young Children (NAEYC) describes a high-quality [education] program as providing "a safe, nurturing environment that promotes the physical, social, emotional and cognitive development of young children while responding to the needs of families" (NAEYC, 2020).

Early childhood education research defines several key programmatic elements (see Table I.1).

Table I.1:
NAEYC Key Program Elements

- Low teacher to student ratios and safe environments, which promotes more intimacy between the teacher and the child
- Teacher-parent communication, which enables parents to be an active part of their child's education
- Developmentally appropriate curriculum, which is based on a child's age appropriate tasks and learning styles
- Sufficient teacher training, which includes a focus on pedagogy and developmental psychology

National Association for the Education of Young Children, 2020

Our growing scientific understanding of the developing brain leads to increasing emphasis on the importance of the in-class relationships with teachers as key elements to healthy child development (Schore, 2012; Ahnert, et al., 2013; de Wilde, et al., 2015; Maldonado-Carreno, & Votruba-Drzal, 2011; Rudasill, et al., 2010; Lei, et al., 2016). Using this framework, we want to focus less on the importance of defining the quality of early childhood education as a function of teacher-student ratios, classroom size, physical class environment, and curriculum (although we acknowledge their importance) and more on the crucial nature of advanced, specialized early childhood teacher training that complements NAEYC standards.

Currently, there are state-based standards (competencies) for early education professionals. The core standards of practice and the related domains are defined by each state, as they are for many other professions (American Psychological Association, 2020). The features within each competency are broken down into sub-categories of beginning, intermediate, and advanced in order to address each teacher's individual skill level. Although there is much common ground, there are state-by-state differences in the expectations of early childhood teachers and the knowledge base they need to master. This knowledge base coalesces around these baseline competencies (see Table I.2).

Table I.2:
Core Standards of Practice for Early Childhood Educators

- administration and management of classroom
- child growth and development
- child wellness, health, safety, and nutrition
- diverse populations
- family dynamics and community outreach
- learning environment and curriculum
- observation and assessment techniques
- professionalism and leadership

- special needs
- teacher-student interactions
- understanding and guiding child behavior

National Association for the Education of Young Children, 2020; American Psychological Association, 2020

We weave a thread between all of these competencies, as they affect the individual early childhood teacher, by supporting attempts to understand children in a more complete and precise manner regardless of the nature or purpose of the interaction. By enhancing the skills and awareness of understanding child communication, we hope to strengthen and ground early childhood education pedagogy in a more "in-the-moment" teaching technique, one that focuses on our thoughts and feelings as a way of informing our interactions with all the children in our classes. This is one that becomes both a means of intervention and a model for our more complex and challenging students.

This book highlights communication as a primary function of the early childhood teacher/child relationship. We accomplish this by exploring communication as the glue that creates a mutual, emotional connection between teacher and child. We expand on this by describing and examining early childhood teaching as an interpersonal process. We believe growing an awareness and understanding of what our students are trying to communicate augments both the teaching and the learning experience. In this way, we strive to enrich the professional teaching experience by creating a sense of empowerment, fulfillment, and reward.

Research shows that when a teacher has high regard for a student, that student excels (Hattie, 2009). We believe that this research and its use of the word "regard" describe the same dynamic as Carl Rogers' "unconditional positive regard" (Rodgers, 1951). Rogers conveys the belief that all individuals strive to better themselves and evolve (through both their successes and missteps). We theorize that behind the conclusions of this research data is a hidden world of interactions between teacher and child in which teachers acknowledge and accept their students' difficulties. Children thrive on being understood and valued. This is never more noticeable to them than when they are struggling. The power of this book lies in the confirmation that, as early childhood teachers, we can indeed have a classroom full of children that we "appreciate" based on our participation in and understanding of the hidden or obscured levels of communication between us and our students (Saft & Pianta, 2001; Spilt, et al., 2012a).

There is a fascinating world embedded in the communication of a child's play, art, non-verbal cues, and behavior (Webb, 2007; Webb & Terr, 2016; Axline, 1947; Paley, 2004; Guerrero, et al., 2008, Landreth, 2012; Saracho & Spodek, 1995). It is composed of what we can observe on the surface and what we assess may be lying beneath (Freud & Stratchey, 1990). First developed by Sigmund Freud in 1909 in his case study of "Little Hans," the connecting of unspoken thoughts and feelings to behaviors has been a tenet of child psychotherapy for almost a century (Freud, 1909). "Little Hans" was afraid to leave his house. Freud worked with "Little Hans'" father (not with the son directly) to "interpret" what his son was communicating through his drawings. In his artwork were clues to the child's fears (Freud, 1909).

This knowledge enabled the father to respond empathically and, ultimately, alter his child's behavior. We contend that this skill is not proprietary in nature. No couch or psychotherapy training is required. Most importantly, it is too integral to the understanding of children not to provide it as a tool for early childhood teachers.

Relationships in early childhood have a profound effect on the child who ultimately develops into an adult. We know through recent neurobiological research that attachment alters the inner structures of the brain and that the learning that flows from these relationships, whether it is social, cognitive, or creative, changes the individual (Van Der Kolk, 2014; Noble, et al., 2015; Schore, 2012). The brain of a young child is highly flexible and fluid more so than at any other time in human development (Siegel & Mazabel, 2014). We see this moment as an opportunity and one that can be optimized for success—the child's and our own. Yes, your enjoyment, sense of accomplishment and gratification are important aspects of being an effective early childhood educator.

The goal of this book is not to turn teachers into child therapists, but to open up the world of communication in order to help reach and teach children in positive and meaningful ways. We believe that this requires a melding or merging of educational practice and psychological theory; in other words, developing a working, practical knowledge base of child development principles that can be used at a moment's notice, in the classroom, as a way of supplementing and augmenting teaching. This requires us to revisit and rework the basic psychology concepts that teachers may have run across earlier in their careers or previously in their training. We may even be able to provide some concepts that are new and stimulating. In this book, we will explore a variety of child developmental theorists from the past 75 years (Table I.3).

Our exploration of child psychology will center on those child development theorists who expanded our knowledge base within the social-emotional realm of children—trust and autonomy; ways of relating; the quality of interpersonal connections; self-esteem and self-efficacy; and control and initiative. Many of these theorists will be familiar. What may not be familiar is how to apply these theories in practical ways to help address common classroom situations, problems, and worries. We believe a theory is only worth knowing when we can use it in our daily professional lives.

Table I.3:
Child Developmental Theorists and Their Theories

- Mary Ainsworth & John Bowlby and attachment theory. (Ainsworth, et al; 2014; Bowlby, 1969; 1982; Harlow, 1959; Krumwiede, 2014).
- Stella Chess and Alexander Thomas a child's temperament (Thomas & Chess; 1956; 1977; Chess & Thomas, 1990; 1996).
- Erik Erikson and his concept of developmental crises (Erikson, 1950; 1968).
- Margret Mahler and her concepts of separation and individuation (Mahler, et al., 1975).
- Abraham Maslow and the Hierarchy of Needs (Maslow 1943, 1968; 1971; 2013)
- D. W. Winnicott and his dual concepts of the holding environment and good-enough parenting (Winnicott, 1953; 1963; 1990).

- Anna Freud and her theories around psychological ego defenses in children (Freud, 1966; Freud & Burlingham, 1967).
- Sigmund Freud and his theories on the conscious and the unconscious (Freud; 1914; Freud & Strachey, 1990).
- Robert Regoli and John Hewitt's and others' theories on oppression's deleterious effects on child development (Regoli and Hewitt, 2001; Graff, 2014; Eyerman, 2001; Kingston et al., 2003; Sroufe, et al., 2005; Sonn & Fisher, 2013; Sotero, 2006; Sar, et al., 2013; Quintana & Segura-Herrera 2003).
- Carl Rogers and his theory of unconditional positive regard and warm acceptance (Rogers, 1939; 1951; 1995; Zimring, 2000).

The first and second sections of the book create a theoretical, yet practical, foundation focused on achieving our overall goal—to help us determine the most effective ways of managing behavior "in-the-moment" in our classrooms. We begin by describing children in multi-layered, holistic terms, highlighting school relationships and related dynamics. We explore behavior in terms of the many forms that a child's communication may take in the classroom and the different levels of the communication, including aspects we can observe and the aspects we can only deduce. This recasts behavior as communication and creates a link between what a child does and his or her internal life. With this information in hand, we provide tools to decipher various types of child communication and, more importantly, to increase our sense of competence in developing empathic responses to the messages these communications contain. Finally, we enhance assessment of children's communication style and the various elements that contribute to how children communicate within their environment and to the people in it.

Using the concepts from the first and second sections, the book's third section examines and deconstructs many of the behaviors that our challenging students present in the classroom setting. From elopement to bullying, from "hyperactivity" to mutism, studying child behavior from a variety of angles provides us with an opportunity to explore the varying choices we can make in terms of responding to what and how a child is presenting. We determine that there are many ways to respond and that these options are crucial to individualizing our work with each child and optimizing outcomes.

We start the third section of this book with an acknowledgment that there is often an understandable urgency to resolve issues or change dynamics. To address this, we provide a week by week planning and intervention structure as a way of creating some balance between urgency and theory. We realize that rarely do teachers have the luxury of coping with one problem at a time or taking a patient approach to an intense situation. While we recommend a structured methodology, feel free to pick and choose which sections and chapters you are most interested in or that may provide the possibility of immediate recourse. We assure you there is no need to read our book in any particular order. Any increase in knowledge will benefit the students.

We sincerely hope our book will help make the crucial time that you spend educating and caring for children more gratifying, fulfilling, and empowering.

Developing understanding, empathy, and responsiveness as of way of helping young children to develop a joy of learning, cooperating, and respecting others is essential for the type of world that values children and childhood. After all, this is a main reason we dedicate ourselves to early childhood education in the first place.

List of Figures and Tables

Introduction

Table I.1 NAEYC Key Program Elements	4
Table I.2 Core Standards of Practice for Early Childhood Educators	4
Table I.3 Child Developmental Theorists and Their Theories	6

Chapter 1: Children in the Round: A Holistic Approach to Understanding Children

Figure 1.1 Components of a Child	17
Table 1.1 Erikson Stages of Development	18
Figure 1.2 Maslow's Hierarchy of Needs	22
Table 1.2 General Characteristics of Each Temperament	23
Table 1.3 The Eight Feelings of Childhood Attachment	25

Chapter 2: Who Needs a Diagnosis, Anyway? Understanding Behavior as Communication

Figure 2.1 Holistic Communication	30
Table 2.1 Actions and Manifest Communication	32
Figure 2.2 The Parts of Latent Communication	34
Table 2.2 Connecting Manifest and Possible Latent Communication	36

Chapter 3: A Child's Communication Scaffolding

Figure 3.1 Hierarchy of Holistic Understanding of Behavior	43
Figure 3.2 Communication Scaffolding	44
Table 3.1 Attributes of Child's Temperament	46
Figure 3.3 Temperaments—Internality versus Externality	48
Figure 3.4 Conscious Mind and Under Reactivity versus Over Reactivity	51
Figure 3.5 Child Personas	53
Figure 3.6 Child Personas with Associated Communications and Behaviors	53

Chapter 4: The Child Who Is "Troubling": Loud and Over Reactive

Table 4.1 Self-Fulfilling Prophecy of the Troubling Child	63

Figure 4.1 Continuum of Responses — 65
Table 4.2 Personas and Responses — 66

Chapter 5: The Child Who Is "Testing": Loud and Under Reactive

Table 5.1 Self-Fulfilling Prophecy of the Testing Child — 78
Table 5.2 Personas and Responses — 79
Table 5.3 Matilda's Monday Behavior Chart — 81

Chapter 6: The Child Who Is "Worrying": Quiet and Over Reactive

Figure 6:1 Possible Effects of Adverse Childhood Experiences — 89
Figure 6.2 Self-Portrait with No Face — 91
Figure 6.3 Self-Portrait with Scratched Face — 91
Table 6.1 Types of Introjects — 93
Table 6.2 Self-Fulfilling Prophecy of the Worrying Child — 95
Table 6.3 Personas and Responses — 96
Figure 6.4 Cross-section of Tree as Child Psyche — 99

Chapter 7: The Child Who Is "Hiding": Quiet and Under Reactive

Figure 7.1 Hiding Child's Boundaries versus Neuro-Typical Child's Boundaries — 109
Table 7.1 Self-Fulfilling Prophecy of the Hiding Child — 111
Table 7.2 Personas and Responses — 112
Figure 7.2 Decision Tree — 115
Figure 7.3 Stephanie's Decision Tree — 115
Figure 7.4 Drawing of Mind-Body Connection — 116
Table 7.3 Self-Disclosure versus Transitional Space Use of Self — 118

Chapter 8: A Week-by-Week Guide for Behavior Assessment, Prioritization, and Planning

Table 8.1 Child Persona Tracker — 123
Table 8.2 Triage Rating System — 126
Table 8.3 Triaged Child Persona Tracker — 126
Figure 8.1 Response Matrix — 128

Chapter 9: Distractibility, Daydreaming, and Attention-Related Issues

Figure 9.1 The Connection Between Attention, Concentration, and Focus — 131
Table 9.1 Behavior Frequency by Persona — 132

Chapter 10: Elopement and "Moving Away"-Related Issues

Table 10.1 Elopement Safety Scale — 160
Table 10.2 Behavior Frequency by Persona — 161

Chapter 11: Excessive Clowning

Figure 11.1 Degrees of Excessiveness	184
Table 11.1 Behavior Frequency by Persona	185

Chapter 12: Aggression, Bullying, Fighting, Out-of-Control Temper

Figure 12.1 Levels of Aggressiveness	199
Table 12.1 Behavior Frequency by Persona	199

Chapter 13: "Hyperactivity"

Figure 13.1 Forms of Energy Discharge	225
Figure 13.2 Intensity of Energy Discharge	226
Table 13.1 Behavior Frequency by Persona	226

Chapter 14: Difficulty Observing Personal Space and Other Boundary Problems

Table 14.1 Potential Problems with Boundary Maintenance	247
Figure 14.1 Lack of Boundary Safety and Descriptors	249
Table 14.2 Behavior Frequency by Persona	249

Chapter 15: Not Speaking

Table 15.1 Forms of Non-Verbal Communication	277
Table 15.2 Behavior Frequency by Persona	278

Chapter 16: Toileting Accidents and Toilet-Related Issues

Figure 16.1 Nature of Problematic Toileting Behavior	301
Table 16.1 Behavior Frequency by Persona	302

Chapter 17: Upsetting Artwork, Writings, and Play

Table 17.1 Types of Creative Expressions and Attributes	320
Table 17.2 Behavior Frequency by Persona	321

List of Challenging Behaviors

Chapter 9: Distractibility, Daydreaming, and Attention-Related Issues

Asking questions that are not on topic	134
Not staying on task	138
Not starting tasks	142
Not following directions	146
Staring off into space, "daydreaming"	150
Wandering around the classroom or on field trips	153

Chapter 10: Elopement and "Moving Away"–Related Issues

Running out of the classroom/school	163
Leaving the school grounds or premises	167
Moving away from teacher when asked to come closer	169
Leaving the confines of a group when asked to stay within it	173
Going missing (inside of school during school hours)	177
Going missing (outside of school on a field trip)	179

Chapter 11: Excessive Clowning

Creating a humorous and/or disruptive sound or expression	186
Falling out of a chair or throwing an object (physical humor)	189
Making a humorous and disruptive statement during a lesson	191

Chapter 12: Aggression, Bullying, Fighting, Out-of-Control Temper

Arguing with peers/teachers	201
Bullying peers	205
Feeling irate with peers/teachers	206
Getting into physical altercations with peers/teachers (hitting, biting, pushing, kicking, etc.)	209
Self-harming (persistent nail-biting, cutting oneself, hitting head, running into walls, pulling one's hair, playing with scissors, etc.)	212
Teasing peers	216
Throwing temper tantrums	219

Chapter 13: "Hyperactivity"

Excessive talking or verbalizing	228
Fidgeting and/or moving body around excessively	232
Frenetically moving from one activity to another (prior to achievement)	236
Getting up from seat excessively	240

Chapter 14: Difficulty Observing Personal Space and Other Boundary Problems

Altering another child's work without asking	251
Exhibiting distress during and/or after a caregiver's departure	253
Lying	256
Not waiting for one's turn	260
Sharing too much personal information	264
Stealing	266
Touching and/or displaying genitals in public	268
Touching another person's body without asking	270

Chapter 15: Not Speaking

Mumbling and/or whispering	279
Not speaking to peers during play	281
Not speaking with peers during group work	284
Only speaking when spoken to	287
Responding to teacher's question with minimal reply	289
Responding with non-verbal communication frequently (when words are known)	292
Responding with sounds frequently (when words are known)	295

Chapter 16: Toileting Accidents and Toilet-Related Issues

Demonstrating excessive need to use the toilet	303
Exhibiting an unwillingness to use the toilet when needed	307
Urinating/Defecating "accidentally" in place other than the toilet	310
Urinating/Defecating "on purpose" in place other than the toilet	312
Using toilet paper excessively (wiping)	314

Chapter 17: Upsetting Artwork, Writings, and Play

Creating artwork that appears overly regressed	323
Generating play that appears overly regressed	327
Generating writing that appears overly regressed	331
Creating artwork that includes sexual content	335
Generating play that includes sexual content	340
Generating writing that includes sexual content	344
Creating artwork that includes violence (self or others)	348
Generating play that includes violence (self or others)	353
Generating writing that includes violence (self or others)	357

Part One

A Different View of the Children in Your Classroom

Chapter 1

Children in the Round

A Holistic Approach to Understanding Children

On December 14, 2012, Victoria Soto died trying to protect her first-grade students from a gunman entering her classroom (Brumfield, 2012). Soto was not a trained police officer or security guard. True, she was responsible for keeping her children safe in her classroom, but her training hardly prepared her for a gunman. Nevertheless, her reaction typifies how many teachers feel responsible for their students, not just their minds, but their bodies as well—the entirety of the child. Soon after the tragedy, her sister Carlee shared Victoria's thoughts about her students, "She loved them more than life" (Warren, 2012). Her sister's characterization of Ms. Soto's belief—that was so profoundly corroborated by her actions on that day—is a holistic one. The commitment that many teachers, especially early-childhood educators, have to their children can only be truly enacted by an "all-in" view of children. To accomplish this entails believing that our children are much more complex than what we may see upon first glance.

We use the term holistic, to speak to the many parts that make up every child. Understanding our children holistically means that as teachers we consider the totality of the child. This does not mean we subscribe to the notion that it is appropriate to make schools and the teachers in them solely responsible to fix all of the ills of society, upbringing or genetics. Early childhood educators cannot be psychological Sherpas leading their children through the complexities of poverty, oppression, trauma, family dysfunction, or other hardships. Yet, we do believe that it is essential that we try to be aware of the many components that comprise each child sitting in our classroom (Weiner & Gallo Silver, 2015). The awareness of these components can lead to the correction or repair of much of what goes on in our classroom, as well as setting in motion, other more involved outcomes.

As a jumping off point, the nature and nurture paradigm of child development provide a helpful platform. The "nature" of a child focuses on heredity, driving a child's overall development including thoughts, decisions, and choices by biological determinants (DNA and genes). The "nurture" of a child centers on a child's environment, shaping a child through interaction, caring, and experiences. Melding these two forces allows us to paint a nuanced and accurate picture of a whole child (Bateson & Gluckman, 2011; Blumberg, 2005; Gottlieb, 2007; Jablonka & Lamb, 2005; Lickliter,

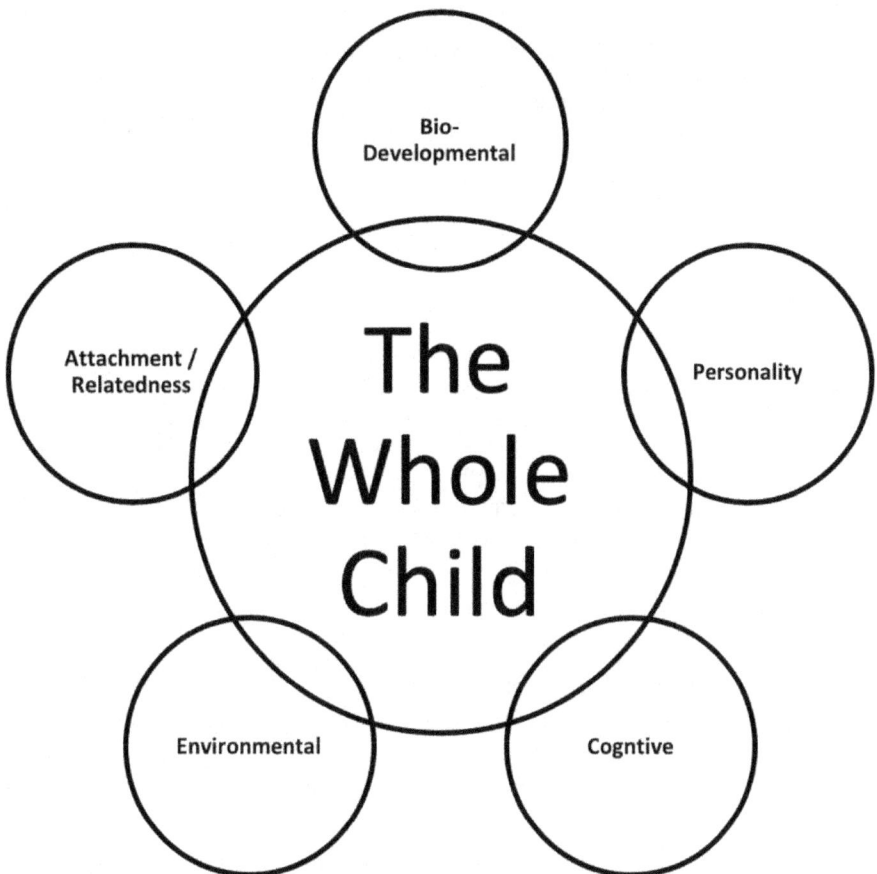

Figure 1.1: Components of a Child

2008; Gander, 2003; Tabery, 2014; Oyama, 2000). This holistic view incorporates five components of a child's developmental world, pulling from both the innate and experiential—the bio-developmental, the cognitive, the environmental, the temperamental, and the relational (see Figure 1.1).

Bio-Developmental Component

Bio-development refers to the inter-connection between a child's psychological, social, and physical development. Many theorists have conceptualized this component of a child's inner life as a series of stages or phases including Ronald Fairbairn, Sigmund Freud, Karen Horney, Melanie Klein, Heinz Kohut, Margaret Mahler, Abraham Maslow, and Jean Piaget, among others (Fairbairn, 1954; Freud & Strachey, 1990; Horney, 1945; 1950; Klein, 1932; 1955; Kohut, 1971; Mahler, et al., 1975; Maslow, 1943; Piaget, & Cook, 1952; Piaget & Inhelder, 1969; Brofenbrenner, 1981; 2004). One of the more useful conceptualizations of psycho-social development for identifying and understanding early childhood behavior was developed by Erik Erikson (Erikson, 1950).

Table 1.1:
Erikson Stages of Development

Crisis	Approximate Age*	Developmental Goal(s)	Potential Future Issue
Trust vs. Mistrust	Birth to 1 or 1½	Works to maximize comfort while minimizing uncertainty; creates trust in others	Isolation; Difficulty with separation
Autonomy vs. Shame and Self Doubt	1 or 1½ to 3 or 4	Works to master physical environment while maintaining sense of self; begins to have opinions	Excessive Caution; Wariness
Initiative vs. Guilt	3 or 4 to 5 or 6	Begins to initiate more complex activities, not only imitate others; develops ideas; makes plans	Inhibition; Difficulty with taking risks
Industry vs. Inferiority	5 or 6 and onward	Tries to develop a sense of self-worth by refining skills, practicing	Indifference; Apathy

*Ages are always approximate as children develop individual skills at different paces.

Erikson believed that the stages that children develop through are centered around working through a series of crises (see Table 1.1). He posited that navigating a specific crisis is dependent on a variety of inter-related environmental, social, and relational factors. We can readily see how trust, sense of self, and creativity and productivity have obvious roles in our work with young children (Erikson, 1950).

Erikson theorized that how children (with their caregivers' participation) manage one crisis affects how they navigate subsequent crises. For example, the first crisis is Trust vs. Mistrust occurring roughly from birth to 1½ years old. During this stage, children learn to trust their initial environments and primary caregivers through receiving attuned, timely, and appropriate responses to their physiological, social, and emotional needs. Successful navigation of this crisis enhances children's overall ability to trust others, especially their early-childhood teachers, and creates a solid foundation for each successive stage. This includes expressing themselves, making choices, developing ideas, as so on. Difficulties within this crisis leave children feeling a great deal of uncertainty about themselves, other people, settings, and situations. Without a trusting foundation, the social-emotional and academic work that children are expected to participate in during school, becomes potentially challenging. Teaching and instruction—focused on learning and integration—require an interpersonal relationship that is predicated on trust. The lack of a trusting foundation prevents children from developing an openness and accessibility to the world and the people in it, including, and especially, their teachers (Erikson, 1950).

This theory creates a framework for what is reasonable to expect of a child based on a set of objective psychological and social criteria. Theories of child development have established what is called a baseline of functioning for a child of a specific age range. Our baseline expectations for how a child relates to others are based on what we have learned about what is typical. This encompasses dexterity and related motor skills as well as sensory abilities that are required to relate to a world filled with other people.

Betsy, 7 years old, 2nd grade and Ms. Feliciano

Ms. Feliciano, a second-grade teacher, notices that at recess Betsy is often by herself. Betsy is a good student, smart and respectful. The other students like her but often baby her as she is much smaller than most of them. Several times, Ms. Feliciano asks other children not to lift Betsy up in their arms and carry her around. Ms. Feliciano notices this frustrates Betsy who feels that she cannot say "no." When she talks to Betsy about it, her student seems to be very insecure about herself. Even though her body language says otherwise, Betsy tells Ms. Feliciano that she likes being picked up.

Betsy's lack of trust in Ms. Feliciano is unmistakable, but subtler is the lack of trust in her classmates that could allow her to stand up to them and say "no" to them. Her physiological realities affect her emotional and relational development, and she, regardless of her physical appearance, communicates this through her presence as an emotionally and socially "small" child. According to Erikson, Betsy has not navigated the Trust vs. Mistrust crisis in a successful way, and this pushes her teacher to patiently build a sense of security and trust over the school year—mainly focused on identifying and honoring her boundaries and personal space and reinforcing the importance of self-advocacy. This step cannot be skipped, if Betsy's sense of self and creativity is to grow and flourish in her subsequent school experience. Allowing our expectations as early childhood educators to be shifted based on where our students "are" is a helpful guideline. The bio-developmental component enables early childhood educators to gauge and identify children who stray from the baseline. It also can provide a window into what a child such as Betsy may find useful in terms of teacher-student interaction (Erikson, 1950).

Cognitive Component

Certainly, as teachers, we are acutely sensitive to and aware of the cognitive development of our students. This includes how a child thinks, organizes thoughts, shares ideas, makes decisions, integrates new skills, or transfers learning from one situation to another. Like the bio-developmental component, this area of focus creates another set of criteria to assess a student's baseline functioning. We want to see children move from thinking concretely to abstractly over the course of their development. We expect a certain amount of black and white thinking from children in early childhood and look forward to the day when our students become more aware and accepting of the ambiguity of different opinions.

This component also covers developmental material that veers into the child neurological realm. There is increasing pressure on parents to identify and determine, as soon as possible, any delay or any organic reality that may affect their child's ability to learn. As some of the first teachers who work with our students, this burden can easily get transferred to the early-childhood educator as the most knowledgeable authority figure in the room. We see this as somewhat unfair, but we do believe that a certain amount of knowledge of this area enhances our ability to understand and communicate with our students.

With this in mind, our ideas about learning and thinking as aspects of neurological growth (brain/nervous system) have been challenged in recent years with our increasing awareness of neurodiversity. Neurodiversity is a relatively new theory that has its roots in both neuroscience and the disability rights movement. We have come to understand the distinctiveness of each human brain as it develops and individuates in various ways due to genetics, experience, and learning. The structures are all similar, but brain imaging has discovered that the size of certain structures varies among all of us. What we now see as a disability in terms of Autism Spectrum Disorders (ASD) and the apparent growing numbers of children being diagnosed with these disorders may be a natural variation in brain development (Silberman, 2015; American Psychiatric Association, 2013).

Some neuroscientists have posited that the autistic brain may be an evolutionary adaptation to the need of our world for computation, technological sagacity, and focused attention (Silberman, 2015). The same may be true for what we call Attention Deficit Hyperactive Disorder (ADHD). We could look at the symptoms less as disruptive to our current system of less-active, didactic education and more as a communication for the need for a kinetic learning environment. Perhaps this is also a natural adaptation of people who are experiential, dynamic learners. While the theory of neurodiversity is beyond the scope of this book, it is important to include it as part of the cognitive component of children.

Sage, 5 years old, kindergarten and Ms. Amato

Ms. Amato is uncomfortable with a 5-year-old student in her kindergarten class who sniffs everyone and everything in the classroom—her fingers, toys, food, and even, toilet paper. At times, Sage puts her nose on classmates' clothes. The other children find her behavior annoying, but sometimes funny. Ms. Amato fears there is something very wrong with Sage and is not sure how to help her. Sage's ability to relate to the other children seems less well developed in a noticeable way. Ms. Amato wonders if Sage needs a neuro-psychological evaluation to find out what her sniffing behavior means and how to help her.

Sage appears to be exhibiting some need for olfactory reinforcement in order to take in information and navigate the classroom. Beyond sensory seeking, this activity communicates information about the nature of Sage's emotional state, her sense of insecurity, and her regressed cognitive development. With this information, early childhood educators like Ms. Amato can open the door to discussions about her structural needs within a school setting and acquiring additional information about any underlying issues. The neurodiversity material can help normalize Sage's presentation in the near term and get the process moving forward. While we seek more input from outside the classroom, helping Sage increase her awareness of personal space and aiding her in controlling her anxious impulses can connect her more securely to her surroundings. As early childhood educators, like child psychotherapists, we have to be comfortable in the knowledge that we are waystations along the journey for these children. Sometimes the best resolution that we can hope for is just stabilizing the here and now and providing a push in the right direction for others to take up later.

Environmental Component

When we speak of a child's environment, we are referring to the accumulation of the experiences that a child has had with his or her primary caregivers, family, community, and society since birth. This encompasses several areas including: (1) the nature of the family life; (2) the makeup of the home and immediate surroundings; (3) any significant changes and losses; and (4) the overarching messages that the child's community and society communicate regarding status, safety, and inclusion. Within these four groupings, we find myriad interactions that shape the children in our classrooms.

Families, indeed all relationships, are constructed using rules, roles, and boundaries. The nature of these factors establishes a child's understanding of how the world inside the family works and provides a model for how the world outside the family may function. It is made up of parental roles, sibling interaction, matriarchal or patriarch family dynamics, cultural norms, rigid rules system or laissez faire ones, and family boundaries, ranging from enmeshed (a lack of) to detached (too rigid). Effective and clear boundaries, rules, and roles prevent confusion, diminish anxiety, provide structure, and can be vehicles of love, affection, comfort, support and learning. The family life aspect of a child's environment provides an understanding of who is the parent and who is the child, of expectations for the adults and the children, of ways of interacting with others, and of a hierarchy of priorities in the family (school, sports, communication, respect for elders, etc.). For each child, these details are distinct, and, as they enter and begin to interact in our classrooms, adjustments are required of each of them. Why are these rules at school ones I have to follow if my rules at home are different? My dad says that he is always right because he is the parent, why do I have to listen to you, you're only the teacher? I don't like sharing with my little brother, why do I have to share with my classmates? My parents yell at me when I am bad, why is yelling not allowed in school? I get punished when I say "no" at home, why do you give me choices at school?

A second element of a child's world is made up of customs, routines, and practices. These include mealtimes, bedtimes, sleeping arrangements, habitants living in the home, the existence of multiple homes, connections to religious institutions, the neighborhood's relative safety, and significant community dynamics (including racism, sexism, and ageism); they create for each child a foundational structure. This structure provides another platform on which a child develops. Abraham Maslow theorized his Hierarchy of Needs with this in mind (Maslow, 1943). Maslow believed that each child has certain base-line requirements that are needed for a child to develop: food, air, water, and shelter, the first requirements, and so on. Without these

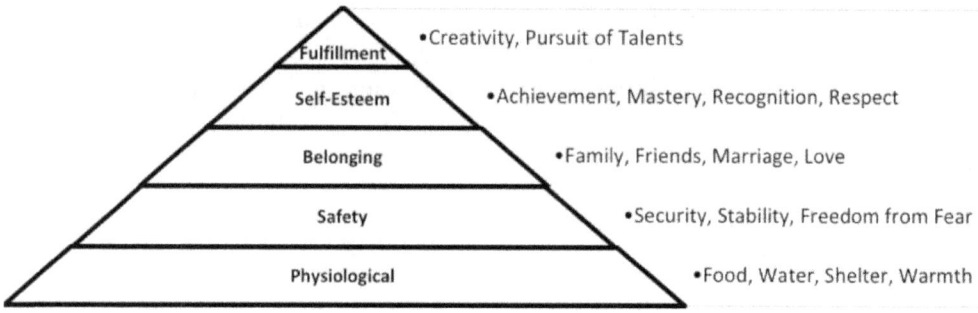

Figure 1.2: Maslow's Hierarchy of Needs

basic elements, subsequent "developmental needs" like safety, love, and friends are challenging to navigate and difficult to acquire (see Figure 1.2).

The last factor within the environment component is change. We know from current research that children, although displaying significant resilience, are greatly affected by environmental change and transitions of any kind. The alteration of a routine ranging from a new bed, to a new home, to a new family member, to a new school, class or teacher are all experienced in one way or another as loss. Loss of the old way that comes with it a sense of vulnerability and insecurity. We cannot emphasize enough that we must see change in this way so as not to underestimate our students' reactions. The end of summer, a change to the daily schedule, the end of the student teacher placement, a vacation, a substitute teacher, no recess outside due to weather. These are only some of the changes that can happen at school. We can add to this list those that are happening at home—divorce, deaths, births, health-related issues, or moving—and in the surrounding community—micro-aggressions, oppression, violence, poverty and racism. We recommend that each of these are thought of in terms of loss with the potential for an emotional and behavioral reaction, from a mild one to one that is more extreme, from a momentary one to one that is long lasting.

Victor, 8 years old, 2nd grade in Ms. Friedman's Class

Ms. Friedman is worried about Victor in her second-grade class because he rarely completes his homework assignment and sometimes does not do it at all. When she asks him about it, Victor just shrugs and says, "I didn't know there was more of the homework to do" or "I didn't know we even had any homework at all." He often seems very tired in class and yawns frequently. She notices that sometimes he sleeps during lunch period. Ms. Friedman asks Victor about his family. He tells her he is the oldest child and has two younger brothers. His mother works at night in a restaurant and Victor cares for his brothers until she comes home. He feeds them and then puts them to bed. Victor says that he is afraid to go to sleep until his mother comes home.

Victor's story is but one of the many heartbreaking situations that children face. Sometimes it is hard to imagine how a child can cope with stress and uncertainty while managing the work of physically, emotionally, and cognitively growing up. Naturally, it is problematic for Victor to have these enormous responsibilities, and, in many states, it is against the law. But until other professionals can help Victor's family, we can make some minor changes that might have enormous impact on Victor. Altering his routines in school may create a counterbalance for unstable structures at home. Check-ins as the day begins and ends provide him with (1) a caregiver-driven structure to offset a home situation in which he must be in charge and (2) empathic moments in which he feels noticed and understood. Maybe the teacher can provide him with a quiet, private space for his naps. Perhaps reviewing his homework assignments before the end of the school day or identifying a "safe and quiet" time for him to do homework before his mother finishes work. Seeing, hearing, and responding to a child in the school can create another set of experiences that adds to a child's environmental component.

Personality Component

We believe that infants are born with innate dispositions already displaying aspects of their eventual personality. Newborns react to the world in such individually distinct ways that neo-natal nurses can differentiate which infant is crying just by the sound and tenor of the cry. These raw "personalities" or temperaments, researched and developed by Stella Chess and Alexander Thomas in the 1950s and 1960s, come in many shapes and sizes (Thomas & Chess; 1956; 1977; Chess & Thomas, 1990; 1996; Allport, 1937; 1954; 1955; 1961; Cattell, 1946; 1957; Boeree, 2006).

During their research, they were able to identify nine attributes with which all children are born. They described a child's temperament in terms of the varying combinations of these elements—activity level, rhythmicity, approach/withdrawal, adaptability, intensity level, mood, persistence level, distractibility level, and sensory sensitivity level (see Table 3.1). Chess and Thomas were the first to categorize temperaments into three main types: feisty, flexible, and cautious (see Table 1.2) (Thomas & Chess; 1956; 1977; Chess & Thomas, 1990; 1996).

Table 1.2:
General Characteristics of Each Temperament

Characteristic	*Feisty*	*Cautious*	*Flexible*
Energy Level	Vigorous	Still	Calm
Response to Control	Resistant	Guarded	Resilient
Social Dynamics	Opposing	Avoidant	Interactive
Outlook	Negative	Worried	Positive
Reactions	Intense	Withdrawn	Calm

Weiner, Gallo-Silver & Lucas, 2020; Based on Thomas & Chess; 1956; 1977

As children mature into adolescents and young adults, their temperaments become the foundation for their overarching personalities, affecting how they relate to and experience other people and the world around them (Allport, 1937; 1954; 1955;

1961; Chess & Thomas, 1990; 1996; Erikson, 1968; Thomas & Chess, 1956; 1977). Are they people who prefer quiet, people who enjoy crowds, people who jump out of planes, people who play sports, or people who prefer to read? Are they leaders, followers, or loners?

It is often easier for parents when their child's temperament feels complimentary to their own temperament. In these cases, the child and the parents fit together comfortably—a flexible kid who has strong-willed parents or a feisty kid who has easy-going parents. This is called "goodness of fit" (Winnicott, 1990). Teachers and students experience a similar dynamic. Our connection with students can be experienced as pleasant, or unfortunately at times, abrasive. Fit becomes an essential aspect of how we feel within our classroom. It is one of the reasons why, in certain years, we feel like we have easy classes and in other years, very difficult ones.

Mr. Clyne and Jamal, 7 years old, 1st grade

Mr. Clyne is often telling Jamal to stop talking to his neighbors and to sit down during class time when he is wandering around. While Jamal's behavior is not unlike many of the other boys in his first-grade class, Jamal seems to have more difficulties following instructions. Mr. Clyne mentions these issues to Jamal's mother during a regular parent/teacher meeting. Jamal's mother becomes insulted and accuses Mr. Clyne of implying that Jamal is hyperactive because he is a child of color. Mr. Clyne tries to discuss his understanding of Attention Deficit Hyperactivity Disorder, but Jamal's mother refuses to engage in this discussion. She describes her son as a nervous and fearful child, with a lot of energy, and says that he has been this way since he was very little. She tells Mr. Clyne that she could never put Jamal down when he was a baby, or he would cry. She also shares with him that it is so difficult to get Jamal to sit at the table for dinner that sometimes she lets him eat standing up. Mr. Clyne points out that Jamal is very bright and often finishes tasks much sooner than the other children in his class, but that his behavior is disruptive to the class.

Jamal's mother's description of him as an energetic child takes on a significant meaning when we consider his temperament. As opposed to defining him, Jamal's high activity level becomes one of many factors in our attempt to understand him—why does he need to move around so much, how does he feel when we try to confine him, how does he experience the rules in school like sit in your seat, stay in line, be quiet, wait your turn?

We see the more challenging elements of this component, not as a set of "unwelcome" choices that a child makes volitionally, but as involuntary forces that are simply part of his or her essence. By taking temperament into account, we may find a way of reframing the power struggles that we sometimes experience with challenging children. We can try to become allies, working together to manage difficult instincts. Temperament is a multifaceted component that has great impact on a child's communication with the world and the people in it. For this reason, we will rely heavily on temperament in subsequent chapters as we discuss how children communicate and behave.

Attachment/Relatedness Component

This component encompasses all of the child's interpersonal relationships with the people in his/her life. It is important at this point to introduce the concept of attachment. We are using this word in the psychological sense. This is the emotional bond that exists between a child and his significant others (Ainsworth, et al., 2014; Bowlby, 1969; 1982; Solomon & George, 2011). Research about attachment is typically focused on the quality of this connection and the effect that the quality has on children through their developmental process.

Attachment is a two-way street. The child needs to be attached to parents and likewise, parents need to be attached to their child. The mutuality (or lack thereof) within the relationship becomes the road map for all of the child's current and future relationships. We can simplify the different types of attachment into four main forms (see Figure 1.3).

Table 1.3:
The Eight Feelings of Childhood Attachment

- Safe and Loved—relationship is attuned and responsive (corresponds to Secure attachment)
- Uncertain and Anxious—relationship is inconsistently attuned and intermittently responsive (corresponds to Ambivalent attachment)
- Withdrawn and Suspicious—relationship is poorly attuned and unresponsive (corresponds to Avoidant attachment)
- Distressed and Afraid—relationship is not attuned and chaotically responsive (corresponds to Disorganized attachment)

Ainsworth, et al., 2014; Solomon & George, 2011; adapted by Weiner, Gallo-Silver, & Lucas, 2020

Revisiting the dynamics from several of the early components, problematic attachment can affect a child's ability to trust, make friends, connect to teachers, and generally feel safe and secure in school. Attachment is also the jumping-off point to the next stage of development. As children leave infancy behind, they pull away from their parents, beginning to crawl and walk, to say "no," to test limits, to tantrum, to have their own ideas, and so on. This is the process of separation and individuation (the expansion of autonomy and a sense of self). This progression is how a child becomes her own person and develops a growing comfort and wish to be independent (Mahler, et al., 1975). Often a challenging developmental stage for parent and children alike, teachers and their classrooms become the repositories for relationship dynamics from home that have not been addressed or sufficiently worked through. This is not a glitch, but a feature of the early childhood education environment.

A theory that we will weave throughout this book is called the "corrective emotional experience" (Alexander, 1946). It serves as the foundational tenant of all our responses in Part Three. Simply stated, the concept enables non-parental authority figures to help children redo and undo some of the difficulties they have developed within their relationships—due to family complications or broader social issues such as poverty or racism, among others. Early childhood educators, through their empathy, love, and protection, can affect children deeply, especially when teachers interact with students in ways that are different and more positive than those the children have experienced outside of the classroom. This aspect of being an early-childhood educator receives little attention, but this does not make it a less powerful tool for teachers. If we make it purposeful and conscious it can become even more so.

Fatima, 4 years old, Pre-K with Ms. Lee

Ms. Lee is worried about Fatima. Fatima has just started attending pre-K and cries inconsolably when her mother leaves each morning. Not only does Fatima cry, but her mother often cries as well, seemingly unable to leave her daughter. The mother's tears make Fatima even more distressed. When the school day is over, Fatima is frantic and distracted until she sees her mother again. The reunion is heartfelt and tearful for both mother and daughter. Ms. Lee has spoken to the mother the best she can but does not speak the mother's language. Ms. Lee sends a note home with Fatima's mother requesting that a meeting be set up with a relative who speaks both their language and English in order to translate for the mother. Ms. Lee is surprised when Fatima's father comes to see her without the mother. He speaks fluent English. He explains that his wife has not been educated and does not understand that girls must go to school in the United States the same as boys. He is fine with his daughter becoming an educated person but knows his wife misses her tremendously while she is in school.

There are two issues at work in Fatima's world that need to be processed by her teacher. First, whether we teach in small rural communities, larger urban centers, or diverse suburbs, we are likely to work with families from different cultures with cultural norms. When a family's norms fit comfortably within what is expected by the community at large, there is ease, support, and respect. Yet at times world views, societal customs, or familial traditions are misunderstood or in conflict with the surrounding environment. Fatima's family's beliefs about school and women may create a challenge for her teacher. Broadening our awareness of multi-cultural dynamics can only strengthen us as early childhood educators; and, within this book, we will creatively address some of these difficult and complex cultural disconnects that might affect our classrooms.

The other dynamic displayed in Ms. Lee's class is that of Fatima's separation anxiety. It is the age-old difficulty, but in this case, it is complicated by cultural issues including assimilation stress and a loss of role and purpose (for Fatima's mother). Her mother's distress and the way it manifests create a great deal of uncertainty in Fatima. Will my mother be okay when I cannot see her? Is she mad at me? Are her tears because I did something wrong? Is going to school wrong because it upsets my mother so much? As teachers we try to empathize with the sadness and worry that this complicated dynamic engenders. Our words and acts can create a holding environment which can model security for our student and her mother (Winnicott, 1953; 1990).

Taking a holistic approach to understand students is a natural complement to early childhood education. We teach the whole child, not just parts. True, we engage a child's mind; yet we know the mind is affected by the body and the emotions, as well as the circumstances outside of school. Our teaching makes more of an impact when we see all parts of the child and try to have all parts tended to in the most attuned ways possible.

Chapter 2

Who Needs a Diagnosis, Anyway?

Understanding Behavior as Communication

Psychiatric diagnoses are subjective constructs. They are developed by professional consensus as summaries of the components of certain behaviors and what to call these component constellations. While diagnoses such as Attention Deficit Hyperactivity Disorder, Autism Spectrum Disorder, Oppositional Defiant Disorder, to name a few, may be viewed as objective descriptors of specific behaviors, they are by no means definitive (American Psychiatric Association, 2013). There are no blood tests or MRIs, no biopsies or exploratory procedures. The diagnoses that teachers typically interact with are based on assessments taken from anecdotal information and survey tools. That said, diagnoses do serve important purposes in the treatment of certain childhood disorders in the following ways:

- Diagnoses can help professionals (mental health and medical, among others) organize around a specific treatment plan for a child (which can include higher levels of intervention such as medication);
- Diagnoses can be required by institutions and other professionals making decisions regarding supplementary services for a child (i.e., Individualized Education Plans, therapies such as occupational and speech, among others);
- Diagnoses allow insurance companies to categorize billing options.

From our perspective, understanding behavior as communication is a far more useful intervention tool for a teacher in the classroom than knowing a child's diagnosis. It is derived from making educated deductions based on the various elements we see, hear, and viscerally experience and does not necessarily need to be definitively "correct." In this chapter, we address this difference between behavior as symptom of a diagnosis and behavior as a communication of a message. Chapter 1 provided a great deal of theoretical background as we form an understanding of childhood, in general. We want you to hold on to this material but set it aside for the moment. It will become essential as we develop well-conceived, targeted responses to a variety of child behaviors in Part Three of the book. For Chapter 2, we want to turn to basics, to the definition of communication, the seen and unseen parts of a behavior, the underpinnings of child messaging, and how we can use all these to begin the process of deciphering childhood behavior in a new way.

As teachers, we can be frustrated by the disruption that certain behaviors can cause in our classroom. We may be troubled about the ways that these child behaviors set off related behaviors in other children, derail our lesson plans, require our attention, and generally put undue pressure on the flow of the day. Attempting to eliminate, prevent, or reduce a disruptive behavior before it reaches this point, inevitably becomes one of our roles as teachers.

In our ongoing effort to manage disruptive behaviors, some teachers may feel like they are pressed into "policing" the students in the classroom or the playground, instead of teaching. We may find ourselves reactively raising our voices, giving consequences out of irritation, "throwing our hands up" in exasperation, and sending children out of the classroom. On the other hand, some of us may attempt to employ one or more of the many recommended behavior modification techniques. All of these practices work sometimes, and other times they do not. When they do, we feel successful, as if we have had a breakthrough, but this accomplishment is often fleeting. Disappointingly, these strategies do not always work the same way with each child and, in reality, do not always work with the same child the second or third time around. What to do? Which strategy to try? When is the right time? What will the results be? As the mystery around a student's behavior deepens for us, our frustration and search for a solution may increase dramatically.

We believe that focusing on behavior as a communication of information and issues about a child, with little or no empathy for a teacher's complex position in the classroom, is one-sided. In reality, scrutinizing behavior is time-consuming and impinges on the limited time teachers already have for classroom management, the expectations of the administration, and the demands of the curriculum. Indeed, what teacher actually has the time to examine, understand, and decipher behaviors when they are disruptive? We often feel we need to act, rather than contemplate.

We are offering a "compromise" process that can be described as follows. First, we acknowledge that, as educators, we often feel pulled in multiple directions in our classes as we endeavor to both meet our curriculum benchmarks and simultaneously acknowledge and focus on the social-emotional realm of our students. To this end, our priority is straightforward: a functional, safe classroom environment that supports learning. Realistically, however, during class time, we are able to comfort and try to support children within the classroom but cannot do much about disruptive behaviors except manage them.

Our proposed change in the process comes once the class is over. We advocate that critical time be allotted to thoughtfully analyzing what the disruptive behaviors might mean. We cannot emphasize this enough. The work to understand and address behaviors happens outside the classroom. The thoughtful and holistic process that we offer in this book provides educators the opportunity to feel empowered as professionals while doing this. The book promotes the ideas of being proactive instead of reactive, intervening earlier, having more attuned responses, and getting ahead of the problem, as opposed to feeling like we are always chasing it or waiting for it to happen and then reacting.

For clarification of terminology, any kind of activity that a child engages in is called an action. A behavior is a series or patterns of these actions. In this book, we will be examining behaviors. We feel that if a child in your classroom does something once, you will note it, address it and move on. Behaviors by their very nature tend to linger and recur and need to be addressed and understood with more acuity, intensity, and sensitivity. Behaviors, therefore, are a series of repetitive actions that recur over time.

In order to begin the process of deciphering the communication behind or within a behavior, we first need to introduce you to two concepts that we will use throughout this book. They are psychological terms that have fallen into disuse within some mental health professions, but we feel that they are critical to working with children and successfully managing their behaviors. Incorporating them into our explorations in this book will give us a common language to comprehend the complicated child behaviors that we confront on a daily basis.

Defining Manifest and Latent Communication

As a rule, we see behaviors as having two distinct levels of communication. First, there is the level that we can see. We call this the "manifest" part of the communication—it is the visible action. Whenever we see a child engaging in an action—running, jumping, sharing, crying, yelling, laughing, scratching, reading, biting, or hitting—these are manifest. Like the tip of an iceberg cracking the surface of the ocean, manifest communications are observable to us as we follow children through school. Second, there exists the level that we cannot easily see or discern. Called the "latent" part of the communication, this level is built on deductions and inferences and centers on a child's feelings, thoughts, and/or personality. Like the vastness of the iceberg that lies beneath the surface of the water, latent communication is the motivation, impetus, or purpose underlying what we are seeing (Weiner & Gallo-Silver, 2015). Latent communication is the engine behind manifest communication. Together they form a complete holistic communication that takes into account the many parts of the child. We can see the child who is crying, but why is he crying? He may be overwhelmed because his parents are divorcing, angry because he has a new sibling, sad because he does not understand the school material, or anxious because of his difficulty connecting to his classmates (see Figure 2.1).

The ideas of manifest and latent communication are the foundation pieces of the child's language that we use to decode what we are experiencing. What are we seeing? What could it mean? What are the manifest aspects of the behavior? What are the possible latent ones? What is the holistic communication? We ask these questions over and over again until the process is second nature. It is a mantra that we use in order to take in and administer this complex world of child behavior and its multiple

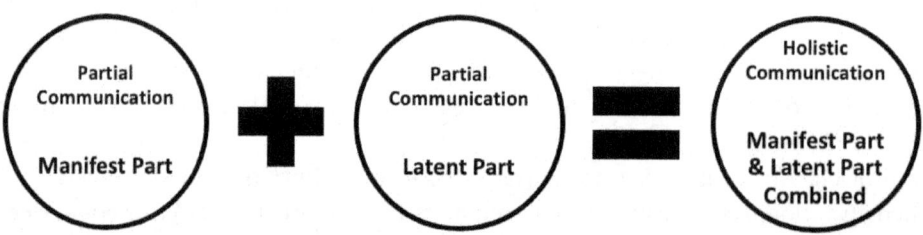

Figure 2.1: Holistic Communication

dimensions. To this end, linking the manifest and latent communication is the key. Over time, we start to notice connections and themes.

Organizing Manifest Communication

Let's begin with developing a coherent way of organizing and operationalizing our exploration of communication. In child psychology, to arrange our thinking about a child's presentation and functioning within a variety of environments—about their ways of thinking, acting, and feeling—we might use developmental theories like John Bowlby and Mary Ainsworth's attachment theory, Margaret Mahler's ideas on separation and individuation, Erik Erikson's stages of psycho-social development, or Abraham Maslow's hierarchy of needs. (Bowlby, 1969; Ainsworth, et al., 2014; Erikson, 1950; 1968; Maslow, 1943; Mahler, Pine & Bergman, 1975). Because we are examining classroom behavior, we think it is most advantageous to use a structure that is both familiar to teachers and one that teachers already use on a regular basis to evaluate a child's functioning.

To this end, early childhood education provides us with a useful construct—the developmental skill sets and areas of focus that each student navigates as they move through their schooling:

- creative skills
- listening skills
- literacy skills
- motor skills (gross and fine)
- social skills
- speaking, language, or expressive skills
- thinking/problem solving skills

National Association for the Education of Young Children, 2020

These areas become a helpful backdrop for our examinations of child communication. A communication within the realm of creative skills may require a different analysis, understanding, and intervention than a communication centered on a child's gross motor activity (Davies, 1983). Some skill areas tend toward the individual child (creativity, problem solving, or impulse control), while others focus more on a child's mutuality and connectedness with others (listening, sharing, socializing).

What do a child's gross motor skills communicate? Is she energetic or still? What do his interpersonal skills look like? Does he share? Does he fight? Does he withdraw? How would you describe a child's listening skills? Does she appear to be focused? Is she distracted? Often children who have behavior difficulties will communicate the underlying issues in myriad ways and at various moments during a day, so it is imperative that, as problem solvers, we are able to break these communications down in order to build a clear understanding of what is being conveyed. The developmental skills areas become a first layer of ordering what may feel chaotic and confusing.

As we stated early in the chapter, a child's manifest communication is comprised of all that we can observe. Under this umbrella, these observations can include both a child's verbal (words, vocabulary, paucity/plethora of speech, articulation, volume, timing of verbalization) and non-verbal communication (movements, attire, facial expressions, gestures, body position, proximity to others, etc.). It is important to make these distinctions, as some children will be more likely to communicate within the verbal realm, while others will prefer the non-verbal realm. This can be based on a variety of factors that we will discuss later in this chapter and during future chapters.

Manifest communication occurs anytime and anywhere during the school day: at drop-off, walking into the school with a caregiver, during rug-time discussion, in the bathroom, on the playground, while eating lunch, when moving around the school, while travelling on field trips. When we combine a child's "choices" of method of communication with a location and time, we begin to see the richness and complexity of manifest communication. Yelling on the playground is one communication; yelling in the classroom is a very different one. Playing firefighter during imaginary play is one communication; drawing a picture of a burning building during art seems like a very different one.

The figure below contains the developmental skill areas, expected activities within each skill set, and some possible manifest communication (both verbal and non-verbal) that may draw our closer attention (see Table 2.1):

Table 2.1:
Actions and Manifest Communication

Skills Area	*Action*	*Concerning Manifest Communication*
Creative Skills	Playing, Drawing, Building Structures, Pretending	Scary drawings, breaking buildings, destructive instead of creative, conflict with peers in unstructured play, difficulty with imaginary play
Listening Skills	Following Instructions, Paying Attention	Not listening, not paying attention, difficulty concentrating, mind wandering, staring off, daydreaming
Literacy Skills	Following Sequences, Reading, Writing, Interpretation, Identification of Objects, Idea and Themes	Refusing to read or write, not doing homework, lacking focus during structured learning, avoiding schoolwork or expressing frustration about that work
Motor Skills (Gross)	Moving, Physicality, Big Body Play, Climbing, Running, Jumping	Falling down regularly, crashing into another child, problems with personal space, lack of core strength and body control, kicking peers, hitting peers, hyperactivity
Motor Skills (Fine)	Holding Objects, Manipulation of Objects, Writing, Coloring	Poor handwriting, difficulty hold pencil or crayon, difficulty with manipulatives, avoidance of activities that require writing, drawing, scissors
Social Skills	Empathy, Identifying Feelings in Self and Others, Sharing, Collaborating, Separation, Managing Frustration	Playing alone, missing social cues, not having friends, emotional at beginning of day or at end of day, refusal to participate in activities, conflict with peers

Skills Area	Action	Concerning Manifest Communication
Speaking, Language or Expressive Skills	Articulating, Public Speaking, Sharing Ideas with Others, Naming Feelings	Refusing to speak in class, stuttering, not answering teacher's questions, mumbling
Thinking/ Problem Solving Skills	Processing New Information, Decision Making, Judgment, Impulse Control, Identifying Difficulties, Organizing	Impulsive behavior, calling out in class, fighting, walking out of class, disorganized work, conflict with peers, having regular tantrums, difficulty making choices regarding activities, talking during teacher instruction, difficulty with transitions

Weiner, Gallo-Silver, & Lucas, 2020

Organizing Latent Communication

Having set up a structure for categorizing and collating manifest communication, we now move on to processing a child's latent communication. Unlike manifest communications, latent communications are often obscured because they lie within the realm of inference and require our imagination. Its abstract nature makes understanding latent communication a subjective and inexact process. The objectivity we have when describing the observable nature of a child's actions, such as a child's inability to sit still in our classroom, is not available when we are asked why this behavior is taking place or what is generating it. This requires vision and educated guesswork. Think of being asked what you believe is going on with a child in your class who is not sitting still. What possible answers come to mind? There are many. You may deduce that the child has:

- an active learning style
- anxiety
- boredom
- difficulty concentrating
- excitement for learning
- fatigue
- issues with control
- hostility toward authority
- hyperactivity
- a personal issue (life stressor)
- physical discomfort (hunger, thirst, toileting)
- a developmental issue (surge in testosterone or estrogen)

The ongoing practice of making educated suppositions, guesses and inferences regarding a child's latent communication is a common practice for parents and child mental health professionals. The speculations are attempts to discern the meaning or purpose of a child's actions. Is a child crying because he is hungry? Is the child angry because she misses her parent? Is the child anxious because her parents regularly argue? The guesswork symbolizes a caregiver's desire to provide connection, attunement, and empathy. We believe that teachers instinctually use this process. Our goal here is to it to make it more conscious, structured, and integral in the day-to-day practice of teaching.

> ### The "Good Enough" Teacher
>
> While getting the correct answer is important and can be helpful, it is more essential that we are seen to be <u>trying</u> to get it right. For primary caregivers, D.W. Winnicott called this concept "good enough parenting" (Winnicott, 1968). Winnicott theorized that there can be no such person as the perfect parent. According to him, a parent being good enough was meant to emphasize the appreciation a child has for a parent who tries her hardest to do the right thing even though she might make inadequate or incorrect choices, at times. Correspondingly, we conceptualize a good enough teacher as an educator who, through a process of trial and error, tries her hardest to understand and respond to her students. The teacher who continues this effort of exploration, regardless of whether she is ultimately successful, is a "good enough teacher." It is this effort that is noticed by children and is often the highest order of compliment you can give them.

To operationalize this process, we want teachers to consider the two pillars of latent communication—a child's feelings or emotions and a child's thoughts or cognitions (see Figure 2.2). Each of these becomes an area of focus and speculation for us as we examine a child's actions within our classroom (see Table 2.3). One is no more important than the other. They may overlap, simultaneously contributing to a child's behavior, or may independently prompt and motivate a child to act. Let us look at each of these areas more closely.

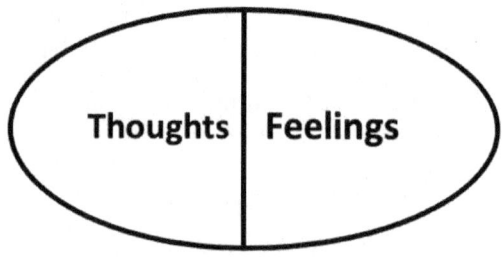

Figure 2.2: The Parts of Latent Communication

Types of Feelings

Feelings and emotions are a child's affectual responses and reactions to his perceptions of day to day experiences, situations, and encounters with people, places, things, and time. These feelings and emotions exist on a continuum:

- Angry—From Annoyed to Enraged
- Afraid—From Concerned to Phobic
- Happy—From Content to Ecstatic
- Nervous—From Worried to Anxious
- Sad—From Unhappy to Heartbroken

We understand that many more feelings exist than those listed above. We encourage teachers to use any feeling name that they can identify—keeping in mind age-typical language. We believe that all more nuanced feelings are derivatives or combinations of these basics (i.e., being confused may a derivation of being nervous or may be a combination of being angry and nervous).

Types of Thoughts

Thoughts are a child's cognitive formulations regarding his perceptions of day to day experiences, situations and encounters with people, places, things, and time. These ideas cover a wide range of productions, including:

- Concerns—thoughts that cause mild emotional discomfort
- Conclusions—thoughts that indicate causality
- Constructions—thoughts that identify a link between two ideas
- Distortions—thoughts that have been modified based on personal narrative only
- Dreams—thoughts about a possible future
- Fears—thoughts that cause moderate to severe emotional discomfort
- Fantasies—thoughts about an altered reality
- Interpretations—thoughts that indicate an understanding of motivation or connection
- Observations—thoughts about something seen or noticed
- Wishes—thoughts about a possible change to one's reality

Understandably, these demonstrations of a child's thought process can vary greatly depending on a child's developmental progress. That said, all school-age children generate thoughts about the world regardless of where we find them on the developmental continuum and how understandably they convey these thoughts. They may be difficult to detect and grasp, at times, but they are there.

Combining Manifest and Latent Communication

With manifest and latent communication defined and deconstructed, we now merge the two, in order to achieve the holistic communication and understanding of a child's behavior. A child's manifest communications, whether they be verbal or non-verbal, *always* correlate with latent communications whether they be the child's feelings or thoughts. Let us break these down for further clarification.

First, some manifest communications track closely to a child's feelings. Some connect to sadness, such as a crying at drop-off time; others to anger, such as shouting "unfair" when losing a game; and yet a different set to nervousness, such as feeling sick before an unfamiliar activity. Second, we can pinpoint that some manifest communications are closely associated with a child's cognitions. They may correlate with children's ideas about their sense of control (I am Superman and I am the strongest), about their willingness to share (I have a younger brother who takes everything of mine), about right and wrong (mom says that adults are always right, kids are always wrong), or about risk taking (dad says I always have to be safe no matter what). Inevitably, blending these latent communications can make our reasoning about children's behavior more compelling and comprehensive (see Table 2.2).

Table 2.2: Connecting Manifest and Possible Latent Communication

Skills Area	*Concerning Manifest Communication*	*Possible Latent Communications*
Creative Skills	Scary drawings, breaking buildings, destructive instead of creative, conflict with peers in unstructured play, difficulty with imaginary play	Difficulty with imaginary play may be a **Sad** (type of feeling) **Conclusion** (type of thought) i.e., "Nothing I do matters" Scary drawings may be an **Angry** (type of feeling) **Wish** (type of thought) i.e., "My mom and dad fight a lot. I want it to stop."
Listening Skills	Not listening, not paying attention, mind wandering, staring off, daydreaming	Not listening to teacher during instruction may be an **Angry** (type of feeling) **Distortion** (type of thought) i.e., "Grownups don't care about what I think" Daydreaming may be a **Nervous** (type of feeling) **Construction** (type of thought) i.e., "I have to stay away from the loud noises"
Literacy Skills	Refusing to read or write, not doing homework, lacking focus during structured learning, avoiding schoolwork or expressing frustration about that work	Refusing to read may be an **Afraid** (type of feeling) **Interpretation** (type of thought) i.e., "Grownups don't like it when I make mistakes" Not doing homework may be a **Nervous** (type of feeling) **Fear** (type of thought) i.e., "If I need help, I will get yelled at"
Motor Skills (Gross)	Falling down regularly, crashing into another child, problems with personal space, lack of core strength and body control, kicking peers, hitting peers, hyperactivity	Crashing into another child may be a **Happy** (type of feeling) **Fantasy** (type of thought) i.e., "She is my best friend" Hyperactivity may be a **Nervous** (type of feeling) **Concern** (type of thought) i.e., "I am not in charge"
Motor Skills (Fine)	Poor handwriting, difficulty hold pencil or crayon, difficulty with manipulatives, avoidance of activities that require writing, drawing, scissors	Poor handwriting may be an **Angry** (type of feeling) **Conclusion** (type of thought) i.e., "I am all alone. No one helps me." Difficulty with manipulatives may be a **Nervous** (type of feeling) **Conclusion** (type of thought) i.e., "I will get it wrong"

Skills Area	Concerning Manifest Communication	Possible Latent Communications
Social Skills	Playing alone, missing social cues, not having friends, emotional at beginning of day or at end of day, refusal to participate in activities, conflict with peers	Playing alone may be a **Sad** (type of feeling) **Fear** (type of thought) i.e., "No one like me." Missing social cues may be a **Happy** (type of feeling) **Observation** (type of thought) i.e., "I like the way that works"
Speaking, Language or Expressive Skills	Refusing to speak in class, stuttering, not answering teacher's questions, mumbling	Refusing to speak in class may be an **Afraid** (type of feeling) **Distortion** (type of thought) i.e., "People think I'm stupid and like to make fun of me." Not answering the teacher's questions may be a **Sad** (type of feeling) **Interpretation** (type of thought) i.e., "She doesn't think I'm good enough."
Thinking/Problem Solving Skills	Impulsive behavior, calling out in class, fighting, walking out of class, disorganized work, conflict with peers, having regular tantrums, difficulty making choices regarding activities, talking during teacher instruction, difficulty with transitions, bizarre behavior/statements	Calling out in class may be a **Nervous** (type of feeling) **Construction** (type of thought) i.e., "When I call out, I might be noticed." Walking out of class may be a **Happy** (type of feeling) **Dream** (type of thought) i.e., "I like being a grownup."

Weiner, Gallo-Silver, & Lucas, 2020

The following scenarios are explorations of manifest and latent communications. In them, we offer preliminary ideas for addressing the behaviors. More detailed responses will be offered in later chapters. For now, our goal is to primarily focus our attention on the underlying communications as a first step in the process.

Renaye Draws Zombies in Ms. Ortiz's class

Renaye is an eight-year-old girl in the second grade who draws a picture of zombies with a heading that reads, "Zombies are not allowed in this classroom." Her teacher, Ms. Ortiz, considered this a worrisome drawing. While it is true that there has been a resurgence of popularity in zombie-focused entertainments, they are typically prohibited in the classroom, and their appearance as part of the drawing is worrisome. It seems that Renaye cannot rule out completely that zombies could find her in the classroom, even though the classroom is supposed to feel safe. They are inside the classroom, because the ideas are inside her head. Renaye insists on posting her sign on the classroom door and becomes tearful and upset when Ms. Ortiz tells her that she cannot leave her sign there. Ms. Ortiz comforts her, and the immediate crisis and disruption of the class is successfully contained. Renaye is permitted to post this sign on her desk. She crosses out part of the prohibition and alters "in this classroom" to "at this desk."

This containment does not address all the latent parts of Renaye's communication. Manifestly, Renaye tries to introduce disturbing, "inappropriate" content into the classroom. Underneath, she feels frightened, unsafe, and personally threatened. Why she feels this way, we may not discover, but this is not critical to our ability to respond within the classroom. She also seems scattered and distracted. This latent communication can provide her teacher with more insight into Renaye's behavior. This will help the staff begin to slowly create and weave a greater sense of safety into the classroom for Renaye. This security can be derived from containment intervention, such as keeping the sign close and checking in with her about whether her desk feels safe. Creating a safe spot for her allows the teacher to use this space as a point from which to build.

Ms. Garcia and Bobby, the Biter

Bobby is a five-year-old kindergartener who has a history of biting other children. When he becomes frustrated with another child, for a variety of manifest reasons such as having to share or having someone stand too close to him, Bobby bites the child on the finger. He suddenly grabs the child by the hand and brings it to his mouth to facilitate the bite. Numerous times, Ms. Garcia has comforted a bitten child and has that child brought to the school nurse. She explains to Bobby that biting is not allowed and that he needs to use his words instead. Also, Bobby is frequently contained in the corner of the classroom, kept away from his classmates, as a safety measure.

Ms. Garcia's strategies are appropriate. Manifestly, Bobby is using a physical way of interacting with other children in his class. Bobby seems angry when he bites, but there are other ways a five year old can communicate anger and frustration. Biting is often associated with extreme anger, such as rage. It is a physical form of seeking control and it makes the biter feel powerful. Because it is a behavior of a younger child, we may assume that Bobby feels small, vulnerable, and lacking control in those moments. Although, it is unclear exactly why Bobby chooses to bite, looking at the possible latent communications can provide ideas as to how to manage and prevent the behavior. If the teacher chooses to focus on the child's underlying need for control, they can provide responses that increase a biter's sense of power by (1) helping a child understand how her behavior impacts others and (2) offering concrete alternatives that include safer types of touch (i.e., pat on the hand).

Kevin and the Reading Quandary in Mr. Doyle's class

Kevin is a six-year-old first grader who continues to have difficulty reading by himself and listening to others read. He typically refuses to read aloud during teacher-student reading assessment and during the class read-aloud time. When anyone but the teacher is reading, Kevin covers his ears with his hands and hums. This behavior bothers his classmates, and they often complain and ask him to stop, disrupting the lesson. In these situations, Mr. Doyle tells Kevin to stop humming and listen to the other children. He responds to this by continuing to cover his ears, sulking, closing his eyes, and laying his head upon his desk, sometimes lightly banging it. From time to time, Mr. Doyle must have Kevin removed from the room by one of the other adults in the class, in order to continue with the reading portion of the lesson.

Manifestly, Kevin hums when his peers read aloud. There is something about hearing his voice reading or hearing the voices of his classmates reading that greatly upsets Kevin. His distress is to such a degree that he avoids the experience by refusing to participate or by making noise in order to seemingly drown out the sounds. He appears anxious, afraid, or at the very least uncomfortable. Some of latent communication may not be revealed without an evaluation for learning or processing issues, but any information gleaned from this type of assessment, in and of itself, does not solve the classroom difficulties. The part of the latent communication that could be useful by his teacher is based upon Kevin's isolation—the closing of his eyes and ears—and his apparent need for self-soothing. His teacher may be able to devise a response or set of responses to Kevin that decrease his sense of aloneness while keeping him connected to the class. These could include helping Kevin understand his behavior as possible protection for a perceived danger. Empathizing in this way creates an alliance and allows for the teacher to make further suggestions.

Mr. Bond and Kelly, Who Picks Her Nose

Kelly is a seven-year-old girl in the second grade who picks her nose and then eats the "boogers." The other children in the class tease Kelly because of this behavior. Her classmates do not want to sit next to her, nor do they want her to join them in large or small group activities. Kelly cries when her classmates tease and push her away. She also has a great deal of difficulty sitting still and paying attention, which requires Mr. Bond's constant reminders. Her parents have sent in a behavior chart to school for Mr. Bond to fill out at the end of each day noting any nose picking—a green sticker if she does not pick her nose, a yellow for once and a red for more than once. Kelly cries when she gets yellow or red stickers at the end of the day and tells Mr. Bond that her father is going to be angry with her. This makes Mr. Bond uncomfortable and worried about this end-of-day routine.

Manifestly, Kelly is picking her nose. Her latent communication centers on her preoccupation with sensations around her nasal passage which seem to demonstrate a nervousness and sadness. She does not seem to feel secure and cannot calm her body. These issues may be medical in nature, as the nasal discharge, the agitation, and the disproportionate emotionality can all speak to an underlying physical issue such as apnea, which can affect a child's sleep routine and level of fatigue. That said, this does not help Mr. Bond necessarily, as he would have to get her parents involved. It is the latent communication that can help the mystery of how to help in-the-moment. From this perspective, Kelly may be using her behavior as (1) a reinforcement of her poor sense of self ("I am gross. I do gross things.") and (2) a self-comforting mechanism to address the agitation derived from these negative feelings about herself. The tactile nature of touching the inside of the nose may serve as a tension-reducer, almost like a mini-massage. These ideas may be helpful to the teacher as he formulates ways of helping Kelly slow down, appreciate herself, and connect to others—altering the ways that picking her nose seems to push her friends away and isolate her, when she really just wants to be close.

No Diagnosis Required

Renaye, Bobby, Kevin and Kelly are some of many examples of children that we encounter in our day to day work, and each is located somewhere on a wide continuum of behavioral issues. These children, and children like them, require in-class understanding and interventions from teachers. In some cases, children may even need to be evaluated for additional services, augmented support plans, or alternative class placements. This assessment process, recommended to parents by school staff or initiated by parents unilaterally, brings into our discussion the concepts of diagnosis and diagnosing.

A diagnosis is part of a medical model of understanding a person's behavior. More and more, it is the cornerstone of the way our society views and discusses child behavioral issues. The medical model views difficulties as a construct that requires an examination or evaluation, a diagnosis or label for the difficulties, and then a treatment, with an end goal of a cessation of symptoms (a cure). The medical model points to the idea that the knowledge for helping an individual is proprietary and resides with the "expert" helper. You go to a doctor, and get a diagnosis, because he or she knows how to help and will give you the material necessary for a change in symptoms (Weiner & Gallo-Silver, 2015).

As a *medical* concept, a diagnosis is the result of a detailed history of a child's problem and a physical examination of a child's body that are then augmented by the results of any necessary medical tests. Based on the results of these examinations, the finding of certain symptoms, or the absence of others, the doctor makes a diagnosis and then determines a course of treatment. For medical problems, this process makes sense (Weiner & Gallo-Silver, 2015).

This model is highly effective in addressing manifest problems. Things we can observe and quantify, such as cells, fractures, infections, injuries, etc. Think about it this way ... if someone has a headache, it may be caused by a variety of issues. Using the process of elimination, a doctor can work through possible problems. If we wanted to know for certain, a physical examination of the head or a medical test, like an MRI or a CAT scan, would provide a clear picture. And that is how it should be for these types of problems, because what is causing the head pain is objectively knowable—a migraine, dehydration, poor vision, allergies, etc. (Weiner & Gallo-Silver, 2015).

In the medical model, patterns of behavior, that seem to be obstacles to optimal functioning and learning, are defined as symptoms. Yet, symptoms by their very nature tend to be manifest communications, and we are proposing that a significant part of a child's behavior is made up of latent communication. We tend to give that which is "medical" a wide berth, believing that by the virtue of being medical it is more accurate than other ways of understanding behavior. But we want teachers to become comfortable with the idea that a diagnosis of your student's behavior is only professional *opinion*, not a fact. A fact requires a level of certainty that, with regards to the nature of latent communication, we cannot have. Because of actual subjectivity regarding a child's latent communication, we find that different professionals can view the same child behavior in very different ways.

We are not dismissing diagnoses. In fact, it is important we acknowledge that the need to search for a diagnosis is understandable and useful. Professionals, parents, even children, often want a name for what is happening. It is the simplification of complexity that is a core aspect of human nature; the security derived from knowing. Receiving a diagnosis for a child in our classroom may serve to help us:

1. Gain a sense of control (i.e., this has been described and named by others; I am now in charge of this).
2. Reduce the sense of isolation (i.e., this has been experienced by others; I now am not alone with this).
3. Acquire a plan of action (i.e., there is an agreed upon set of strategies to address this; I now know what to do).

It is the old adage that information is power, and we as teachers need to feel empowered. That said, the categorizing of a child's behavior with a diagnostic label typically adds very little information that aids in our efforts to manage situations in our classrooms in real time. And regardless of the State in which we teach, the assessment process that provides these labels and the subsequent services is often slow and frustratingly methodical. While an external process of examination is taking place, these children and their behaviors remain ours to contend with, and we are expected to continue teaching.

To this end, our belief is that a diagnosis cannot be a holistic understanding of a child's behavior because of the absence of the child's latent communication. This requires us to look elsewhere for answers. The missing part simply makes a diagnosis less useful in the classroom environment. In each of these cases, there are response strategies that, with a bit of digging and thoughtful consideration of the latent communication, are readily available to teachers but do not flow from a child's diagnosis. Accumulating additional information, psychiatric evaluations, familial histories, and formal diagnoses may be helpful but are not prerequisites to developing effective strategies to seemingly complex and entrenched behaviors.

We believe that a more useful model of understanding child behavior is the humanistic model. This model of understanding behavior (that we call AURA) is based on:

- Acknowledging—acknowledging the whole child (observing both manifest communication and latent communication including feelings and thoughts to identify the holistic communication)
- Understanding—understanding the holistic communication (reconciling and linking manifest communication with latent communication)

- Responding—responding to the holistic communication (coordinating our reactions to the holistic communication)
- Affirming—affirming the child's change in behavior (identifying new holistic communications by recognizing the child's attempts, changes and novel decision-making)

When Renaye feels safer, Bobby feels less vulnerable, Kevin feels less overwhelmed, and Kelly feels less isolated, we as teachers affirm these changes. Stronger than praise, having more depth than a compliment, an affirmation is a type of interpersonal positive reinforcement. Manifestly, the changes in behavior (new holistic communication) could look like: (1) Renaye believing that zombies will *not* disrupt her classroom; (2) Bobby ceasing to bite and using his words; (3) Kevin listening while using ear plugs; and (4) Kelly picking her nose less often. These changes cannot be considered cures for a diagnosis. They are behavioral reactions of children being responded to in ways that are empathic and helpful by their caregivers. Identifying a diagnosis—that Renaye has early signs of Mood Disorder, that Bobby has Disruptive Behavior Disorder, that Kevin has Autism Spectrum Disorder, or that Kelly has an Anxiety Disorder—will not change their behaviors. The behaviors will continue to be the same. Any behavioral changes that occur will do so because we try to understand their possible latent communication underneath the label and respond to it, even if we are not certain that we completely understand.

The child's perception of our unconditional efforts develops an environment that encourages change. The "good enough teacher" is a very powerful force in a child's life. In Part Three of this book, we will examine manifest communications of specific problematic behaviors, possible understandings of the latent communications, potential responses, and affirmations. The goal is to become the "good enough teacher" that we all wish to be.

CHAPTER 3

A Child's Communication Scaffolding

Before we delve into identifying response strategies for specific problematic classroom or playground behaviors, we want to explore another layer of understanding that will enhance our overall discussion. When we use the word layer, we want teachers to visualize tiers in a pyramid. We must build each layer, one at a time, setting them carefully on top of one another, until our structure is complete, solid, and useful. Each layer, and its connection to the one beneath it and above it, is critical to the overall construction of the pyramid. As the pyramid grows, we move "higher," feeling more empowered. Without each layer, the pyramid is incomplete, and so is our ability to respond to the child behaviors that are so important to comprehend (see Figure 3.1).

In the previous chapter, we began our discussion of the AURA (Acknowledging, Understanding, Responding, Affirming) process of understanding behavior and its underlying communications. Constructed as a pyramid, the initial layer of AURA is our identification of manifest communications—what we can see and observe. This layer refers to the "Acknowledging" part of the AURA process (the first A in AURA)—we "see" the children by the examining and taking in of information they provide. The pyramid is further strengthened through our developing comprehension of what they are truly communicating. Our belief in the existence of possible meanings or motivations behind the manifest aspects of a given behavior. This is the "Understanding" (the U in AURA) of the child's whole communication, not just our observations of their behavior. To be fully utilized, this "Understanding" requires the next layer of the pyramid.

In this chapter, we will focus on and begin to recognize the third layer of our

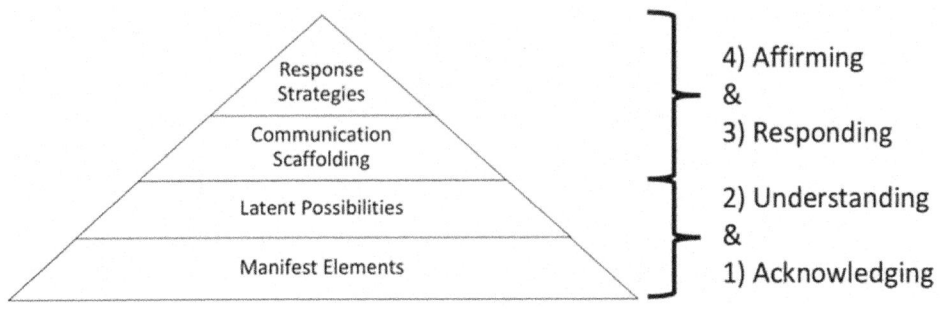

Figure 3.1: Hierarchy of Holistic Understanding of Behavior

understanding of behavior—what we call a child's communication scaffolding. How a child organizes his communication with others is built using Structural layers ("scaffolding") that provide support for the way a child communicates. These layers define the general manner or approach by which a child manages all interactions but are exaggerated when he, she, or they are having a challenge. They are made up of characterological structures that outline and influence a child's "choices" with regard to manifest and latent communication. Why does he cry so much? Why is she always so loud? Why do they seem so meek? What makes her take over the play? In other words, how does a specific child typically react to a problem he, she, or they are having? It is our contention that to fully "Acknowledge" and "Understand" a child's behavior is to consider three elements of communication—manifest communication, latent communication, and the child's communication scaffolding. It is also our belief that to do so dramatically increases our opportunities for successful intervention.

Elements of Communication Scaffolding

We think it is easiest to understand the characterological nature of communication scaffolding by breaking the concept down into a couple of parts and using case studies to concretize these ideas. We call these parts: (1) Temperament and (2) the Conscious Mind (see Figure 3.2). These two elements are inter-connected within a child, woven together into this scaffolding. While we can examine and explore each of these separately and will do so in this chapter for learning purposes, we want to emphasize that, as developmental and functional concepts, they work together in concert within a child. Either of these elements is no more or less important than the other, but, as we get to understand and use the concepts, we may find that for a specific child,

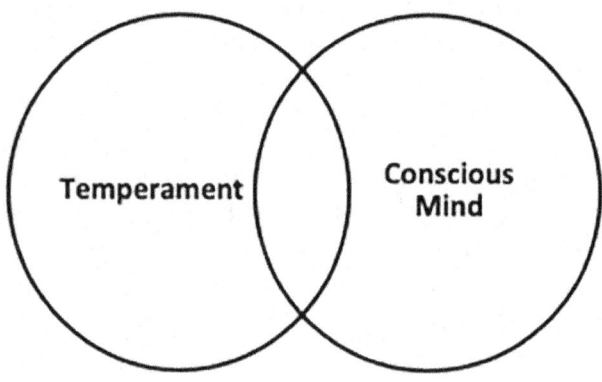

Figure 3.2: Communication Scaffolding

one of these may be more of a determining factor with regard to communication and behavior. We may also find that, as individuals, we are more adept at noticing one of the elements over the other.

Disruptive Abner in Ms. Dawson's Class

Abner is eight years old and in the second grade. He has a history of hitting and pushing other children, calling out during lessons, and running from the classroom, among other behaviors. He is often sent out of class, either to other classrooms or to the office, when he becomes too disruptive. Recently, when he became frustrated during an arts and crafts project, he threw a pair of scissors and hit another student in the leg with them. The scissors were rounded, but they still left a bruise. Abner was suspended from school for three days and his parents were called to meet with the principal. As this was just the most recent of many incidents, and since the incidents seem to be escalating in danger, a psychological evaluation was recommended. At the time of the meeting, there were three months left to the school year, and it was very unlikely the psychological evaluation and resulting Individualized Education Plan (IEP) would be completed and acted on before the end of the term. In the meantime, Abner was allowed to return to his class, and a para-professional was temporarily provided for the classroom in order to provide increased supervision for Abner. Regardless of outside interventions, it remains Ms. Dawson's responsibility to manage Abner in the classroom.

Temperament

By any measure, Abner's behavior may be considered atypical; on this matter we can all agree. But why is he so demonstrative in his behavior? Why does he get in trouble so often? Why did he throw scissors? What makes him "act out" or "act up" so much? To further our discourse about Abner's behaviors and others like him (and not like him), we want to provide an in-depth discussion of temperament and the function of the conscious mind.

As we indicated in Chapter 1, temperament is a multifaceted aspect of human nature that governs children's sense of connection to their environment and helps shape how that child interacts within it. Through their studies of young children in the 1980s, Stella Chess and Alexander Thomas were able to identify nine attributes of temperament with which all children are born—activity level, rhythmicity, approach/withdrawal, adaptability, intensity level, mood, persistence level, distractibility level, and sensory sensitivity level (see Table 3.1) (Chess & Thomas, 1990; 1996). They went on to propose that the properties of each of these attributes, combined in a variety of ways, color the way a child experiences the world. They called these ways of experiencing the environment, temperaments, and categorized them into three main types. They are as follows:

- Feisty or difficult—speaks to children's tendency toward needing control over their environment in an *expansive* and *intense* way. Struggling with the perceived impingements of any structures placed around them, these children tend toward letting out thoughts and feelings or outwardly expressing their latent communication. Feisty children feel first and think second. Abner is impulsive, head strong, unpredictable, reactive and passionate. His instinctual responses rule him, and they drive him forward in a highly external manner. While it may be helpful and an important goal to work toward, it will produce significant discomfort if Abner is pressed to express himself in a more contained way without preparation. For him, this feels unnatural.

- Slow to warm or cautious—speaks to children's tendency toward needing control over their environment in a *watchful* and *guarded* way. While these children can become fearful, loudly protesting their experiences of vulnerability, they tend toward keeping thoughts and feelings inside, indirectly expressing their latent communication. In contrast to Abner's externality, these children tend to express themselves more internally. In contrast to Abner, these children think first and struggle to express themselves. They keep their own counsel, contemplate, are inclined to perseverate (compulsively think); expressing themselves openly will produce discomfort, as it is experienced as a lack of containment.
- Flexible or easy—speaks to children's tendency toward feeling secure within their environment, being comfortable with adapting to changes that may take place, and requiring reasonable amounts of control and pacing to manage most day-to-day situations. In how they manage and express their feelings and thoughts, these children present a balance between needing to let information out (externality) and needing to keep it in (internality).

Children typically can be described using one temperament but may share aspects of multiple temperaments. For example, a child may be primarily feisty but also exhibit flexibility at times when that child is feeling particularly secure.

That said for our planning, identifying a child's primary temperament is useful and should not be viewed as limiting or pathologizing. Seeing a child as he or she is can be experienced as empathic. Social work has a helpful adage, "Start where the client is," not where we want them to be. Similar to child's feelings and emotions, the individual attributes that comprise a child's overall temperament exist on a continuum and therefore are not fixed. (Thomas & Chess; 1956; 1977). For each child, some of these attributes are more central to their character, while others may have less of an impact.

Because of this, we feel it is important to be familiar with each attribute. It may also be interesting for us to note that, over the years, some of these attributes have been given singular importance on their own (i.e., Distractibility and lack of focus, Activity Level and hyperactivity, and Sensory Threshold and sensory-seeking issues), as a way of understanding behavior. We believe it is important to consider these attributes as part of an overall picture, as opposed to unconnected contributors to or drivers of behavior.

Table 3.1:
Attributes of Child's Temperament

Attribute	*Meaning*	*From*	*To*
Activity Level	how a child physically engages with his/her environment	Sedentary	Energetic
Adaptability	how a child manages the changes or transitions that occur in everyday life	Resilient	Resistant

Attribute	Meaning	From	To
Distractibility	how a child is able to manage external factors like sounds or smells while trying to engage in a typical task	Focused	Scattered
Intensity	how a child reacts to an everyday situation that is not in his/her control	Calm	Reactive
Mood	how a child feels in general about typical life events and experiences	Positive Outlook	Negative Outlook
Persistence	how a child reacts to every-day adversity or challenges, like learning a new skill or figured out a problem	Driven	Passive
Regularity	how often, when, and in what pattern a child's everyday physiological needs (like hunger, thirst, sleep, or excretion) are expressed	Consistent	Unpredictable
Relatedness	how a child interacts with other people on a day-to-day basis, including children and adults	Social	Withdrawn
Sensory Threshold	how a child interprets the effect of external stimuli (sound, light, touch, smell) on his/her physical and emotional boundaries	Insensitive to External Stimuli	Sensitive to External Stimuli

(Thomas & Chess; 1956; 1977)

Abner's temperament can be identified as feisty. We can describe his nine temperament attributes as follows:

- energetic
- resistant to change
- scattered in terms of focus
- reactive to situations
- negative in his outlook
- driven in what he wants
- unpredictable in terms of his actions
- socially interested
- sensitive to external stimuli

Abner acts out, intensely, as do most temperamentally feisty children. He is a highly "external" child, communicating by expelling information. He lets his feelings drive his behavior, thinking through his feelings only minimally before he communicates to the world around him. His innate need for control and the feeling that his classmates and, teachers are controlling him, push him to communicate outwardly in ways that gets him in trouble.

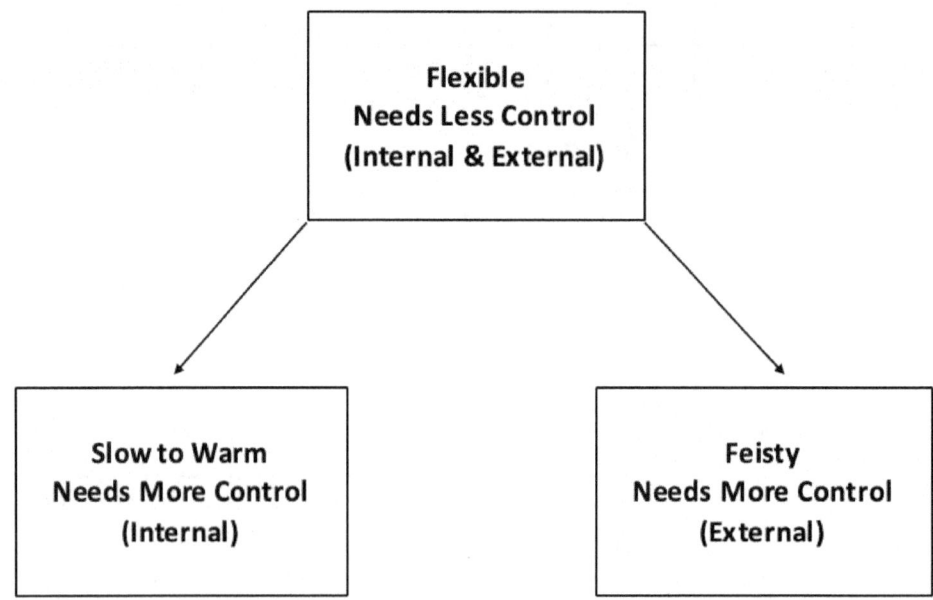

Figure 3.3.: Temperaments—Internality versus Externality

Tommy Keeps His Head Down in Ms. Anderson's Class

Tommy is eight years old and often sits at his desk with his head down especially when the class gets loud and boisterous. He answers questions when they are posed directly to him but otherwise is quiet and does not engage with the other students. His work is age appropriate, and he does his homework accurately and on time. At recess, he tends to stay by himself, drawing in his notebook. Ms. Anderson asked to see his drawings, and they are full of explosions, people being hanged, stabbed, and shot, and other worrisome imagery. He has even labeled some of the people with the names of his classmates. Naturally this is of great concern to Ms. Anderson, who plans to reach out to the guidance counselor immediately to discuss the disturbing drawings.

Tommy is a slow-to-warm child. He is as equal in need of control over his environment as Abner is; he simply goes about it in a different way. He removes himself (reducing his emotional and/or physical proximity from other children) from the environment when he becomes upset. This can be seen in the withdrawing behavior of putting his head down on the desk. The upset feelings connected to his frustration with his classmates and the impulses to express these feelings would be anathema to him. Feeling vulnerable, Tommy moves "inward," withdrawing, perseverating about what his classmates are doing, and possibly becoming upset with himself. In this way, we call Tommy an "internal" child (as are most slow to warm children), who keeps his information inside, communicating through more subtle means, such as via his concerning drawings and his "closed-off," non-verbal communication.

Tommy and others like him, who struggle with their classmates and the loss of control that comes with interacting with others, may be more subtle in their presentation, due to the fact that they do not "act out" and clamor. We must remain vigilant for these types of deceptively quiet communicators, as "acting in" can be misinterpreted as being content or just "shy."

For our purposes in describing communication scaffolding, we want to provide a convenient way of referring to temperament, its associated behaviors and communication scheme. While we still think it important to examine and consider all the various attributes of child temperament for thoroughness (as time allows), providing challenging children in our classroom with a straightforward classification can begin to help organize our thoughts with regard to their behavior and communication. For simplicity sake, let's characterize feisty, external children as "Loud" and slow to warm, internal children as "Quiet." These are not value judgments, but only streamlined identifiers.

The Functioning of the Conscious Mind

The second part of a child's communication scaffolding is what we call the functioning of the conscious mind. By conscious mind, we are referring to an idea that was originally developed by Sigmund Freud (Freud, 1914). Freud, and many subsequent theorists, posited that a child's conscious mind is the psychological mixture of brain elements that are tasked with administering a variety of activities of thinking (May 1953; 1967; Piaget, 2001; Ellenberger, 1970; Hurlburt & Heavey; 2008; Lerner, 1982; Meichenbaum, 1977). These mental processes, most of which fall under the current concept of executive functioning, are central to the quality of a child's day-to-day functioning and behavior. These include:

- Decision-Making (judgment, thoughtful balance of impulses, the understanding of society's rules, and life's realities)
- Impulse Control & Attention (reliable self-control of impulses)
- Memory (reliable access to past experiences for current application)
- Psychological Defenses (ingenious methods of reducing challenging anxiety of maturation and development)
- Regulation of Emotions (moment to moment self-control of raw and ever-changing feeling states)
- Stress Management (self-soothing of the difficulty adapting to rules)

We like to describe the conscious mind as a child's internal chaperone—helping with the many undertakings that home, school, and society at large demands of them on a daily basis: how to manage a relationship, how to share, what to do after one uses the bathroom, how to wait one's turn, how to control one's emotions, what to feel when disappointed or frustrated. When a child's conscious mind is working in a reliable manner, it provides an essential, internal, supervisory, and guidance service for these and many other childhood tasks and dynamics.

Problems begin to occur for a child when the direction that the conscious mind provides is not commensurate with the expectations or rules of the environment—when the internal chaperone is not overseeing sufficiently. It is important to acknowledge the potential for subjectivity in this concept. As teachers, we have our own styles, our own expectations and buttons that can get pushed. Some of us are strict; some of us are easy going; some of us allow for talking in the class; some of us do not. That said, we believe there is a baseline of objective structure that exists in every school, and it is this to which we are referring when we discuss the school environment.

Abner's feisty temperament and his related externality often affect his ability to modulate his feelings and lead to the overwhelming of his thoughts as he struggles to feel in control. He may know that throwing scissors is wrong but has great difficulty controlling himself. While he knows right from wrong, the functioning of his conscious mind (specifically his decision-making, impulse control, and emotional regulation) does not seem to provide him with the needed ability to manage the situation. Consequently, we can determine that, at this moment, the current functioning of Abner's conscious mind is such that it cannot prevent him from:

1. becoming overcome by his thoughts and feelings which are challenged by the structure of the school environment, and
2. displaying the feelings via extreme behaviors that communicate his sense of overwhelm.

More specifically, Abner's teacher can identify that the functioning of his conscious mind compromises his ability to manage particular tasks such as:

1. Remembering the safety rules of the class
2. Coping with the limits of the class rules
3. Helping him identify and control his anger
4. Considering different choices of action when he is angry
5. Stopping the impulse to throw the scissors at his classmate

Fortunately, unlike a child's temperament which caregivers and children must learn to adapt to and accommodate for, the conscious mind is dynamic and malleable. As Abner develops, his conscious mind will incorporate new information and ways of thinking from caregivers and peers alike and will use these new skills to help him navigate his more and more complex life experiences.

Tommy presents with the functioning of a conscious mind that is constricted, closed-off with highly contained emotions. He has a slow-to-warm temperament shaping his basic internality. He is aware that his behaviors are different from the other children; no one else keeps their heads on their desk. He sees others being jocular and sometimes silly in class and knows that their behavior makes him feel uncomfortable.

His angry feelings may frighten him, but he cannot express them. In fact, he may not even be aware of them. That said, we can know they exist because they splash out in his drawings in great detail. Tommy is aware that his drawings depict mayhem and death but does not understand that this may be connected to his angry impulses. The functioning of his conscious mind (specifically his judgment and impulse control) does not seem to provide him with the needed ability to manage the realities of feeling different, isolated and upset by children in his class. Consequently, we can determine that, at this moment, the current functioning of Tommy's conscious mind is such that it cannot prevent him from:

1. becoming overcome by his thoughts and feelings and fearfully needing to hide and obscure them, and
2. displaying the feelings via extreme drawings and obvious withdrawing behaviors.

More specifically, Tommy's teacher can identify that the functioning of his conscious mind compromises his ability to manage particular tasks such as:

1. Coping with the social norms of the classroom
2. Helping him identify and control his anger
3. Considering different choices of action when he is angry
4. Participating in group-based activities in the classroom
5. Asking for help, comforting, and support from his teacher and family

Like our streamlined classification of challenging child temperaments as "Loud" or "Quiet," we want to provide a straightforward way of characterizing the functioning of the conscious mind. This can be described as follows:

- "Over Reactive" to denote students who seem overwhelmed by their thoughts and feelings; whose conscious mind cannot contain these thoughts and feelings, allowing for the uncontrolled, chaotic expression of these thoughts and feelings (as illustrated with Abner).
- "Under Reactive" to describe students who seem disconnected from their thoughts and feelings; whose conscious mind has clamped down on these thoughts and feelings, allowing little freedom of thoughtful expression or even an awareness that they exist (as illustrated with Tommy) (see Figure 3.4).

Getting positive, attuned feedback from grownups aids the healthy development of the conscious mind. Obviously, the level of expected functioning varies based on the environment that the child is in (i.e., school has a set of rules, home has a set of rules, the playground has a set of rules), but a child's conscious mind is constructed and has the potential to accommodate and adjust for these variations.

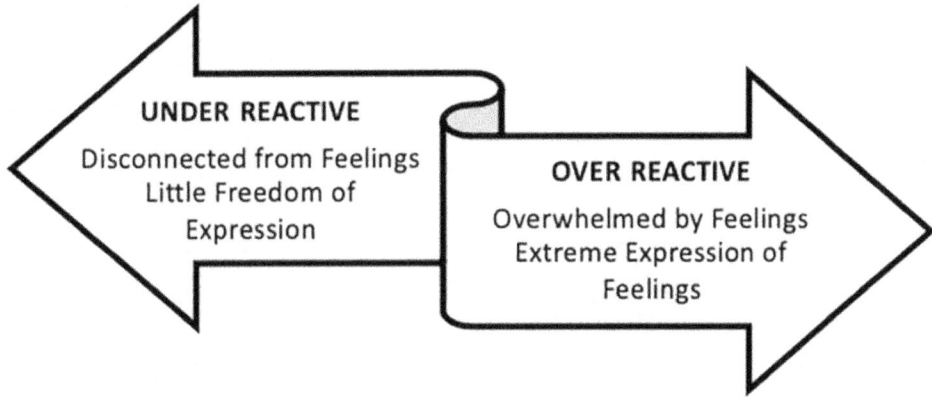

Figure 3.4: Conscious Mind and Under Reactivity versus Over Reactivity

Child Scaffolding Personas

With temperament and the conscious mind in place as the foundational elements of the child's communication scaffolding, we want to present teachers with a way of using these concepts for the purpose of responding to students' communication and managing behavior. This process centers on the reality that children utilize these two elements of their communication scaffolding to engage with the world around them. When combined, a child's temperament (Quiet or Loud) and their level of conscious mind function (Over Reactive or Under Reactive) create the ways of engaging what we call Personas. We have given these Personas names based on the typical reaction these combinations elicit from teachers (see Figure 3.5). The four Personas available are:

The Troubling Child
- Loud—Temperamentally feisty and externalizes their thoughts and feelings; acts "out" as a way of striving for control
- Over Reactive—The conscious mind is overwhelmed by their thoughts and feelings with extreme and chaotic expression of these thoughts and feelings

The Testing Child
- Loud—Temperamentally feisty and externalizes their thoughts and feelings; acts "out" as a way of striving for control
- Under Reactive—The conscious mind is disconnected from their thoughts and feelings with little freedom of expression of thoughts and feelings

The Worrying Child
- Quiet—Temperamentally slow to warm and internalizes their thoughts and feelings; acts "in" as a way of striving for control
- Over Reactive—The conscious mind is overwhelmed by their thoughts and feelings with extreme and chaotic expression of these thoughts and feelings

The Hiding Child
- Quiet—Temperamentally slow to warm and internalizes their thoughts and feelings; acts "in" as a way of striving for control
- Under Reactive—The conscious mind is disconnected from their thoughts and feelings with little freedom of expression of thoughts and feelings

Some of us may find delving into the details of each child (the nine temperament attributes, or the nuances of the conscious mind) to be a fulfilling intellectual pursuit. Yet the realities of the pressures of curriculum, administration, and scheduling seem to require that we offer a more user-friendly, practical, and speedier approach to defining the makeup of each child (see Figure 3.5). Thus, the reason for creating child Personas is so that we rapidly identify a specific child's needs and are able to recognize the preliminary manner that we will approach and address these needs.

While there may be variations based on individual details and specific behaviors, each Persona will have its own overarching methodology that will be thematically similar. For instance, Abner is, for the most part, Loud and Over Reactive, while Tommy is primarily Quiet and Under Reactive. We are not required to extemporaneously develop responses for Abner or Tommy. Their specific child Personas allow us

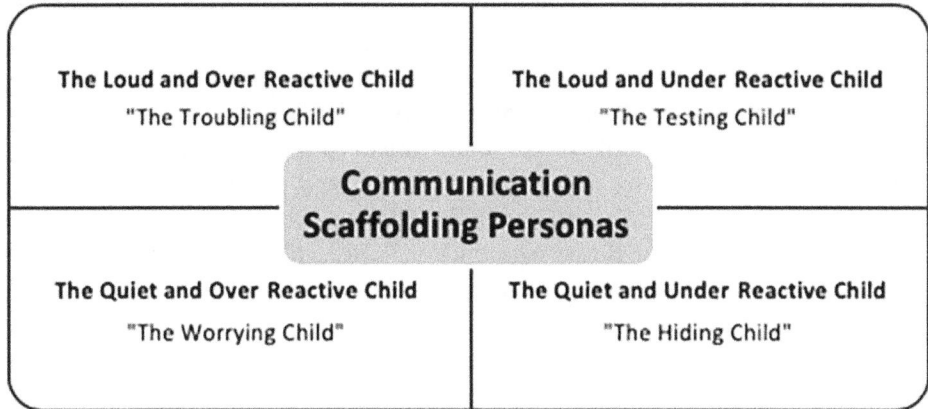

Figure 3.5: Child Personas

to home in on the type and quality of the strategy, increasing the possibility of a successful intervention.

There is overlap between these Personas, and by no means are we suggesting that a child always reacts exactly the same way; but we find there are tendencies to the way children present themselves when under some level of duress (see Figure 3.6). Regardless of what each child's approach to a problem is, we believe a child's communication scaffolding is a crucial piece to the puzzle, a linchpin, for creating a holistic response to any type of behavior.

In next section, we will look at a variety of children who, in some way or another, disrupt the classroom. There will be children like Abner, who create dangerous situations, and children like Tommy, who present other subtler, but equally challenging

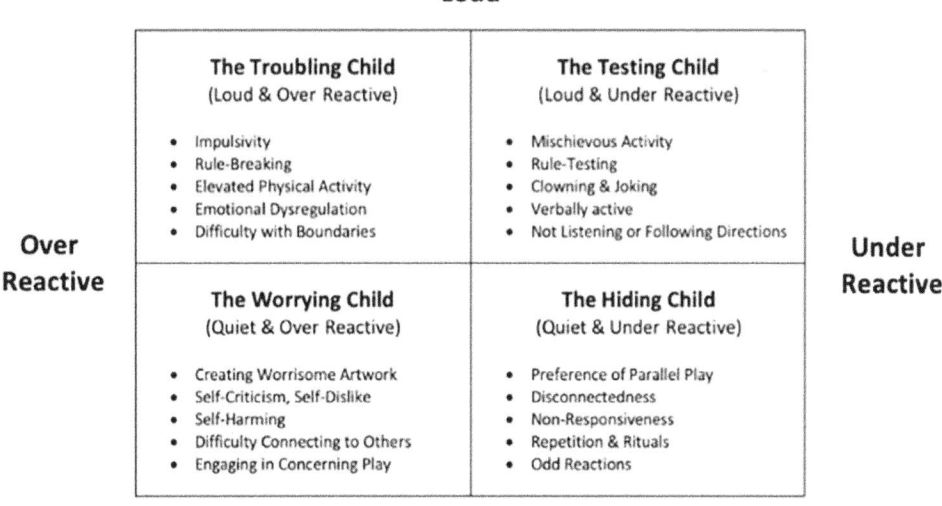

Figure 3.6: Child Personas with Associated Communications and Behaviors

behaviors. We will explore in depth what it means to be "Quiet" or "Loud," "Under Reactive" or "Over Reactive." We will examine each of the Personas—the Troubling child, the Testing child, the Worrying child, and the Hiding child—in detail in order to better understand how their temperaments and the functioning of their conscious minds affect their ability to communicate both manifestly and latently. With this information in hand, we will also begin to map out the framework of response strategies that each communication scaffolding Persona requires. As we complete our pyramid, we address the final two segments of AURA (the Responding and Affirming), which will allow us to successfully react to any number of child behaviors and situations.

Part Two

The Children Communicating in Your Classroom

Chapter 4

The Child Who Is "Troubling"

Loud and Over Reactive

Loud—<u>Temperamentally</u> feisty and externalizes thoughts and feelings; acts "out" as a way of striving for control

Over Reactive—The <u>conscious mind</u> is overwhelmed by thoughts and feelings with extreme and chaotic expression of these thoughts and feelings

* * *

AURA (Acknowledging, Understanding, **Responding**, **Affirming**)

This chapter will explore the behavior of the "Troubling" child and many of the possible aspects of this child that contribute and produce these challenging types of communications. The Troubling child is characterized by a Loud and Over Reactive communication scaffolding, and we will cover both in our attempts to gain a workable understanding of how to respond in a sustainable, helpful, and empathic fashion.

Imagine a pressure cooker sitting atop our stove with its small metal release valve letting out steam. Now recast that pressure cooker with a child's mind and a child's body and allow that child to leave the confines of the kitchen. The ensuing pressured release of behavior/communication of that child is what we describe as Troubling.

Within our confined classroom, this group of children present their Loud aspect of communication as significantly demonstrative behavior that requires our immediate focus. Troubling children do more than test the limits, often grabbing them and shaking them. Their Over Reactive nature heightens a sense of overwhelm that can be felt by everyone, as the chaotic attention these children seek clamors against any boundary it finds. We tend to push these children away because of the scale of their disruption. Unfortunately, their presentation can lead directly to their actual needs being missed. In reality, the Troubling child is yearning to be contained by compassionate strength and desperate for the healthy release of pressure that this type of response can bring.

Chapter 4. The Child Who Is "Troubling" 57

> *Am I Mandated to Share?*
>
> There may be times when a teacher deems it necessary to involve individuals outside the classroom to address the needs of the Troubling child (including but not limited to, other school professionals, administration, parents, child protective services, and law enforcement). The material in this chapter addresses what a teacher can accomplish with a Troubling child within the classroom setting, but does not, in any way, suggest that these issues need only be managed within the classroom setting. If a teacher has significant concerns about a child, we always suggest discussing these concerns immediately with other individuals.

Over the next four chapters, we will explore the four previously identified child Personas. We will present each by conveying the information in an organized structure. This structure—starting with the Troubling child—will track with the AURA format, describing manifest and possible latent communications to bolster our understanding and then laying out the beginnings of a response strategy. For this chapter, the sections are as follows:

- Child scenarios
- Manifest communication (temperament) from scenarios in this chapter—Loud
- Latent communication (temperament) from scenarios in this chapter—Loud
- Manifest communication (conscious mind) from scenarios in this chapter—Over Reactive
- Latent communication (conscious mind) from scenarios in this chapter—Over Reactive
- Structured responses for Loud & Over Reactive (Troubling) children

There may be some overlap of information from section to section within a chapter (remember, all things "children" are rarely orderly, neat, or organized).

Scenarios—Lloyd and Victoria

Scenario—Lloyd, 7 years old, 1st grade in Mr. Barnett's class

Lloyd is a 7 year old boy and in 1st grade. His disruptive behavior makes day-to-day functioning of the class very challenging for Mr. Barnett and for the other students. Since the school year began, Lloyd consistently calls out in class, calling the teacher names like "Ugly" and "Stupid," and making animal noises while the teacher is trying to interact with other students. Mr. Barnett asks him (sometimes demands him) to stop when he engages in these behaviors, but he rarely does, and Mr. Barnett is forced to bounce Lloyd to another classroom (where he typically continues behavior). Lloyd seldom stays in his seat for an entire lesson, often wandering around, talking to other students, taking their papers and crumpling them, or removing books from shelves and tossing them on the floor. Recently, things seemed to escalate when Lloyd walked out of the classroom and actually left the school grounds. After he was found, Lloyd reported to the school administrators that the reason he ran away was that Mr. Barnett told him "to get out of my sight!!"

Scenario—Victoria, 4 years old, Pre-Kindergarten in Ms. Kressler's class

Victoria's behavior in class has disturbed Ms. Kressler all year. Victoria seems fine at times and then, seemingly without cause, throws herself on the ground and has a temper tantrum that can last for quite some time. Victoria performs well in school activities and does her solitary work (drawing, painting, sand-table, block building, etc.) without incident, but she has difficulties with group work and playground activity. When she is with other children, she often gets into physical and verbal altercations with them when she disagrees with their ideas—she will push them, bite them, spit on them, or tell them that she hates them. At the parent/teacher conference in December, Victoria's parents acknowledged they were having the same problems at home. They reported that they had taken Victoria to see a psychiatrist because of her "hyperactivity" and "impulsivity" and that she had been diagnosed with ADHD and prescribed, Daytrana TM, one of the ADHD medications. They indicated that they were intending to start Victoria on her medication in January after the winter break. It is now April, and Ms. Kressler has not noticed a dramatic difference in Victoria's behavior.

Manifest Content—Loud

The child who wants to be, indeed demands to be, noticed could be described in terms of child communication scaffolding, as a "Loud" child. When we turn to the Merriam-Webster's dictionary, we find it defines the word loud as "producing or capable of producing much noise; easily audible" (Merriam-Webster, 2020). From a manifest perspective, when we consider "Loud," we tend to first think of volume. In the car or at a club, we may listen to loud music; we are aware when someone is speaking loudly in certain settings; or when we are trying to concentrate or sleep, we can be distracted or bothered by loud noises. We may also think of "Loud" as something that is clearly visible. Our eyes are drawn to someone walking down the street wearing loud clothing that is colorful and brash, or we are preoccupied by a person with a loud personality who "makes a scene."

Typically, we know when something is "Loud" because we are motivated to use "defenses" to shelter ourselves from it—cover our ears, shield our eyes, or shy away from the sensation. This type of "Loudness" is unpleasant to us, and we try to avoid it or escape from it. In our scenarios, Victoria and Lloyd use Loud physical expressions, Loud language, and Loud feelings. Within the realm of communication, whether we are talking about volume or conspicuousness, the notion of being Loud conveys the inevitable reality of being noticed by others. It is very difficult to be Loud and not to be observed.

Latent Content—Loud

The behaviors connected to "Loud" also have their own meaning that cannot be found in a dictionary without some interpretation. The additional information that we find critical to our understanding of the concept of "Loud" comes from deductions and inferences about the internal life of these children. We believe that being "Loud" comes from a tacit wish or demand to be noticed and responded to by others. For children, this feeling of not being noticed is akin to being hungry (for attention, for nurturance, for empathy). Using this metaphor, we can imagine that the louder children are, the hungrier they are. Loud children, we might say, are "starving" for attention. In terms of priorities, the requirement to be noticed (or to be fed) exists as bedrock for these children.

As a way of reinforcing this idea, let us look at Maslow's Hierarchy of Needs from Chapter 1. We want to present a slightly altered view of his theory for early childhood educators. In it, the first three levels of need—Physiological, Safety and Belonging/Love—are merged because of a child's vulnerability and dependence on adults. There is no real separation between the need for water, air, shelter (physiological), security and protection (safety), and attachment (belonging and love). While Maslow placed these on separate and increasingly advanced levels, we suggest that children experience them as one (Maslow, 1943).

For our purposes, the concept of *acting-out* is defined as behavior that is fueled by the external expression of a person's thoughts and/or emotions. It is typically exaggerated in its presentation, requiring some level of containment from others and, therefore, is considered an inefficient and less effective means of communicating one's needs. For Troubling children, this acting out takes the form of the "Loud" hungry cry for attention and speaks to their desperate and persistent demand for any and all of Maslow's bedrock needs. The repercussions and ramifications that this tenacious request for their basic necessities of life has on their day-to-day school functioning are essential to our understanding of and empathy for these children. Whether the Loud child or the receiver(s) of this type of communication are consciously aware, the unspoken need and hunger exist and demand a thoughtful and measured response.

Manifest Content—Over Reactive

As you will recall from the previous chapter, we define "reactivity" in relation to communication as:

1. a child's connection to his or her thoughts and feelings
2. a child's manner of expression of those same thoughts and feelings

In general, "Troubling" children tend to exhibit a surplus of energy and power within both of these realms of reactivity. This is where the "over" in over reactivity comes from. They are like supernovas. These children are explosive and typically unable to contain their potent thoughts and feelings, allowing unfiltered expression of these raw communications. They are also angry at not having their needs met, and this is expressed in the aggressiveness of their behaviors.

Some children may catch themselves with self-soothing techniques or a hesitancy stemming from an awareness of how their intense behavior may be negatively perceived. Without external intervention, Lloyd and Victoria, (even with some self-awareness) unfortunately, do not curtail the intensity of their communication. Their feelings and thoughts are expressed as physical or verbal communications of significant forcefulness, with little or no conscious consideration of surroundings or consequences. In this way, we want you to consider that both hyperactivity and impulsivity are Over Reactive behaviors. Victoria's tantrums, Lloyd's elopement from the school grounds, Victoria's spitting, biting, and pushing, Lloyd's incessant calling out and crumpling of papers, are all examples of their Over Reactive communications.

Latent Content—Over Reactive

Over reactivity, like being Loud, contains a tacit demand to be responded to, but with a different end goal. In the case of over reactivity, the child's demand is to be stopped—not the type of being stopped with the definitiveness of a security guard detaining someone, but more like the empathic feel of being held back by a caregiver from something that could lead to injury. We want you equate "being stopped," with these children providing much needed developmental resources including:

- Supportive Responsiveness
- Non-threatening Containment
- Compassionate Security

In this way, we are talking about providing rules, limits and consistency in conjunction with Carl Rogers' theory of "unconditional positive regard." This theory carries the message that every child is innately good and that anything a child does, we accept as having an important purpose (Rogers, 1951). Rogers saw this as the way to create a corrective emotional experience (Alexander, 1946); meaning, in this regard, that the teacher creates with the Troubling child a relationship where he is "fed," and that his hunger for attention is sated in a productive, helpful, and learning-enhancing manner. In addition, Rodgers developed the notion of client-centered psychotherapy. This theory has as its core the notion that the client is the focus of the work in psychotherapy and it is directed by the client rather than the therapist. This creates a sense of partnership based on mutuality.

We extrapolate from his theory a student-centered way of assessing and evaluating a child's communication by becoming a partner in the process with the child. What this achieves is the depersonalizing of a child's behavior. Although we can all agree that hearing "don't take it personally" often feels unhelpful, Rogers' student-centered framework can help us by reminding us to continually shift our focus from how the situation may be impacting us to what the children's difficulties and problems may be communicating about them.

We are also talking about D.W. Winnicott's "holding environment." This concept is based on a message to the child that anything he, she, or they feel will not overwhelm their caregivers (Winnicott, 1953; 1990). This creates an environment of safety for the child that can handle, manage, understand, and soothe the child's feelings. Underneath the Troubling child is often a child with a deep sense of sadness. The holding environment indicates it is safe to express that sadness instead of acting it out through attention-seeking behaviors in the classroom.

The latent communication of the Over Reactive child is a wish to be stopped and the fears that: (1) no one will be able to or (2) that no one will want to. It is the desire to trust someone and to have that someone care, love, and nurture enough to take charge in an empathic and understanding way that provides a sufficient sense of security.

And so, when Lloyd feels the impulse building to express his fears or discomfort about himself, the following occurs: (1) he calls out in class and uses offensive language in order to diminish those around him and help himself to feel more powerful, and (2) the dramatic, outward communication works to overshadow his vulnerability in the ensuing commotion. When Victoria senses that she is not in control within a group setting and begins to feel vulnerable, she spits on other children, screams, physically accosts her peers, and throws a tantrum. This creates a similar theatrical tumult that distracts from her discomfort. Is it really possible that these two children are actually seeking a person to stop them, to hold them back from their behaviors? Can we imagine that they are looking for a firm and caring hand to say, "Absolutely not?" We want you to consider that the answer to both of these is "yes."

We understand that, manifestly, the behavior exhibited by the Troubling child appears to communicate the exact opposite message. However, we strongly believe that:

- Lloyd would not consciously choose for his teacher to abandon him and want nothing to do with him any longer;

and

- Victoria in no way would want her teacher to reject her and remove her from the classroom.

In Lloyd and Victoria's cases, neither child feels particularly safe nor trusts that the adults around them will know how or will even want to respond to their needs. Unfortunately, all of the logical reasoning and verbal discourse one might use to respond to their behavior seems not to register with them at all.

Building Responses for Scenarios—Loud & Over Reactive

By our definition, both Lloyd and Victoria are "Loud" and "Over Reactive" communicators. Their communications demand to be noticed, and they often receive the teacher's undivided attention, as well as the attention of their classmates. Under AURA, once these behaviors are acknowledged, without the added element of understanding, these children often receive frustration, dismay and rejection from those around them. These are the most common and, understandable responses that the Troubling child consistently generates in teachers and peers.

While we are suggesting that Lloyd and Victoria both want to be noticed and stopped from self-harm, we also acknowledge that their behaviors motivate teachers and classmates to give them space, shy away, or try and rid themselves of these problematic children. In fact, these children often end up more and more isolated as the school year progresses. While we may feel some transient empathy for Troubling children, they are challenging. Their behaviors and the negative feelings they provoke often cause feelings of anxiety and inadequacy in responsible adults. Mr. Barnett and Ms. Kressler may wonder, "What is it about me that I cannot reach or handle this child?" How do we as teachers begin to get around this seemingly intractable dilemma?

Answering these questions requires an understanding of what triggers the Troubling child's manner of communication. Since the times of Greek tragedies to the theories of Sigmund Freud, we have been aware of the connection of the wish and the fear behind human aspirations (Freud 1966, La Farge, 2014). For these children the wish and fear are two sides of the same reality. When we apply this to Lloyd and Victoria, we find that they:

1. have a *wish* to be noticed, cared for and valued (which unfortunately may stem from the likely reality, either overt or covert, that they do not feel this is so within the family);

and simultaneously

2. have a *fear* of being ignored, unloved, rejected, and abandoned (which sadly may be connected to the likely reality, either overtly or covertly, that plays out within the family).

We want to look at this multi-layered dilemma in two ways. First, let us look at their behavior's self-fulfilling prophetic nature. A self-fulfilling prophecy flows as follows:

- An individual, in this case, a child, makes a false assumption about himself within the context of their current environment, in this case, at school (**I am a bad person, and no one at school loves me**).
- The individual, then sets about trying to address this false assumption by engaging others, often in roundabout and indirect ways, in order to prove or disprove its validity (**I demand to be comforted by you so as to prove you love me**).
- Because the assumption is misaligned with the environment and the individuals in it, in this case classmates and teachers, attempts to remedy the false reality are invariably misunderstood by others (**while I like you, I do not always want to comfort you; I want to play with you, teach you; stop asking me to always comfort you**).
- The confused, frustrated, or annoyed reactions by others lead the individual to believe he has confirmed the false assumption (**see, they do not want to**

comfort me, they keep telling me to stop, therefore I must be bad and unlovable).

Robert Merton (1948) believed that all people, and this includes children, were susceptible to self-fulfilling prophecies. While the reasons behind a person's false assumptions may be beyond our abilities to decipher, we can make an educated guess that they are not purely conjured for the purposes of making life complicated. They are based in and derived from some reality that the person has experienced. For our purposes, it is important to remember that children carry their false assumptions and act them out within the school environment—they enter the school like a cold gust of wind on a wintery day. These false assumptions have no place in the warmth of the classroom, but make their presence known just the same.

Let us examine Lloyd's self-fulfilling prophecy based on his fear that he will be ignored, unloved, rejected, and abandoned:

Table 4.1:
Self-Fulfilling Prophecy of the Troubling Child

Steps in a Self-Fulfilling Prophecy	*Example*
A person makes a false assumption about himself in the context of the current environment.	Because of his life experiences, Lloyd feels that he is always ignored, unloved, rejected and abandoned. These thoughts and feelings manifest in Lloyd as a belief that no one will listen to/hear him at school.
The person takes action to test the false assumption.	Convinced of these dynamics, this creates a great deal of consternation in Lloyd, and he tries to enact a solution. Lloyd speaks very loudly so that those around him will be forced to hear him and listen to him.
Others react to the action and misunderstand.	The request for being noticed challenge the teachers and his classmates in its pervasiveness and intensity. They feel unable to listen to Lloyd because of his loud volume and try to stop Lloyd from being Loud by giving him consequences (the teachers) or withdrawing from him (his classmates).
The others' reactions/responses to the person's action, confirm the false assumption for the person.	Based on the teacher's and classmates' reactions, Lloyd confirms to himself that no one listens to/hears him (and he maintains the feeling of being ignored, unloved, rejected, and abandoned).
The person takes more extreme action to further test the false assumption.	Lloyd escalates, speaking more loudly or with more extreme language.

Merton, 1948; Weiner, Gallo-Silver, & Lucas, 2020

Second, we believe that the Troubling child's false assumption stems from difficulties that can best be understood if we return to Erik Erikson's theories that we discussed in our first chapter. One could speculate or deduce that both Lloyd and Victoria did not trust that their cries, as infants, would be answered or responded to in helpful, empathic and loving ways. This disrupts the very foundation of interpersonal relationships as it thwarts the basic human need for connection (Fairbairn, 1954; Fairbairn, et al., 1995). This disruption of the first stage of Erikson (leading to mistrust) and its lack of resolution can cause the need to overcompensate during Erikson's second stage of development (shame/self-doubt) (see Figure 1.1) (Erikson, 1950). Because of the development of mistrust in one's surroundings, we could very easily observe:

- pressure to be Loud and noticed (because of a dependence on others) in order to get one's needs met,
- requirement to be in control (not dependent on others) in order get one's needs met,
- intense shame and self-doubt (vulnerability) when feeling an absence of either of the first two

This shame is a powerful, emotional feeling that is always initiated and generated from outside the person who feels the shame. It is like an unwanted gift that a child cannot return, and it isolates the shame-feeling individual further and further from any people who could offer support.

The behavior of the "Troubling" child is a request for intervention, a plea to be stopped, to no longer perpetuate the mistrust and shame. In this case, "stopped" is a euphemism that can have many meanings. All of them include a structured response (either verbal or non-verbal) that brings about the momentary cessation of the problematic behavior:

- Addressed by a teacher
- Noticed by a teacher
- Responded to by a teacher
- Attended to by a teacher
- Held back by a teacher
- Talked to by a teacher
- Explained to by a teacher
- Contained by a teacher

Utilizing our student-centered approach, and adding into the mix, the self-fulfilling prophecy and the mistrust of others, we now have a workable outline for understanding the Troubling child's behavior. This includes the manifest communication, a likely framework for latent communication and this child's typical communication scaffold. With this understanding, we can move into the response stage of AURA.

Based on their individual natures, experiences, and early relationships, children find intuitive and instinctual ways of asking for help from others (Horney, 1945; Horney, 1950). It is our contention that these ways of asking for help are linked to the latent communications and communication scaffolding of our four Personas. Troubling children ask for help and responses in their own specific ways, as do Testing children, Worrying children, and Hiding children. Within each of these categories, there is variability to be sure, but the central themes are consistent.

Types of Responses

From the needs of these four Personas (we will discuss the Testing, Worrying, and Hiding children in subsequent chapters), we have derived four types of empathic responses:

- Structural
- Verbal
- More Emotional
- Less Emotional

Each type of empathic response presents to these children a new and healthier model of interacting. We organized them based on what we believe are the two most essential and foundational aspects of a child's relational development—their sense of connection and their sense of security. The four types exist on two continuums and should be viewed as follows:

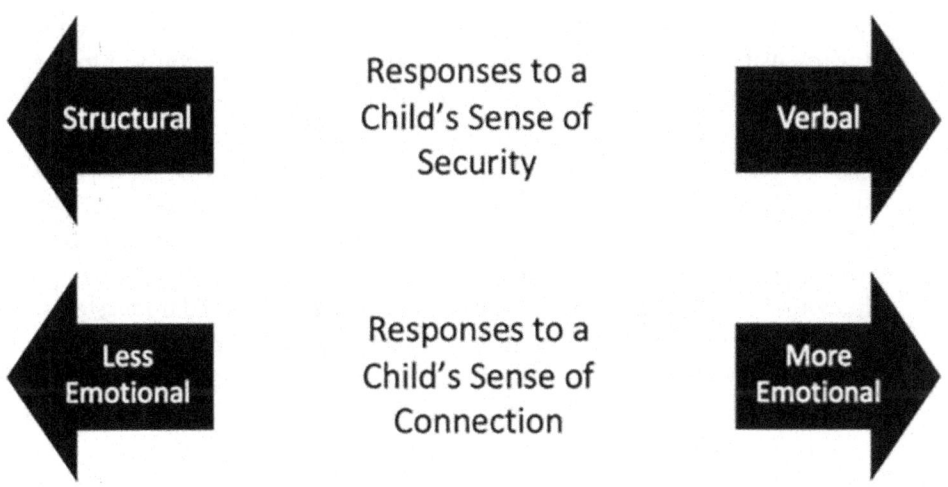

Figure 4.1: Continuum of Responses

By providing and modeling skill sets that are underdeveloped or, even missing, our intent is to balance out the presentation of the child communication Persona. Imagine this as a response to a vitamin deficiency. If a child needs Vitamin B, then we give them more greens in their diet. If Vitamin D, we take them outside and get them some sun. Our responses can allow for a child to learn (at least during school hours) to communicate in a more holistic fashion and may even work to slowly undermine the self-fulfilling prophecy. The over-arching descriptions of the four basic ways that we can respond are as follows:

> *Structural Response*—an intervention in response to "Loud" communications that includes using a teacher's practical abilities to alter the environment, changing a routine, getting down on one knee, sitting close, making physical contact, and/or identifying some one-on-one time. These types of

interventions are focused on physical containment and relate to visceral comforting. This is connected to the basic physical attention that a parent provides and harkens back to infancy—holding, swaddling, rocking, hugging, or finding a quiet room to nap.

Verbal Response—an intervention in response to "Quiet" communications that includes using one's words, talking through a problem, describing a perspective, conveying empathy, and/or explaining a process. These types of interventions are focused on spoken containment and relate to aural comforting. This is connected to the way that parents use sounds and words to calm their distressed children such as specific encouragement ("you'll be okay"), relational assurances ("I got you"), or soothing speech patterns and tones ("there, there, now" or "just breathe").

Less Emotional Response—an intervention in response to "over reactivity" that centers on the teacher remaining calm and providing as little personal emotion into the intervention as possible. These interventions anticipate the likelihood that the child is already bringing a great deal of intensity to an interaction and is overwhelmed by his/her emotions. By not adding to the intensity of the interaction, teachers are more likely to connect to the child by diminishing the overall emotional stimulation of the moment—like pulling a window shade down because the sun is too bright.

More Emotional Response—an intervention in response to "under reactivity" that centers on the teacher providing some amount of personal disclosure of feelings and displaying some of their underlying emotion that has been generated by an interaction. These types of interventions anticipate the likelihood that a child is having difficulty connecting to and understanding his/her own important emotions during an interaction. By highlighting the underlying intensity of the interaction, teachers are more likely to connect to the child by increasing the child's overall self-awareness—like pulling a window shade up because a room is too dark.

Table 4.2:
Personas and Responses

Persona	*Responses*
Loud & Over Reactive (Troubling)	**Requires Structural & Less Emotional Response from teacher**
Loud & Under Reactive (Testing)	Requires Structural & More Emotional Response from teacher
Quiet & Over Reactive (Worrying)	Requires Verbal Response & Less Emotional Response from teacher
Quiet & Under Reactive (Hiding)	Requires Verbal Response & More Emotional Response from teacher

Weiner, Gallo-Silver, & Lucas, 2020

Let us recall from Chapter 3, the basic behaviors that the Troubling child may exhibit.

- Impulsivity (lack of control over one's instinctual urges to act)
- Rule Breaking (the disregarding of guidelines set by one's environment)
- Elevated Physical Activity (the increase in one's body movement)
- Emotional Dysregulation (difficulty in managing one's expressive output)
- Difficulty with boundaries (trouble accepting or working with the physical and emotional restrictions of other people and environments)

As we stated earlier, the heat and intensity generated from Troubling children are actually designed to have us move toward these children. Think about it like putting out a fire. If we saw someone in danger from a flame, we would move to put out the flame, to smother it in order to keep the child safe. And we do not put out fires by dowsing them with more flame. A child's intensity can take many forms:

- The child who is always moving around in an uncontained manner (hyperactivity)
- The child who consistently acts before thinking (impulsivity)
- The child who displays intense emotional outbursts (tantrums)
- The child who breaks others' creations (destruction)
- The child who breaks his own creations (self-destruction)
- The child who consistently runs away (lack of self-care)
- The child who consistently hits, spits, bites, harms others (aggression)

For our purposes, we work toward containing and diluting the Troubling child's loss of control, impulsivity, movement, outbursts, boundary violations and irritability. By way of their behavior, we can identify that Lloyd and Victoria need help corralling their frenetic pace, unpredictability, chaotic natures, and the underlying mistrust and fear that these behaviors signify. Because of the communication scaffolding that the Troubling child presents, we can most effectively accomplish this goal by providing:

    1. a secure, clear and solid environment through the use of *Structural responses*, to show that we are not overwhelmed; and
    2. a cool calmness through the use *Less Emotional responses* to show that we are in control, responsive and listening.

Let's put some these responses into action. Beginning with the Structural responses, the following are several generic interventions that fit our scenarios:

Examples of Structural Responses

- Altering the time and place of contact
  Meeting with the child outside of class time can begin forming a different type of relationship that mirrors the relationship the teacher has with the other children in the class. **These touch bases do not need to be long (i.e., one or two sentences or comments, for 10 seconds or so).** Creating the needed "holding environment" in the classroom requires this type of preparation outside of class time. How can Lloyd or Victoria learn to trust

their teachers if their only experience with them is when their teachers are anxious and irritated by their behavior? While it may briefly take away from some of our planning time, consistently meeting with Lloyd and Victoria before class, for part of lunch, or prior to going out for recess, is a sacrifice that can have a significant upside. Meeting after school tends to lessen the effectiveness of this intervention because post-school fatigue (the wish to leave for both teacher and student) and its identification with punishment.

- Creating close physical proximity

  Lloyd and Victoria both require some type of physical cue that helps contain and "hold" them (stop them). This might include a request to stand next to the teacher, hand holding, placing our hand on their shoulder, or some other non-aggressive physical contact. This would be followed by the teacher insisting on as much direct eye contact as possible (at the child's eye level) and then a firm (and calm, see below) indication that the child cannot continue the behavior.

  Ongoing physical proximity maintenance may also be necessary. This might include moving a desk or a seat closer to a teacher. While this may look like a punishment, we view this as increasing secure structure. It can be characterized as "you need to stay near me until we can manage and control your actions."

- Altering the locus of control

  Outside of class, it may be profitable to ask the child (give them some control) what might help when they "have big feelings" (become Loud) and "want to push someone, run, or call out in class" (feel Over Reactive). If the children can offer suggestions, that is wonderful, as long as it fits in the model of increased security. If not, we can offer Structural responses, such as Lloyd spending time in a chair by Mr. Barnett's desk so that he might feel more noticed by the closeness of the teacher. Victoria might suggest that she needs to sit in a corner of the classroom with her favorite doll in order to try and self-comfort herself or under a table if that feels more containing.

- Creating novel activities

  Sometimes being given a separate individual assignment helps the child feel both heard and held. While we are not advocating writing "I will behave" one hundred times, the repetitive nature of that assignment can be relaxing to some children. A drawing assignment might be more fruitful, such as, "Draw a picture of yourself when you are happy (or when you are angry)." No matter what they actually draw, this can relax and refocus a child, as well as produce further insights into the child's feelings and thoughts.

Examples of Less Emotional Responses

- Altering tone of discourse

  We conduct in-class interactions between child and teacher in a tone that is purposefully reserved. This peaceful, measured tone is in stark contrast to the child's Loud behavior and compels them to quiet their presentation in order to hear us. We also use "calm" statements, simple phrasing and simple ideas because this is all they can hear at these moments. "I see you." "I hear you." "You are safe." "I got you." Working with Lloyd and Victoria, we can use their names in the statements. "Victoria, I see what you are doing. I am here, Victoria. I will stay with you, Victoria, until you feel calm." Using a person's name over and over again can help both focus them and connect them to their surrounding environment. This also has a hypnotic quality that can calm a child. In those newly created opportunities to interact outside of class time, because of the decrease in stimulation, we may be able to use more complex phrasing and concepts.

- Changing the speed and pace
  In addition to altering the tone that we speak with, we can produce a "calming" pace to our interaction. Slowing down, talking and moving slower, requires children to mirror us, to match our speed, in order to process what we are saying and doing. If Mr. Barnett says the phrase "I see you," with a heartbeat in between each word, Lloyd will have to wait to hear, "I … See … You." As Ms. Kressler moves across the room, she walks and breathes slowly, holding hands, Victoria walks next to her, matching her gait. We know from meditation that slowing one's body, decreases one's heart rate. This intervention, combined with a less stimulating setting, helps to manage these children's emotionality.

As we have stated throughout this chapter, the attention we provide needs to be conveyed in specific ways for the Troubling child. Lloyd and Victoria need extra "attention" at this time, yet we acknowledge it is complicated giving a child extra attention when they are acting out in the classroom. Frustratingly, addressing the behavior of Troubling children take time away from the rest of the class. Being "kind" to them may, thus, seem paradoxical.

That said, we do not believe the common wisdom that "gratifying" a Troubling child with our attention reinforces their "negative" behavior. Ignoring the behavior and/or laying out consequences for the behavior as the primary or only response is not sufficient and will not work long term. If Troubling children believe that they are being misunderstood (feeling rejected or abandoned), the behaviors will continue and/or escalate. We are suggesting a more holistic empathic attention that overtime will address the underlying nature of the Troubling child.

While we cannot rely on getting additional information from the parents, if we do come by some, it can be used, with parents' permission, to help their child. These pieces of background information do not excuse, nor do they completely explain a child's behavior. They do identify stressors in a child's home life that could be acted-out in the classroom. These bits of history can be used to augment our empathic responses. For instance: "Victoria, it's so upsetting upset when our home life is changing, but it is still not safe to spit in the classroom," or "Lloyd, it is really hard to have a new brother, but we are never allowed to be unsafe and throw things in the classroom."

Affirmations That Help Children Hold On to Their New Coping Skills

The final "A" in AURA is the practice that helps children integrate and consolidate a change in their behavior. Once any of these responses work, once we see that a "helpful" empathic response resonates with a child's manifest communication, their latent communication, and their communication scaffolding, the next step is affirmation. An affirmation is a meaningful statement about the child's worth and value. It can come in a variety of forms:

- "The way you were able to breathe and calm yourself was amazing."
- "You showed how clever you were when you made that great decision."
- "You are so athletic, and you show it by the way can really control your body when you are upset."
- "Your big thoughts are so important; I am impressed by the way you tell me about them."

As Lloyd and Victoria respond to the new responses, the affirmations would focus on the good qualities of each child, such as acknowledging and highlighting their decision-making, courage, or creativity. This might sound something like this: "Lloyd, everyone can see how hard you are working to keep your body safe."

These statements make children think about themselves. It is more than just a teacher's manifest observation. It has a latent component, and it speaks to the uniqueness of a specific child—who a child is; what that child can do; what the meaning of that ability might be. All these components link up to create a memorable statement that provides positive recognition. It is memorable because of the detail and allows a teacher's hard work to travel on with the child well after class is over.

Chapter 5

The Child Who Is "Testing"

Loud and Under Reactive

Loud—<u>Temperamentally</u> feisty and externalizes thoughts and feelings; acts "out" as a way of striving for control

Under Reactive—The <u>conscious mind</u> is disconnected from thoughts and feelings with little freedom of expression of thoughts and feelings

* * *

AURA (Acknowledging, Understanding, **Responding, Affirming**)

This chapter will explore the behavior of the "Testing Child" and all the possible aspects of this child that contribute and produce these types of communications. The Testing Child is characterized by a Loud and Under Reactive communication scaffolding. We will cover the Under Reactive aspect of communication in depth. As we looked into the Loud component of a child's communication scaffolding in Chapter 4, we will only briefly touch on the details again here. That said, we will link any previously covered concepts to this chapter's new scenarios.

This group of children is given the "Testing" moniker for their ability to "test" or try our patience. They also "test" the typical limits for comportment in the classroom. Inherent in these children's presentation is their subtle, yet tenacious way of irritating us and at times provoking us. In their Loud way, they seek our (and everyone's) attention, but their Under Reactive nature dampens their attention seeking to more of a persistent poke.

We tend to take the Testing child "home" with us because they preoccupy us with their Loud "negative attention seeking" behaviors/communications that we cannot seem to shake off. Their needs may be overlooked because they typically bother us to the point of annoyance and frustration. If left unattended, our feelings about the Testing child can spiral, and so we must be cautious. Sadly, all these dynamics mask an unhappiness within the Testing child and that tends to be difficult, but not impossible, to access. The same persistence that we experience in their behavior needs to be returned back to them in equal measure with empathy, thoughtfulness, and caring.

> ### *Am I Mandated to Share?*
>
> There may be times when a teacher deems it necessary to involve individuals outside the classroom to address the needs of the Testing child (including but not limited to, other school professionals, administration, parents, child protective services, and law enforcement). The material in this chapter addresses what a teacher can accomplish with a Testing child within the classroom setting, but does not, in any way, suggest that these issues need only be managed within the classroom setting. If a teacher has significant concerns about a child, we always suggest discussing these concerns immediately with other individuals.

For this chapter, the sections will flow as follows:

- Child scenarios
- Manifest communication (temperament) from scenarios in this chapter—Loud
- Latent communication (temperament) from scenarios in this chapter—Loud
- Manifest communication (conscious mind) from scenarios in this chapter—Under Reactive
- Latent communication (conscious mind) from scenarios in this chapter—Under Reactive
- Structured responses for scenarios in this chapter—Loud & Under Reactive

Scenarios—Pedro and Matilda

Pedro, 7 years old and in Ms. Reynolds' 2nd grade class

Pedro is 7 years old and in 2nd grade. Ms. Reynolds has become very frustrated with Pedro this school year. She finds herself constantly having to tell him to sit down, go back to his seat, stop touching other children. Pedro also has the ability to find that exact "perfect" time to do something that sets off the class—requiring Ms. Reynolds to spend a great amount of effort to refocus the students. He might make a joke, generate a silly sound, or fall off his seat in an exaggerated way. While none of these actions are significant in and of itself, taken as a group they make Pedro a constant hassle for her. Ms. Reynolds finds that the amount of redirection he needs can consume her day and exhaust her. Recently, she needed to intervene during a State test prep class because Pedro, in a quiet voice, repeatedly announced his answers to the students sitting around him. Pedro told the teacher that he was joking and that he would not do it again.

Matilda, 5 years old and in Ms. Gutierrez's Kindergarten class

Matilda is a 5-year-old kindergartener. Her teacher, Ms. Gutierrez, is becoming increasingly concerned with Matilda's behavior with other students. This precocious little girl is very bossy. She tries to dominate all the children in her group, telling her classmates what to do, pushing forward her ideas regardless of what her peers are saying, and rarely listening to suggestions from others. She is not mean about it, just relentless. Ms. Gutierrez has asked her numerous times to consider and accept her classmate's ideas, and Matilda says she will, but this only lasts as long as Ms. Gutierrez is monitoring the group. When she walks away the behavior re-commences. She has also noticed that Matilda has a way of pitting students against one another. Ms. Gutierrez noticed this herself in the group activities, but the lunch aides also report that they have overheard Matilda have problems with other children. She may say to a student, "I don't want you to sit next to me" and then ask another to sit down. She will comment negatively on what other children are having for lunch. Ms. Gutierrez finds that she does not like Matilda very much and wants to defend the other children from Matilda's overbearing nature.

Manifest Content—Loud

Recall in Chapter 4, we discussed the noticeable nature of being "Loud." Being Loud has a "cannot look away" or "cannot ignore" quality, and for "Testing" children this manifest quality takes on great importance. It is this aspect of loudness, not the volume and chaos of the Troubling child, which defines the Testing children. Like the drip of a faucet or a mosquito buzzing in one's ear, it is their persistence (and the specific ways that they exhibit this persistence) that catches our attention, that grabs us and does not let go, as well as distracts us from paying attention to the other children in the class. Being one of the underlying aspects of a feisty temperament, the driven and controlling nature of these children's behavior tends to ignore or, at least, overlook our limit setting or structures we try to put in place.

One definition of persistence is the insistent or obstinate continuance in a course of action in spite of difficulty or opposition (Merriam-Webster Dictionary, 2020). It is this version of Loud behavior that can be quite subtle, even noiseless, yet intensely present and obvious. Like making a joke in the class at an inopportune moment, moving around the room when everyone is calm and needing to focus, or playing favorites and creating classroom discord, the Testing child's Loud behavior needles teachers and creates a great deal of frustration. In these scenarios, Pedro and Matilda are Loud. Their behaviors grab the attention of the teachers, the aides, and their fellow students. The difference between the Troubling child and these children is that Pedro and Matilda are not always shunned by their classmates. In fact, Testing children have a charisma that attracts other children. Their manifest behavior is not so disquieting that it pushes people away; quite the opposite—it can be funny, it can be considered cool to the other children, and it can be clever. Yet, it also creates a great deal of anxiety in the other children in the class that we as teachers need to manage and redirect.

Latent Content—Loud

Remember that the behaviors connected to Loud also have meaning, but we believe that they are slightly different than those of the Troubling child. In the case of the Testing children, this version of Loud, of needing to be observed, noticed and responded to, is "asking" for teachers to be aware of these children's underlying sadness and anger related to loss. Their "choices" of behavior speak to the latent loneliness of the Testing child. Pedro makes jokes when the mood is too serious. He gets up and walks around, feeling happier to see and touch his friends, when the work or rules of class make him feel vulnerable and alone. Matilda orchestrates interactions with her classmates that create alternating closeness and distance to work through her feelings. She uses her assertive "bossiness" as a way of managing the connections and relationships that she desires but that she also fears may ultimately abandon her. Recalling the self-fulfilling prophecy, these versions of behavior that seek connections both sadly result in the children being more isolated.

Manifest Content—Under Reactive

When Testing children want to make a joke because something humorous has dawned on them, they do it, and to them it feels funny. When they want to get up and move around or touch their classmates because they have experienced an impulse to do so, they do it, and to them it feels enjoyable. When they do not like someone or feel upset with a situation, they take steps to diminish that person or those involved (by teasing, being mean or not listening), and to them, it feels better.

The frustrating, and sometimes disorienting, aspect of the Testing child's behavior is that to these children, their behavior feels perfectly reasonable and appropriate. Yet, we suspect that something is not reasonable or appropriate. It is as if there is a pressure or an intensity that we are not be able to put a finger on in the moment, but we feel irritated. These behaviors grab the attention of classmates and teachers because they are often loud, yet unlike those of Troubling children, the behaviors are quite ordinary and so should not pose a problem. What child has not joked around, not listened, tried to control a situation, or been mean to another child? Yet these do. In addition to the relentlessness of these "Loud" aspects of these behavior, the "Under Reactive" dynamic exhibited through the Testing child's disconnectedness from the intensity of the communication makes these behaviors a uniquely frustrating challenge.

Latent Content—Under Reactive

The "under" component of Testing children's reactivity stems from the fact that their actual feelings are not purposely represented in their outward behavior. We believe that this is due, in part, because these thoughts and feelings (anger, sadness, and fear) may just be too difficult for these children to consciously experience.

To "protect" themselves, the Testing children *disconnect* from the essence of these thoughts or feelings and end up expressing them in alternative ways. With these children, their feelings of anger or fear can become avoidance and rigidity, sadness or worry can become hyperactivity and silliness. Thus, the Testing child's request for attention is indirect. We may feel annoyed and pushed away from this child by the manifest component of the behavior, while the latent component simultaneously calls to us for help.

In the Introduction of this book, we referred to Anna Freud and development of psychological defenses for children (Freud, 1966; Freud & Burlingham, 1967). These defenses are like protective mind tricks that a child's mind uses to maintain a sense of emotional and cognitive balance when difficult feelings challenge this equilibrium. What is important to remember is that these defenses are not conscious, meaning that a child is never aware that they are in use, even if it may seem difficult at times for us to believe that is so. Some defenses that you may have heard of are:

- Denial is blocking an unwanted thought because of its self-threatening nature. For example, a child strikes another child and then "denies" doing so, because of what the act may show about the hitter's own anger.
- Regression is moving to an earlier developmental state as a way of managing a stressor. For example, a potty-trained child "regresses" when his parents separate and starts to have toileting accidents similar to when he was younger. Depending on the details, silliness can be understood as a form of regression.
- Projection is disowning one's own unacceptable thought and assigning it to another person or institution. For example, a child gets in trouble in class and as a response states that "everyone in the class hates her" and "projects" her anger at being disciplined onto her classmates.

The disconnected part of the Testing child, what we call under reactivity, stems from one of the psychological defenses called dissociation. Anger, sadness or fear can trigger this emotional reaction. These emotions cause a disconnection from thoughts that are too difficult to feel. Dissociation, then, is the removal of certain aspects of an upsetting experience (i.e., feelings, details, etc.) from one's awareness as a way of managing the intensity of that experience. To accomplish this, a person may remove some or all of his attention or connection to challenges happening around him. The person is somehow not quite there in the moment (Janet, 1965; Freud, 1990). We all engage in a version of this to a certain extent. Daydreaming is one example of dissociating from one's surroundings, leaving a person unaware for a period of time. Other examples can be when we only partly recall a particularly difficult time in our lives, or when we complete a conversation with someone to realize we have only partial memory of the whole conversation. In these ways, we have all dissociated or disconnected.

This idea becomes important for understanding under reactivity in three specific ways. First, because of dissociation, Testing children are even less connected their latent thoughts and feelings than other children might be. The lack of awareness of their actual feelings and its effect on other people can be so profound that it seems improbable or unbelievable (Janet, 1965; Freud, 1990). This leads to the unfortunate, yet understandable, conclusion that the Testing child's behavior may be consciously purposeful. When we examine our case studies, we notice that something must be motivating Pedro's and Matilda's behavior, but neither child can consciously acknowledge this. To them all is as it should be—to Pedro, his jokes are timely and funny and to Matilda, her classmates are simply not as capable as she is. This unique and often frustrating quality of the Testing child leads us to believe that the Testing child is "reluctant" to address challenging behaviors. In actuality the emotional difficulties that create the energy for their Testing behavior lurks in a hidden state (from them and from us).

Second, because of the dissociative nature of the behaviors, Testing children create a sense of antagonism within relationships. Some of us may know people described as passive-aggressive. This too is a form of dissociation. In these cases, their passive emotion (latent) is "dis-associated" from the way they directly communicate their anger or aggression (manifest). In one example, person A may say to person B that a situation is "fine." Meanwhile, person B distinctly feels, based on facial expression and tone of voice, that they have done something to upset person A. The angry part of the communication is outside person A's awareness, but its intensity is still being transmitted to person B. This behavior can make person B feel quite put upon. In another example, person A may say to person B that he has done something wrong. Meanwhile, person B cannot understand what could have happened to draw person A's ire. The actual cause of person A's anger is outside person A's awareness, but its intensity is still being transmitted to person B. This behavior can make person B feel quite put upon. Pedro's joking behavior in class, while manifestly funny and silly, is actually quite contrary to the structure of the class and to the authority of the teacher and so frustrates the teacher who is attempting to maintain decorum in the classroom. Matilda's behavior (while not overtly mean) shows favoritism of one child over the another, causing hurt feelings in the rejected child. The preferred child is left under Matilda's control (albeit subtly), which may also cause hurt feelings eventually.

Third, because of the dissociative nature of the Testing child's behavior—their lack of awareness and their passive antagonism—the latent thoughts and feelings that they express are rarely, if ever:

- heard as their "actual" meaning by another
- empathically responded to by another
- thoughtfully reorganized by another

Their important latent communications remain in an Under Reactive (and under reacted to) state within the child's conscious mind. This type of communication is called unsymbolized because it is unspoken and never addressed by another person. Hurburt and Heavey described this type of thought as follows: "thinking a particular, definite thought without the awareness of that thought's being conveyed in words, images, or any other symbols" (Hurlburt & Heavey, 2008, p. 802; Gregory, 2018). This unfortunate reality keeps the Testing behaviors static and never changing. This, in turn, ramps up the tension within their relationships, causing ever increasing problems between them and those around them.

Building Responses for Scenarios—Loud & Under Reactive

In our scenarios, Pedro and Matilda are "Loud" and "Under Reactive" children, those we describe as Testing children. We have established that these children are inwardly upset, feeling alone, and unsupported, but have also identified that this is a nuanced version of their isolation. The Testing child's overall presentation sets her apart and determines the nature of our responses. Understanding these dynamics can lead to the question, how did these children relational interactions and communication get so convoluted? And what can we do about it?

Often the answer lies in some type of family dysfunction. There is something about the parent/child interaction and communication in a Testing child's life that makes these children feel alone, unsupported, and upset. Salvador Minuchin, Virginia Satir and other family therapists believed that in dysfunctional family systems—such as those in which psychiatric problem exist, alcoholism or substance abuse is present, or significant unresolved losses have taken place—the children are often pressed into specific roles within the family that become fixed, often completely ignoring the child's needs (Satir, 1972; Minuchin, 1974; Belsky, 1981; Morgan, 2014). The roles are typically expressed as follows:

- The Hero—the golden child, the over-achiever, the perfectionist; holds the family's hope
- The Helper—the parent's assistant, the parentified overly compliant, "can't say no" child; takes care of the family
- The Clown/Mascot—the jokester, the excessively upbeat child; distracts the family
- The Scapegoat—the rule breaker, the black sheep, the negative child; takes blame for the family's problems
- The Lost Child—the unseen child, the quiet child; hold the family's secrets

Wegscheider-Cruse, 1981

The coopting of a child's autonomy such as this, according to Erikson's second stage of development, leads to a crisis and a significant level of internal shame and uncertainty (Erikson, 1950). It is not our role to assess or evaluate this, yet the child is in our class and is (1) causing disruption and, (2) often, evoking negative feelings in us. We are less inclined to want to spend time with Testing children or understand them. We are more likely to want to reprimand, limit, or push them away. Simply put, they can annoy us and we, often, do not like them.

For the sake of the child, we should know why we have negative feelings about him. We believe that this somehow mirrors the nature of the dynamics in their lives. These children feel in school the same way they feel outside of school—alone, unsupported, and upset. With these statements, we do not stand in judgment of families of Testing children. There may be many reasons as to why these children feel the way they do. That said, we, as teachers, can unwittingly play a part in perpetuating or exacerbating these feelings.

This perpetuation is called a re-enactment. Sigmund Freud called it a repetition compulsion (Freud, 1914). It is defined as a current situation or relationship that mirrors the same elements as a historic and concurrent "unsuccessful" situation or relationship. Re-enactments are important for a child's (or adult's) development because they serve as a "re-do" for relationships or interactions whose outcomes have left a child unfulfilled. In a way, these children are "testing" to see if we will act differently than the other caregivers with whom they are familiar. They are trying to gain some control over the dynamics by trying them again and again. Both sides of a relationship can get caught in these re-enactments (Bibring, 1943). It does not occur to us to approach Pedro or Matilda in a different way because we often get caught mirroring the patterns that are familiar to the Testing child (the ones that stem from their lives complications and/or dysfunction). Re-enactments can feel powerfully urgent to the child and therefore are often relentlessly repeated.

We want to acknowledge the connection between re-enactments and self-fulfilling prophecies. These re-enactments have their foundations in the self-fulfilling prophecy dynamics that we discussed in the previous chapter.

Table 5.1:
Self-Fulfilling Prophecy of the Testing Child

Steps in a Self-Fulfilling Prophecy	Example
A person makes a false assumption about himself in the context of the current environment.	Because he feels ignored, unsupported, and abandoned, Pedro believes that no one cares about him. These feelings are too upsetting for him, and so Pedro does not let himself think about this. He only thinks about the need to work hard to get people's attention and connection.
The person takes action to test the false assumption.	Pedro makes jokes in class. He presents the that he is worthy of attention and connection by presenting that he is happy and by being a clown for his peers.
Others react to the action and misunderstand.	Even though the children laugh, Pedro feels only a brief moment of attention and connection. The teacher, who feels annoyed by Pedro because of the disruptiveness and because of the rule breaking, gives him increasingly onerous consequences each time he makes a joke.
The others' reactions/responses to the person's action, confirm the false assumption for the person.	Based on the teacher's reaction, Pedro feels negative attention and less of a connection. This confirms to him that no one cares about him (and continues to feel ignored, unsupported, and abandoned).
The person takes more extreme action to further test the false assumption.	Pedro tries new and more disruptive ways to get the class' attention and connection.

Merton, 1948; Weiner, Gallo-Silver, & Lucas, 2020

The following responses follow the format we laid out in the previous chapter. The "Loud" aspect of the behavior requires the Structural responses as a way of helping to control the intensity of the behaviors such as the silliness, bossiness, and antagonism. The "under reactivity" and the disconnectedness requires us to respond with more of ourselves, modeling a relationship and interaction that displays self-awareness and matching of feelings to behavior. For the purposes of our discussions here, we describe these interventions and responses as "More Emotional." Figure 5.2 Personas and Responses reiterates this.

**Table 5.2:
Personas and Responses**

Persona	Responses
Loud & Over Reactive (Troubling)	Requires Structural & Less Emotional Response from teacher
Loud & Under Reactive (Testing)	**Requires Structural & More Emotional Response from teacher**
Quiet & Over Reactive (Worrying)	Requires Verbal Response & Less Emotional from teacher
Quiet & Under Reactive (Hiding)	Requires Verbal Response & More Emotional from teacher

Weiner, Gallo-Silver, & Lucas, 2020

Let us recall from Chapter 3, the basic behaviors that the Testing child may exhibit:

- Rule Testing (the systematic pushing, but not breaking, of rules, boundaries and norms)
- Mischievous Activities (acting out in a way that displays a playful, yet disobedient stance toward authority figures)
- Clowning and Joking (verbally and/or non-verbally attempting to elicit laughter from other individuals)
- Verbally Active (trouble accepting or working with the restrictions related to talking)
- Not Listening or Following Directions (the emotional disconnecting from verbal and written messages and/or control coming from other individuals)

Let us remember that the power generated from the Testing child is still designed to have us move toward these children by calling out for our attention, but, in the case of these children, the nature of their re-enactments and their passive-aggressive emotionality push us away. Our job is to figure out a way to "enjoy" Testing children even though how they behave, often times, comes across as intensely unenjoyable. We all know children like this:

- The child who is always right and never wrong
- The child who always wants to help (in the way the child wants to)
- The child who is always joking around
- The child who raises his hand too much
- The child who corrects us
- The child who always says "no"
- The child who always has to win
- The child who convinces others to break the rules

- The child who always says he knows how to do it
- The child who has to be first

For these children, *Structural responses* allow us to reshape the unproductive and unhealthy ways they conduct themselves in the classroom. The *More Emotional responses* are focused on helping these children re-discover their internal self—the one that has been hidden as self-protection—and allowing them to connect to others in more authentic ways.

Let's put some of these responses into action. Beginning with the Structural interventions, the following are several generic responses that fit our scenarios:

Examples of Structural Responses

- Altering the time and place of contact

    Meeting with the Testing child outside of class time can begin to form a new pattern for our relationship. This meeting becomes a regular occurrence and is not directly connected to a given days challenging behaviors. The idea behind this is to create a sense that these children are "valued" by us, that they feel worthy of this special type of contact. This intervention is grounded in the ideas of unconditional positive regard that we discussed in Chapter 4 and attempts to address the child's need to "test" whether we care about them. How can Pedro or Matilda learn to alter their interactions if their repeated experiences with their teachers (their co-re-enactors) involve their teachers being frustrated by their behavior?

- Altering the Locus of Control

    While we understand that behavior charts are typically used as a form of ongoing information transfer and evaluation of a child's manifest behavior, we see behavior charts as important in a different way. A behavior chart can be a helpful way to enhance the communication between two sides of a relationship. It can become a tangible manifestation of an evolving positive student-teacher relationship.

    A typical behavior chart has three columns, the objective, success or failure, and teacher comments. Let's look at these as forms of communication:
    ◊ Column (1) contains a teacher's communications about the structure of the environment (our expectations),
    ◊ Column (2) contains the child's manifest communications and the behavior associated with student's willingness comply with the expectations, and
    ◊ Column (3) is the teacher's communication to the parents about the child's behavior.

    This is actually a linear discussion (from teacher, through the child, to the parents) and is difficult to manage in terms of the communications that can occur outside the classroom between child and parent. We cannot control for what parents will say about these interactions and we believe that this, more often than not, decreases the effectiveness of this intervention.

We propose altering this chart thusly:

◊ Column (1) providing our ground rules for these relationships (different from relationships that she may have as models at home)
◊ Column (2) identifying her manifest communication about these rules (her ability to comply with the rules)
◊ Column (3) receiving reinforcement of our beliefs about her
◊ Column (4) beginning the process of identifying her latent communication about herself

The fourth column alters the re-enactment by tacitly communicating that we believe that what the child thinks is important. In addition, it undermines the under reactivity by helping the testing child express an aspect of the child's relationships that is typically hidden. It also keeps the relationship intact (from teacher, to the child, and back to the teacher) by affecting a third-party interpretation of material that may be happening outside the classroom.

Providing a behavior chart for Matilda which focuses on how she interacts with her classmates can serve to increase her positive connections within these relationships.

Table 5.3:
Matilda's Monday Behavior Chart

Monday 9/18 Task	Matilda accomplished her task	Teacher's thoughts about Matilda's task	Matilda feelings or thoughts about her task
I listened to my classmate	🙂	Matilda listened closely to her classmate's ideas about what to build. I was very proud of her for listening so well.	I feel happy.
I followed my classmate ideas	☹	Matilda said her classmate's building was ugly and did not want to build with her. I think Matilda was upset that she did not get her way.	I feel mad.
I helped my classmate	☹	Matilda made her classmate cry and did not say sorry. I know it is hard for Matilda, but I want her to keep trying to say sorry when she hurts someone's feelings.	I feel sad.

Weiner, Gallo-Silver, & Lucas, 2020

We recommend separate charts for the parents and for students (they can be a copied). While they convey the same information, once a chart is handled by a parent, its meaning changes for the child. In addition, if the re-enactments that we are trying to address include the parent-child relationship, then the information we are trying to convey to the child will be more effective (and have more of a positive impact in pattern alteration) if it is kept separate. We do not always know how interventions are handled away from our presence, and, unfortunately, they can be contaminated. We can make suggestions to parents who then either do or do not follow our recommendations. At times, our suggestions may be distorted by parents as a way of maintaining their own view of their child.

- Creating specialized activities

Sometimes being given a separate individual assignment helps the Testing child feel cared for—instead of one of many, he or she is one of one. We have all done this from time to time. Making a child our "helper," sending them on tasks, asking them to make "choices" or "decisions" about the class, aids in altering their latent sense that they are unimportant and alone.

This intervention centers on altering a child's role within the classroom. Allowing a child to have new roles allows that child the opportunity to communicate in new ways. If a child is only allowed to use one form of communication, all information must be narrowly expressed within that form—it is inherently limiting. As examples, pushing Matilda to be a "helper" instead of a "hero" can feel empowering for her. Similarly, moving Pedro from the "mascot" to the "hero" by helping achieve star-of-the-day status alters his view of himself.

Examples of More Emotional Responses

- Altering content of discourse toward self-awareness

To explore this intervention, we refer back to the term *unsymbolized*. Remember, this means that the underlying issue has never been spoken about, addressed or empathically reacted to by a witness (parent, caregiver, or teacher). It is unsymbolized and remains in an Under Reactive state within the conscious mind. Symbolization—the taking on of a conscious, tangible form—comes from talking about these "secret" feelings and "naming" them in a productive way, such as with words, play, art, dance, etc. We may have a feeling that exists in the abstract—like sadness over the loss of a loved one. Without symbolizing it and putting form to it, the feeling remains outside our ability to shape or change. While remaining outside of our consciousness, unsymbolized feelings and thoughts can be the fuel for acting out and acting in behaviors. If we put words to our thoughts and feelings, they begin to evolve, and even subside.

Both Pedro and Matilda need to begin to symbolize their feelings and thoughts before the Testing behavior will be curtailed and ultimately stopped. As Pedro wanders around the class, we can name the feelings he may be having, and connect them to the behavior. "Pedro, I think that you are upset and that causes you to wander around, but please take your seat." This link, although not necessarily accepted, remains in the Testing child's mind as a possibility. Repetition of this type of intervention begins to connect manifest communication with latent communication, positively addressing the child's under reactivity.

In addition, this intervention requires that we move toward Pedro and try to take educated guesses as to how a given activity or assignment is making him feel. This act creates a sense that we care enough about him to notice him and try to understand him.

- Modeling our feelings about the behavior

    The re-enactment that Testing children engage in includes a message that one does not (possibly is not allowed to) communicate their feelings to another person. For this reason, an intervention that conveys our comfort with communicating our feelings or thoughts about a situation is a helpful way of altering this fixed and unproductive dynamic.

    This requires teachers to participate in a measure of self-disclosure. Self-disclosure is the practice of sharing information about oneself to another person. Teachers often have private lives that they do not share with their students, as well as emotions and thoughts that they keep to themselves. For Testing children, because their connection to their actual thoughts and feelings is tenuous at best, having teachers model this process, in a controlled way, can be enlightening and liberating. We say controlled because in some homes, it may not be unavailability, but the over-sharing of a parent's information, that leaves a child feeling unheard and unloved.

    To this end, it is important to be aware of the different types of self-disclosure. First is *content* self-disclosure. This includes all of our personal details—our age, likes and dislikes, family make-up, marital status, etc. Second is *process* self-disclosure and is the more complicated of the two types. Process self-disclosure centers on communicating how we feel about a situation in the moment. "I am confused about what you are saying." "It is really hard for me to hear you say this." Of the two types of self-disclosure, process self-disclosure is the one we can use as a modeling intervention for Testing children by including both a feeling and the behavior.

- "Matilda, it makes me sad when you say that you don't like your classmates."
- "Pedro, I am sad when you get up out of your seat when I have told you not to. It feels like you are pushing me away."

Affirmations That Help Children Hold On to Their New Coping Skills

As teachers, we cannot alter the realities for the Testing child, but we can add to the child's life experiences in a profound way. Teachers are able to provide children with a "corrective emotional experience" (Alexander, 1946). Our relationships with the children whom we teach and spend considerable time with during the day are so central that an understanding and emotionally accessible teacher can add to children's life what may be missing or compromised in other parts of their life.

Some children see and interact with their teacher far longer during each day than with their parents, who may be working or caring for others. In this environment, teachers can provide an emotional experience that adds to a child's life. It may seem odd for us to recommend spending time with and increasing our focus on children who anyone would find frustrating or irritating, yet that is just what Testing children, like Pedro and Matilda, need from their teachers. During the times in class when we structure an opportunity for Pedro or Matilda to express (symbolize) their latent feelings, we create the opportunity to act as the empathic witness to their struggles. Our consistent attention to their feelings, gives them a sense of value, belonging and worth and is the "corrective emotional experience" these children crave.

To be the person who alters the pattern, by modeling other methods for addressing the needs of these children, provides teachers with the opportunity to have a profound effect on the Testing child—one that can last well beyond our class year. Jean Piaget understood this opportunity as a foundational aspect to children's development. From Piaget's perspective, the Testing child has a relational *schema* (a way of thinking and feeling that results in a response pattern) that can be highly problematic for interacting with both peers and adults. Providing the Testing children with different responses (with new *schemas*) requires them to *assimilate* this new information. This entails the Testing child to "test out" these new responses. Hopefully this leads to *accommodation,* the alteration of their old *schema* based on our more helpful, empathic responses to what they are communicating (Piaget & Cook, 1952).

Carl Rogers ("unconditional positive regard") and Piaget believed in the inherent goodness of children and their innate desire to improve their functioning and succeed in life (Piaget & Inhelder, 1968; Rogers, 1939; 1951; 1995). We can employ their humanistic view of this challenging group of children as a way of affirming them and of understanding that their behaviors do not have to define them. More than any other group of children that we discuss in this book, it is our thoughtful relationships with the Testing child that can have the greatest impact.

Chapter 6

The Child Who Is "Worrying"

Quiet and Over Reactive

Quiet—<u>Temperamentally</u> slow to warm and internalizes thoughts and feelings; acts "in" as a way of striving for control

Over Reactive—The <u>conscious mind</u> is overwhelmed by thoughts and feelings with extreme and chaotic expression of these thoughts and feelings

* * *

AURA (Acknowledging, Understanding, **Responding, Affirming**)

In this chapter, we will look at the behavior of the "Worrying Child." In terms of Persona, these children are distinguished by their Quiet and Over Reactive communication scaffolding. The Quiet aspect of their communication presents a level of complexity that is not always initially apparent. We tend to find Quiet children less challenging, as they typically test limits less often than Loud children do. Their needs may be overlooked because they typically do not overtly break the rules and are not disruptive to the class or the lesson plans. Even so, they are silently communicating difficulties and are emotionally struggling. They sit and appear to listen and follow, and so their sadness can slip our attention. While their over reactivity tends to result in a significant level of expression of emotions and thoughts, it is of an "indirect" nature. In reality, they are expressing a serious level of self-dislike and low self-esteem.

For teachers, these children act as powerful magnets for empathy and concern. There is an obviousness about the Worrying child's plight that tugs at our wish to protect someone who is smaller and vulnerable, yet they can also make us anxious. They give the impression that, if they just received enough care, all would be "fixed." Sadly, this is not the case. We may want to rescue these children from their current situation (sometimes called a "rescue fantasy"), but that is often unrealistic for us to do as individuals and may, in fact, not be what the child needs.

86   Part Two—The Children Communicating in Your Classroom

Am I Mandated to Share?

There may be times when a teacher deems it necessary to involve individuals outside the classroom to address the needs of the Worrying child (including but not limited to, other school professionals, administration, parents, child protective services, and law enforcement). The material in this chapter addresses what a teacher can accomplish with a Worrying child within the classroom setting, but does not, in any way, suggest that these issues need only be managed within the classroom setting. If a teacher has significant concerns about a child, we always suggest discussing these concerns immediately with other individuals.

For this chapter, the sections will flow as follows:

- Child scenarios
- Manifest communication (temperament) from scenarios in this chapter—Quiet
- Latent communication (temperament) from scenarios in this chapter—Quiet
- Manifest communication (conscious mind) from scenarios in this chapter—Over Reactive
- Latent communication (conscious mind) from scenarios in this chapter—Over Reactive
- Structured responses for Quiet & Over Reactive (Worrying) children

Scenarios—Kayla and Ethan

Kayla, 4 years old, Pre-K in Ms. Ellie's class

Kayla is 4 years old and in Pre-Kindergarten. Since the beginning of the school year, her teacher, Ms. Ellie, has noticed a variety of worrisome aspects of Kayla's behavior. The most concerning of these behaviors is that Kayla spends a great deal of time in the bathroom each day and often clogs and overflows the toilet with a large of amount of toilet paper. Ms. Ellie has called for maintenance three times in the past month. This behavior leads to Kayla missing other activities because of the amount time she spends in the bathroom. In addition, Ms. Ellie notices that Kayla is not able to do anything—draw a picture, build something with blocks, or tell a story—without having to "undo" her work. She tears up drawings, erases writing, and rebuilds towers over and over again because she says that she does not like what she has created. This dynamic leads to Kayla rarely finishing any projects. Ms. Ellie worries that Kayla does not like herself very much.

Ethan, 7 years old, 2nd grade in Ms. Colligan's class

Ethan is 7 years old and in 2nd grade. He typically comes to school somewhat disheveled. By the end of the first two weeks in the school year, it has become clear to his teacher, Ms. Colligan, that Ethan has very poor personal hygiene. His hair is almost always unwashed, he wears the same few pieces of clothing each week, and he smells of body odor and, sometimes she believes, even dried urine. The other children shun him and do not want to be near him. During recess, he is teased about being "smelly and dirty," and some of the boys in his class run up to him and hit him and then run away taunting him. Ms. Colligan has explained she has zero tolerance for teasing in the class or during recess and has disciplined the students who continue to tease Ethan. Ethan's work is on grade level, but he rarely participates in class. Ms. Colligan is trying to cope with the fact that Ethan does smell and that his smell is not getting any better as time goes on. She asks Ethan how "things" are at home, and he gives vague non-specific answers. Even more troubling than the odor, when asked about bathing or laundering his clothes, Ethan just stares at her. His art projects and writing assignments make her uncomfortable, as they all seem to be quite "violent" including images of explosions, blood, death, injuries, and war. He shows all the signs of possible maltreatment.

Manifest Content—Quiet

The word quiet brings to mind the absence of noise, or silence. We seek quiet in order to be able to think, to concentrate and focus. In this way, Quiet, as opposed to Loud, is typically viewed by teachers as positive. There is a serenity to the word quiet, especially if we are thinking about a class filled with 25 to 30 young children, the lesson plans we have to get through, the curriculum requirements we must meet, or testing we need to prep within a limited time frame. The children who sit quietly in our classrooms are, through their outward presentation, extremely helpful to us or, at the very least, far less a hindrance than those who are loud and boisterous. In this way, we may often describe these children as behaved.

Another way of defining the word quiet is by identifying something as subtle or obscure, such as in the following statements:

- "This quiet life was not for her; she needed energy, movement, and vitality."
- "The boy was so reserved, his difficulties quietly slipped through the cracks."

This understanding of the word quiet is based on perception rather sound. It's about the connection between something and the environment in which it exists. For our purposes, of the two—silent or subtle—the second usage is more useful.

In this book, we use the word Quiet to define manifest communication that is less outward and less other-directed. The more typically disruptive student (with "Loud" manifest content) acts out his or her difficulties. From a temperament standpoint, Worrying children are more cautious in how they express themselves—using forms of manifest communication over which they have a significant level control. Inwardly, though, these children often feel out of control. A primary way that these children retain a sense of control over their communications is by establishing a transitional space for these communications. This concept, developed by D.W. Winnicott, describes an "in-between" area that exists between two people attempting to communicate (Winnicott, 1951). Using a medium through which to communicate increases a sense of security because of its indirect nature. The "distance" created through the use of the transitional space decreases closeness and provides each party to the interaction some "space" or "breathing room." Transitional spaces can be anything that serves as a vehicle to communicate a message in an indirect and often less intimate way. These can include:

- Art (drawings, paintings, coloring, sand, clay, etc.)
- Games (board games, card games, etc.)
- Imaginary Play (doll play, building blocks, trains, dress up, etc.)
- Gross Motor Movements (repeated patterns like falling down, wandering off etc.)
- Fine Motor Movements (repeated patterns like touching, picking at self, pulling out hair, etc.)
- Writings (poems, stories, charts, etc.)
- Activities (throwing a ball, toileting, organizing, cleaning, running etc.)

Looking at our scenarios, the messages from the transitional spaces are worrisome. From Kayla's chaotic toileting activities and destruction of her own handiwork to Ethan's hygiene, violent drawings, and written assignments, both children are communicating in powerfully intense ways. They are providing their teachers with clues to the mystery of their existence outside the classroom and their thoughts about themselves.

Latent Content—Quiet

There is an innate caution in the Quiet child that is important to note. On a latent level, this uneasiness speaks to the notion that, at their core, these children do not feel secure and take a tentative approach to sharing their inner worlds. This type of communication conveys an uncertainty about being responded to by others, a wariness of relationships, at times a fear of reprisals, poor self-esteem, and low self-worth. It declares "If you get to know me, you may think that I am unlovable and undeserving."

We believe this negative self-image is derived from some number of adverse childhood experiences (ACEs) in the child's life. This concept is derived from the research of Drs. Vincent Felitti of Kaiser Permanente Health Centers and Robert Anda of the United States Centers for Disease Control and Prevention and their 1998 study entitled *The Adverse Childhood Experiences (ACE) Study*. With regard to children, this study indicated that traumatic childhood experiences could result in both compromised neurodevelopment, an impaired health status, and disruptions to social, emotional and cognitive growth (Felitti, et al., 1998). The ACE studies and other later studies demonstrate that a child's (and subsequently an adult's) ideas about life, identity and the self, relationships, and the greater world, when shaped by traumatic and/or oppressive experiences such as maltreatment, racism, poverty, violence or other abuses of power, can create thought processes and communications that demonstrate a great deal of negativity and self-blaming (see Figure 6.1).

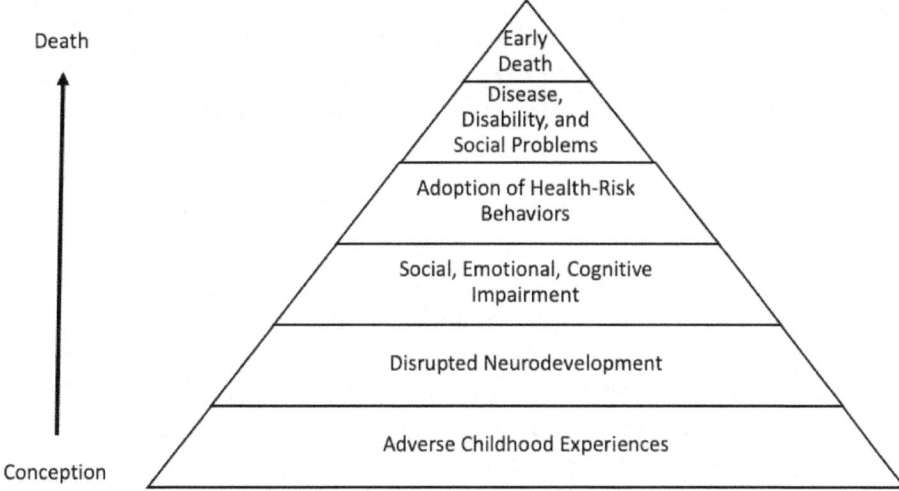

Figure 6.1: Possible Effects of Adverse Childhood Experiences

There are many sources of these ACEs—loss, sudden or dramatic life change, maltreatment (neglect or abuse), oppression, effects of a disability or health condition, parental mental illness, etc. (Felitti, et al., 1998). Whether the reasons are environmental, developmental, characterological, physiological, or a combination, these challenging experiences of the Worrying child often include a compromised relationship dynamic (caregiver-child) that leaves the child to believe:

- I was not cared for
- I was hurt
- I was ignored
- I was punished
- I was misunderstood
- I was not loved
- I was unimportant

These concepts, whether based on truth or only on perception of truth, become part of how Worrying children understand themselves. In light of this, the manifest forms of communication exhibited by the Quiet child suffering from ACEs are typically driven by:

- The child's negative self-worth and a transfer of this negative belief onto others; and/or
- The child's fear that creating closeness will lead to rejection similar to his, her or their own self-rejection.

Both Kayla and Ethan's behaviors separate them from the adults and peers in the classroom. This fits their view of themselves—quietly distant. Kayla's frequent long bathroom trips and Ethan's poor hygiene isolate them from people who they believe do not want to have anything to do with them. To explain this in detail, we must return to our *ego defenses* discussion from Chapter 4.

In that section, we introduced the concept of *projection*—that a person can unconsciously take a significantly unwanted feeling and pass it or transfer it on to another person. For example, "I don't like myself" becomes "people don't like me"; or "I want to hurt someone" becomes "people want to hurt me." This is a commonly used defense that we see in people of all ages. Kayla displays this ego defense. "I am bad" becomes "Ms. Ellie thinks I am bad." She feels terrible about herself and, in addition to feeling unclean when toileting, projects these feelings onto her school projects. Her creations become not good enough, unwanted and flawed (just like her). This is a projection of her negative sense of herself—that she feels she deserves to be rejected, criticized, even maltreated. These projections are at the core of the Worrying child's form of interaction and their lack of connection to us. They simply do not believe people will help them. They dread the negative response to come and may even believe that they deserve this treatment. While a tiny bit of hope may remain, generally they do not trust anyone will find them worthy of help or love.

Unfortunately, in scenarios such as these, Ethan and Kayla's expectation that they will be rejected at school, just as they are elsewhere, is problematic. While this may be true in certain parts of their lives, at school, with us, it is not. When we apply Erikson (see Chapter 1) we see that Kayla and Ethan demonstrate a high level of mistrust (signifying that the crisis between trust and mistrust in the initial stage of child development remains unresolved) (Erikson, 1950). We may also speculate about the existence of ACEs that date back to their earliest experiences in infancy. Kayla and Ethan display behaviors that demonstrate that even though their teachers may be empathic and safe and may, in practice, be excellent caregivers, these children typically do not feel safe enough to approach them directly with their thoughts and feelings.

Manifest Content—Over Reactive

When we observe the behavior of a Worrying child, there is a subtle nature to it. The communications these children outwardly display can be angst-laden and upsetting in content but may exist in understated packaging. Expanding on our earlier list of transitional spaces, the communications can take on many forms:

- creating disquieting artwork
- erasing until the paper tears
- inappropriate touching of self or others
- maintaining poor boundaries
- chewing/tearing of clothing
- engaging in concerning imaginary play
- picking at scabs/wounds
- twisting or pulling out hair
- biting nails to the quick

Chapter 6. The Child Who Is "Worrying"

Left: **Figure 6.2: Self-Portrait with No Face.** *Right:* **Figure 6.3: Self-Portrait with Scratched Face**

The drawings above do not look like typical self-portraits. Their differentness forcefully calls out with a silent voice. The thoughts and feelings that these children communicate jump out of the page (the transitional space) without conscious thought. Their conscious minds cannot contain them. We can guess at the many possible meanings of what we are seeing, but we do not have to guess that something is off because it is right there in front of us. The creation in Figure 6.2 evokes descriptors such as: faceless, hidden, secretive, unfeeling, detached, lost. There is a depressed emptiness. The face in Figure 6.3 is scratched out and there seems to be a large down-turned mouth. There is an agitated, angry, hostile, and injured quality to the drawing.

Both Kayla and Ethan are not able to contain their scared, hurt feelings. Even though they do not create a level of drama that derails the class, they most certainly demand to be noticed. Their Quiet, cautious nature precludes them from acting out their sense of overwhelm, but, as attuned caregivers, their communications are nearly impossible for teachers to miss. For Kayla, the intensity of her over reactivity gets communicated through the tactile, in-your-face, agitated, uncontained nature of the constant rubbing and wiping that cries out to be soothed. For Ethan, it is the olfactory bombardment of his ever more pungent scent that screams to be cleansed. These behaviors and the communications they convey may at times make us uncomfortable and detach us from Worrying children. Yet it is their helplessness and hopelessness that we see in these transitional spaces that draw us towards them. We cannot ignore them because, within these transitional spaces, Worrying children are so raw and vulnerable.

Latent Content—Over Reactive

While we mention the concepts of *process* and *content* within the context of self-disclosure in the previous chapter, we want to go over them in a slightly different way for this chapter. This discussion will frame our discussion of over reactivity in Worrying children. In psychological terms, process refers to the "how" and content refers to the "what." If one is making ice-cream, the content is the milk, the sugar, the heavy cream, etc. The process is how one endeavors to put these ingredients together. With this in mind, the latent material of the Worrying child's over reactivity can be understood in these two distinct ways.

First, from a process perspective, there is a bigness or a pervasiveness to the Worrying child's latent communication. The "how" is its intensity. For the Worrying child, it overwhelms the classroom environment for her or him and creates a great deal of difficulty in learning, focusing, and staying on task. The feelings continuously push their conscious minds for outlets, finding cracks and expression in many of the transitional spaces that are available to school-age children. The distress that Worrying children feel has an underlying force that preoccupies and dominates their communications and invariably creates uneasiness in their classmates and at times their teachers. Over time, this process pushes these children further and further from helpful connections and results in isolating them even more. In other words, the Worrying children's projection of their own self-dislike leads others to "dislike" and reject them as well.

Second, this process is continually fed by the "what" of the Worrying child's life experiences outside of school—content that is typically generated from the traumatic nature of the ACEs. This has led to these children experiencing feelings of self-dislike and low-self-esteem. For Worrying children, we can see the substance of their distress and resulting poor self-image in their latent communication. Recalling from Chapter 4, we discussed that within the context of children's behavior, over reactivity contains a tacit wish to be responded to and contained. While this wish can be severely undermined by ACEs' effect on a child's self-image and self-worth, it still exists, as observed within the transitional spaces. In the scenarios from this chapter, we can surmise that both children feel "dirty." Kayla's need to excessively clean herself in the bathroom and Ethan's poor hygiene demonstrate their negative sense of self, lack of belonging, and self-disgust. The latent communication communicates not only neglect, but sadly the notion that, to these children, the neglect feels deserved.

Building Responses for Scenarios—Quiet & Over Reactive

In our scenarios, Kayla and Ethan are "Quiet" and "Over Reactive" children, whom we describe as Worrying children. We have established that these children are feeling hurt, hopeless, helpless, unsafe, and neglected. Even with their belief that no one will listen or notice, their over reactivity drives an unfiltered and urgent though indirect communication. The resulting vulnerability can create heart-felt responses to liberate the Worrying children from their situations. Their behaviors and related communications worry us so greatly that we feel compelled to do something, anything, to help them. Acknowledging these dynamics can lead to the question, how much can we do? And the more nuanced question, how much should we do?

That the quietly intense behaviors of Worrying children can create strong reactions in their teachers, who have been given the task to care for them, should not surprise us. The activation we feel when we see a troublesome drawing, a concerning written assignment, or disquieting play, is a function of how Worrying children often induce a paradoxically "Loud" response in others as they present their "Quiet" sufferings. In fact, there are laws written in many states to specifically look out for and respond to the behaviors of Worrying children. Depending on the severity of our suspicions, the reporting laws "mandate" a response that includes calls to parents, child protective services, and possibly law enforcement.

This is our society's attempt at a response system for these children and, to a large extent, it is pre-determined. In being pulled along by the flow of the programmed and mandated responses to the Worrying child's behavior, there is an unspoken expectation that we should be involved in the "rescue" of these children from their ACE–related fate. We want to acknowledge that the impulse to swoop in and save the Worrying child is formidable and persuasive. However, we believe that our work in this chapter is to shape helpful strategies to aid these children within our classrooms, based on the idea that there are many ways to "rescue" a child.

Worrying children have *taken on* and *taken in* the harmful thoughts and feelings of a parent, caregiver, or environment that did not respond to them in loving or protective ways. This process of taking on and taking in can be described as integrating a relationship interaction. We call these types of relational integrations "introjects." They are typically powerful aspects of a relationship that become a part of our internal psychological make-up. It is akin to absorbing a repeated pattern of relating that the child has experienced with another person. That form of interacting is preserved within the child's memories, to be drawn on later (Fairbairn, 1954). For example, an introject is at work when we suddenly realize that we sound like one of our parents when interacting with our children. Instinctually, the introject affects our response to others based on these integrated memories of significant caregivers and the way they interacted with us. See Table 6.1.

Table 6.1: Types of Introjects

Negative	*Positive*
Humiliating	Uplifting
Critical	Praising
Questioning	Empowering
Undermining	Loving
Demeaning	Compassionate
Punishing	Inquisitive

Weiner, Gallo-Silver, & Lucas, 2020; Fairbairn, 1954

In the case of the Worrying child, the negative self-talk and problematic sense of self is evidence of the existence of "negative" introjects. We teachers have the opportunity to be "positive" and "supportive" introjects that may stand in direct opposition to these children's detrimental ones.

As we develop our responses to Worrying children, let us begin with a two-part ego defense called *projective-identification* that this group of children unconsciously employs (Freud, 1966; Freud & Burlingham, 1967). We are going to explain the concept in reverse order. It is the second part, that of *identification*, that we wish to focus on first. This is the teacher's part of the process, and it is the motivation for the drive (and even the compulsion) to help and aide the Worrying child. The definition of *identification* is an intensely, personal connection to a feeling, thought, or characteristic of another person. And it requires a special foundation, an unspoken association. For example, an individual is sitting and eating alone at a restaurant. Someone viewing that person may suddenly have a powerful sense of loneliness, while another person may not even notice. Another example of this phenomena is, a little boy or girl watching the championship game and imagining themselves as a professional athlete with all the emotion, feelings and thoughts that accompany the intense moment. A teacher's ability to "identify with" the Worrying child is an important piece of connecting and communicating with the Worrying child.

Now for the *projection* part of the process. In the case of Worrying children, their feelings of hopelessness and/or helplessness (generated by their negative introjects) are *projected* out on to other people in their lives, such as us. By projection, we mean the act of taking an undesirable feeling and casting it out, like throwing away junk mail. One typically does this when the feeling that is being experienced is uncomfortable, distasteful, or downright scary to the point that disowning it becomes the only option. This process is not conscious but dwells in the deeper recesses of our mind that is often referred to as the subconscious (Freud, 1966; Freud & Burlingham, 1967). A person does not know they are projecting. It is not planned or thought out, it is simply done. For example, a person who is unhappy in a marriage, and feeling that she may stray, may projects these feelings onto her spouse and become convinced that her spouse is thinking about being unfaithful. Or, a child who does not like himself may become convinced that no one likes him by projecting his own feels of self-dislike, which he cannot face, onto others. If we tell someone directly that they are projecting, they typically, will deny our observation.

Because we are caring, available, helping professionals (and see ourselves as potential positive introjects), the negative projections of the Worrying child find fertile ground within us (Fairbairn, 1954; Freud, 1966; Freud & Burlingham, 1967). We see the pain within these children, and we notice, *identify* with it, connect to it, and accept it into our consciousness. This *identification* process can have powerful and challenging effects on us. On the one hand, it can induce in us the very desperation that these children are experiencing. In these situations, teachers may feel compelled to urgently and spontaneously act in order to bring this quiet, overwhelming despair to a "positive" resolution as soon as possible. This type of resolve is quite understandable. Conversely, we may mirror the Worrying child's helplessness and hopelessness which can lead to:

1. feeling that the help we could offer is not nearly sufficient or not remotely suitable, or
2. feeling that we are alone in this situation, and there is simply no help available at all.

As examples of these latter identification reactions, Ms. Ellie may be very sad about Kayla's presentation and believe that trying to just keep her connected to the class is woefully inadequate for this sweet little girl. She may feel overwhelmed by this realization to the point of questioning herself and the possible courses of action she may want to take. Ms. Colligan may be angry and even somewhat fearful about Ethan's hygiene issues and believe that they are beyond her abilities to address in the classroom. She may feel that something terrible is happening to Ethan and be convinced that only a call to child protective services will suffice.

In terms of identification, it is very important to keep in mind that these projected feelings are not ours but are given to (induced in) us. We can imagine that Ms. Ellie's thoughts and feelings mirror Kayla's own thoughts and feelings:

- "Nothing I do can clean me enough."
- "My work is terrible, I question all my work, doing anything just feels wrong."

While, Ms. Colligan's thoughts mirror Ethan's:

- "I cannot keep myself clean no matter what I do, so what is the point in even trying?"
- "I will just let someone else do it; the act is beyond me."

That said, the projected feelings and thoughts absolutely can feel like they are ours and can dominate our waking hours. We want to remind teachers not to be surprised when they find themselves feeling anxious, agitated, or disquieted by any of the behaviors that these Worrying children exhibit. In these situations, we want teachers to comfort themselves first and not feel compelled to act impulsively or without thoughtful consideration.

Unlike with Troubling children or Testing children, whose Loud aspect can be challenging, Worrying children's Quiet nature tends to draw teachers in. The intolerable paradox of a teacher's identification with these children's quiet anguish can at times feel overwhelming. We can feel jolted into action, anything to help these children, but not have a direction or plan. In these moments, it is important to slow down, breathe, and talk to colleagues and other professionals in order to get perspective and make decisions.

We want to acknowledge the connection between projective-identification and self-fulfilling prophecies. The inducing nature of this construct has its foundations in the self-fulfilling prophecy dynamics that we discussed in the previous chapters.

Table 6.2:
Self-Fulfilling Prophecy of the Worrying Child

Steps in a Self-Fulfilling Prophecy	Example
A person makes a false assumption about herself in the context of the current environment.	Because of her life experiences, Kayla, believes that if she asks for help, there will be negative repercussions. This fear accompanies other feelings like being ignored, unloved, rejected, hurt, and abandoned; and convinces her that she is alone.

Steps in a Self-Fulfilling Prophecy	Example
The person takes action to test the false assumption.	Overwhelmed by these feelings, Kayla cannot stop herself from calling for help. However, because she is afraid of the consequences, she disguises her calls for help with her frequent bathroom wiping and destructive frustration with everything she produces.
Others react to the action and misunderstand.	The disguised calls for help are often seen by her peers and teachers as disquieting or distressing behavior that further isolates Kayla. It provokes reactions—either too intense or too inadequate—that do not address her underlying issues.
The others' reactions/responses to the person's action, confirm the false assumption for the person.	Based on the others' reaction, Kayla confirms to herself that she is alone and unable to be helped. The others' responses, along with Kayla's perception of their missteps, rejections, and abandonments, serve as proxies for those punishments she is so familiar with.
The person takes more extreme action to further test the false assumption.	Kayla creates more provocatively disguised communications to see if her teacher will come to her aid and "get it right."

Merton, 1948; Weiner, Gallo-Silver, & Lucas, 2020

The following responses follow the format we laid out in the previous chapter. The "Quiet" aspect of the behavior requires the teacher's "verbal" responses. This matches the child's cautiousness and includes the using of one's words through talking, explaining, and questioning. This provides "auditory" comforting that is connected to the many ways loving parents calm distressed children. The "over reactivity" and its intensity require us to respond with Less Emotional content, less of our own reaction, than we might be experiencing. This creates a gentleness and softness that can be useful, as the child is bringing a lack of containment to the interaction. For the purposes of our discussions here, we describe these interventions and responses as "Less Emotional." Figure 6.3 Personas and Responses reiterates this.

Table 6.3:
Personas and Responses

Child's Persona	Teacher's Responses
Loud & Over Reactive (Troubling)	Requires Structural & Less Emotional Response from teacher
Loud & Under Reactive (Testing)	Requires Structural & More Emotional Response from teacher
Quiet & Over Reactive (Worrying)	**Requires Verbal & Less Emotional Response from teacher**
Quiet & Under Reactive (Hiding)	Requires Verbal & More Emotional Response from teacher

Weiner, Gallo-Silver, & Lucas, 2020

Let us recall from Chapter 3, the basic behaviors that the Worrying child may exhibit and look at these in greater detail.

- Creating Worrisome Artwork
  - violent, dark imagery
  - negative sense of self images such as faceless or scratched out faces, disquieting representations of the body such as no hands, no feet, injuries, scary eyes
  - age-inappropriate portrayals of relationships between individuals such as sexual, violent, or menacing
- Self-Criticism, Self-Dislike
  - comments indicating a lack of patience with or appreciation of the self
  - "I hate myself"
  - "I am bad"
  - "No one likes me"
  - erasing until the paper tears
  - rejection of trying new, unknown activities
- Self-Harming Behavior
  - nail-biting-especially to the quick
  - picking at scabs/wounds
  - clothes chewing/ripping
  - twisting, pulling out hair
  - hitting, pinching oneself
  - inappropriate touching of oneself
- Difficulty Connecting with Peers
  - poor hygiene
  - odd anxiety-provoking behaviors such as suddenly walking away, tics
  - "inadvertent," yet consistent, destruction of others' projects
  - inappropriate touching and boundary maintenance (no understanding of personal space, touching the other inappropriately)
- Engaging in Concerning Play
  - age-inappropriate sexual content
  - violent content (death, killing, injuries, gore)
  - menacing or coercive content
  - neglectful content

For these children, acknowledging their struggles is a crucial part of the response. In both of our scenarios, the teachers are very concerned about the children and feel tense and restless as to how and when to best help them. They are not hopeful that involving others will help the children. Yet, without additional supports, these children's situations will remain unchanged.

Let us put some these responses into action. Beginning with the Structural interventions, the following are several responses that fit our scenarios:

Examples of Verbal Responses

- Describing Intentions and Creating Transparency
  Optimally, we want children to develop a deep, positive connection to their

teacher, class, and school. In psychological terms, a child's feelings about any new connection to another person are part of an emotional and cognitive reaction called transference and are based on positive or negative experiences and memories of past relationships. Think of it as a template we use to understand each new relationship—a starting point for comparison. Often, transference is discussed as an aspect of interpersonal relationships between people. "Kayla quickly developed a positive transference to her teacher." "Ethan's transference to his teacher was quite mistrusting at the beginning of the school year." What we are proposing for the Worrying child is that an "institutional" transference is needed. This means helping the child develop a positive attachment to an "entire" environment and the collection of people within that environment. With Worrying children, this can only happen (and be maintained) through clear, open, and authentic communication from the teacher. There is a great deal of mistrust in these children, temperamentally and environmentally driven, as well as strengthened by negative messaging. Teachers can respond to this by methodically describing to the child their thoughts and ideas about how they intend to work with them. The idea of transparency is to announce "emphatically" that we have nothing to hide, no secret agendas, no ulterior motives, that we may not be like the other people in the child's life. This process can reduce the child's fearful, anxious distortions and undermine any re-enactments that stem from any uncertainty that their lives have produced. Recall from Chapter 5, a re-enactment is a repetition of an unsuccessful relationship from the past.

We recommend this way of interacting with Worrying children in every circumstance, but especially when we feel it is necessary to respond to a worrisome communication or behavior. "Kayla, I want to know about what you are thinking when…. It helps me to make decisions for children when I understand them better. I want to help you, and this information might let me help you better." In order to maintain the positive connection to the teacher, the classroom and the school, words become a powerful means that challenge any negative messaging.

- Putting Words to Feelings and Ideas

  This may seem like a basic activity in the world of children, and, for the most part, it is.

  "The people in your drawing look angry."

  "That painting is very sad."

  "The building you constructed is very tall and strong but fell down suddenly."

  "The letters you drew look carefully written yet you ripped up the page."

  For the Worrying child, unfortunately, this is not the case. For some of the reasons we have mentioned throughout this chapter, the process of consciously communicating their thoughts and feelings is fraught with trepidation and fear of negative responses. Our responses can actively react to this reticence by beginning to create a more connected (more secure) relationship. As we sit with the child and their non-verbal creations (or in Kayla's case her destroyed artwork), we talk about what we see and ask questions for clarification. Recall from Chapter 5 that feelings and thoughts that remain secret and verbally unexplored are called unsymbolized. They never get aired out or responded to and fester inside a child's mind in a sea of self-recrimination and shame (Hurlburt & Heavey, 2008; Gregory, 2018). Symbolization is the process where thoughts and feelings are put into words and responded to with empathy and compassion by another person.

Gradually, the children may open up and tell us the "story" behind their work (and maybe even some of their "actual" difficulties). We may become an "empathic witness" to their suffering—an ally, companion, or fellow traveler—helping them feel less alone. When we demonstrate that we want to know them and understand them, they may begin to trust us. The purpose of the bark of a tree is to be protective, and so it can be quite tough and resistant to allowing us inside. Similarly, the interpersonal process of getting underneath the bark and putting words to the creations "symbolizes" them for use in future discussions and exploration.

- Using Words to Enhance Boundaries

    We can use our words to emphasize and empower the Worrying child's sense of safety and autonomy by developing and teaching the where, the when, and the what of boundaries. The healthy and appropriate norm regarding where the child physically begins and ends, when their needs are realized or ignored, and what they are allowed to say and to feel, can be taught explicitly through our verbal responses. There are words and phrases that evoke a sense of security and limits. These may feel awkward or clunky to weave into our discussions and interactions with these children, but they speak to the Worrying child at a deep level.

    Imagine the Worrying child's "pain" within the context of this cross-section of a tree—the trust we are trying to reach lies within (see Figure 6.4). The heart of the tree, the heart of the child—walled off by a rough, protective exterior. We can hear (respond to) the latent communication by moving past the bark and positively connecting to the receptive core that is so in need of this type of empathic attachment. This creates attunement, when two people are feeling and thinking similarly in a compassionate manner. For the Worrying child, we cannot hack away at the bark (the child's defenses) because of the possibility

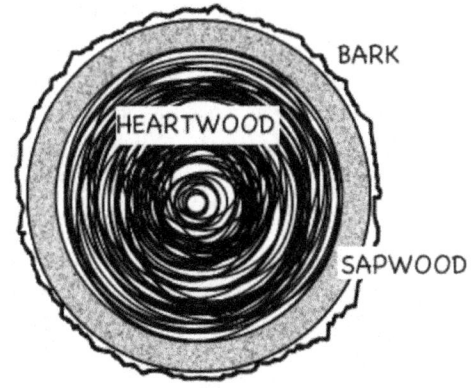

Figure 6.4: Cross-section of Tree as Child Psyche

of injuring the tree. Also, because we only spend a limited amount of time with the child, we do not want to remove the protections they may need to use elsewhere. Rather we need to use interventions that gently pass through the protective bark without disrupting it too much. This is similar to how a tree is tapped to obtain its sap. To accomplish this, we suggest using words and phrases such as:

Word	*Example of Usage*
Control	"Kayla, I am not going to stop you from ripping up your drawings. You are in **control**. The next time you feel like ripping it or erasing it, I wonder if you could try something new. I am not trying to take your **control** away, but I was hoping that you could raise your hand and I will come over and stand by you, before you begin changing the drawing."
Personal Space	"Ethan, no one is allowed to come into your **personal space** without your permission. That means the other children cannot come in the area around you without your permission, and they cannot try to make you feel bad. Your **personal space** is very important, and I want to know if anyone is trying to come into it without your permission. Maybe we can also take care of your personal space. I want you to wash your hands and your face each day. I can help if you want me to because staying clean is an important part of caring for our personal space."
Safety	"Kayla, I want you to feel **safe** when you go to the bathroom. I am sorry you feel like you need to use so much toilet paper. It looks like you feel upset when you need to use all that toilet paper. I will not come into the bathroom with you, but I was wondering if you could let me know when you feel like you have to go, and I could be nearby just in case you need help feeling **safer**."

Examples of Less Emotional Responses

- Using the Speed and Pace as Containment

  The Worrying child requires adults to approach him in a slow, methodical and measured way. This is based on a concept called pacing. Pacing is the act of determining an optimally secure flow of information passing to and from an individual. In the case of the teacher-child relationship, it is based on the needs of the child you want to reach and not on our needs to help the child as quickly as possible. This requires us to manage the tension that inevitably exists between the expectations of school and the ability of the Worrying child to meet those expectations. Because of this, going slow, speaking slow, finding quiet moments to speak alone with these children, sometimes feel like holding back a powerful force that is pushing to move them faster than they can bear.

  Worrying children cannot move quickly in their relationships with new people. The slow pace increases a sense of control within the Worrying child, enabling the child to better manage any anxiety about the increased closeness of an adult. In this way, the slow pace contains the emotional responses of the child and helps prevent a flooding of feelings that would overwhelm him or her. The slow pace silently says, in effect, "I think you are in pain; I will not inflict more; I will meet you where you are." This is akin to tapping through the bark of the tree rather than hacking away at it.

- Respecting Intensity of Communication

  Because of how intense some of these non-verbal communications can seem to us, we think that honoring this "forceful" expression in terms of self-care is critical. Using the earthquake metric, if the communication of upset from the Worrying child is a 6.7 on the Richter scale, then adding our own, unfiltered 5.5 level of upset dramatically increases the shaky quality of the relationship. If our goal is to respond in a helpful, intensity reducing way, then it is very important to understand the transmittable (or vicarious) nature of trauma.

  Trauma can get passed on from a survivor to the caretakers of that survivor. Think about how fatigued we can be after attending a funeral or after watching media coverage of a tragedy. After 9/11, the repetitious news coverage of the World Trade Center collapsing caused a great deal of vicarious trauma to individuals that were not even directly affected by the tragedy. When working with the trauma of a Worrying child, we must take action to be kind to ourselves and practice self-care. It is not enough to make plans for the child. We also must make similar plans for ourselves by actively engaging in activities that comfort us, re-energize us, and "feed" us emotionally. This is not a passive process. If we are to help the Worrying child, give the child a part of us in order to heal, then we must refill ourselves. We can do this by undertaking some of the following:

  ◊ Exercising (running, jogging, walking, swimming, biking, dancing, etc.)
  ◊ Keeping a journal of any thoughts and feelings about these children
  ◊ Participating in relaxation exercises (yoga, guided imagery, massages, etc.)
  ◊ Talking to colleagues other than your teammates and co-teachers (for other perspectives)
  ◊ Prayer
  ◊ Enjoying activities with friends and family
  ◊ Artistic endeavors and activities
  ◊ Visiting a counselor or psychotherapist

Self-care is our form of pacing ourselves when it comes to working with Worrying children. In fact, it can be a form of self-pacing when working with any child who challenges us.

Affirmations That Help Children Hold On to Their New Coping Skills

The commitment and understanding that teachers have for Worrying children are essential for attentive responses to their behaviors. While these children may very well need help beyond the classroom, Ms. Ellie and Ms. Colligan can become conduits for changes within the classroom.

The Worrying child's difficulties are not so easily solved, but their over reactivity obliges us to identify and implement measures to keep them secure within our classrooms while the issues central to their underlying difficulties are being addressed. Creating a safe school environment where the child feels a sense of belonging and empathy helps to develop and reinforce their sense of self, inner strength, and power. For Worrying children, all three of these developmental necessities are a constant challenge. A safe school environment functions as a "holding environment" for their trauma-related communications—an aptly named safe space that protectively envelopes the child (Winnicott, 1990).

What will not help these children is for us to overreact, move too quickly, or respond without contemplation. While our worries and fears are often justifiable, we must distance ourselves from the understandable and compelling fantasy to rescue or fix the Worrying child. Finding a loving home, changing a destructive living situation, altering any toxic relationships with their parents, are critically important to the development of any child. Yet, for the Worrying child, finding the right individuals to carry out these caretaking responsibilities is even more important. Endemic to the trauma of the Worrying child is a sense of hopelessness. We do have the opportunity to undermine and contain this hopelessness by systematically strengthening the clear, safe, and realistic boundaries of an empathic, caring teacher-child relationship. Unfortunately, giving in to fanciful and overly unrealistic fantasies of quick fixes and miraculous salvation, will more likely create false expectations and an increased sense of betrayal for the Worrying child to manage.

What we can do is to create a series of responses in the classroom that affirms the inherent goodness that lives within the Worrying child. The process we describe in this chapter has one main purpose—to embed a vital idea deep within the Worrying child's mind, an idea that their current living environment may not allow for, an idea that these children can learn in the "transitional space" that is our classroom and keep for the future. This idea is like a seed that will remain underneath the earth and be nourished by the memories of our interactions. And when the Worrying child feels secure, sometime later in life, the seed will sprout and grow. This idea is, of course, hope—a hope that the Worrying child can find happiness, thrive and flourish.

These "seeds" can sound like the following:

> "Kayla, I believe in you … you are such a powerful and strong girl."
> "Ethan, your feelings are so big and bright and powerful. They shine like the sun."
> "Kayla, what you create in your artwork is so thoughtful and impressive."
> "Ethan, you are such an important part of this class. It is better because you are in it."

For the Worrying child, we must retain a long-term view with regard to the affirmations we provide. We suggest thinking in terms of years rather than days or even months. Our role is to provide hope for safety, for love, for companionship, for a better future, one that can outshine the present day.

Chapter 7

The Child Who Is "Hiding"

Quiet and Under Reactive

Quiet—Temperamentally slow to warm and internalizes thoughts and feelings; acts "in" as a way of striving for control

Under Reactive—The conscious mind is disconnected from thoughts and feelings with little freedom of expression of thoughts and feelings

* * *

AURA (Acknowledging, Understanding, **Responding, Affirming**)

In this chapter, we will look at the behavior of the "Hiding Child." In terms of Persona, these children are distinguished by their Quiet and Under Reactive communication scaffolding. Our discussion about the Hiding child should start with the old adage, "the squeaky wheel gets the grease." To understand and respond to the communications of this group of children is to be aware of their nature—they are the precise opposite of the squeaky wheel. Making little to no noise outwardly (to their environment) or inwardly (to themselves), Hiding children present a challenge in that we often must make a concerted effort even to notice them.

With the Hiding child, we are presented with a group of children who need to communicate something important, but whose communication scaffolding obscures this communication to the point where it is nearly buried. Let us be honest with one another. With managing a significant number of children on a day-to-day basis—including those who actively preoccupy us such as the Troubling, Testing, or Worrying ones—the idea of having to go and find a Hiding child may just be a bridge too far. If these children are not affecting the lesson plan, the environment, the flow of the class, why is it necessary to add to our teaching burden? The straightforward and unfortunate answer centers on the concept of neglect. Neglect is "the state of being uncared for." If not addressed, it is both the impetus behind Hiding children's presentations and the unhappy outcome of their experiences at school. These children instinctively hide—they hide from others, and they even hide from themselves—and in their acts of hiding, it becomes very difficult for us to provide them care and education.

> *Am I Mandated to Share?*
>
> There may be times when a teacher deems it necessary to involve individuals outside the classroom to address the needs of the Hiding child (including but not limited to, other school professionals, administration, parents, child protective services, and law enforcement). The material in this chapter addresses what a teacher can accomplish with a Hiding child within the classroom setting, but does not, in any way, suggest that these issues need only be managed within the classroom setting. If a teacher has significant concerns about a child, we always suggest discussing these concerns immediately with other individuals.

For this chapter, the sections will flow as follows:

- Child scenarios
- Manifest communication (temperament) from scenarios in this chapter—Quiet
- Latent communication (temperament) from scenarios in this chapter—Quiet
- Manifest communication (conscious mind) from scenarios in this chapter—Under Reactive
- Latent communication (conscious mind) from scenarios in this chapter—Under Reactive
- Structured responses for scenarios in this chapter—Quiet & Under Reactive

Scenarios—Stephanie and Harley

Stephanie, 4 years old, Pre-K in Mr. Royce's class

Stephanie is 4 years old and in Pre-Kindergarten. She and her twin sister were both adopted from Russia when they were infants. Their parents have informed the school's administration that Stephanie's sister has developmental issues which require the assistance of a full-time paraprofessional while in school. Mr. Royce has observed Stephanie with her sister, and their dynamic is very sweet, with Stephanie "taking care" of her sister by bringing her toys to play with and attending to her needs. That said, when Stephanie is on her own, she seems listless and floats around the room from activity to activity. She does not stay long at each and often does not seem to have a plan. Mr. Royce has noticed that if he speaks to Stephanie about a task, such as creating with Play-Doh, he can leave Stephanie at a desk with the Play-Doh, then come back minutes later and she will still be sitting there with the ball of Play-Doh untouched. If Mr. Royce asks Stephanie about what she wants to make with the Play-Doh, she will not respond. With all his concerns, he must admit to himself that Stephanie does not seem unhappy.

Chapter 7. The Child Who Is "Hiding"

Harley, 6 years old, first grade in Ms. Cox's class

Harley is a 6-year-old boy in first grade. Everyone in the class calls Harley shy. He is quiet and reserved. Ms. Cox describes him to her colleagues as a "watcher." On the playground, Harley stands off to the side while his classmates play chase and tag, imaginative games derived from the cartoon and comic books that they read and watch. He seems very connected to the play but remains apart. In the classroom, Harley never initiates an activity but will participate and collaborate. At reading time, Ms. Cox notes that Harley will not raise his hand in response to her questions. He will answer a question when asked directly, with a volume that borders on inaudible. Compared to the more challenging boys in the class, Ms. Cox finds Harley's overall presentation curiously odd but sweet and unassuming, and she is happy that he is in her class.

Manifest Content—Quiet

For the Hiding child, the nature of Quiet looks demonstrably different than that of the Worrying child. Where the Worrying child makes herself visible through transitional spaces, the Hiding child conveys his version of Quiet with signs on his front door such as "Please Keep Out" or "No One Home at the Moment." It is best characterized as a "staying away," an avoidance that presents as a separateness from others. It is a castle wall, tall and sturdy, impenetrable, behind which these children hide or shelter. It is Superman's "Fortress of Solitude," Batman's "Bat Cave," or Snoopy's "Doghouse." It is not only the outside world that is being kept out but the inside world as well. The inside world seems as chaotic and turbulent as the outside world to these children (see Latent Under Reactive). The Hiding child has difficulty making sense of both the outside or their inside worlds and guards against too much contact with and awareness of either (Bellak, 1973).

The behaviors of a Hiding child typically appear like avoidance or disconnectedness. This disengagement invariably results in the unobtrusive circumvention by the Hiding child of the routines, rules, and norms of a classroom. This evasion is not a glitch of the Hiding child; it is the feature. To this end, the Hiding child may:

- avoid social situations
- intrude into a classmates' space (without acknowledgment)
- make inappropriate statement about others
- look past someone who is speaking to them
- not make eye contact
- not participate in group activities
- not reciprocate with others
- not respond to questions/statements from others
- play in ways that do not include others
- stand off to the side
- stare at others

These behaviors allow for Hiding children to be more than cautious. Their disconnectedness creates an outward solitude that provides them with a semblance of control. Unfortunately, this is a false sense of control. We use the word false because we believe Hiding children are not peacefully aloof. The Quiet outward presentation covers for an internal world that experiences a significant level of pressure from the expectations of the outside world. Their internal world does, at times, bubble up and over, as their inner unrest can no longer be contained.

Latent Content—Quiet

A boundary is the point at which one thing ends and another thing begins. The meaning of boundaries can also center on the transfer of information in and out of a system. For this discussion, we want you to have an expansive view of this concept. There are tangible boundaries. We can imagine a boundary as a wall or a fence or a door, like a castle wall or a moat around that castle. But we can also understand boundaries as something more abstract—let's call these intangible boundaries. Personal space can be a boundary; a set of beliefs can be a boundary; mental illness can be a boundary; and the unique workings of neurobiological structures can be a boundary. Each of these shapes the way information moves back and forth. Simply put, a boundary allows for:

- information from outside a system to be incorporated within
- information from within a system to be communicated out

For example, a family system watches a movie about climate change. During the movie, information is provided about the importance of doing one's part to address the different aspects making up this issue. The family members discuss the idea from the film of reducing the amount of garbage they produce and decide to increase their activities of recycling and composting. In this scenario, the family's boundary permitted the incorporation of concepts about (1) climate change and (2) the importance of recycling and composting, and allowed these to alter the family's behavior.

To use the notion of boundaries in order to understand a child, especially a Hiding one, it is important to discuss the idea of boundary permeability and acknowledge that it can vary. Boundary permeability is the quality and quantity of information that is allowed to pass in and out of a boundary. The extremes of boundary permeability can be characterized as follows:

- Rigid—allowing little or no information to pass in or out of a boundary
- Diffuse—allowing most if not all information to pass in or out of a boundary

Why is this important? Because communication and relationships are impacted significantly by the nature of the boundary that exists between two people. When we discussed Worrying children in the previous chapter, we focused the idea of a child who portrays "Quiet" by expressing this quality through a means of indirect communication (transitional spaces). Using the concept of boundaries to explain this presentation, the indirect communication means that the information leaves the child through a permeable boundary, but very cautiously and tentatively. We would describe these boundaries as somewhat rigid.

In Hiding children, their internal world is reflexively held close and guarded, so very little information gets out. Alternatively, information we may try to provide to them is overly vetted to the point of often being summarily rejected. In this way, we see that being "Quiet" for Hiding children is more a way of coping and enduring. It is just so hard for them to manage the outside and inside worlds. For this reason, their boundaries are harder, higher, and more rigid—being far less permeable than that of Worrying children. This is not a fence, but a concrete wall. "Quiet" signifies the wish within these children to limit engagement in the typical back and forth between child and anyone else, parents, teachers and classmates alike.

Manifest Content—Under Reactive

As educators, we are comfortable when we can connect A to B to C; when two plus two equals four; when cause and effect make sense. From the perspective of an observer, the Hiding child upsets this comfortable predictability. These children typically go about their days with a lack of mindfulness to their actions. Hiding children may act a certain way, move in a given direction, or play in a specific way that seems unusual or atypical. These and other acts will seem confusing to those tasked with interacting with them—classmates and teachers. Responses, questions or interventions may seem lost on them or seem not to make contact with them in any discernable way.

It is almost as if they, themselves, do not know the reasons or thoughts behind what they are doing—only that they want to or sense they should. They can appear as instinct machines, behaving as impulse-driven, sensory seeking individuals, marching to a different drumbeat than those around them. In addition, there is often a layer of "being different" to their actions, statements, and presentation. This differentness, which can come across as "odd," does not, typically, create a self-consciousness in the Hiding child. While the behaviors are almost too varied to create an exhaustive list, some of what we may typically see a Hiding child do are as follows:

- Engaging in play on their own
- Flapping their hands or making other motor movements
- Humming/singing to themselves
- Making odd facial expressions
- Making repeated sounds/verbalizations, almost "tic" like
- Needing activities to follow certain procedures (that are defined unilaterally)
- Repeating specific behaviors excessively (ritualistic)
- Seeming to be daydreaming
- Spontaneously laughing
- Talking/mumbling to themselves

As with the "Quiet" behaviors, the "Under Reactive" behaviors create their own distancing as classmates and teachers can feel put-off by their unusual nature. One teacher described her experience of a Hiding child by comparing it to feeling like she was floating in the air and losing focus while interacting with him. Without seeming to know they are doing so, Hiding children employ their under reactivity in ways that keep others off balance and allows them to remain hidden in plain sight. Classmates' and teachers' puzzlement regarding these behaviors acts like a fog of war, throwing off relationship-building activity with a level of uncertainty and tentativeness. This further emphasizes these children's apparent isolation.

Latent Content—Under Reactive

Children actively or passively try to grasp how they think and feel about situations, experiences, relationships, environments, and their place in the world. We call this practice developing self-awareness. It is the skill of reflection and reviewing as a way of processing their own thoughts about the world around them. This may seem straightforward, but let's go over the steps of this process so that we have a common baseline for future discussions.

The child's exploration for understanding typically tracks a course such as this:

Step (1) encounters an experience
Step (2) searches inward (to oneself) for options of how to think or feel (understanding) about the encounter
Step (3) based on the results of the search, reflects and develops "self-aware" responses (managing or coping) to that experience

This process is opaque to an outside observer—it happens within the children, although we may see them reflecting and processing. It is the ubiquitous work of childhood, and it is conducted over and over again, in homes, at schools, on playgrounds, in museums and parks, really anywhere children can be found.

The Hiding child finds Step 2 of above-described process to be particularly challenging. As we said earlier in this chapter, Hiding children perceive their inside world to be as confusing and unavailable as the outside world. This conflicted relationship with their own feelings and thoughts creates an unfortunate disconnect. Cut off from mindful use their internal resources (such as self-soothing, problem solving, prioritizing, compromising, preparing, planning, etc.), the Hiding child's very ability to cope and manage daily activities is constantly tested and at times thwarted.

In exchanges with Hiding children, the disconnect from the self is experienced by us as a persistent sense that something is missing or absent. Due to their lack of self-awareness, there is a lack of consistency and an unexpectedness in the Hiding child's interactions. This may continually surprise us and, while we will discuss this more at length later in this chapter, we want to acknowledge, now, the intense uncertainty that these children may provoke in us.

What their under reactivity "hides" is the mutuality we typically feel with children when helping them navigate life situations or relational dynamics. Even if a child initially struggles with being helped, we typically expect a level receptivity and maybe, eventually, even an alliance. Mutuality is the connective tissue of relationships. However, Hiding children as collaborative "partners" are concealed—from us

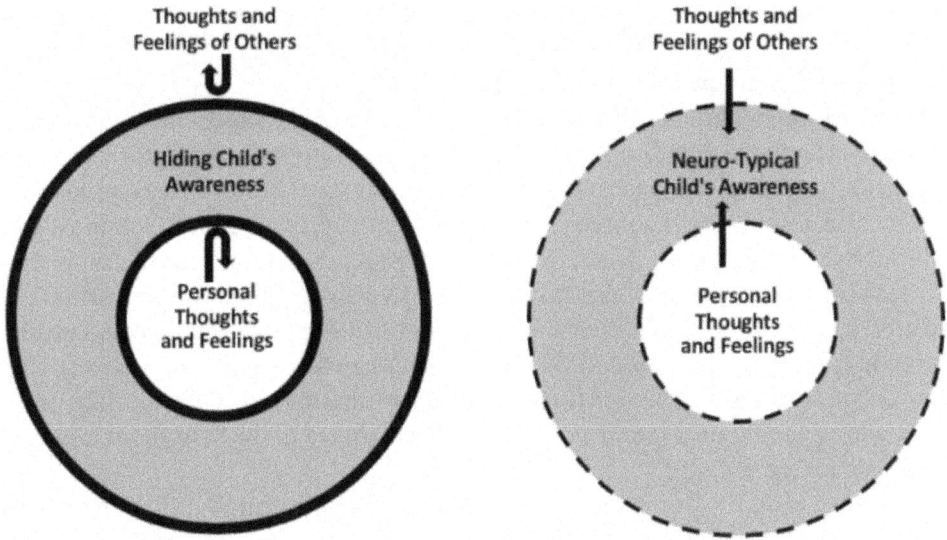

Figure 7.1: Hiding Child's Boundaries versus Neuro-Typical Child's Boundaries

and from themselves, keeping us and their personal thoughts and feelings behind substantial rigid boundaries.

Visualize the tall, sturdy walls that keep the outside world out. Now, we want you to imagine the same set of walls that seems to protect the Hiding child from the outside are also constructed within the Hiding child. From this perspective, this under reactivity could better be seen as a self-imposed solitary confinement.

Is this a conscious choice to willfully reject information from themselves that could help communicate their needs? We think not. The latent communication of this under reactivity is instinctual. There is a widespread flinching from input that seems more protective in nature than defiant. Unfortunately, having difficulty processing and using how they feel and think about a situation leaves Hiding children with a dearth of self-awareness from which to draw on.

With all this, when a teacher is compelled to interact with Quiet, Under Reactive Hiding children, he or she may feel a sense of initial discouragement, as characterized in the typical questions: "where do I even begin with this child?" or "is this child even in the appropriate setting?" We want to convey empathy for this feeling, for we believe that this may be connected to the Hiding child's own experience of discouragement. That said, there are common themes to their communications that we can respond to in order to build a productive school experience.

Building Responses for Scenarios—Quiet and Under Reactive

In our scenarios, Stephanie and Harley are "Quiet" and "Under Reactive," those we describe as Hiding children. As we have established, there are a couple of common themes to their latent communication. First, these "Quiet" children are inwardly struggling, feeling alone, and often ambivalent about getting help. Second, there is a complexity to the Hiding children's access to their internal world which creates confusion about how to understand their own experiences and leaves them at a loss as to how or what to communicate to caregivers.

With these two themes noted, we want to assert that Hiding children can present with a level of variability that creates its own unique challenges for us in identifying and creating responses. Our personal individual emotional responses to a child can be described as counter-reactions to them. The counter-reaction most common with this group of children is a sense of strangeness, an off-putting impression, that leaves us with a sense of not knowing exactly which way to proceed. This is the counter-reaction to the child's sense of confusion and displacement. Recognizing this dynamic is a key to creating helpful responses. It can lead to the questions such as: How do these children manage their day-to-day functioning? How do they understand what is going on around them? And what can we do to help them move forward even incrementally?

At this point, it is important to note that the Hiding child's difficulties are frequently organic in nature. This means the difficulties are a function of a unique brain structure and brain functioning. Rather than see these children as "abnormal" or even "disabled," they are instead representative of a newly identified group of people who are now considered "neuro-diverse."

Neurodiversity is a new term used to normalize the notion that there are myriad ways for people to think and learn. It supports the idea that these children, the ones that we call Hiding children, exhibit natural, and often distinctive, cognitive variations that require the adults working with them to establish personalized and tailored responses (Silberman, 2015). For our purposes, neurodiversity includes children:

- with behaviors that are identified within the Autism Spectrum;
- with learning problems and related challenges (such as dyslexia, dysgraphia, dyscalculia, processing issues); and
- with difficulties of thinking, including disorganized thoughts and odd thoughts (such pre-psychotic thought-related disorders).

The inclusion of a concept like neurodiversity within our discussion is a more useful way to understand child behavior as non-pathological. Neurodiversity-related issues manifest themselves in different aspects of the brain and brain functioning and can seem extreme in the way they affect a child's behavior at times. These children may differ from neuro-typical children in a variety of ways that result in profound challenges in certain areas of functioning and remarkable expertise and skill in others. For example:

- Some children who have been diagnosed with Attention-Deficit Hyperactivity Disorder may be able to focus when their bodies are in motion (C8Sciences, 2016; American Psychiatric Association, 2013; Hartanto, et al., 2015).
- Some children who have been diagnosed with Autism Spectrum Disorder can excel in working with computers, as well as with numbers, charts, maps, or other highly structured areas (American Psychiatric Association, 2013; Mayor, 2008; Szczerba, 2015; Wei, et al., 2014).

- Some children who have been diagnosed with Dyslexia can achieve extraordinarily heights in areas such the culinary arts, theater or music performance, where tasks are not dependent on compulsory, time constrained reading (American Psychiatric Association, 2013; Everatt, et al., 1999).
- Some children who have disorganized thinking or unusual thoughts can be highly artistic due, in part, to the disinhibited nature of their cognitive framework (American Psychiatric Association, 2013; Kaufman & Paul, 2014).

Acknowledging that children's brains and their neurobiological expression exist on a continuum of functionality does not mean that neuro-diverse children can forgo needed support, counseling, and higher levels of structured care (including, at times, medication). These can be important accommodations for neuro-diverse children, to help them productively benefit from our teaching and the overall school environment.

The foundation of mental health treatment and intervention as a general practice is its pursuit of self-awareness. Regardless of the therapeutic modality, the goal is to assist an individual in gaining a sense of control through increased understanding, insight, and connections. Neuro-diverse children can and do greatly benefit from this type of assistance (whether offered in school or elsewhere) as a way of cultivating self-awareness. This will be the basis of our strategies in this chapter.

Table 7.1: Self-Fulfilling Prophecy of the Hiding Child

Steps in a Self-Fulfilling Prophecy	Example
A person makes a false assumption about herself in the context of the current environment.	Stephanie has the sense that no one truly understands her, and this leaves her quite isolated. While she may be upset with this, her own thoughts and feelings, in general, are difficult for Stephanie to process and can easily overwhelm her. Due to these reinforcing dynamics—her isolation, a lack of self-awareness, and her difficulty communicating, Stephanie thinks it is better to avoid being challenged by the demands of the outside world.
The person takes action to test the false assumption.	Stephanie tries to control her world through disentanglement by (1) limiting her interactions with others and going unnoticed, when she can, or (2) protesting (passively or more vigorously) requests for engagement.
Others react to the action and misunderstand.	Behaving in this way, Stephanie seems odd and/or aloof to teachers (and classmates), and they struggle to understand exactly how to engage her in the work of school. Attempts often miss the mark, leaving teachers (and classmates) confused, discouraged, or frustrated. To them, leaving Stephanie alone seems the easiest path.

Steps in a Self-Fulfilling Prophecy	Example
The others' reactions/responses to the person's action, confirm the false assumption for the person.	Based on the teacher's (and classmates') reaction, Stephanie confirms that no one understands her or really cares to try—and, for Stephanie, because of her discomfort with others and her difficulty understanding how she feels, this result may feel "right" to her.
The person takes more extreme action to further test the false assumption.	Stephanie's solitary behaviors continue, and may even increase, deepening her isolation.

Merton, 1948; Weiner, Gallo-Silver, & Lucas, 2020

These responses follow the format we laid out in previous chapter. The "Quiet" aspect of the behavior requires the teacher's "verbal" responses. This matches the child's cautiousness and includes the soft use of one's words through talking, repetition, explaining and taking educated guesses, and slowly inquiring. This is reminiscent of the "auditory" structure that is connected to the earliest ways that parents inform children they are present—cooing, humming, or singing. The "under reactivity" and the disconnectedness require us to respond with more of ourselves, modeling a relationship and interaction that display self-awareness and matching of feelings to behavior. We describe these interventions and responses as "More Emotional"; however, our emotional presentation for this group needs to be measured and titrated for each individual child so as not to overwhelm (see Table 7.2).

Table 7.2:
Personas and Responses

Persona	Responses
Loud & Over Reactive	Requires Structural & Less Emotional Responses from teacher
Loud & Under Reactive	Requires Structural & More Emotional Responses from teacher
Quiet & Over Reactive	Requires Verbal & Less Emotional Responses from teacher
Quiet & Under Reactive	**Requires Verbal & More Emotional Responses from teacher**

Weiner, Gallo-Silver, & Lucas, 2020

Let us recall the basic behaviors that Hiding children may exhibit from Chapter 3.

Preference for Parallel Play Over Collaborative Play

- Playing in ways that do not include others
- Seeming developmentally younger than peer group
- Engaging in repetitious play on their own
- Not reciprocating with others

Disconnectedness

- Seeming to be daydreaming
- Talking to themselves/mumbling
- Not making eye contact
- Looking past someone who is speaking to them
- Distress in social situations

Non-responsiveness

- Not participating in group activities
- Not responding to questions/statements from others
- Standing off to the side

Repetition and Rituals

- Flapping their hands or make other repetitive movements
- Humming/singing to themselves
- Selecting regressed self-soothing behaviors
- Making repeated sounds/verbalizations, almost "tic" like

Odd Reactions

- Making odd facial expressions
- Spontaneously laughing
- Intruding into classmates' space (without acknowledgment)
- Having tantrums when overwhelmed
- Staring at others

Of all the children we discuss in this book, we believe that this group may be the most complex to approach as teachers. This is due, in large part, to the dynamic that the majority of their "resources" are being committed to pushing others away and staying away themselves. It should not be lost on us that the least taxing approach with Hiding children would be to allow them to move about the classroom at their own pace, in their own time, with their own agendas. This cannot be said for Troubling, Testing or Worrying children, as these groups would quickly, or at least eventually, create issues in the classroom that we would have to address directly.

For these children, the question is how to reach them as they "hide" in plain sight. Operationally, we attempt to establish a connection that we recognize may create some level of discomfort in the Hiding child. We utilize a counterweight to this discomfort by choosing an approach vector that offers the Hiding child a sense of control. To accomplish this, *verbal responses*—the thoughtful use of words, tone, repetition and pace—can provide a level of security that enables Hiding children to permit our information through their boundaries. In addition, titrated and measured *More Emotional responses* can provide a useful model for children who are having difficulties accessing and processing their own thoughts and feelings. Our self-awareness serves as a lighthouse in their own darkness.

While the *More Emotional responses* follow the same pattern as previous chapters, we want to augment this chapter's version of *verbal responses*. When we think of verbal, we typically think of speaking to someone. However, we do not believe this is sufficient for this group of Hiding children. The boundary difficulties that impact the ability of Hiding children to take in information require the additional prompt of a written communication. Writing down the thoughts and ideas that we want these children to consider offers them an added sense of control. These augmented *verbal responses* accomplish this task in several ways:

1. Reduces intimacy of communication by having the information conveyed through a transitional space
2. Allows for a choice about when to initially take in the communication (offering control)
3. Enables the ability to keep the communication and revisit it numerous times if necessary, as repetition creates comfort and comfort increases the possibility for the communication to pass through the child's boundaries

Thoughts and ideas communicated by these augmented *verbal responses* can be shown and explained through any number of mediums, including:

- Drawings (of facial expressions connected to feelings, situations, metaphors)
- Picture Books (of stories with useful themes)
- Word/Number Scales (of level of feelings, importance of specific thoughts)
- Video (of situations to be examined and explored from a distance)

Let's put some these responses into action. Beginning with the verbal interventions, the following are several generic interventions that fit our scenarios:

Examples of Verbal Responses

- Identifying (and concretizing) choices and decisions
    Creating a decision tree allows for the Hiding child to (1) participate in the creation of plans and options and to (2) develop an ongoing awareness of how teacher/school expectations interface with the child's ideas. The teacher discusses options and possibilities with the Hiding child—what to do when he enters the room, what to do if she gets frustrated. These then are written on a sheet of paper to memorialize them and be able to refer back to them (see Figure 7.2). The decision tree is a transitional space between the teacher and the student and provides that additional security that the Hiding child can use for integration.
    When we apply this response to Stephanie, our discussions with her might initially focus on how to move through an activity or even how to choose an activity. We would create a decision tree that began with Play-Doh. Next, we would identify with her input two undertakings she could engage in with the

Chapter 7. The Child Who Is "Hiding" 115

Figure 7.2: Decision Tree

Play-Doh—roll it out or flatten it. Next, we would identify two items she could make with rolled Play-Doh and two with flattened Play-Doh (see Figure 7.3). Having written this down in an age-sensitive way, we would then leave her to see how she could manage the activity.

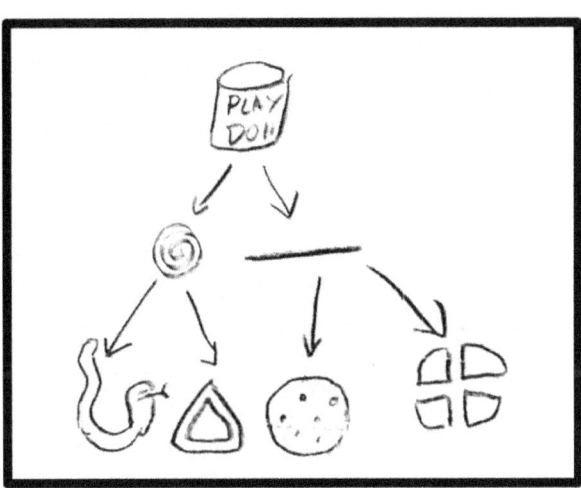

Figure 7.3: Stephanie's Decision Tree

- Identifying (and concretizing) thoughts and feelings

As we stated earlier, when a Hiding child feels something, there may be some difficulty in making the connections necessary to act on those ideas in a self-aware manner. As demonstrated in Figure 7.4 below, describing the way objects work (the body, the mind, the class, the student-teacher relationship) provides an operational understanding that serves as a foundation to help the child feel more competent. Like a blueprint for a construction project, a picture like the one below creates a visual reality different than the child's and decreases intimacy. This helps in two important ways:

◊ the words and images are integrated at a pace the Hiding child needs, which is more in keeping with the need for control.
◊ the complexity (and overwhelming nature) of the abstract notions of

feelings, relationships, thoughts, etc., are made into words and images that can more easily pass through the Hiding child's boundaries.

Returning to Harley's scenario, Ms. Cox recently implemented a new recess curriculum called the Empowered Playground (Coffield & Weiner, 2015) as a way of addressing the problematic rough-and-tumble play that was causing some of the students to get injured and upset during recess. The goal of the curriculum is to provide clear playground procedures that can be easily integrated and applied by children. This process leads to a sense of security through efficacy and control.

Figure 7.4: Drawing of Mind-Body Connection

The Empowered Playground follows a series of steps for teacher and children:

1. video the children playing on the playground
2. have the children watch themselves playing (on video)
3. discuss the types of play, naming them and describing their features
4. talk about their thoughts and feelings about each type of play
5. identify some basic guidelines for playground time
6. guide the children in making their own safety rules for each type of play including rough and tumble play, that they can implement themselves
7. have the children choose what type of play they will engage in prior to going out on the playground as a way of preparing them

Ms. Cox was surprised when Harley, after participating in the new rule-creation for playground time, immediately chose to participate in the "rough" play. Over several weeks she watched him "come out of his shell" both on the playground and in the classroom.

The practical nature of the rules, Harley's ability to engage in the discourse that went into their creation, and the mandate to speak out about his choices with regard to the play created an environment of security on the playground for this Hiding child. The observations of himself on video, the discussions around self-awareness and awareness of others, and the subsequent rules developed through this process, gave Harley the voice he needed to leave his hiding place.

Examples of More Emotional Responses

- Encouraging the development of self-awareness

    As when we discussed symbolizing thoughts and feelings of the Testing child, the same process is useful for the Hiding child with variations to accommodate their difficulties with boundaries and the need for individualized pacing. The differences in the responses center on the nature of empathy and the building of trust (as well as the need to titrate responses in terms of pacing). Empathy (showing someone that we truly understand) establishes the reality that the person receiving empathy is not alone. The complication with providing empathy to Hiding children is their penchant to push away connection. We realize that this creates somewhat of a paradox. The solution is preparation and pacing.

    Central to this process is the importance of our own awareness that interactions, relationships and day-to-day functioning that may be straightforward to some children are complicated and demanding for the Hiding child. We begin with a definitive notion that, for a Hiding child, relational dynamics are arduous. Setting this baseline and remembering it during our interactions with this group of children creates the opportunity for empathic statements that will prepare the Hiding child to do something arduous. The speed with which we introduce concepts can be paced at a level that meets the individual child's needs. Our statements simultaneously can provide control to the Hiding child and allow us to share our knowledge of their inner world:
    - ◊ "Harley, I would like to share something with you … (pause) … I wonder if it may be hard for you to choose feeling words."
    - ◊ "Stephanie, I was wondering if I could make a comment … (pause) … I imagine it may make you feel good to help your sister and it's maybe hard for you when she is not around."
    - ◊ "Harley, there is something I was noticing … (pause) … Sometimes it seems that playground time without rules makes you feel confused."
    - ◊ "Stephanie, I had a thought, maybe I could share it with you … (pause) … I noticed that it could be hard to decide what to do when your sister is not near you."

    The pacing mechanism used in the above teacher responses is called posing a *tentative* question/statement. This is a question/statement that (1) offers an initial caveat that allows for a Hiding child to prepare for what comes next, and (2) leaves room for the child to reject the notions behind the question or indeed to accept them. These less-than-definitive statements/questions are easier for the Hiding child to "hear," as they do not force their way past his/her/their boundaries.

    Both Harley and Stephanie need this assistance in describing their inner world. Our empathic, educated guesses can be helpful touchstones for them, like breadcrumbs to follow. This process creates a tentative connection, and we should not expect any sort of obvious acknowledgment. Like most Hiding-child communications, the feeling of increased trust will be subtle.

- Modeling our feelings about the behavior

    Again, following the format of the Testing child's More Emotional paced response, these Hiding child interventions require teachers to use themselves as an example. Where the interventions diverge is in the specific nature of the use of self. For Hiding children, we recommend the use of self that functions more like a story or allegory. The story or allegory need not necessarily be true (although a seed of truth is always more authentic), just believable, and of course associated with the situation.

    The narrative intervention that we are suggesting creates an added layer between teacher and student which helps with any boundary discomfort. We do not share how we feel about the Hiding child or his behavior—that is more like process self-disclosure (see Chapter 5). Instead, we report how we feel or think about a comparable instant that we may have experienced. Like the video, the drawing, or the story book, our story is a transitional space—one that the Hiding child can draw on for understanding. This type of transitional space (our use of self) models for the Hiding child the way we access thoughts and feeling, but with less intimacy.

Table 7.3:
Self-Disclosure versus Transitional Space Use of Self

Self-Disclosure	*Transitional Space Use of Self*
"Harley, it makes me sad when you are not playing with your classmates."	"Harley, when I am in a big group of people, I sometimes feel <u>confused</u> by what to do—should I talk, should I stand on the side? Sometimes it makes me feel <u>sad</u>."
"Stephanie, it makes me worried when are having trouble figure out what to do."	"Stephanie, when I was little and my mom left me at school, I would feel <u>afraid</u> and not want to do anything. It made me feel better when my teacher helped me make choices."

Weiner, Gallo-Silver, & Lucas, 2020

These interventions are not structured to enable Hiding children to escape their isolation. They are devised to metaphorically empower the Hiding child to open a window, crack a door, or peer over a wall. Trust is built one slow step at a time and the school year is long enough to make strides.

Affirmations That Help Children Hold On to Their New Coping Skills

When we understand and accept that a Hiding child may experience the innate need to remain behind his or her fortifications, we open up the opportunity of being able to join them there. Social work, as a philosophy, espouses the idea that to establish a successful working relationship with a client (in our case a student), we must "start where the client is." Obviously the "where" for each child is different, but we believe that as a group, Hiding children need us to start where they are in terms of their interpersonal abilities and skills.

The responses we describe above will work using certain criteria. These criteria rely on our being mindful and present.

> 1. Take the time (even if we do not feel that we have it) to notice the specific details of the Hiding child's presentation—the curious nuances, the interesting behaviors, any atypical social interactions, and the non-verbal communications (facial expression, posture, eye contact, etc.). We want to remind you that the confusion, frustration and/or discomfort that these children generate in us tend to limit interaction. This requires you to detour around these feelings and re-double your efforts to reach these children.
>
> 2. Do not inflate expectations of how quickly the Hiding child will or can absorb our responses. It is critical that we do not rush the Hiding child and spend sufficient time reinforcing these interventions—even though, at times, progress may seem excruciatingly slow. We want to remind you that progress is not necessarily defined by discernible movement, that just being exposed to your responses can create change in these children.

Metaphorically speaking, we first "find" the Hiding child and then we "stay" with them, just like the popular variant on the child's game of hide and seek, called "Sardines." In this game, everyone searches for the hidden child and then hides with them, keeping them company—just like the cans of those little fish. While we do not suggest that we take on the Hiding child's presentation, we believe that honoring it by accepting it offers the most efficient way of leading Hiding children out from behind their boundaries. This demonstrates the concept of *attunement*, which is defined as two people occupying the same emotional space. This is an example of enhanced empathy. Attunement is a powerful tool in reaching Hiding children because it comforts these children and provides them with the experience that they are not alone.

We want to close this chapter by reminding teachers that it is very probable that Hiding children will ultimately need outside resources to fully engage with their environment. This is a part of the process when you indicate to parents that their child may need an evaluation for additional services. The augmented care for the child is then shepherded (or unfortunately sometimes avoided) by the parents. Whether it be with para-professionals, occupational therapists, speech therapists, physical therapists, psychotherapists, or psychiatrists, each Hiding child will eventually require outside assessment and/or participation to structure the most beneficial configuration of support. That said, our support as described above, while limited, is not contingent on this involvement. Any little bit is useful, and our empathic engagement can be an essential component of the Hiding child's overall growth, maturation, learning, and enjoyment.

PART THREE

Pulling Back the Curtain on Specific Communicative Behaviors

Chapter 8

A Week-by-Week Guide for Behavior Assessment, Prioritization, and Planning

The goal of this book is to provide a path for teachers to find a sense of unity with the classroom. This path is centered on an increase in awareness of, the teachers themselves, initially and then their students. It is a path that is really no different from how all caregivers move their charges forward—figure out what a person needs and then provide it.

We have included a great deal of theory in this book. That said, we know that theory is only as good as the structure through which it flows. If we cannot use a theory in the classroom, if it is not practical or operational, then it just adds to our work, or may even detract from it. With this in mind, we think it is important that first stepping-stones of the path are set in place. We cannot know exactly where the path will lead each of us. How far we go with each individual child is a mystery that has yet to unfold, but we can know how to begin. And it starts on Day 1:

Week 1

The first step is to take the temperature of your classroom. This is a step of engaging your awareness of the environment around you. It is a process that takes time and focus. It cannot be done instantly or with urgency (even if the problems seem pressing). Understanding how you feel about a child or a dynamic is an internal process and needs to be considered and re-considered before you can be clear on the feeling. Also be open to the idea that it may evolve. Here are some ideas to get you started:

- Take time to get a sense of your class. You may have heard about children that are entering your class from other teachers, but make sure you take your own read. Try to tune out those preconceived notions.
- Let the feelings wash over you, trying to get a sense of the children that seem, on the one hand, to draw your attention, or, on the other, to slip completely under your radar (almost avoiding notice).
- Make a list of these children and do not be cautious. You can always add or subtract.
- Questions you can ask yourself:

Chapter 8. Behavior Assessment, Prioritization, and Planning 123

◊ What children do I have strong feelings about?
◊ What are my feelings about these children?
◊ Am I worried about him/her?
◊ Do I feel confused by his/her behavior?
◊ Does he/she make me feel uncomfortable?
◊ Do I like him/her?
◊ Do I dislike him/her?
◊ Am I drawn to him/her in a way that I am not usually affected?
◊ Do I want nothing to do with him/her?
◊ Do I find myself not thinking about him/her at all during the day?
◊ Do I think about him/her when I leave the school?

Week 2

The next step is to create a working document that will enable you to track your evolving thoughts about the children in your class that are presenting curious, complex, or challenging behaviors/communications (see Chart 8.1.). This chart will have four sections:

- Child's Name
- Manifest Communications/Behavior
- Your Personal Feelings
- Your best guess as to when the child is Loud or Quiet
- Your best guess as to when the child is Over Reactive or Under Reactive
- Child's Persona

Table 8.1:
Child Persona Tracker

Child Name	*Manifest Communication/ Behavior*	*My Personal Feelings*	*Possible Persona(s)*
Ellie R.	She is always on her own, does not talk to other children, seems sad	I am concerned about her	Worrying Child
Nat O.	He won't leave me alone, asks too many questions	I am irritated by him	Testing Child
Olive R.	Wanders off, daydreams, have to call her name multiple times	I am frustrated because I don't have time to devote to her, freaking out that she is going to disappear off the playground	Hiding Child

Child Name	Manifest Communication/ Behavior	My Personal Feelings	Possible Persona(s)
Ben L.	Throws tantrums and cries everyday	I am annoyed with him, sometimes I am not sure his crying is real	Testing Child
Freya J.	Very disruptive, gets up all the time, pushes other children, spits on floor	I would like her out of my classroom	Troubling Child
Tess E.	Has these very quirky behaviors that are kind of sweet, squeezes her eyes shut and squishes her face when she gets nervous	I am fascinated by her, kind of want to take her home	Hiding Child or Worrying Child
Noa C.	Seems younger than she is, needs to be told what to do, not a self-starter	I feel a combination of concern and worry that she is not able to do more on her own	Testing Child or Worrying Child

Weiner, Gallo-Silver, & Lucas, 2020

Week 3

At this point, we want to introduce a term typically used in the medical profession—triage. For our purposes, we are going to use the non-medical form of this word. According to Merriam-Webster, triage is "the assignment of priority to projects on the basis of where … resources can best be used, are most needed, or are most likely to achieve success is when you focus on the person with the most acute needs first" (Merriam-Webster, 2020). Prioritization is the work of the next step. There is not one way to do this; no right or wrong order. We must acknowledge that teachers will prioritize their students differently due to their own specific sensitivities, background, training, experiences, and classroom structures.

In the medical profession, triage is a systematic dispassionate process of prioritizing patients' level of need. The higher the level of need, the more imperative a quick response is required. If there is more than one patient seeking attention, the one with the highest level of need is treated before others. The levels are:

- Immediate
- Urgent
- Pressing
- Standard

Triage is driven by a set of yes/no questions that are asked of medical staff. For example, a child is brought to an emergency room that is filled with other patients already waiting to be seen. The parents tell the triage nurse that the child is lethargic and feels

Chapter 8. Behavior Assessment, Prioritization, and Planning

warm. The nurse checks the child's temperature and blood pressure and how responsive the child is and finds that he can answer as follows:

- Is child's temperature over 103.5? Yes
- Is child's blood pressure above 120 systolic and 80 diastolic? Yes
- Is the child responsive to external stimuli? No

With these responses, the nurse performs triage with the patients under his care and decides that this child is to be give a priority level of "immediate" and is moved ahead of all the patients in the waiting room.

Using this metaphor, our students who have been identified as having specific Personas that require your attention need to be triaged by us. It would be overwhelming to try to simultaneously address all the problematic behaviors we see. We cannot re-work the connections with all of them at once and need to create an order that is based on the level of disruption. If we return to the examples in Chart 8.1, one teacher might want to focus on Freya because of the negative feelings she provokes, while another teacher might want to focus on Tess because of the protective feelings she provokes. That said, we think that this process can be standardized using the following questions.

1. If left unaddressed for the moment, will this child's behavior lead to emotional danger (being isolated or experiencing fear) to this child or other children?
2. If left unaddressed for the moment, will this child's behavior lead to physical danger to this child or other children?
3. If left unaddressed for the moment, will this child's behavior alter the overall functioning of my class (by requiring more of my attention or the attention of other children in the class)?
4. If left unaddressed for the moment, will this child's behavior get worse?
5. Does this child create a feeling of anger or elevated frustration in me (remember, we need to be honest with ourselves)?
6. Does this child create a feeling of fear or elevated anxiety/worry in me (remember, we need to be honest with ourselves)?

With "yes" or "no" answers to these, we run through the follow triage decision-making progression:

- If we can answer yes to 5 or 6 of these questions, then we must set our "triage priority" to **immediate** meaning we set AURA in motion
- If we can answer yes to 3 or 4 of these questions, then we must set our "triage priority" to **urgent** meaning we set AURA in motion, unless there are two or more children with **immediate** designations in our class
- If we can answer yes to 1 or 2 of these questions, then we must set our "triage priority" to **pressing**, meaning we set AURA in motion, unless there are two or more children with **immediate** or **urgent** designations in our class
- If we can answer yes to none of these questions, then we must set our "triage priority" to standard, meaning we set AURA in motion, unless there are two or more children with **immediate** or **urgent** or **pressing** designations in our class

Table 8.2:
Triage Rating System

Child Name	Question 1	Question 2	Question 3	Question 4	Question 5	Question 6	Total	Priority Level
Ellie R.	Y	N	N	N	N	Y	2	Pressing
Nat O.	N	N	Y	N	Y	N	2	Pressing
Olive R.	Y	Y	Y	N	Y	Y	5	Immediate
Ben L.	Y	N	Y	Y	Y	N	4	Urgent
Freya J.	Y	Y	Y	Y	Y	Y	6	Immediate
Tess E.	N	N	N	N	N	N	0	Standard
Noa C.	N	N	Y	Y	N	Y	3	Urgent

Weiner, Gallo-Silver, & Lucas, 2020

Remember this is not a static list or priority order. It is a snapshot in time. With new information and/or new behaviors, we may decide to move someone up or down in terms of priority level. For example, if Ellie R produces artwork that is disturbing to us, this would require us to go through our triage progression again, possibly altering our answers to questions 2 (about physical danger) and question 3 (about our increased attention) to Yes's. This would increase her priority level from Pressing to Urgent.

Reworking our Child Persona Tracker, we get the following plan of action:

Table 8.3:
Triaged Child Persona Tracker

Child Name	Manifest Communication/ Behavior	My Personal Feelings	Possible Persona(s)	Triage Priority
Ellie R.	She is always on her own, does not talk to other children, seems sad	I am concerned about her	Worrying Child	Pressing
Nat O.	He won't leave me alone, asks too many questions	I am irritated by him	Testing Child	Pressing
Olive R.	Wanders off, daydreams, have to call her name multiple times	I am frustrated because I don't have time to devote to her, freaking out that she is going to disappear off the playground	Hiding Child	Immediate

Chapter 8. Behavior Assessment, Prioritization, and Planning

Child Name	Manifest Communication/ Behavior	My Personal Feelings	Possible Persona(s)	Triage Priority
Ben L.	Throws tantrums and cries everyday	I am annoyed with him; sometimes I am not sure his crying is real	Testing Child	*Urgent*
Freya J.	Very disruptive, gets up all the time, pushes other children, spits on floor	I would like her out of my classroom	Troubling Child	*Immediate*
Tess E.	Has these very quirky behaviors that are kind of sweet, squeezes her eyes shut and squishes her face when she gets nervous	I am fascinated by her, kind of want to take her home	Hiding Child or Worrying Child	*Standard*
Noa C.	Seems younger than she is, needs to be told what to do, not a self-starter	I feel a combination of concern and worry that she is not able to do more on her own	Testing Child or Worrying Child	*Urgent*

Weiner, Gallo-Silver, & Lucas, 2020

The plan to address this group of children will begin with creating responses for the children with behaviors rated as needing Immediate focus: Olive R. and Freya J. Next, Ben L. and Noa C. are triaged as Urgent. They are followed by Ellie R. and Nat O. as Pressing. Tess E., while on the list, is categorized as Standard and can wait for our direct intervention until we feel more in control of the rest of these children. The exact Priority List is as follows:

1. Freya J
2. Olive R
3. Ben L
4. Noa C
5. Ellie R
6. Nat O
7. Tess E

Week 4

By the fourth week, with our plan in place, we can begin to apply AURA with our students that address their specific behaviors and the needs of their particular Personas. The graphic below is a tool to remind you that each child Persona needs something different from you as a teacher. We recommend using it as a way of recalling and organizing your responses and the goals and themes of each (see Figure 8.1). It is divided into quadrants, highlighting the goals (to contain, to notice, to support, and to validate) and themes (boundaries, self-care, self-awareness, and connection) required for empathically addressing the latent communications of each child Persona. There is a symmetry between the goals of your responses and the themes conveyed within these responses. Each goal corresponds with a theme:

- For "Loud" communications, the goal of being "contained" is responded to with statements that include a theme of "boundaries"
- For "Quiet" communications, the goal of being "noticed" is responded to with statements that include a theme of "connection"
- For "Over Reactive" communications, the goal of being "supported" is responded to with statements that include a theme of "self-care"
- The "Under Reactive" communications, the goal of being "validated" is responded to with statements that include a theme of "self-awareness"

In this way, your responses deeply join the child as they recognize that you have received their message and attuned your stance. For example, Troubling children ask for their "loud" behavior to be **contained** (goal). The corresponding latent communication from this Persona can be addressed by a reply that speaks to setting up **boundaries** (theme) for that child. Similarly, their "Over Reactive" behavior is addressed when the Troubling child feels **supported** (goal). This latent communication is responded to through **self-care** (theme) statements. Together, the overarching message that Troubling children receive from us is thoughtful and secure containment:

Remember this is not an easy or quick fix, but a gradual process. As always, children need a great deal of repetition to help them integrate new ideas.

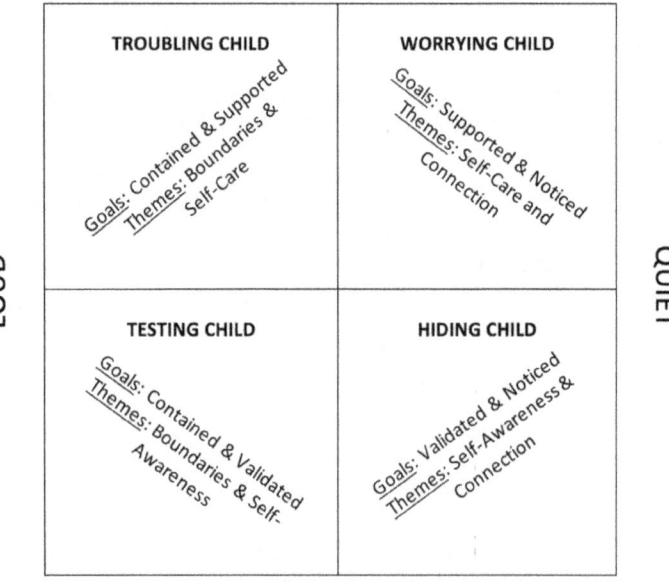

Figure 8.1: Response Matrix

Chapter 9

Distractibility, Daydreaming, and Attention-Related Issues

"What other people see as your distraction can simply be your need to occupy multiple channels at the same time."
—Lara Honos-Webb, Ph.D.

How to Use This Chapter

1. As you prepare to read this chapter, choose one child from your class on whom you wish to focus. Selecting one child at a time allows for a more concentrated exploration of the material and how it relates to each child uniquely. **As a guide, we will use "Melody," a second grader who asks seemingly random questions.**

2. Read the paragraphs from the following headings to begin the process: *Format and Theme* and *Common Forms of the Behavior*.

3. Choose one behavior that the selected child is exhibiting. Selecting one behavior at a time allows for a more concentrated exploration of the material centering on how the child communicates using this specific behavior. **Melody's behavior of asking random questions at odd moments.**

4. Read the paragraphs from the following headings to learn more about the general category that this behavior falls within from a more holistic perspective: *Manifest Communication* and *Latent Communication*.

5. Read the paragraphs from the heading *Responses and Affirmations* as background to how we structured the proposed responses and the expectation that you will ultimately personalize the responses provided in this chapter.

6. Turn to the page that contains the behavior in question. There you will find the number of the behavior and its name. **We select Behavior (1) Asking questions that are not on topic.**

7. On that page, below the number and name, you will find all the possible latent communication prompts for that behavior, ranging from (1) to (4). From these prompts, choose the prompt that most closely reminds you of how this child exhibits this behavior. Your choice may not fit one prompt exactly. If your sense

is that multiple prompts could fit, choose the closest one to begin the process. You can return to the other prompts later. You will notice that each prompt corresponds with a child communication Persona (i.e., Troubling, Testing, Worrying, Hiding). **For Melody, we choose "disconnected from material; possibly odd and/or confusing to follow (see Hiding Child)."**

8. After choosing a latent communication prompt, use the child communication Persona and read the corresponding Core Feelings, Core Wish, Core Question. This information describes the underlying meaning of the behavior and creates an empathic guide for you to keep in mind when responding to the child's behavior.

9. On the following page(s), you will find responses and affirmations for the number and name of the behavior in question. **We select Responses for:** *Behavior (1) Asking question that is not on topic* section **The Hiding Child**. Find and read the responses and affirmations for the behavior in question that corresponds with the child communication Persona.

10. **Try the responses and affirmations with Melody and determine how they feel to you.**

Format and Theme

All of the behavior chapters in this section of the book track the following format.

- Common Forms of This Behavior (list of variations on the theme)
- Manifest Communication (narrative description of the behavior)
- Latent Communication (underlying meanings of what we are observing)
- Table of Behavior Frequency based on Persona (which type of child exhibits these behaviors)
- Responses and Affirmations (for each form of these behaviors)

Each section of the chapter should be considered with the concept of theme in mind. In this chapter, we focus on **distractibility and attention-related issues**. These are behaviors/communications that we try to understand holistically in order to create more effective interventions and responses. That said, the behaviors in the title of this chapter are umbrella descriptors, and are just several examples that comprise a larger theme or group of communications. We note these manifest communications as thematic, as there are many permutations and nuanced differences within a category of behavior.

Common Forms of This Behavior

- Asking questions that are not on topic
- Not staying on tasks
- Not starting tasks

- Not following directions
- Staring off into space, "daydreaming"
- Wandering around the classroom or on field trips

Manifest Communication

The definition of distracted is "having one's thoughts or attention drawn away" (Merriam-Webster Dictionary, 2020). We like this definition because of its dynamic take on distractibility. The behavior inherently involves movement and is therefore fluid. It can move in either direction: from less attention, less concentration, and less focus to more attention, more concentration, and more focus.

To operationalize these abstract ideas, we think it is important to begin the response discussion by getting on the same page. In this chapter, the language we will use to describe the elements of this manifest communication are:

- Attention—The act or state of applying the mind to something. This is a more global response to applying one's mind.
- Concentration—The direction of attention to a single object. This solidifies the direction in which your mind's application is attending to.
- Focus—The pinpointed thought, feeling or action the mind is concentrating on.

For example, if one pays *attention* to the United States, one might *concentrate* on the State of Texas and then *focus* in on the City of Houston. The mind's application to a thought, feeling, or action is ultimately telescoped down into the specific details of that thought, feeling, or action (see Figure 9.1).

From an outside observer, a child's distractibility may appear as a general disconnect or a refusal to attend. A refusal, though, is a conscious act of behavior, and we believe that distractibility is an automatic response to stimuli—albeit with a variety of possible latent meanings. There is no thought *not* to attend or concentrate or

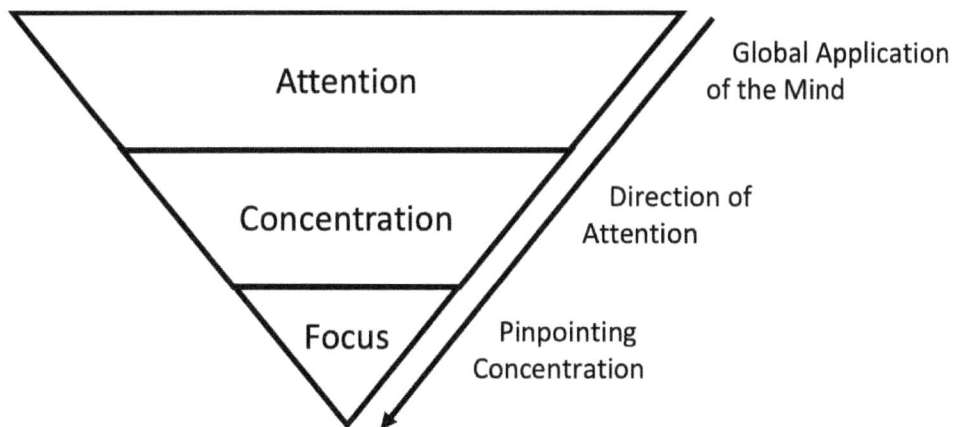

Figure 9.1: The Connection Between Attention, Concentration, and Focus

focus. While we may feel otherwise, these are not "head-strong" or stubborn children but rather children reacting to the stimulation of the classroom in a detached manner. They stand out from the rest of your student body and require more connection, direction, and reminding than their peers.

There is a range to the behaviors associated with distractibility from what seems like daydreaming to general preoccupation and all the way to sleepiness. The terms *daydreaming*—when a child's eyes are distant and calmly oblivious to the surrounding environment—and *sleepiness*—when a child is yawning with eyes that are bleary, heavy and fluttering shut—are readily understood. Preoccupation requires some clarification. It differs from daydreaming in its subtle lack of calm. We can observe preoccupation when a child appears strained and inattentive simultaneously. As we will discuss later in this chapter, disturbing or worrisome thoughts or feelings typically push this form of distractibility.

In the frenetic times of a typical school day, we can have a tendency to group all these types of distractibility together. This approach is understandable due to the fact that there are many similarities between these attention-related issues. As we explore distractibility more deeply, we believe that identifying and understanding the nuances may be very helpful in determining useful responses.

Using the child Personas of the Troubling child, the Testing child, the Worrying child, and the Hiding child, we will explore specific teacher responses for each type of communication pattern (see Table 9.1). We understand that in cases of distractibility, we may or may not be the ones who intervene. Our focus for this chapter centers on what we can do within the classroom setting to diminish the frequency and/or intensity of these related behaviors. For more detailed information about the most productive teacher response configurations for each Persona, please refer back to their respective chapters.

Table 9.1: Behavior Frequency by Persona

Behavior	*Persona*			
	Troubling Child Loud & Over Reactive	Testing Child Loud & Under Reactive	Worrying Child Quiet & Over Reactive	Hiding Child Quiet & Under Reactive
Asking questions that are not on topic	X	X	X	X
Not staying on task	X	X	X	X
Not starting tasks	X	X	X	X
Not following directions	X	X	X	X
Staring off into space, "daydreaming"	X		X	X

Chapter 9. Distractibility, Daydreaming, and Attention-Related Issues

	Persona			
Behavior	Troubling Child Loud & Over Reactive	Testing Child Loud & Under Reactive	Worrying Child Quiet & Over Reactive	Hiding Child Quiet & Under Reactive
Wandering around the classroom or on field trips	X	X	X	X

The absence of an "X" indicates that this Persona does not typically engage in this type of behavior/communication.

Latent Communication

This process is not an exact science and should be conducted more as trial and error. We would like you to take your best professional guess as to your answers to the following inquiries and evaluations. If you find that after working through the latent communication material and identifying a set of responses, they do not work as you hoped, you can always revise and try again. Just remember, children integrate learning following repetition, so do not give up too soon.

Responses and Affirmations

Children do not learn the first time we teach them a new concept or a task. We say this in order to manage our expectations about how quickly or completely these new interventions will change or extinguish any given behavior.

Let's keep in mind the following factors. First, the development of these behaviors has typically occurred over an extended period of time. Based on the ages of the children we address in this book, any behavior grew over at least two years and up to eight. As much as we would wish it, a behavior that has been developing over a lengthy period of time cannot change "overnight." Actually, rapid change is often poorly integrated by children and cannot be sustained. Second, children integrate responses at different rates based on a variety of factors, including temperament, environment, learning styles, family involvement/support, etc. We have addressed these earlier in the book. Last, we are constructing foundations from which to grow, one brick at a time, foundations that these children will be able to build on and rely on for years to come. To this end, we want you to know that each of your responses is remembered and cataloged by these children for future use—even if it does not outwardly appear to have been during your time with the child. This relates to the corrective emotional experience we wrote about earlier in this book. Your interactions become part of the child's long-term memory, exchanges that are saved for future use.

That said, we want us to have some benchmarks for our expectations. First, we believe that one month is a sufficient timeframe for some level of change in a behavior, given that a specific teacher response is maintained with consistency and repetition. Second, as we cannot factor in changes that are occurring in real time within these children and with their families, the one-month benchmark may need to be altered accordingly. Third, the one-month duration allows for these challenged children to test us. They will imagine that what we are doing cannot be sustained, that it is too good to last. Our consistency and repetition in responding to the underlying message ultimately quiet their negative thoughts. It is then when the child's expectations of the people around them begin to change to an inner message that is more hopeful and positive. This hopefulness alters their communications and behaviors and can become a more embedded part of their future interpersonal relationships.

Behavior (1)
Asking questions that are not on topic

If you find the child's disruptive question *seems* for the most part to be:

1. purposefully provocative; seemingly inflammatory and challenging (see Troubling Child)

2. purposefully silly; mildly pushing limits and redirecting attention (see Testing Child)

3. disconnected from material; possibly upsetting to you or others (see Worrying Child)

4. disconnected from material; possibly odd and/or confusing to follow (see Hiding Child)

- **The Troubling Child**

Core Feeling:	The more outrageous the child's question is, the greater the **sadness/anger** is being experienced by the child.
Core Wish:	Communicates unconscious wish to be **contained** and **supported** as a way of decreasing sense of **danger** and **rejection**.
Core Question:	Limit-testing question—I am being triggered by events because this discussion feels overwhelming; can you accept me and handle me?
Responses:	**Structural & Less Emotional** (see Responses section)

- **The Testing Child**

Core Feeling:	The more outrageous the child's question is, the greater the **sadness/anger** is being experienced by the child.

Core Wish:	Communicates unconscious wish to be **contained** and **validated** as a way of increasing sense of **security** and decreasing sense of **abandonment**.
Core Question:	Limit-testing question—I am feeling bad about myself and need to show this by creating a distraction; do you care about me enough to stop me?
Responses:	**Structural & More Emotional** (see Responses section)

- **The Worrying Child**

Core Feeling:	The more outrageous the child's question is, the greater the **fear/anger** is being experienced by the child.
Core Wish:	Communicates unconscious wish to be **noticed** and **supported** as a way of decreasing sense of **danger** and **abandonment**.
Core Question:	Limit-testing question—I am being triggered by events and this is an expression of how afraid I am; do you care enough to protect me?
Responses:	**Verbal & Less Emotional** (see Responses section)

- **The Hiding Child**

Core Feeling:	The more outrageous the child's question is, the greater the **fear/anger** is being experienced by the child.
Core Wish:	Communicates unconscious wish to be **noticed** and **validated** as a way of increasing sense of **security** and decreasing sense of **rejection**.
Core Question:	Limit-testing question—My question is a diversion from just how uncomfortable I feel right now; can you accept the way I am and contain me?
Responses:	**Verbal & More Emotional** (see Responses section)

Responses for: Behavior (1) Asking questions that are not on topic

The Troubling Child

- *Structural*:
    - ◊ Clear and calm voice (supportive).
    - ◊ Before class: Check in. Hold eye contact. "I'm with you. Let's keep working on this."
    - ◊ During class: Hand on shoulder; down on knee at eye level. Hold eye contact. Use the Less Emotional responses below.
    - ◊ After class: Check in. Hold eye contact. Reiterate response themes (boundaries, self-care). Track progress with chart.

- *Less Emotional*:
  - ◊ *Self-Care and Boundaries*: "I want you to try to stop and control your question. You are more in charge when you don't push me away with your question."
  - ◊ *Self-Care*: "Take a deep breath and let it out very slowly when you have a question."
  - ◊ *Boundaries*: "I want you to think to yourself, 'I can make a choice to let out my questions or not.'"
  - ◊ *Self-Care and Boundaries*: "Waiting to make a sound or say something that pops into your head is like saving a piece of candy for after dinner. It's difficult, but sometimes we just have to do it and then maybe we get to have more dessert later because we waited."
- *Affirmation*:
  - ◊ "You have such important and impressive ideas."
  - ◊ "Anyone can see what huge effort you made to hold onto your questions."

The Testing Child

- *Structural*:
  - ◊ Clear and crisp voice (supportive).
  - ◊ Before class: Check in. Hold eye contact. "I'm with you. Let's keep working on this."
  - ◊ During class: Hand on shoulder; down on knee at eye level. Hold eye contact. Use More Emotional responses below.
  - ◊ After class: Check in. Hold eye contact. Reiterate response theme (boundaries, self-awareness). Track progress with chart.
- *More Emotional*:
  - ◊ *Self-Awareness and Boundaries*: "It saddens me when you ask a silly question, because I feel like it pushes us apart."
  - ◊ *Self-Awareness*: "When you ask a silly question, I think you feel bad."
  - ◊ *Self-Awareness and Boundaries*: "Sometimes bad thoughts just feel like popping out of us. They are like balloons that blow up too big. We have to ask for help to let some air out before it pops because this can make us feel worse."
  - ◊ *Boundaries*: "Try to take a breath and say to yourself, 'I will be okay,' before you ask the question."
  - ◊ *Self-Awareness and Boundaries*: "Your questions are important. Try to raise your hand if you have one, and I will come over."
- *Affirmation*:
  - ◊ "I am proud of you for trying so hard to manage your questions."
  - ◊ "You took good care of yourself by holding your questions."

The Worrying Child

- *Verbal*:
  - ◊ Clear and calm voice (quiet).

Chapter 9. Distractibility, Daydreaming, and Attention-Related Issues 137

  - ◊ Before class: Check in and talk about previous day. Occasional eye contact. "I want to check in with you to see how our talk felt for you. We can do this each day."
  - ◊ During class: Occasional eye contact. Maintain distance (two feet at least). No physical contact. Use sound or words to get attention (Less Emotional responses below).
  - ◊ After class: Occasional eye contact. Reiterate response themes (connection, self-care).
- **Less Emotional**:
  - ◊ *Self-Care*: "Take a deep breath and let it out very slowly when you have a question. The question can wait a moment."
  - ◊ *Self-Care and Connection*: "It can help us feel safer if we try and slow down a little. By putting one finger in the air when you have a question, I can see it and will come over."
  - ◊ *Connection*: "Sometimes your questions help me understand what you are thinking."
  - ◊ *Connection*: "Your question makes me think that I would like to hear more about your thoughts."
- **Affirmation**:
  - ◊ "The questions you think of are so imaginative."
  - ◊ "You are brave to ask that question."

The Hiding Child

- **Verbal**:
  - ◊ Clear and calm voice (quiet).
  - ◊ Before class: Check in and talk about previous day. Occasional eye contact. "I want to check in with you to see if you remember our talk. We will do this each day."
  - ◊ During class: Occasional eye contact. Maintain distance (two feet at least). No physical contact. Use sound or words to get attention (More Emotional responses below).
  - ◊ After class: Occasional eye contact. Reiterate response themes (connection, self-awareness).
- **More Emotional**:
  - ◊ *Self-Awareness and Connection*: "That question is so important. I think you are excited, and I want you to try and raise your hand before you ask. I can help with that."
  - ◊ *Self-Awareness*: "It looks like you just can't wait to share what you are thinking. Waiting is a way to be strong."
  - ◊ *Connection*: "Look at my face. I am concerned that you are having difficulty waiting to ask your question."
  - ◊ *Self-Awareness*: "Try to think to yourself, 'I can control my questions,' like your question is water coming out of a faucet. Just try to turn it off for a moment."

- *Affirmation:*
    - ◊ "The questions you think of are so creative."
    - ◊ "Impressive how you came up with such a thoughtful question."

Behavior (2)
Not staying on task

If you find the child's inability to stay on task *seems* for the most part:

1. willfully escaping; rebuffing of attempts at redirection (see Troubling Child)
2. actively shirking; mildly, but constantly, pushing boundaries/limits (see Testing Child)
3. disconnected from events, daydreamy, like being "lost in the sauce" (see Worrying Child)
4. disconnected from events; confusing and/or odd by observation (see Hiding Child)

- **The Troubling Child**

    Core Feeling: The more frequently or intensely disorganized the child is, the greater the **sadness/anger** is being experienced by the child.

    Core Wish: Communicates unconscious wish to be **contained** and **supported** as a way of decreasing sense of **danger** and **rejection**.

    Core Question: Limit-testing question—I am being triggered by events and am so upset that I feel all over the place; can you accept me and handle me?

    Responses: **Structural & Less Emotional** (see Responses section)

- **The Testing Child**

    Core Feeling: The more frequently or intensely disorganized the child is, the greater the **sadness/anger** is being experienced by the child.

    Core Wish: Communicates unconscious wish to be **contained** and **validated** as a way of increasing sense of **security** and decreasing sense of **abandonment**.

    Core Question: Limit-testing question—I feel bad about myself and have the need to show this by creating a distraction; do you care about me enough to redirect me?

    Responses: **Structural & More Emotional** (see Responses section)

Chapter 9. Distractibility, Daydreaming, and Attention-Related Issues

- **The Worrying Child**

    Core Feeling: The more frequently or intensely disorganized the child is, the greater the **fear/anger** is being experienced by the child.

    Core Wish: Communicates unconscious wish to be **noticed** and **supported** as a way of decreasing sense of **danger** and **abandonment**.

    Core Question: Limit-testing question—I am being triggered by events and am afraid to be too present; do you care enough to protect me?

    Responses: **Verbal & Less Emotional** (see Responses section)

- **The Hiding Child**

    Core Feeling: The more frequently or intensely disorganized the child is, the greater the **fear/anger** is being experienced by the child.

    Core Wish: Communicates unconscious wish to be **noticed** and **validated** as a way of increasing sense of **security** and decreasing sense of **rejection**.

    Core Question: Limit-testing question—I feel uncomfortable and strange and suddenly need to divert myself; can you accept and contain me?

    Responses: **Verbal & More Emotional** (see Responses section)

Responses for: Behavior (2) Not staying on task

The Troubling Child

- *Structural*:
    ◊ Clear and calm voice (supportive).
    ◊ Before class: Check in. Hold eye contact. "I'm with you. Let's keep working on this."
    ◊ During class: Hand on shoulder; down on knee at eye level. Hold eye contact. Use the Less Emotional responses below.
    ◊ After class: Check in. Hold eye contact. Reiterate response themes (boundaries, self-care). Track progress with chart.
- *Less Emotional*:
    ◊ *Self-Care and Boundaries*: "I want you to try to stay with me (us). You are more in charge when you don't push me (us) away."
    ◊ *Self-Care:* "When you start to leave the task, take a deep breath and let it out very slowly; and say, 'It's okay, I can stay.'"
    ◊ *Boundaries*: "I want you to think, 'I can stay with my teacher (my class).'"

- ◊ *Self-Care and Boundaries:* "I want you to think about a big tree, swaying in the wind. The wind wants to push it over, but you are strong, like the tree, and you can stay focused even when it's windy. It's difficult, sometimes the wind is strong."
- *Affirmation*:
  - ◊ "You have so many impressive ideas, sometimes they want to pull you away."
  - ◊ "Anyone can see what a huge effort you made to stay with the work."

The Testing Child

- *Structural*:
  - ◊ Clear and crisp voice (supportive).
  - ◊ Before class: Check in. Hold eye contact. "I'm with you. Let's keep working on this."
  - ◊ During class: Hand on shoulder; down on knee at eye level. Hold eye contact. Use More Emotional responses below.
  - ◊ After class: Check in. Hold eye contact. Reiterate response themes (boundaries, self-awareness). Track progress with chart.
- *More Emotional*:
  - ◊ *Self-Awareness and Boundaries*: "It makes me sad me when you leave the task, because I feel like it pushes us apart."
  - ◊ *Self-Awareness*: "When you leave the task, I think you are feeling bad."
  - ◊ *Self-Awareness and Boundaries*: "Sometimes bad thoughts are like little splinters in our hands that hurt. We have to ask someone to take out the splinter or the hurt will just get bigger."
  - ◊ *Boundaries*: "Try to take a breath and say to yourself, 'I will be okay if I stay on task.'"
  - ◊ *Self-Awareness and Boundaries*: "Your concentration is so important to me. When you notice yourself leaving the task, try to raise your hand and I will come over."
- *Affirmation*:
  - ◊ "I am proud of you for trying so hard to manage your concentration."
  - ◊ "You took good care of yourself by trying to stay on task."

The Worrying Child

- *Verbal*:
  - ◊ Clear and calm voice (quiet).
  - ◊ Before class: Check in and talk about previous day. Occasional eye contact. "I want to check in with you to see how our talk felt for you. We can do this each day."
  - ◊ During class: Occasional eye contact. Maintain distance (two feet at least). No physical contact. Use sound or words to get attention (Less Emotional responses below).

Chapter 9. Distractibility, Daydreaming, and Attention-Related Issues 141

- ◊ After class: Occasional eye contact. Reiterate response themes (connection, self-care).
- **Less Emotional**:
  - ◊ *Self-Care and Connection*: "If I notice you are losing concentration, I will come over and say your name and calmly remind you that you are safe and that you are able to continue the work."
  - ◊ *Self-Care and Connection*: "Attention is when we sit down to do something, concentration is when we really think about doing it. I think you sometimes lose concentration and I can help with that."
  - ◊ *Self-Care and Connection*: "Do you want to come up with a word that is just between you and me that means, 'I see you are losing concentration?' This is a way of us working as a team."
- **Affirmation**:
  - ◊ "It is impressive to see you trying to stay on task."
  - ◊ "It takes a lot of courage to stay on task."

The Hiding Child

- **Verbal**:
  - ◊ Clear and calm voice (quiet).
  - ◊ Before class: Check in and talk about previous day. Occasional eye contact. "I want to check in with you to see if you remember our talk. We will do this each day."
  - ◊ During class: Occasional eye contact. Maintain distance (two feet at least). No physical contact. Use sound or words to get attention (More Emotional responses below).
  - ◊ After class: Occasional eye contact. Reiterate response themes (connection, self-awareness).
- **More Emotional**:
  - ◊ *Self-Awareness*: "When you are having strong ideas that pop up, I think you get really excited. Try your best to hold them for later."
  - ◊ *Self-Awareness and Connection*: "Look at my face. I am concerned that if you don't think about our task, then you might get lost from the group."
  - ◊ *Self-Awareness and Connection*: "You can control you strong ideas. I want you to try and raise your hand and let me know that your ideas are distracting you. I can help with that."
- **Affirmation**:
  - ◊ "The ideas you think of are so creative."
  - ◊ "Impressive how you tried to keep working with you having your strong ideas."

Behavior (3)
Not starting tasks

If you find the child's inability to start a task *seems* for the most part:

1. willfully stonewalling; diminishing and deriding activity (see Troubling Child)
2. actively avoiding; finding many "practical" reasons to not begin (see Testing Child)
3. disconnected and inattentive; missing basic steps needed to begin (see Worrying Child)
4. disconnected and rigid; unwilling without satisfactory explanation (see Hiding Child)

- **The Troubling Child**

    Core Feeling: The more frequently or intensely disorganized the child is, the greater the **sadness/anger** is being experienced by the child.

    Core Wish: Communicates unconscious wish to be **contained** and **supported** as a way of decreasing sense of **danger** and **rejection**.

    Core Question: Limit-testing question—I am being triggered by events and feel confused and scattered; can you accept me and handle me?

    Responses: **Structural & Less Emotional** (see Responses section)

- **The Testing Child**

    Core Feeling: The more frequently or intensely disorganized the child is, the greater the **sadness/anger** is being experienced by the child.

    Core Wish: Communicates unconscious wish to be **contained** and **validated** as a way of increasing sense of **security** and decreasing sense of **abandonment**.

    Core Question: Limit-testing question—I feel bad about myself and have the need to show this by avoiding; do you care about me enough to redirect me?

    Responses: **Structural & More Emotional** (see Responses section)

- **The Worrying Child**

    Core Feeling: The more frequently or intensely disorganized the child is, the greater the **fear/anger** is being experienced by the child.

Chapter 9. Distractibility, Daydreaming, and Attention-Related Issues 143

Core Wish: Communicates unconscious wish to be **noticed** and **supported** as a way of decreasing sense of **danger** and **abandonment**.

Core Question: Limit-testing question—I am being triggered by events and am afraid to be too present; do you care enough to protect me?

Responses: **Verbal & Less Emotional** (see Responses section)

- **The Hiding Child**

Core Feeling: The more frequently or intensely disorganized the child is, the greater the **fear/anger** is being experienced by the child.

Core Wish: Communicates unconscious wish to be **noticed** and **validated** as a way of increasing sense of **security** and decreasing sense of **rejection**.

Core Question: Limit-testing question—I feel uncomfortable and overwhelmed suddenly and need to divert myself; can you accept the way I am and contain me?

Responses: **Verbal & More Emotional** (see Responses section)

Responses for: Behavior (3) Not starting tasks

The Troubling Child

- *Structural*:
    ◊ Clear and calm voice (supportive).
    ◊ Before class: Check in. Hold eye contact. "I'm with you. Let's keep working on this."
    ◊ During class: Hand on shoulder; down on knee at eye level. Hold eye contact. Use the Less Emotional responses below.
    ◊ After class: Check in. Hold eye contact. Reiterate response themes (boundaries, self-care). Track progress with chart.
- *Less Emotional*:
    ◊ *Self-Care and Boundaries*: "I want you to try to start when we start, even if it feels hard."
    ◊ *Self-Care*: "When you don't feel like starting your work, take a deep breath and let it out very slowly; and say to yourself, 'It's okay, I can start and do just a little at a time.'"
    ◊ *Boundaries*: "I want you to think, 'my teacher will help me start this project.'"
    ◊ *Self-Care*: "I want you to think about a big train engine. It takes a lot of energy to get that train moving, it's really heavy, but it can be done. It

just needs a great train conductor, like you, to be in charge and move it forward one bit at a time. All the projects are like this. One bit at a time."
- *Affirmation*:
    ◊ "When you push yourself to start you work, I can see how strong you are."
    ◊ "Anyone can see what big effort you made to start your work, one step at a time."

The Testing Child

- *Structural*:
    ◊ Clear and crisp voice (supportive).
    ◊ Before class: Check in. Hold eye contact. "I'm with you. Let's keep working on this."
    ◊ During class: Hand on shoulder; down on knee at eye level. Hold eye contact. Use More Emotional responses below.
    ◊ After class: Check in. Hold eye contact. Reiterate response themes (boundaries, self-awareness). Track progress with chart.
- *More Emotional*:
    ◊ *Self-Awareness and Boundaries*: "It makes me sad when you do not start a task, because I feel like it pushes us apart."
    ◊ *Self-Awareness*: "When you cannot start a task, I think you are feeling bad."
    ◊ *Self-Awareness and Boundaries*: "Sometimes bad thoughts are like very bright lights that shine in our eyes and make it hard to see. When we can't really see because of the bright bad thoughts, we need to ask someone to help us or we might not be able to figure out where to go."
    ◊ *Self-Awareness*: "Try to take a breath and say to yourself, 'I will be okay, I can start this work.'"
    ◊ *Self-Awareness and Boundaries*: "Your first steps are so important to me. When you are having trouble starting the task, try to raise your hand and I will come over."
- *Affirmation*:
    ◊ "I am proud of you for trying so hard to begin your work on time."
    ◊ "You took good care of yourself by trying start your work with everyone else."

The Worrying Child

- *Verbal*:
    ◊ Clear and calm voice (quiet).
    ◊ Before class: Check in and talk about previous day. Occasional eye contact. "I want to check in with you to see how our talk felt for you. We can do this each day."
    ◊ During class: Occasional eye contact. Maintain distance (two feet at

Chapter 9. Distractibility, Daydreaming, and Attention-Related Issues

  least). No physical contact. Use sound or words to get attention (Less Emotional responses below).
  ◊ After class: Occasional eye contact. Reiterate response themes (connection, self-care).
- **Less Emotional**:
  ◊ *Self-Care and Connection*: "Look around the class and see that everyone is working. They are safe and so are you."
  ◊ *Self-Care*: "When you don't feel like starting your work, take a deep breath and let it out very slowly; and 'It's okay, I am okay, I can begin and do just a little at a time until I'm more comfortable.'"
  ◊ *Self-Care and Connection*: "Try and think, 'my teacher is here, my classmates are here, I am here. Let's work.'"
  ◊ *Self-Care and Connection*: "Starting any task takes courage. Let's see if you can be courageous with my help."
- **Affirmation**:
  ◊ "Getting ready to begin your work takes planning and courage."
  ◊ "You are being brave each time you start your work."

The Hiding Child

- **Verbal**:
  ◊ Clear and calm voice (quiet).
  ◊ Before class: Check in and talk about previous day. Occasional eye contact. "I want to check in with you to see if you remember our talk. We will do this each day."
  ◊ During class: Occasional eye contact. Maintain distance (two feet at least). No physical contact. Use sound or words to get attention (More Emotional responses below).
  ◊ After class: Occasional eye contact. Reiterate response themes (connection, self-awareness).
- **More Emotional**:
  ◊ *Self-Awareness and Connection*: "Starting your work is sometimes difficult. I think that you get big feelings about beginning and I am worried. Just try to take a deep breath and let it out very slowly; and start with the first step."
  ◊ *Connection*: "Look at my face. I am concerned that if you do not begin your work that you will get lost from the group."
  ◊ *Self-Awareness and Connection*: "You can control your excitement long enough to start your work. You can raise your hand and let me know that your excitement is stopping you from starting. I can help you with that."
- **Affirmation**:
  ◊ "I can see how you are trying to use your powerful ability to focus."
  ◊ "Impressive how you are able to control yourself and begin your work."

Behavior (4)
Not following directions

If you find the child's difficulty following directions *seems* for the most part:

1. willfully insubordinate, rejecting attempts at redirection (see Troubling Child)
2. actively dodging, mildly, but constantly, pushing boundaries/limits (see Testing Child)
3. disconnected, seemingly forgetful, like getting confused and lost (see Worrying Child)
4. preoccupied, going off in confusing/odd directions (see Hiding Child)

- **The Troubling Child**

  Core Feeling: The more regularly or dramatically the child moves off course, the greater the **sadness/anger** is being experienced by the child.

  Core Wish: Communicates unconscious wish to be **contained** and **supported** as a way of decreasing sense of **danger** and **rejection**.

  Core Question: Limit-testing question—I am being triggered by events and am so upset that these rules feel confining; can you accept me and handle me?

  Responses: **Structural & Less Emotional** (see Responses section)

- **The Testing Child**

  Core Feeling: The more regularly or dramatically the child moves off course, the greater the **sadness/anger** is being experienced by the child.

  Core Wish: Communicates unconscious wish to be **contained** and **validated** as a way of increasing sense of **security** and decreasing sense of **abandonment**.

  Core Question: Limit-testing question—I feel bad about myself and have the need to show this by disregarding the rules; do you care about me enough to pull me back?

  Responses: **Structural & More Emotional** (see Responses section)

- **The Worrying Child**

  Core Feeling: The more regularly or dramatically the child moves off course, the greater the **fear/anger** is being experienced by the child.

Chapter 9. Distractibility, Daydreaming, and Attention-Related Issues   147

Core Wish:	Communicates unconscious wish to be **noticed** and **supported** as a way of decreasing sense of **danger** and **abandonment**.
Core Question:	Limit-testing question—I am being triggered by events and am afraid to be too present; do you care enough to protect me?
Responses:	**Verbal & Less Emotional** (see Responses section)

- **The Hiding Child**

Core Feeling:	The more regularly or dramatically the child moves off course, the greater the **fear/anger** is being experienced by the child.
Core Wish:	Communicates unconscious wish to be **noticed** and **validated** as a way of increasing sense of **security** and decreasing sense of **rejection**.
Core Question:	Limit-testing question—I feel uncomfortable and uneasy and suddenly need to go off on my own path; can you accept the way I am and contain me?
Responses:	**Verbal & More Emotional** (see Responses section)

Responses for: Behavior (4) Not following directions

The Troubling Child

- ***Structural***:
    - ◊ Clear and calm voice (supportive).
    - ◊ Before class: Check in. Hold eye contact. "I'm with you. Let's keep working on this."
    - ◊ During class: Hand on shoulder; down on knee at eye level. Hold eye contact. Use the Less Emotional responses below.
    - ◊ After class: Check in. Hold eye contact. Reiterate response themes (boundaries, self-care). Track progress with chart.
- ***Less Emotional***:
    - ◊ *Boundaries*: "I want you to try your best to follow my directions, even if you do not want to."
    - ◊ *Self-Care and Boundaries*: "When you start to want to go your own way, take a deep breath and let it out very slowly; and say to yourself, 'It's okay, I can follow the teacher this time.' I will remind you that you can do it."
    - ◊ *Self-Care and Boundaries*: "I want you to think about a fast-flowing river. Imagine you are trying to cross it, but the current is strong, and it is pulling on you. It's difficult, sometimes the current is super powerful. But you are more powerful than the river. You can make it across."

- *Affirmation*:
    - "You are powerful when you are in charge and sometimes that means you choosing to follow me."
    - "Anyone can see what big effort you made to follow my directions."

The Testing Child

- *Structural*:
    - Clear and crisp voice (supportive).
    - Before class: Check in. Hold eye contact. "I'm with you. Let's keep working on this."
    - During class: Hand on shoulder; down on knee at eye level. Hold eye contact. Use More Emotional responses below.
    - After class: Check in. Hold eye contact. Reiterate response themes (boundaries, self-awareness). Track progress with chart.
- *More Emotional*:
    - *Self-Awareness and Boundaries*: "It makes me sad when you don't follow directions, because I feel like it pushes us apart."
    - *Self-Awareness*: "When you don't follow directions, I think you feel bad."
    - *Self-Awareness and Boundaries*: "Sometimes bad thoughts are like a powerful wind that can push very hard. When it pushes in the wrong direction, we need someone to help pull us back and fight the wind's power. If not, we may be pushed in the wrong direction."
    - *Self-Awareness*: "Try to take a breath and say to yourself, 'I will be okay if I follow the directions.'"
    - *Self-Awareness and Boundaries*: "Following me and the class is so important. When you feel like not following directions, try to raise your hand and I will come over."
- *Affirmation*:
    - "I am proud of you for trying so hard to follow directions."
    - "You took good care of yourself by following directions and staying with the class."

The Worrying Child

- *Verbal*:
    - Clear and calm voice (quiet).
    - Before class: Check in and talk about previous day. Occasional eye contact. "I want to check in with you to see how our talk felt for you. We can do this each day."
    - During class: Occasional eye contact. Maintain distance (two feet at least). No physical contact. Use sound or words to get attention (Less Emotional responses below).

Chapter 9. Distractibility, Daydreaming, and Attention-Related Issues

  - ◊ After class: Occasional eye contact. Reiterate response themes (connection, self-care).
- **Less Emotional:**
  - ◊ *Self-Care and Connection*: "If I notice you are not following directions, I will come over and say your name and calmly remind you that you are safe and that I believe that you can follow my directions."
  - ◊ *Self-Care and Connection*: "Attention is when we sit down to do a task, focus is when we follow the steps to work through that task—I think you sometimes lose focus. I can help you with that."
  - ◊ *Self-Care and Connection*: "Do you want to come up with a word that is just between you and me that means, 'I see you are not following my directions?' This is a way of us working as a team."
- **Affirmation:**
  - ◊ "It is impressive to see you trying to follow directions."
  - ◊ "It takes a lot of courage to follow directions."

The Hiding Child

- **Verbal:**
  - ◊ Clear and calm voice (quiet).
  - ◊ Before class: Check in and talk about previous day. Occasional eye contact. "I want to check in with you to see if you remember our talk. We will do this each day."
  - ◊ During class: Occasional eye contact. Maintain distance (two feet at least). No physical contact. Use sound or words to get attention (More Emotional responses below).
  - ◊ After class: Occasional eye contact. Reiterate response themes (connection, self-awareness).
- **More Emotional:**
  - ◊ *Self-Awareness*: "Having difficulty following my directions makes me think you are having strong ideas of your own."
  - ◊ *Self-Awareness and Connection*: "Look at my face. I am concerned that you are going to get separated from the group when you don't choose to follow my directions."
  - ◊ *Self-Awareness and Connection*: "Try to think, 'I can control my choices and follow the teacher.' If you are having difficulty, I can help with that."
- **Affirmation:**
  - ◊ "I can see how hard you are trying to follow my directions."
  - ◊ "Impressive how you are able to make the difficult choice to follow directions."

Behavior (5)
Staring off into space, "daydreaming"

If you find the child's staring off or daydreaming *seems* for the most part:

1. disregarding, as if a wall is constructed and a "keep out" sign hung (see Troubling Child)

2. disconnected, seeming "out-of-it," absent or lost (see Worrying Child)

3. preoccupied, as if contemplating an alternative set of specific ideas (see Hiding Child)

- **The Troubling Child**

  Core Feeling: The more regularly the child disconnects, the greater the **sadness/anger** is being experienced by the child.

  Core Wish: Communicates unconscious wish to be **contained** and **supported** as a way of decreasing sense of **danger** and **rejection**.

  Core Question: Limit-testing question—I am being triggered by events and am so upset that my feelings are too intense for me to handle; can you accept me and handle me?

  Responses: **Structural & Less Emotional** (see Responses section)

- **The Worrying Child**

  Core Feeling: The more regularly the child disconnects, the greater the **fear/anger** is being experienced by the child.

  Core Wish: Communicates unconscious wish to be **noticed** and **supported** as a way of decreasing sense of **danger** and **abandonment**.

  Core Question: Limit-testing question—I am being triggered by events and am afraid to be too present; do you care enough to help me feel safe?

  Responses: **Verbal & Less Emotional** (see Responses section)

- **The Hiding Child**

  Core Feeling: The more regularly the child disconnects, the greater the **fear/anger** is being experienced by the child.

  Core Wish: Communicates unconscious wish to be **noticed** and **validated** as a way of increasing sense of **security** and decreasing sense of **rejection**.

Chapter 9. Distractibility, Daydreaming, and Attention-Related Issues   151

   Core Question: Limit-testing question—I feel overwhelmed and uneasy and need to "think about" things that I know and make be comfortable; can you accept me and stay connected to me?

   Responses: **Verbal & More Emotional** (see Responses section)

Responses for: Behavior (5) Staring off into space, "daydreaming"

The Troubling Child

- *Structural*:
    - ◊ Clear and calm voice (supportive).
    - ◊ Before class: Check in. Hold eye contact. "I'm with you. Let's keep working on this."
    - ◊ During class: Hand on shoulder; down on knee at eye level. Hold eye contact. Use the Less Emotional responses below.
    - ◊ After class: Check in. Hold eye contact. Reiterate response themes (boundaries, self-care). Track progress with chart.
- *Less Emotional*:
    - ◊ *Boundaries*: "I want you to try to pay attention to me."
    - ◊ *Self-Care and Boundaries*: "When you don't want to hear me, take a deep breath and let it out very slowly; and say, 'It's okay, I can try to hear this time.' I will remind you that you can do it."
    - ◊ *Self-Care and Boundaries*: "Hearing me does not mean you have to agree me."
    - ◊ *Self-Care*: "I want you to think about a person running a marathon. It is long, but the person wants to finish. Slowing down helps them finish. Stopping does not. When you don't hear me, you are stopping. I want you to finish the race."
- *Affirmation*:
    - ◊ "You work so hard, when you are trying to pay attention."
    - ◊ "Anyone can see the effort you make to hear me."

The Worrying Child

- *Verbal*:
    - ◊ Clear and calm voice (quiet).
    - ◊ Before class: Check in and talk about previous day. Occasional eye contact. "I want to check in with you to see how our talk felt for you. We can do this each day."
    - ◊ During class: Occasional eye contact. Maintain distance (two feet at least). No physical contact. Use sound or words to get attention (Less Emotional responses below).
    - ◊ After class: Occasional eye contact. Reiterate response themes (connection, self-care).

- *Less Emotional*:
    - *Self-Care*: "Daydreaming is a way of losing attention that we don't realize is happening."
    - *Self-Care and Connection*: "If I notice you are losing attention, I will come over and say your name and calmly remind you of where you are and that you are safe."
    - *Self-Care and Connection*: "Do you want to come up with a code word that is just between you and me that means, 'I see you are daydreaming?' This is a way of us working as a team."
- *Affirmation*:
    - "It takes a powerful imagination to daydream."
    - "Your daydreaming is an important talent."

The Hiding Child

- *Verbal*:
    - Clear and calm voice (quiet).
    - Before class: Check in and talk about previous day. Occasional eye contact. "I want to check in with you to see if you remember our talk. We will do this each day."
    - During class: Occasional eye contact. Maintain distance (two feet at least). No physical contact. Use sound or words to get attention (More Emotional responses below).
    - After class: Occasional eye contact. Reiterate response themes (connection, self-awareness).
- *More Emotional*:
    - *Self-Awareness*: "Thinking about other thoughts is a way of losing attention that we don't realize is happening."
    - *Self-Awareness and Connection*: "When you have strong ideas pop into your head, sometimes they are so interesting that grab your attention away from the class."
    - *Self-Awareness and Connection*: "Look at my face. I am concerned that you are paying attention to your own thoughts and might get lost from the class."
    - *Self-Awareness and Connection*: "You can control the other thoughts that you are having that grab your attention from me. I can help you with that."
- *Affirmation*:
    - "It takes a creative mind to have interesting thoughts."
    - "I am impressed how you are trying to control your other thoughts."

Chapter 9. Distractibility, Daydreaming, and Attention-Related Issues 153

Behavior (6)
Wandering around the classroom or on field trips

If you find the child's wanderings *seem* for the most part:

1. insubordinate, rejecting attempts at redirection (see Troubling Child)
2. actively dodging, mildly, but constantly, pushing boundaries/limits (see Testing Child)
3. disconnected, seeming forgetful, aimless and lost (see Worrying Child)
4. preoccupied, seeming derailed, going off in confusing/odd directions (see Hiding Child)

- **The Troubling Child**

    Core Feeling: The more regularly or noticeably the child wanders around, the greater the **sadness/anger** is being experienced by the child.

    Core Wish: Communicates unconscious wish to be **contained** and **supported** as a way of decreasing sense of **danger** and **rejection**.

    Core Question: Limit-testing question—I am being triggered by events and I am upset that the rules feel too confining; can you accept me and handle me?

    Responses: **Structural & Less Emotional** (see Responses section)

- **The Testing Child**

    Core Feeling: The more regularly or noticeably the child wanders around, the greater the **sadness/anger** is being experienced by the child.

    Core Wish: Communicates unconscious wish to be **contained** and **validated** as a way of increasing sense of **security** and decreasing sense of **abandonment**.

    Core Question: Limit-testing question—I feel bad about myself and have the need to show this by moving around; do you care about me enough to redirect me?

    Responses: **Structural & More Emotional** (see Responses section)

- **The Worrying Child**

    Core Feeling: The more regularly or noticeably the child wanders around, the greater the **fear/anger** is being experienced by the child.

Core Wish:	Communicates unconscious wish to be **noticed** and **supported** as a way of decreasing sense of **danger** and **abandonment**.
Core Question:	Limit-testing question—I am being triggered by events and am afraid to be too still; do you care enough to help me feel safe and protect me?
Responses:	**Verbal & Less Emotional** (see Responses section)

- **The Hiding Child**

Core Feeling:	The more regularly or noticeably the child wanders around, the greater the **fear/anger** is being experienced by the child.
Core Wish:	Communicates unconscious wish to be **noticed** and **validated** as a way of increasing sense of **security** and decreasing sense of **rejection**.
Core Question:	Limit-testing question—I feel uncomfortable and uneasy and suddenly need to move around and go my own path; can you accept me and contain me?
Responses:	**Verbal & More Emotional** (see Responses section)

Responses for: Behavior (6) Wandering around the classroom or on field trips

The Troubling Child

- *Structural*:
    - ◊ Clear and calm voice (supportive).
    - ◊ Before class: Check in. Hold eye contact. "I'm with you. Let's keep working on this."
    - ◊ During class: Hand on shoulder; down on knee at eye level. Hold eye contact. Use the Less Emotional responses below.
    - ◊ After class: Check in. Hold eye contact. Reiterate response themes (boundaries, self-care). Track progress with chart.
- *Less Emotional*:
    - ◊ *Boundaries*: "I want you to try your best to stay where you are supposed to be, even though sometimes it seems really difficult for you do to."
    - ◊ *Self-Care and Boundaries*: "When you start to want to go your own way, take a deep breath and let it out very slowly; and think, 'I'm okay, I can follow the teacher's rules and stay put.' I will remind you that you can do it."
    - ◊ *Self-Care and Boundaries*: "I want you to think about crossing a street. A person has to make good choices when deciding to cross in order to make it safely. The person has to slow down and think, 'should I go move

Chapter 9. Distractibility, Daydreaming, and Attention-Related Issues 155

now or stop and wait?' For you, I want you to think about when you move and when you stay."
- *Affirmation*:
    - ◊ "Choosing to follow the rules and stay where you are supposed to be is a powerful way for you to be in charge."
    - ◊ "Anyone can see what big effort you made to follow the class rules."

The Testing Child

- *Structural*:
    - ◊ Clear and crisp voice (supportive).
    - ◊ Before class: Check in. Hold eye contact. "I'm with you. Let's keep working on this."
    - ◊ During class: Hand on shoulder; down on knee at eye level. Hold eye contact. Use More Emotional responses below.
    - ◊ After class: Check in. Hold eye contact. Reiterate response themes (boundaries, self-awareness). Track progress with chart.
- *More Emotional*:
    - ◊ *Self-Awareness and Boundaries*: "It makes me sad when you keep moving around, because I feel it pushes us apart."
    - ◊ *Self-Awareness*: "When you don't stay where you are supposed to be, I think you feel bad."
    - ◊ *Self-Awareness*: "Try to take a breath and say to yourself, 'I will be okay if I follow the directions.'"
    - ◊ *Self-Awareness and Boundaries*: "Staying where you are supposed to be is important. When you feel like moving, try to raise your hand and I will come over and be with you."
- *Affirmation*:
    - ◊ "I am proud of you for trying so hard to stay where you are supposed to be."
    - ◊ "You took good care of yourself by following directions and staying put."

The Worrying Child

- *Verbal*:
    - ◊ Clear and calm voice (quiet).
    - ◊ Before class: Check in and talk about previous day. Occasional eye contact. "I want to check in with you to see how our talk felt for you. We can do this each day."
    - ◊ During class: Occasional eye contact. Maintain distance (two feet at least). No physical contact. Use sound or words to get attention (Less Emotional responses below).
    - ◊ After class: Occasional eye contact. Reiterate response themes (connection, self-care).
- *Less Emotional*:

- ◊ *Self-Care and Connection*: "If I notice you are not staying where you are supposed to be, I will come over and say your name and calmly remind you that it is important to be safe."
- ◊ *Self-Care and Connection*: "Staying with the group can sometimes feel uncomfortable. When we are uncomfortable, we sometimes need to move around. I think that is what you are doing, and I can help with that."
- ◊ *Self-Care and Connection*: "Do you want to come up with a code word that is just between you and me that means, 'I see you are moving around a lot; do you need my help?' This is a way for us to work as a team."
- *Affirmation*:
  - ◊ "It is impressive to see you being courageous by controlling your movement."
  - ◊ "It takes hard work to follow this type of directions."

The Hiding Child

- *Verbal*:
  - ◊ Clear and calm voice (quiet).
  - ◊ Before class: Check in and talk about previous day. Occasional eye contact. "I want to check in with you to see if you remember our talk. We will do this each day."
  - ◊ During class: Occasional eye contact. Maintain distance (two feet at least). No physical contact. Use sound or words to get attention (More Emotional responses below).
  - ◊ After class: Occasional eye contact. Reiterate response themes (connection, self-awareness).
- *More Emotional*:
  - ◊ *Self-Awareness*: "Having difficulty staying with the group makes me think that you are having strong ideas or your own."
  - ◊ *Self-Awareness and Connection*: "Look at my face. I am concerned that you are going to get separated from the group when you choose to wander and not following my directions."
  - ◊ *Self-Awareness and Connection*: "You can control your movement. If you are having difficulty ignoring your strong ideas and staying with the group, I can help with that."
- *Affirmation*:
  - ◊ "I am proud of you for trying so hard to stay where you are supposed to be."
  - ◊ "You took good care of yourself by following directions and staying put."

Your Evolving Responses

As you have read, there are different motivations for your students' behaviors depending on their latent communication patterns. This demonstrates that your responses cannot be "one size fits all" in nature. While we have provided specific words for you to follow, we intend this chapter and the others like it to be a framework for your responses, not a script. You certainly can use our suggested language as you experiment with the interventions we have described. Overtime, it will be more helpful for you to find your own words to communicate with your students. As you continue to try these techniques, using your own communication style will make the responses to your students' behaviors feel authentic and sincere. This will happen naturally. The proposed interventions that we used in this chapter are a starting point and are meant to evolve and grow with your comfort level. This might take some practice, but it will be well worth it to expand your repertoire of potential responses to concerning or disruptive behaviors. You may find that your own words are more effective or more impactful than the words and phrases we have suggested in this book. The more you are a part of the interventions, the more meaningful they may be to your students. As we know, students need repetition, so please be patient as you try out new ways to respond to them.

Chapter 10

Elopement and "Moving Away"– Related Issues

"If you can't fly, then run."—Martin Luther King, Jr.

How to Use This Chapter

1. As you prepare to read this chapter, choose one child from your class on whom you wish to focus. Selecting one child at a time allows for a more concentrated exploration of the material and how it relates to each child uniquely. **As a guide, we will use "Melody," a second grader who runs out of the class when the teacher is giving a lesson.**

2. Read the paragraphs from the following headings to begin the process: *Format and Theme* and *Common Forms of the Behavior*.

3. Choose one behavior that the selected child is exhibiting. Selecting one behavior at a time allows for a more concentrated exploration of the material centering on how the child communicates using this specific behavior. **Melody's behavior of running out of the classroom room.**

4. Read the paragraphs from the following headings to learn more about the general category that this behavior falls within from a more holistic perspective: *Manifest Communication* and *Latent Communication*.

5. Read the paragraphs from the heading *Responses and Affirmations* as background to how we structured the proposed responses and the expectation that you will ultimately personalize the responses provided in this chapter.

6. Turn to the page that contains the behavior in question. There you will find the number of the behavior and its name. **We select Behavior 1) Running out of the classroom/school.**

7. On that page, below the number and name, you will find all the possible latent communication prompts for that behavior, ranging from 1) to 4). From these prompts, choose the prompt that most closely reminds you of how this child exhibits this behavior. Your choice may not fit one prompt exactly. If your sense is that multiple prompts could fit, choose the closest one to begin the process. You can return to the other prompts later. You will notice that each prompt

corresponds with a child communication Persona (i.e., Troubling, Testing, Worrying, Hiding). **For Melody, we choose "sudden and restless; possibly upsetting and tense for you (see Worrying Child)."**

8. After choosing a latent communication prompt, use the child communication Persona and read the corresponding Core Feelings, Core Wish, Core Question. This information describes the underlying meaning of the behavior and creates an empathic guide for you to keep in mind when responding to the child's behavior.

9. On the following page(s), you will find responses and affirmations for the number and name of the behavior in question. **We select Responses for:** *Behavior 1) Running out of the classroom/school* section **The Worrying Child**. Find and read the responses and affirmations for the behavior in question that corresponds with the child communication Persona.

10. **Try the responses and affirmations with Melody and determine how they feel to you.**

Theme and Format

Each of the following behavior chapters in this section of the book should be considered with the following format in mind. In this chapter, we will focus on **elopement and other running-related issues** as behaviors we see in the classroom and as communications that we try to understand. That said, the title of this chapter is an umbrella descriptor, and these behaviors comprise a theme or group of communications. We observe these manifest communications as thematic, as there are many permutations within a category of behavior.

Common Forms of This Behavior

- Running out of the classroom/school
- Leaving the school grounds or premises
- Moving away from teacher when asked to come closer
- Leaving the confines of a group when asked to stay within it
- Going missing (inside of school during school hours)
- Going missing (outside of school on a field trip)

Manifest Communication

There is little that is more gratifying than to see a child running with abandon. The look on that face is a combination of joy, contentment, and exertion. There is a freedom and a beauty to this activity that we wish for all children. At its core, running is a positive … until it is not. Because with that freedom that running brings comes a level of independence in children that requires the structure of wisdom. The speed, the movement, and the pace create a vulnerability that gives us pause. Phrases like "running into the street," "running away," and "look where you're running" each contain a strain of adult anxiety.

The confined nature of the classroom, the school, and the playground (along with the quantity of students to be attended to) requires teachers to focus not only on the positive physical and emotional benefits associated with running, but also with the real safety concerns that this behavior can create. Elopement as a behavior centers on the idea of a child running (or fleeing) from the structures that exist to provide security—this is why it creates distress in us as academic caregivers. It communicates a manifest disregard of or difficulty with the limits we have placed on the child's environment for the sake of safety, orderliness, and self-control.

So, what exactly does elopement look like? We think the most useful way of deconstructing this behavior/communication is to identify its elements:

- It is the **environment containment,** or how far a child can run and does run (contained or uncontained)
- It is the perceived **level of control** that the child is exhibiting (in control or out-of-control)
- It is the child's **pace/movement** (slow or fast)

These three elements intertwine to produce each moment of elopement and to characterize it as age-typical or atypical, as safe or unsafe. All children run away at times, this is normative behavior and should typically be seen and responded to as understandable limit testing or boundary pushing. Yet, at times, child elopement becomes worrisome, and at these moments teachers will have to address the behavior in a more significant manner and as a real potential hazard for the child, the class, and the school. For our purposes, the following scale may be a helpful tool in determining whether the elopement rises to the level of needing more determined intervention.

Table 10.1:
Elopement Safety Scale

Environmental Containment 2=Yes 0=No	Did the child leave the classroom?	Yes	No
	Did the child leave the school?	Yes	No
	Did the child leave a safe area (i.e., playground, field trip group)?	Yes	No
	Did the child disappear from the teacher's sight?	Yes	No
Level of Control 1=Yes 0= No	Did the child ignore to the teacher's voice?	Yes	No
	Did the child keep moving away when called?	Yes	No
	Did the child look like the act of running was impulsive?	Yes	No
	Did the child laugh if the teacher expressed concern or dismay about the behavior?	Yes	No

Pace/Movement 1= Yes 0= No	Was the child moving quickly?	Yes	No
	Was the teacher unable to catch up with the child?	Yes	No
	Did the child increase speed or dart away when the teacher got close?	Yes	No

Weiner, Gallo-Silver, & Lucas, 2020

The following ratings indicate the level of severity of the elopement behavior and direct the nature of the teacher response including the rapidity, the comprehensiveness, and the personnel involved:

- If our answers to the scale queries tally a score of 15 to 11, then there is reason to identify a child's elopement behavior as acute or severe (requires immediate structural intervention, i.e., adult proximity and supervision, doors closed, etc., in addition to the responses listed below).
- If our answers to the scale queries tally a score of 10 to 6, we can categorize the child's elopement behavior as moderate. (requires possible structural interventions, i.e., adult proximity and/or supervision, doors monitoring, etc., in addition to the responses listed below).
- If our answers to the scale queries tally a score of 5 to 1, we can classify the elopement behavior as mild (Pennington, et al, 2012; Feliciano & O'Connor, 2017).

Using the child Personas of the Troubling child, the Testing child, the Worrying child, and the Hiding child, we will explore specific teacher responses for each type of communication pattern (see Table 10.1). We understand that in cases of elopement, we may or may not be the ones who intervene when the child has left our classroom or other area of supervision. Our focus for this chapter centers on what we can do within the classroom setting to diminish the elopement frequency and/or intensity. For more detailed information about the most productive teacher response configurations for each Persona, please refer back to their respective chapters.

Table 10.2:
Behavior Frequency by Persona

	Persona			
Behavior	Troubling Child Loud & Over Reactive	Testing Child Loud & Under Reactive	Worrying Child Quiet & Over Reactive	Hiding Child Quiet & Under Reactive
Running out of the classroom/school	X	X	X	X
Leaving the school grounds or premises	X			X
Moving away from teacher when asked to come closer	X	X	X	X

	Persona			
Behavior	Troubling Child Loud & Over Reactive	Testing Child Loud & Under Reactive	Worrying Child Quiet & Over Reactive	Hiding Child Quiet & Under Reactive
Leaving the confines of a group after being asked to stay within it	X	X	X	X
Going missing (inside of school during school hours)	X			X
Going missing (outside of school on a field trip)	X			X

The absence of an "X" indicates that this Persona does not typically engage in this type of behavior/communication.

Latent Communication

This process is not an exact science and should be conducted more as trial and error. We would like you to take your best professional guess as to your answers to the following inquiries and evaluations. If you find that, after working through the latent communication material and identifying a set of responses, they do not work as you hoped, you can always revise and try again. Just remember, children integrate learning following repetition, so do not give up too soon.

Responses and Affirmations

Children do not learn the first time we teach them a new concept or a task. We say this in order to manage our expectations about how quickly or completely these new interventions will change or extinguish any given behavior.

Let's keep in mind the following factors. First, the development of these behaviors has typically occurred over an extended period of time. Based on the ages of the children we address in this book, any behavior grew over at least two years and up to eight. As much as we would wish it, a behavior that has been developing over a lengthy period of time cannot change "overnight." Actually, rapid change is often poorly integrated by children and cannot be sustained. Second, children integrate responses at different rates based on a variety of factors, including temperament, environment, learning styles, family involvement/support, etc. We have addressed these earlier in the book. Last, we are constructing foundations from which to grow, one brick at a time, foundations that these children will be able to build on and rely on for years to come. To this end, we want you to know that each of your responses is remembered and cataloged by these children for future use—even if it does not outwardly appear to have been during your time with the child. This relates to the corrective emotional experience we wrote about earlier in this book. Your interactions become part of the child's long-term memory, exchanges that are saved for future use.

That said, we want us to have some benchmarks for our expectations. First, we believe that one month is a sufficient timeframe for some level of change in a behavior, given that a specific teacher response is maintained with consistency and repetition. Second, as we cannot factor in changes that are occurring in real time within these children and with their families, the one-month benchmark may need to be altered accordingly. Third, the one-month duration allows for these challenged children to test us. They will imagine that what we are doing cannot be sustained, that it is too good to last. Our consistency and repetition in responding to the underlying message ultimately quiet their negative thoughts. It is then when the child's expectations of the people around them begin to change to an inner message that is more hopeful and positive. This hopefulness alters their communications and behaviors and can become a more embedded part of their future interpersonal relationships.

Behavior (1)
Running out of the classroom/school

If you find the child's leaving the classroom or school *seems* for the most part to be:

1. persistently willful; seemingly inflammatory and challenging (see Troubling Child)

2. persistent, yet playful; mildly vexing, pushing limits and boundaries (see Testing Child)

3. sudden and restless; possibly upsetting and tense for you (see Worrying Child)

4. sudden and seemingly arbitrary; possibly odd and/or confusing to you (see Hiding Child)

- **The Troubling Child**

    Core Feeling:　The more frequent the child's behavior is, the greater the **sadness/anger** is being experienced by the child.

    Core Wish:　Communicates unconscious wish to be **contained** and **supported** as a way of decreasing sense of **danger** and **rejection**.

    Core Question:　Limit-testing question—I am being triggered by events because this moment in class feels overwhelming; can you accept me and handle me?

    Responses:　**Structural & Less Emotional** (see Responses section)

- **The Testing Child**

Core Feeling:	The more frequent the child's behavior is, the greater the **sadness/anger** is being experienced by the child.
Core Wish:	Communicates unconscious wish to be **contained** and **validated** as a way of increasing sense of **security** and decreasing sense of **abandonment**.
Core Question:	Limit-testing question—I am feeling bad about myself and need to show this by creating a distraction; do you care about me enough to stop me?
Responses:	**Structural & More Emotional** (see Responses section)

- **The Worrying Child**

Core Feeling:	The more frequent the child's behavior is, the greater the **fear/anger** is being experienced by the child.
Core Wish:	Communicates unconscious wish to be **noticed** and **supported** as a way of decreasing sense of **danger** and **abandonment**.
Core Question:	Limit-testing question—I am being triggered by events and this is an expression of how afraid I am; do you care enough to protect me?
Responses:	**Verbal & Less Emotional** (see Responses section)

- **The Hiding Child**

Core Feeling:	The more frequent the child's behavior is, the greater the **fear/anger** is being experienced by the child.
Core Wish:	Communicates unconscious wish to be **noticed** and **valid**ated as a way of increasing sense of **security** and decreasing sense of **rejection**.
Core Question:	Limit-testing question—My behavior is a diversion from just how uncomfortable I feel right now; can you accept the way I am and contain me?
Responses:	**Verbal & More Emotional** (see Responses section)

Responses for: Behavior (1) Running out of the classroom/school

The Troubling Child

- ***Structural*:**
  - ◊ Clear and calm voice (supportive).
  - ◊ Before class: Check in. Hold eye contact. "I'm with you. Let's keep working on this."

Chapter 10. Elopement and "Moving Away"–Related Issues

- ◊ During class: Hand on shoulder; down on knee at eye level. Hold eye contact. Use the Less Emotional responses below.
- ◊ After class: Check in. Hold eye contact. Reiterate response themes (boundaries, self-care). Track progress with chart.

- **Less Emotional**:
  - ◊ *Self-Care and Boundaries*: "I want you to try to stay in the classroom. You are safer when you stay in the room."
  - ◊ *Self-Care*: "Wait, take a deep breath and let it out very slowly when you want to run out of the class."
  - ◊ *Boundaries*: "I want you to think to yourself, 'I can make a choice to run out of the classroom or stay and be safe.'"
  - ◊ *Self-Care and Boundaries*: "I want you to think about us building a dam together across a stream and trying to stop all the water from flowing. If we can do it, it can feel really good when we see that we have stopped the water in the stream completely. Controlling your feet and your body is the same. It's like a victory."

- **Affirmation**:
  - ◊ "Controlling your body and your feet takes great strength."
  - ◊ "Anyone can see what a huge effort you make not to run out of the class."

The Testing Child

- **Structural**:
  - ◊ Clear and crisp voice (supportive).
  - ◊ Before class: Check in. Hold eye contact. "I'm with you. Let's keep working on this."
  - ◊ During class: Hand on shoulder; down on knee at eye level. Hold eye contact. Use More Emotional responses below.
  - ◊ After class: Check in. Hold eye contact. Reiterate response themes (boundaries, self-awareness). Track progress with chart.

- **More Emotional**:
  - ◊ *Self-Awareness and Boundaries*: "It saddens me when you run out of the classroom, because I feel like it pushes us apart."
  - ◊ *Self-Awareness*: "When you run out of the classroom, I think you feel bad."
  - ◊ *Self-Awareness and Boundaries*: "Sometimes bad thoughts just feel like they need to push our body around and move us in directions that are not safe. We have to ask for help to keep our body in a safe place."
  - ◊ *Self-Awareness*: "Try to take a deep breath and let it out very slowly; and say to yourself, 'I will be okay,' before you run out of the classroom."
  - ◊ *Self-Awareness and Boundaries*: "Staying with me is important. Try to raise your hand if you feel like running and I will come over."

- **Affirmation**:
  - ◊ "I am proud of you for trying so hard to not run out of class."
  - ◊ "You took good care of yourself by not running out of class."

The Worrying Child

- **Verbal**:
    - ◊ Clear and calm voice (quiet).
    - ◊ Before class: Check in and talk about previous day. Occasional eye contact. "I want to check in with you to see how our talk felt for you. We can do this each day."
    - ◊ During class: Occasional eye contact. Maintain distance (two feet at least). No physical contact. Use sound or words to get attention (Less Emotional responses below).
    - ◊ After class: Occasional eye contact. Reiterate response themes (connection, self-care).
- **Less Emotional**:
    - ◊ *Self-Care*: "Take a deep breath and let it out very slowly when you want to run out of the classroom. Your body can wait."
    - ◊ *Self-Care and Connection*: "It can help us feel safer if we try and slow down a little. When you want to run, try to come over and see me first."
    - ◊ *Connection*: "Sometimes your movements helps me understand what you are thinking."
    - ◊ *Connection*: "When you run out of class, it makes me think about your safety. I would like to ask you about what you are thinking."
- **Affirmation**:
    - ◊ "Controlling your body takes strength."
    - ◊ "You are brave to stop yourself from running out of the classroom."

The Hiding Child

- **Verbal**:
    - ◊ Clear and calm voice (quiet).
    - ◊ Before class: Check in and talk about previous day. Occasional eye contact. "I want to check in with you to see if you remember our talk. We will do this each day."
    - ◊ During class: Occasional eye contact. Maintain distance (two feet at least). No physical contact. Use sound or words to get attention (More Emotional responses below).
    - ◊ After class: Occasional eye contact. Reiterate response themes (connection, self-awareness).
- **More Emotional**:
    - ◊ *Self-Awareness and Connection*: "When leaving the room becomes very important to you, I think you have big feelings, and I am worried. Try to raise your hand if you want to leave. I can help with that."
    - ◊ *Self-Awareness*: "It looks like you just can't wait when you feel like you have to leave the room. Waiting is a way to be strong."
    - ◊ *Connection*: "Look at my face. I am concerned that you are having difficulty staying in the room."

◊ *Self-Awareness*: "Try to you to think to yourself, 'I can control my body and feet. They are like water coming out of a faucet. I can try to turn the faucet off for a moment.'"
- *Affirmation*:
  ◊ "I see you using your thoughts to control your body and feet."
  ◊ "I am impressed how you decide to stay put and not leave the classroom."

Behavior (2)
Leaving the school grounds or premises

If you find the child's leaving the school grounds *seems* for the most part:

1. persistently willful; seemingly inflammatory and challenging (see Troubling Child)

2. disconnected and seemingly unmindful of repercussions; possibly odd and/or confusing to you (see Hiding Child)

- **The Troubling Child**

Core Feeling:	The more frequent the child's behavior is, the greater the **sadness/anger** is being experienced by the child.
Core Wish:	Communicates unconscious wish to be **contained** and **supported** as a way of decreasing sense of **danger** and **rejection**.
Core Question:	Limit-testing question—I am being triggered by events and I am upset that the rules feel overwhelming and far too confining; can you accept me and handle me?
Responses:	**Structural & Less Emotional** (see Responses section)

- **The Hiding Child**

Core Feeling:	The more frequent the child's behavior is, the greater the **fear/anger** is being experienced by the child.
Core Wish:	Communicates unconscious wish to be **noticed** and **validated** as a way of increasing sense of **security** and decreasing sense of **rejection**.
Core Question:	Limit-testing question—I feel uncomfortable and uneasy and suddenly need to go my own path; can you accept the way I am and contain me?
Responses:	**Verbal & More Emotional** (see Responses section)

Responses for: Behavior (2) Leaving the school grounds or premises

The Troubling Child

- *Structural*:
    - Clear and calm voice (supportive).
    - Before class: Check in. Hold eye contact. "I'm with you. Let's keep working on this."
    - During class: Hand on shoulder; down on knee at eye level. Hold eye contact. Use the Less Emotional responses below.
    - After class: Check in. Hold eye contact. Reiterate response themes (boundaries, self-care). Track progress with chart.
- *Less Emotional*:
    - *Self-Care and Boundaries*: "I want you to try to stay with the group. Your safety is important. It is safer for you to stay."
    - *Self-Care*: "When you start to think about leaving, take a deep breath, let it out very slowly, and say to yourself, 'It's okay, I can stay.'"
    - *Self-Care and Boundaries*: "I want you to think, 'I can stay with my teacher (my class). It makes me safer.'"
    - *Self-Care and Boundaries*: "If you wander off by yourself, maybe you can find your way back; but the people you are with do not know where you went, and they might need to find you and talk to you. You are stronger when people know where you are."
- *Affirmation*:
    - "You are strong inside to be able to stay with us and not leave."
    - "Anyone can see what huge effort you made to control your feet and body."

The Hiding Child

- *Verbal*:
    - Clear and calm voice (quiet).
    - Before class: Check in and talk about previous day. Occasional eye contact. "I want to check in with you to see if you remember our talk. We will do this each day."
    - During class: Occasional eye contact. Maintain distance (two feet at least). No physical contact. Use sound or words to get attention (More Emotional responses below).
    - After class: Occasional eye contact. Reiterate response themes (connection, self-awareness).
- *More Emotional*:
    - *Self-Awareness and Connection*: "When you are having strong ideas that make you want to leave, I think you have big feelings, and I am worried. I really want you to try to control your feet and stay because you are safer when you stay with the group."

◊ *Self-Awareness and Connection*: "Look at my face. I am concerned that if you don't stay with the class then you might get lost from the group."
◊ *Self-Awareness and Connection*: "You can control your strong ideas. I want you to try and raise your hand and let me know that you are having ideas about leaving the group. I can help with that."
- *Affirmation*:
    ◊ "The ideas about leaving are powerful. You are strong when you try to control them."
    ◊ "Impressive how you tried so hard to control your body and feet."

Behavior (3)
Moving away from teacher when asked to come closer

If you find the child's moving away *seems* for the most part:

1. persistently willful; seemingly inflammatory and challenging (see Troubling Child)

2. persistent, yet playful; mildly vexing, pushing limits and boundaries (see Testing Child)

3. cautious and seemingly fearful; possibly upsetting and regretful for you (see Worrying Child)

4. disconnected and arbitrary; possibly odd and/or confusing to you (see Hiding Child)

- **The Troubling Child**

    Core Feeling: The more frequent the child's behavior is, the greater the **sadness/anger** is being experienced by the child.

    Core Wish: Communicates unconscious wish to be **contained** and **supported** as a way of decreasing sense of **danger** and **rejection**.

    Core Question: Limit-testing question—I am being triggered by events and I am upset that the rules feel overwhelming and far too confining; can you accept me and handle me?

    Responses: **Structural & Less Emotional** (see Responses section)

- **The Testing Child**

    Core Feeling: The more frequent the child's behavior is, the greater the **sadness/anger** is being experienced by the child.

    Core Wish: Communicates unconscious wish to be **contained** and **validated** as a way of increasing sense of **security** and decreasing sense of **abandonment**.

Core Question: Limit-testing question—I am feeling bad about myself and need to show this by creating a distraction; do you care about me enough to stop me?

Responses: **Structural & More Emotional** (see Responses section)

- **The Worrying Child**

Core Feeling: The more frequent the child's behavior is, the greater the **fear/anger** is being experienced by the child.

Core Wish: Communicates unconscious wish to be **noticed** and **supported** as a way of decreasing sense of **danger** and **abandonment**.

Core Question: Limit-testing question—I am being triggered by events and this is an expression of how afraid I am; do you care enough to protect me?

Responses: **Verbal & Less Emotional** (see Responses section)

- **The Hiding Child**

Core Feeling: The more frequent the child's behavior is, the greater the **fear/anger** is being experienced by the child.

Core Wish: Communicates unconscious wish to be **noticed** and **validated** as a way of increasing sense of **security** and decreasing sense of **rejection**.

Core Question: Limit-testing question—My behavior is a diversion from just how uncomfortable I feel right now; can you accept the way I am and contain me?

Responses: **Verbal & More Emotional** (see Responses section)

Responses for: Behavior (3) Moving away from teacher when asked to come closer

The Troubling Child

- *Structural*:
    - ◊ Clear and calm voice (supportive).
    - ◊ Before class: Check in. Hold eye contact. "I'm with you. Let's keep working on this."
    - ◊ During class: Hand on shoulder; down on knee at eye level. Hold eye contact. Use the Less Emotional responses below.
    - ◊ After class: Check in. Hold eye contact. Reiterate response themes (boundaries, self-care). Track progress with chart.
- *Less Emotional*:

Chapter 10. Elopement and "Moving Away"–Related Issues

- ◊ *Boundaries*: "I want you to try to stay close to me even if you do not want to."
- ◊ *Self-Care and Boundaries*: "Take a deep breath and let it out very slowly when you feel like moving away from me."
- ◊ *Boundaries*: "I want you to think to yourself, 'I can make a choice to stay close to my teacher.'"
- ◊ *Self-Care and Boundaries*: "I want you to think about a castle. When a ruler wants to keep the people safe, she/he asks them to come inside the castle walls. You can be brave and stay inside my castle."
- *Affirmation*:
  - ◊ "When you push yourself to stay near me, I can see how strong you are."
  - ◊ "Staying close takes great courage."

The Testing Child

- *Structural*:
  - ◊ Clear and crisp voice (supportive).
  - ◊ Before class: Check in. Hold eye contact. "I'm with you. Let's keep working on this."
  - ◊ During class: Hand on shoulder; down on knee at eye level. Hold eye contact. Use More Emotional responses below.
  - ◊ After class: Check in. Hold eye contact. Reiterate response themes (boundaries, self-awareness). Track progress with chart.
- *More Emotional*:
  - ◊ *Self-Awareness and Boundaries*: "It makes me sad me when you choose to move away from me, because I feel like it pushes us apart."
  - ◊ *Self-Awareness and Boundaries*: "When you move away from me, I think you are feeling bad."
  - ◊ *Self-Awareness and Boundaries*: "Sometimes bad thoughts are like loud noises that hurt our ears and make it hard to hear. When we can't really hear because of the loud bad thoughts, we need someone to help us. That means staying close to me."
  - ◊ *Self-Awareness and Boundaries*: "Try to take a breath and let it out very slowly; and then say to yourself, 'I will be okay, I can stay near the teacher.'"
  - ◊ *Self-Awareness and Boundaries*: "Our connection is so important to me. When you are having trouble staying near me when I ask, try to remember that I care about you."
- *Affirmation*:
  - ◊ "I am proud of you for trying so hard to stay near me."
  - ◊ "You took good care of yourself by trying to stay close and not moving away."

The Worrying Child

- **Verbal**:
    - ◊ Clear and calm voice (quiet).
    - ◊ Before class: Check in and talk about previous day. Occasional eye contact. "I want to check in with you to see how our talk felt for you. We can do this each day."
    - ◊ During class: Occasional eye contact. Maintain distance (two feet at least). No physical contact. Use sound or words to get attention (Less Emotional responses below).
    - ◊ After class: Occasional eye contact. Reiterate response themes (connection, self-care).
- **Less Emotional**:
    - ◊ *Self-Care and Connection*: "Take a deep breath and let it out very slowly when I ask you to come talk. You are safe."
    - ◊ *Self-Care and Connection*: "When you don't feel like coming over to me, take a deep breath and let it out very slowly; and think to yourself, 'It's okay, I am okay, I am safe. I can be near my teacher for a moment.'"
    - ◊ *Self-Care and Connection*: "Try and think, 'my teacher is safe, my classmates are safe, I am safe. I can stay close.'"
    - ◊ *Self-Care and Connection*: "Staying near my teacher takes courage. Let's see if you can be courageous with my help."
- **Affirmation**:
    - ◊ "Coming over to talk when you don't want to, shows how much courage you have."
    - ◊ "You are being brave when you stay close."

The Hiding Child

- **Verbal**:
    - ◊ Clear and calm voice (quiet).
    - ◊ Before class: Check in and talk about previous day. Occasional eye contact. "I want to check in with you to see if you remember our talk. We will do this each day."
    - ◊ During class: Occasional eye contact. Maintain distance (two feet at least). No physical contact. Use sound or words to get attention (More Emotional responses below).
    - ◊ After class: Occasional eye contact. Reiterate response themes (connection, self-awareness).
- **More Emotional**:
    - ◊ *Self-Awareness and Connection*: "Coming over to me when I ask you to can be difficult. I think that you have big feelings about what I might say, and that worries me. Try to take a deep breath and let it out very slowly; and just stay near me for a moment."
    - ◊ *Self-Awareness and Connection*: "Look at my face. I am concerned that if

you have big feelings about staying near me when I ask you to, then you won't be able to hear what I need to share with you."
   ◊ *Self-Awareness and Connection*: "You can control your excitement enough to be close to me for a bit. Try to let me know that your excitement is stopping you from coming over to me. I can help you with that."
- *Affirmation*:
   ◊ "I can see how you are trying to control your body and feet when you have big feelings."
   ◊ "Impressive how you are able to control your excitement and stay near me."

Behavior (4)
Leaving the confines of a group after being asked to stay within it

If you find the child's leaving the group *seems* for the most part:

1. persistently willful; seemingly inflammatory and challenging (see Troubling Child)

2. persistent, yet playful; mildly vexing, pushing limits and boundaries (see Testing Child)

3. cautious and seemingly fearful; possibly upsetting and regretful for you (see Worrying Child)

4. disconnected and arbitrary; possibly odd and/or confusing to you (see Hiding Child)

- **The Troubling Child**

Core Feeling:	The more frequent the child's behavior is, the greater the **sadness/anger** is being experienced by the child.
Core Wish:	Communicates unconscious wish to be **contained** and **supported** as a way of decreasing sense of **danger** and **rejection**.
Core Question:	Limit-testing question—I am being triggered by events and I am upset that the rules feel overwhelming and far too confining; can you accept me and handle me?
Responses:	**Structural & Less Emotional** (see Responses section)

- **The Testing Child**

Core Feeling:	The more frequent the child's behavior is, the greater the **sadness/anger** is being experienced by the child.

Core Wish: Communicates unconscious wish to be **contained** and **validated** as a way of increasing sense of **security** and decreasing sense of **abandonment**.

Core Question: Limit-testing question—I am feeling bad about myself and need to show this by creating a distraction; do you care about me enough to stop me?

Responses: **Structural & More Emotional** (see Responses section)

- **The Worrying Child**

Core Feeling: The more frequent the child's behavior is, the greater the **fear/anger** is being experienced by the child.

Core Wish: Communicates unconscious wish to be **noticed** and **supported** as a way of decreasing sense of **danger** and **abandonment**.

Core Question: Limit-testing question—I am being triggered by events and this is an expression of how afraid I am; do you care enough to protect me?

Responses: **Verbal & Less Emotional** (see Responses section)

- **The Hiding Child**

Core Feeling: The more frequent the child's behavior is, the greater the **fear/anger** is being experienced by the child.

Core Wish: Communicates unconscious wish to be **noticed** and **validated** as a way of increasing sense of **security** and decreasing sense of **rejection**.

Core Question: Limit-testing question—My behavior is a diversion from just how uncomfortable I feel right now; can you accept the way I am and contain me?

Responses: **Verbal & More Emotional** (see Responses section)

Responses for: Behavior (4) Leaving the confines of a group after being asked to stay within it

The Troubling Child

- *Structural*:
    ◊ Clear and calm voice (supportive).
    ◊ Before class: Check in. Hold eye contact. "I'm with you. Let's keep working on this."
    ◊ During class: Hand on shoulder; down on knee at eye level. Hold eye contact. Use the Less Emotional responses below.

- ◊ After class: Check in. Hold eye contact. Reiterate response themes (boundaries, self-care). Track progress with chart.
- **Less Emotional:**
  - ◊ *Boundaries*: "I want you to try to stay close to the group even if you do not want to."
  - ◊ *Self-Care*: "Take a deep breath and let it out very slowly when you feel like moving away from us."
  - ◊ *Boundaries*: "I want you to think to yourself, 'I can make a choice to stay close to my class or not.'"
  - ◊ *Self-Care and Boundaries*: "I want you to think about a team. It is really important that a team plays together." Sometimes a player is having trouble, but because he/she is on a team, the rest of the players can help him/her. You can be brave and stay with the class, it's your team.
- **Affirmation:**
  - ◊ "When you push yourself to stay near me, I can see how strong you are."
  - ◊ "Staying close takes great courage."

The Testing Child

- **Structural:**
  - ◊ Clear and crisp voice (supportive).
  - ◊ Before class: Check in. Hold eye contact. "I'm with you. Let's keep working on this."
  - ◊ During class: Hand on shoulder; down on knee at eye level. Hold eye contact. Use More Emotional responses below.
  - ◊ After class: Check in. Hold eye contact. Reiterate response themes (boundaries, self-awareness). Track progress with chart.
- **More Emotional:**
  - ◊ *Self-Awareness and Boundaries*: "It makes me sad me when you choose to move away from the group, because I feel like it pushes you away from your classmates."
  - ◊ *Self-Awareness*: "When you move away from the group, I think you are feeling bad."
  - ◊ *Self-Awareness and Boundaries*: "Sometimes bad thoughts are like loud noises that hurt our ears and make it hard to hear. When we can't really hear because of the loud bad thoughts, we need others to help us figure out where to be. That means staying close to the group."
  - ◊ *Self-Awareness*: "Try to take a breath and let it out very slowly; and say to yourself, 'I will be okay, I can stay near my class.'"
  - ◊ *Self-Awareness and Boundaries*: "Your connection to the class is so important to me. When you are having trouble staying near the group, try to remember that they care about you."
- **Affirmation:**
  - ◊ "I am proud of you for trying so hard to stay in the group."

◊ "You took good care of yourself by trying to stay close and not moving away."

The Worrying Child

- *Verbal*:
    ◊ Clear and calm voice (quiet).
    ◊ Before class: Check in and talk about previous day. Occasional eye contact. "I want to check in with you to see how our talk felt for you. We can do this each day."
    ◊ During class: Occasional eye contact. Maintain distance (two feet at least). No physical contact. Use sound or words to get attention (Less Emotional responses below).
    ◊ After class: Occasional eye contact. Reiterate response themes (connection, self-care).
- *Less Emotional*:
    ◊ *Self-Care*: "Take a deep breath and let it out very slowly when I ask you to stay with the group. You are safe."
    ◊ *Self-Care*: "When you don't feel like staying with the group, take a deep breath and let it out very slowly; and say to yourself, 'I am okay, I am safe. I can be near my classmates for a moment.'"
    ◊ *Self-Care and Connection*: "Try and think, 'my teacher is safe, my classmates are safe, I am safe. I can stay close.'"
    ◊ *Self-Care and Connection*: "Staying with the group takes courage. Let's see if you can be courageous with my help."
- *Affirmation*:
    ◊ "Coming over to talk when you don't want to, shows how much courage you have."
    ◊ "You are being brave when you stay close."

The Hiding Child

- *Verbal*:
    ◊ Clear and calm voice (quiet).
    ◊ Before class: Check in and talk about previous day. Occasional eye contact. "I want to check in with you to see if you remember our talk. We will do this each day."
    ◊ During class: Occasional eye contact. Maintain distance (two feet at least). No physical contact. Use sound or words to get attention (More Emotional responses below).
    ◊ After class: Occasional eye contact. Reiterate response themes (connection, self-awareness).
- *More Emotional*:
    ◊ *Self-Awareness and Connection*: "Staying with the class when I ask you to, is sometimes difficult. I think that you have big feelings about what

might happen, and I am worried. Try to take a deep breath and let it out very slowly; and just stay for a moment."
- ◊ *Self-Awareness and Connection*: "Look at my face. I am concerned that if you have big feelings about staying in the group when I ask, then you won't be able to follow along with what the class is doing."
- ◊ *Self-Awareness and Connection*: "You can control your excitement long enough to stay close for a bit. Try to let me know that your excitement is stopping you from coming over to me. I can help you with that."

- **Affirmation:**
  - ◊ "I can see how you are trying to control your body and feet when you have big feelings."
  - ◊ "Impressive how you are able to control your excitement and stay near me."

Behavior (5)
Going missing (inside of school during school hours)

If you find the child's wandering off *seems* for the most part:

1. defiant, rejecting attempts at containing and not adhering to rules (see Troubling Child)

2. preoccupied, seeming derailed, going off in confusing/odd directions (see Hiding Child)

- **The Troubling Child**

Core Feeling:	The more frequent the child's behavior is, the greater the **sadness/anger** is being experienced by the child.
Core Wish:	Communicates unconscious wish to be **contained** and **supported** as a way of decreasing sense of **danger** and **rejection**.
Core Question:	Limit-testing question—I am being triggered by events and I am upset that the rules feel overwhelming and far too confining; can you accept me and handle me?
Responses:	**Structural & Less Emotional** (see Responses section)

- **The Hiding Child**

Core Feeling:	The more frequent the child's behavior is, the greater the **fear/anger** is being experienced by the child.
Core Wish:	Communicates unconscious wish to be **noticed** and **validated** as a way of increasing sense of **security** and decreasing sense of **rejection**.

Core Question: Limit-testing question—My behavior is a diversion from just how uncomfortable I feel right now; can you accept the way I am and contain me?

Responses: **Verbal & More Emotional** (see Responses section)

Responses for: Behavior (5) Going missing (inside of school during school hours)

The Troubling Child

- *Structural*:
    ◊ Clear and calm voice (supportive).
    ◊ Before class: Check in. Hold eye contact. "I'm with you. Let's keep working on this."
    ◊ During class: Hand on shoulder; down on knee at eye level. Hold eye contact. Use the Less Emotional responses below.
    ◊ After class: Check in. Hold eye contact. Reiterate response themes (boundaries, self-care). Track progress with chart.
- *Less Emotional*:
    ◊ *Self-Care and Boundaries*: "I want you to try to stay with the group. Your safety is important. It is safer for you to stay close."
    ◊ *Self-Care*: "When you start to think about leaving, take a deep breath and let it out very slowly; and say to yourself, 'It's okay, I can stay.'"
    ◊ *Self-Care and Boundaries*: "I want you to think, 'I can stay with my class. It makes me safer and braver.'"
    ◊ *Self-Care and Boundaries*: "If you wander off by yourself you may not be able to find your way back, and the people you are with would not know where you are, and they might need to tell you something. You are stronger when people know where you are."
- *Affirmation*:
    ◊ "You are strong inside to be able to stay with us and not leave."
    ◊ "Anyone can see what huge effort you made to control your feet and body."

The Hiding Child

- *Verbal*:
    ◊ Clear and calm voice (quiet).
    ◊ Before class: Check in and talk about previous day. Occasional eye contact. "I want to check in with you to see if you remember our talk. We will do this each day."
    ◊ During class: Occasional eye contact. Maintain distance (two feet at least). No physical contact. Use sound or words to get attention (More Emotional responses below).

◊ After class: Occasional eye contact. Reiterate response themes (connection, self-awareness).
- *More Emotional*:
    ◊ *Self-Awareness*: "When you are having strong ideas that make you want to leave, I think you have big feelings, and I am worried."
    ◊ *Connection*: "I really want you to try to control your feet and stay because you are safer when you stay with the group."
    ◊ *Self-Awareness and Connection*: "Look at my face. I am concerned that if you don't stay with the class then you might get lost from the group. This would not be safe, and I would be upset."
    ◊ *Self-Awareness and Connection*: "You can control you strong ideas. I want you to try and raise your hand and let me know that you are having ideas about leaving the group. I can help with that."
- *Affirmation*:
    ◊ "The ideas about leaving are powerful. You are strong when you try to control them."
    ◊ "Impressive how you tried so hard to control your body and feet."

Behavior (6)
Going missing (outside of school on a field trip)

If you find the child's wandering off *seems* for the most part:

1. defiant, rejecting attempts at containing and not adhering to rules (see Troubling Child)

2. preoccupied, seeming derailed, going off in confusing/odd directions (see Hiding Child)

- **The Troubling Child**

Core Feeling:	The more frequent the child's behavior is, the greater the **sadness/anger** is being experienced by the child.
Core Wish:	Communicates unconscious wish to be **contained** and **supported** as a way of decreasing sense of **danger** and **rejection**.
Core Question:	Limit-testing question—I am being triggered by events and I am upset that the rules feel overwhelming and far too confining; can you accept me and handle me?
Responses:	**Structural & Less Emotional** (see Responses section)

- **The Hiding Child**

Core Feeling:	The more frequent the child's behavior is, the greater the **fear/anger** is being experienced by the child.

180   Part Three—Pulling Back the Curtain on Communicative Behaviors

Core Wish: Communicates unconscious wish to be **noticed** and **validated** as a way of increasing sense of **security** and decreasing sense of **rejection**.

Core Question: Limit-testing question—My behavior is a diversion from just how uncomfortable I feel right now; can you accept the way I am and contain me?

Responses: **Verbal & More Emotional** (see Responses section)

Responses for: Behavior (6) Going missing (outside of school on a field trip)

The Troubling Child

- *Structural*:
    - ◊ Clear and calm voice (supportive).
    - ◊ Before class: Check in. Hold eye contact. "I'm with you. Let's keep working on this."
    - ◊ During class: Hand on shoulder; down on knee at eye level. Hold eye contact. Use the Less Emotional responses below.
    - ◊ After class: Check in. Hold eye contact. Reiterate response themes (boundaries, self-care). Track progress with chart.
- *Less Emotional*:
    - ◊ *Self-Care and Boundaries*: "I want you to try to stay with the group. Your safety is important. It is safer for you to stay close."
    - ◊ *Self-Care*: "When you start to think about leaving, take a deep breath and let it out very slowly; and say to yourself, 'It's okay, I can stay.'"
    - ◊ *Self-Care and Boundaries*: "I want you to think, 'I can stay with my class. It makes me safer and braver.'"
    - ◊ *Self-Care and Boundaries*: "If you wander off by yourself, you might not be able to find your way back. The people you are with would not know where you are, and they might need to tell you something. You are stronger when people know where you are."
- *Affirmation*:
    - ◊ "You are strong inside to be able to stay with us and not leave."
    - ◊ "Anyone can see what huge effort you made to control your feet and body."

The Hiding Child

- *Verbal*:
    - ◊ Clear and calm voice (quiet).
    - ◊ Before class: Check in and talk about previous day. Occasional eye contact. "I want to check in with you to see if you remember our talk. We will do this each day."

- ◊ During class: Occasional eye contact. Maintain distance (two feet at least). No physical contact. Use sound or words to get attention (More Emotional responses below).
  - ◊ After class: Occasional eye contact. Reiterate response themes (connection, self-awareness).
- **More Emotional:**
  - ◊ *Self-Awareness*: "When you are having strong ideas that make you want to leave, I think you have big feelings, and I am worried."
  - ◊ *Connection*: "I really want you to try to control your feet and stay because you are safer when you stay with the group."
  - ◊ *Self-Awareness and Connection*: "Look at my face. I am concerned that if you don't stay with the class then you might get lost from the group. This would not be safe; and I would be upset."
  - ◊ *Self-Awareness and Connection*: "You can control you strong ideas. I want you to try and raise your hand and let me know that you are having ideas about leaving the group. I can help with that."
- **Affirmation:**
  - ◊ "The ideas about leaving are powerful. You are strong when you try to control them."
  - ◊ "Impressive how you tried so hard to control your body and feet."

Your Evolving Responses

As you have read, there are different motivations for your students' behaviors depending on their latent communication patterns. This demonstrates that your responses cannot be "one size fits all" in nature. While we have provided specific words for you to follow, we intend this chapter and the others like it to be a framework for your responses, not a script. You certainly can use our suggested language as you experiment with the interventions we have described. Overtime, it will be more helpful for you to find your own words to communicate with your students. As you continue to try these techniques, using your own communication style will make the responses to your students' behaviors feel authentic and sincere. This will happen naturally. The proposed interventions that we used in this chapter are a starting point and are meant to evolve and grow with your comfort level. This might take some practice, but it will be well worth it to expand your repertoire of potential responses to concerning or disruptive behaviors. You may find that your own words are more effective or more impactful than the words and phrases we have suggested in this book. The more you are a part of the interventions, the more meaningful they may be to your students. As we know, students need repetition, so please be patient as you try out new ways to respond to them.

Chapter 11

Excessive Clowning

*"I was the class clown at school,
but at home, my family wasn't very funny."*
—Carrot Top (comedian)

How to Use This Chapter

1. As you prepare to read this chapter, choose one child from your class on whom you wish to focus. Selecting one child at a time allows for a more concentrated exploration of the material and how it relates to each child uniquely. **As a guide, we will use "Melody," a second grader who makes silly sounds during class.**

2. Read the paragraphs from the following headings to begin the process: *Format and Theme* and *Common Forms of the Behavior*.

3. Choose one behavior that the selected child is exhibiting. Selecting one behavior at a time allows for a more concentrated exploration of the material centering on how the child communicates using this specific behavior. **Melody's behavior of making silly sounds when the class is trying to read.**

4. Read the paragraphs from the following headings to learn more about the general category that this behavior falls within from a more holistic perspective: *Manifest Communication* and *Latent Communication*.

5. Read the paragraphs from the heading *Responses and Affirmations* as background to how we structured the proposed responses and the expectation that you will ultimately personalize the responses provided in this chapter.

6. Turn to the page that contains the behavior in question. There you will find the number of the behavior and its name. **We select Behavior (1) Creating a humorous and disruptive noise during a lesson.**

7. On that page, below the number and name, you will find all the possible latent communication prompts for that behavior, ranging from (1) to (4). From these prompts, choose the prompt that most closely reminds you of how this child exhibits this behavior. Your choice may not fit one prompt exactly. If your sense is that multiple prompts could fit, choose the closest one to begin the process.

You can return to the other prompts later. You will notice that each prompt corresponds with a child communication Persona (i.e., Troubling, Testing, Worrying, Hiding). **For Melody, we choose "purposefully silly; mildly pushing limits and redirecting attention (see Testing Child)."**

8. After choosing a latent communication prompt, use the child communication Persona and read the corresponding Core Feelings, Core Wish, Core Question. This information describes the underlying meaning of the behavior and creates an empathic guide for you to keep in mind when responding to the child's behavior.

9. On the following page(s), you will find responses and affirmations for the number and name of the behavior in question. **We select Responses for: Behavior (1) Creating a humorous and disruptive noise during a lesson** section **The Testing Child.** Find and read the responses and affirmations for the behavior in question that corresponds with the child communication Persona.

10. **Try the responses and affirmations with Melody and determine how they feel to you.**

Theme and Format

Each of the following behavior/communication chapters in this section of the book should be considered with the following format in mind. In this chapter, we will focus on **excessive clowning** as behavior we see in the classroom and as a communication that we try to understand. That said, the title of this chapter is an umbrella descriptor, and these behaviors comprise a theme or group of communications. We observe these manifest communications as thematic, as there are many permutations within a category of behavior.

Common Forms of This Behavior

- Creating a humorous and/or disruptive sound or expression
- Falling out of a chair or throwing an object (physical humor)
- Making a humorous or witty statement in the middle of a lesson

Manifest Communication

We have all known a class clown or two over our own years of schooling. These are children who stand out, with a quip, a gesture, or a sound placed just to get a laugh (from a classmate) or a glare (from a teacher). The verbal and physical abilities and use of timing by this child create a spotlight that shines brightly on them. At the same time, the clowning suddenly takes attention away from educators and peers alike. This type of behavior creates a commotion in your classroom and disrupts the flow of lessons, transitions, and quiet times alike.

Children who engage in clowning behavior can be endearing at moments, but typically they continue until the conduct must be addressed by teachers in some obvious, overt manner. It is the excessiveness of their comportment that creates reactions from other people. In fact, the various responses of others—which can include amusement, surprise, frustration, or disbelief—often further reinforce the behavior and seem to encourage the child to persist. In this way, there seems to be no end to these inopportune communications.

The form that this type of excessive comportment may take varies dramatically. It can include some sort of physical movement at times or remain exclusively verbal in nature. It can be loud or quiet, subtle or obvious, hurtful or charming. The common thread throughout these variations is that, in each of these moments, a classroom rule is broken to some degree. The form and degree of the communication are important aspects of the behavior to identify and classify. Degrees of Excessiveness can be categorized into three levels. Each level represents a different intensity of communication (see Figure 11.1).

Using the child Personas of the Troubling child, the Testing child, the Worrying child, and the Hiding child, we will explore specific teacher responses for each type of communication pattern (see Table 11.1). For more detailed information about the most productive teacher response configurations for each Persona, please refer back to their respective chapters.

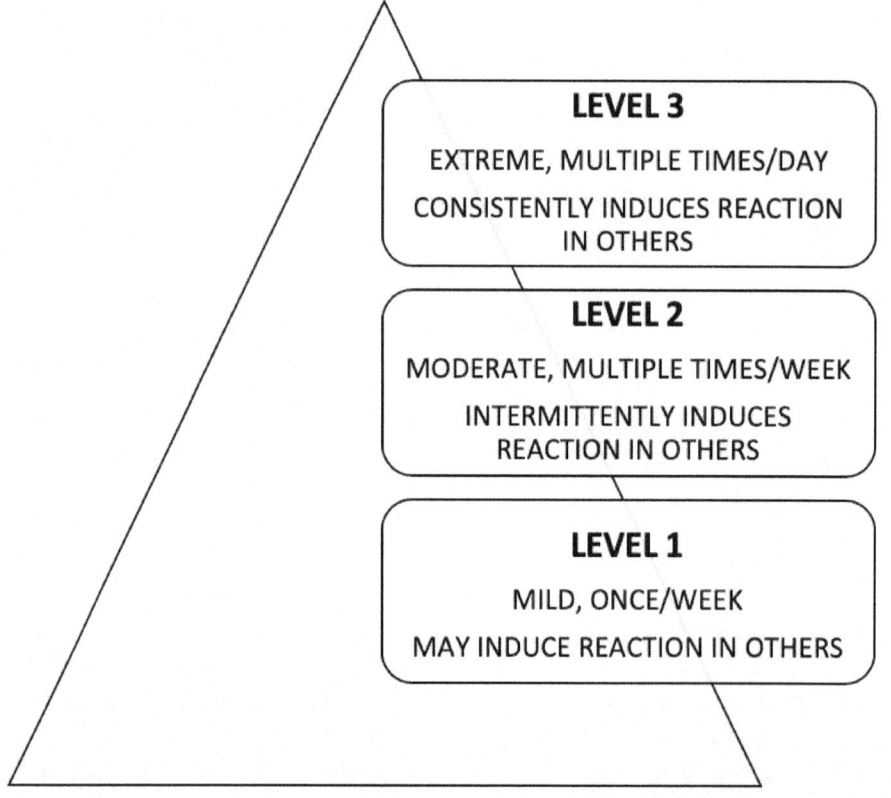

Figure 11.1: Degrees of Excessiveness

Table 11.1:
Behavior Frequency by Persona

Behavior	Persona			
	Troubling Child Loud & Over Reactive	*Testing Child Loud & Under Reactive*	*Worrying Child Quiet & Over Reactive*	*Hiding Child Quiet & Under Reactive*
Creating a humorous and/or disruptive sound or expression	X	X		X
Falling out of a chair or throwing an object (physical humor)	X	X		
Making a humorous and disruptive statement during a lesson	X	X		X

The absence of an "X" indicates that this Persona does not typically engage in this type of behavior/communication.

Latent Communication

This process is not an exact science and should be conducted more as trial and error. We would like you to take your best professional guess as to your answers to the following inquiries and evaluations. If you find that, after working through the latent communication material and identifying a set of responses, they do not work as you hoped, you can always revise and try again. Just remember, children integrate learning following repetition, so do not give up too soon.

Responses and Affirmations

Children do not learn the first time we teach them a new concept or a task. We say this in order to manage our expectations about how quickly or completely these new interventions will change or extinguish any given behavior.

Let's keep in mind the following factors. First, the development of these behaviors has typically occurred over an extended period of time. Based on the ages of the children we address in this book, any behavior grew over at least two years and up to eight. As much as we would wish it, a behavior that has been developing over a lengthy period of time cannot change "overnight." Actually, rapid change is often poorly integrated by children and cannot be sustained. Second, children integrate responses at different rates based on a variety of factors, including temperament, environment, learning styles, family involvement/support, etc. We have addressed these earlier in the book. Last, we are constructing foundations from which to grow, one brick at a time, foundations that these children will be able to build on and rely on for years to come. To this end, we want you to know that each of your responses is remembered and cataloged by these children for future use—even if it does not outwardly appear to have been during your time with the child. This relates to the corrective emotional experience we wrote about earlier in this book. Your interactions become part of the child's long-term memory, exchanges that are saved for future use.

That said, we want us to have some benchmarks for our expectations. First, we believe that one month is a sufficient timeframe for some level of change in a behavior, given that a specific teacher response is maintained with consistency and repetition. Second, as we cannot factor in changes that are occurring in real time within these children and with their families, the one-month benchmark may need to be altered accordingly. Third, the one-month duration allows for these challenged children to test us. They will imagine that what we are doing cannot be sustained, that it is too good to last. Our consistency and repetition in responding to the underlying message ultimately quiet their negative thoughts. It is then when the child's expectations of the people around them begin to change to an inner message that is more hopeful and positive. This hopefulness alters their communications and behaviors and can become a more embedded part of their future interpersonal relationships.

Behavior (1)
Creating a humorous and/or disruptive sound or expression

If you find the child's disruptive sound *seems* for the most part to be:

1. purposefully provocative; seemingly inflammatory and challenging (see Troubling Child)

2. purposefully silly; mildly pushing limits and redirecting attention (see Testing Child)

3. disconnected from material; possibly odd and/or confusing to follow (see Hiding Child)

- **The Troubling Child**

Core Feeling:	The more outrageous the child's noise is, the greater the **sadness/anger** is being experienced by the child.
Core Wish:	Communicates unconscious wish to be **contained** and **supported** as a way of decreasing sense of **danger** and **rejection**.
Core Question:	Limit-testing question—I am being triggered by events because this discussion feels overwhelming; can you accept me and handle me?
Responses:	**Structural & Less Emotional** (see Responses section)

- **The Testing Child**

Core Feeling:	The more outrageous the child's noise is, the greater the **sadness/anger** is being experienced by the child.
Core Wish:	Communicates unconscious wish to be **contained** and **validated** as a way of increasing sense of **security** and decreasing sense of **abandonment**.
Core Question:	Limit-testing question—I am feeling bad about myself and need to show this by creating a distraction; do you care about me enough to stop me?
Responses:	**Structural & More Emotional** (see Responses section)

- **The Hiding Child**

Core Feeling:	The more outrageous the child's noise is, the greater the **fear/anger** is being experienced by the child.
Core Wish:	Communicates unconscious wish to be **noticed** and **validated** as a way of increasing sense of **security** and decreasing sense of **rejection**.
Core Question:	Limit-testing question—My noise is a diversion from just how uncomfortable I feel right now; can you accept the way I am and contain me?
Responses:	**Verbal & More Emotional** (see Responses section)

Responses for: Behavior (1) Creating a humorous and/or disruptive sound or expression

The Troubling Child

- *Structural*:
    - ◊ Clear and calm voice (supportive).
    - ◊ Before class: Check in. Hold eye contact. "I'm with you. Let's keep working on this."
    - ◊ During class: Hand on shoulder; down on knee at eye level. Hold eye contact. Use the Less Emotional responses below.
    - ◊ After class: Check in. Hold eye contact. Reiterate response themes (boundaries, self-care). Track progress with chart.
- *Less Emotional*:
    - ◊ *Boundaries*: "I want you to try to stop making those silly sounds."
    - ◊ *Self-Care*: "Take a deep breath and then let it out very slowly, when you have a silly thought."
    - ◊ *Boundaries*: "I want you to think to yourself, 'I can make a choice whether to let out a silly sound or not.'"
    - ◊ *Self-Care and Boundaries*: "Holding on to that silly sound that suddenly

pops into your head is like saving a really great secret. It's really difficult, but waiting for just the right time makes sharing the secret feel even better."
- **Affirmation**:
    - ◊ "You can be so strong, when you wait for the right moment to express your silly ideas."
    - ◊ "Anyone can see what huge effort you made to hold onto your silly sounds."

The Testing Child

- **Structural**:
    - ◊ Clear and crisp voice (supportive).
    - ◊ Before class: Check in. Hold eye contact. "I'm with you. Let's keep working on this."
    - ◊ During class: Hand on shoulder; down on knee at eye level. Hold eye contact. Use More Emotional responses below.
    - ◊ After class: Check in. Hold eye contact. Reiterate response themes (boundaries, self-awareness). Track progress with chart.
- **More Emotional**:
    - ◊ *Self-Awareness and Boundaries*: "It saddens me when you make a silly sound; I feel like it pushes us apart."
    - ◊ *Self-Awareness*: "When you make a silly sound, I think you feel bad."
    - ◊ *Self-Awareness and Boundaries*: "Sometimes bad thoughts, even when they seem funny, just feel like popping out of us. They are like balloons that blow up too big. We have to ask for help to let some air out before it pops."
    - ◊ *Self-Awareness*: "Try to take a breath, let it out very slowly, and say to yourself, 'I will be okay,' before you make a silly comment or sound."
    - ◊ *Boundaries*: "Your sounds and comments are important. Try to raise your hand if you feel like making one and I will come over."
- **Affirmation**:
    - ◊ "I am proud of you for trying so hard to manage your silly thoughts."
    - ◊ "You took good care of yourself by holding your silly thoughts."

The Hiding Child

- **Verbal**:
    - ◊ Clear and calm voice (quiet).
    - ◊ Before class: Check in and talk about previous day. Occasional eye contact. "I want to check in with you to see if you remember our talk. We will do this each day."
    - ◊ During class: Occasional eye contact. Maintain distance (two feet at least). No physical contact. Use sound or words to get attention (More Emotional responses below).

◊ After class: Occasional eye contact. Reiterate response themes (connection, self-awareness).
- **More Emotional:**
  ◊ *Self-Awareness and Connection*: "That interesting sound is very important. I think you are excited, and I want you to try and raise your hand when you realize that you might want to make it. I can help with that."
  ◊ *Self-Awareness*: "It looks like you just can't wait to share that interesting sound with the class. Holding on to it is a way to be strong."
  ◊ *Connection*: "Look at my face. I am concerned that you are having difficulty holding onto that sound."
  ◊ *Self-Awareness*: "Try to think to yourself, 'I can control my sounds from leaving my mouth,' like your sounds are like water coming out of a faucet. Just try turn them off for a moment."
- **Affirmation:**
  ◊ "The sounds you think of are so creative and are good for the playground."
  ◊ "Impressive how you came up with such an interesting sound for the playground."

Behavior (2)
Falling out of a chair or throwing an object (physical humor)

If you find the child's disruptive behavior ***seems*** for the most part:

1. purposefully provocative; seemingly inflammatory and challenging (see Troubling Child)

2. purposefully silly; mildly pushing limits and redirecting attention (see Testing Child)

- **The Troubling Child**

Core Feeling:	The more outrageous the child's action is, the greater the **sadness/anger** is being experienced by the child.
Core Wish:	Communicates unconscious wish to be **contained** and **supported** as a way of decreasing sense of **danger** and **rejection**.
Core Question:	Limit-testing question—I am being triggered by events because this discussion feels overwhelming; can you accept me and handle me?
Responses:	**Structural & Less Emotional** (see Responses section)

- **The Testing Child**

  Core Feeling: The more outrageous the child's action is, the greater the **sadness/anger** is being experienced by the child.

  Core Wish: Communicates unconscious wish to be **contained** and **validated** as a way of increasing sense of **security** and decreasing sense of **abandonment**.

  Core Question: Limit-testing question—I am feeling bad about myself and need to show this by creating a distraction; do you care about me enough to stop me?

  Responses: **Structural & More Emotional** (see Responses section)

Responses for: Behavior (2) Falling out of a chair or throwing an object (physical humor)

The Troubling Child

- *Structural*:
  - ◊ Clear and calm voice (supportive).
  - ◊ Before class: Check in. Hold eye contact. "I'm with you. Let's keep working on this."
  - ◊ During class: Hand on shoulder; down on knee at eye level. Hold eye contact. Use the Less Emotional responses below.
  - ◊ After class: Check in. Hold eye contact. Reiterate response themes (boundaries, self-care). Track progress with chart.
- *Less Emotional*:
  - ◊ *Boundaries*: "I want you to try to stop your body from doing silly actions."
  - ◊ *Self-Care*: "When you think of a silly action, try to take a deep breath and then let it out very slowly."
  - ◊ *Boundaries*: "I want you to think to yourself, 'I can make a choice whether to let my body do a silly action or not.'"
  - ◊ *Self-Care and Boundaries*: "Keeping your body from doing a silly action is like holding tightly onto a kite string when the kite is way up in the air. Sometimes it is hard, but we have to hold on tightly, so the kite does not fly away."
- *Affirmation*:
  - ◊ "You can be so strong, when you stop your body from doing a silly action."
  - ◊ "Anyone can see what a huge effort you made to hold onto silly actions."

The Testing Child

- *Structural*:
  - ◊ Clear and crisp voice (supportive).

- Before class: Check in. Hold eye contact. "I'm with you. Let's keep working on this."
- During class: Hand on shoulder; down on knee at eye level. Hold eye contact. Use More Emotional responses below.
- After class: Check in. Hold eye contact. Reiterate response themes (boundaries, self-awareness). Track progress with chart.

- **More Emotional:**
  - *Self-Awareness and Boundaries*: "It saddens me when you do a silly action; I feel like it pushes us apart."
  - *Self-Awareness*: "When you do a silly action, I think you feel bad."
  - *Self-Awareness and Boundaries*: "Sometimes bad thoughts, even when they seem funny, just feel like popping out of us. They are like balloons that blow up too big. We have to ask for help to let some air out before it pops."
  - *Self-Awareness*: "Try to take a breath, let it out very slowly, and say to yourself, 'I will be okay,' before you make a silly action."
  - *Boundaries*: "Your silly actions are important. Try to raise your hand if you feel like doing one and I will come over."

- **Affirmation:**
  - "I am proud of you for trying so hard to manage your silly actions."
  - "You took good care of yourself by holding onto your silly actions."

Behavior (3)
Making a humorous and disruptive statement during a lesson

If you find the child's untimely effort at humor *seems* for the most part:

1. purposefully provocative; seemingly inflammatory and challenging (see Troubling Child)

2. purposefully silly; mildly pushing limits and redirecting attention (see Testing Child)

3. disconnected from material; possibly odd and/or confusing to follow (see Hiding Child)

- **The Troubling Child**

    Core Feeling: The more outrageous the child's statement is, the greater the **sadness/anger** is being experienced by the child.

    Core Wish: Communicates unconscious wish to be **contained** and **supported** as a way of decreasing sense of **danger** and **rejection**.

Core Question: Limit-testing question—I am being triggered by events because this discussion feels overwhelming; can you accept me and handle me?

Responses: **Structural & Less Emotional** (see Responses section)

- **The Testing Child**

Core Feeling: The more outrageous the child's statement is, the greater the **sadness/anger** is being experienced by the child.

Core Wish: Communicates unconscious wish to be **contained** and **validated** as a way of increasing sense of **security** and decreasing sense of **abandonment**.

Core Question: Limit-testing question—I am feeling bad about myself and need to show this by creating a distraction; do you care about me enough to stop me?

Responses: **Structural & More Emotional** (see Responses section)

- **The Hiding Child**

Core Feeling: The more outrageous the child's statement is, the greater the **fear/anger** is being experienced by the child.

Core Wish: Communicates unconscious wish to be **noticed** and **validated** as a way of increasing sense of **security** and decreasing sense of **rejection**.

Core Question: Limit-testing question—My statement is a diversion from just how uncomfortable I feel right now; can you accept the way I am and contain me?

Responses: **Verbal & More Emotional** (see Responses section)

Responses for: Behavior (3) Making a humorous and disruptive statement during a lesson

The Troubling Child

- *Structural:*
    ◊ Clear and calm voice (supportive).
    ◊ Before class: Check in. Hold eye contact. "I'm with you. Let's keep working on this."
    ◊ During class: Hand on shoulder; down on knee at eye level. Hold eye contact. Use the Less Emotional responses below.
    ◊ After class: Check in. Hold eye contact. Reiterate response themes (boundaries, self-care). Track progress with chart.
- *Less Emotional:*

Chapter 11. Excessive Clowning

- ◊ *Boundaries*: "I want you to try to stop making those silly statements."
- ◊ *Self-Care*: "Take a deep breath and then let it out very slowly, when you have a silly thought."
- ◊ *Boundaries*: "I want you to think to yourself, 'I can make a choice whether to let out a silly thought or not.'"
- ◊ *Self-Care and Boundaries*: "Holding onto a silly statement that we suddenly think of is like keeping a good surprise from someone. It's really, really difficult, but we just have to do it. And if we can wait for the right time, then we get to surprise them with the silly statement."
- **Affirmation:**
  - ◊ "You can be so strong, when you wait for the right moment to express your silly ideas."
  - ◊ "Anyone can see what a huge effort you made to hold onto silly thoughts."

The Testing Child

- **Structural:**
  - ◊ Clear and crisp voice (supportive).
  - ◊ Before class: Check in. Hold eye contact. "I'm with you. Let's keep working on this."
  - ◊ During class: Hand on shoulder; down on knee at eye level. Hold eye contact. Use More Emotional responses below.
  - ◊ After class: Check in. Hold eye contact. Reiterate response themes (boundaries, self-awareness). Track progress with chart.
- **More Emotional:**
  - ◊ *Self-Awareness and Boundaries*: "It saddens me when you make a silly statement; I feel like it pushes us apart."
  - ◊ *Self-Awareness*: "When you make a silly statement, I think you feel bad."
  - ◊ *Self-Awareness and Boundaries*: "Sometimes bad thoughts, even when they seem funny, just feel like popping out of us. They are like balloons that blow up too big. We have to ask for help to let some air out before it pops."
  - ◊ *Self-Awareness*: "Try to take a breath, let it out very slowly, and say to yourself, 'I will be okay,' before you make a silly statement."
  - ◊ *Self-Awareness and Boundaries*: "Your silly statements are important. Try to raise your hand if you feel like making one and I will come over."
- **Affirmation:**
  - ◊ "I am proud of you for trying so hard to manage your silly statements."
  - ◊ "You took good care of yourself by holding your silly statements."

The Hiding Child

- **Verbal:**
  - ◊ Clear and calm voice (quiet).
  - ◊ Before class: Check in and talk about previous day. Occasional eye contact. "I want to check in with you to see if you remember our talk. We will do this each day."
  - ◊ During class: Occasional eye contact. Maintain distance (two feet at least). No physical contact. Use sound or words to get attention (More Emotional responses below).
  - ◊ After class: Occasional eye contact. Reiterate response themes (connection, self-awareness).
- **More Emotional:**
  - ◊ *Self-Awareness and Connection*: "That interesting statement is very important. I think you are excited, and I want you to try and raise your hand when you realize that you might want to make it. I can help with that."
  - ◊ *Self-Awareness*: "It looks like you just can't wait to share that interesting thought with the class. Holding on to it is a way to be strong."
  - ◊ *Connection*: "Look at my face. I am concerned that you are having difficulty holding onto that thought."
  - ◊ *Self-Awareness*: "Try to think to yourself, 'I can control my thoughts from leaving my mouth,' like your thoughts are like water coming out of a faucet. Just try turn them off for a moment."
- **Affirmation:**
  - ◊ "The thoughts you think of are so creative."
  - ◊ "Impressive how you came up with such an interesting thought."

Your Evolving Responses

As you have read, there are different motivations for your students' behaviors depending on their latent communication patterns. This demonstrates that your responses cannot be "one size fits all" in nature. While we have provided specific words for you to follow, we intend this chapter and the others like it to be a framework for your responses, not a script. You certainly can use our suggested language as you experiment with the interventions we have described. Overtime, it will be more helpful for you to find your own words to communicate with your students. As you continue to try these techniques, using your own communication style will make the responses to your students' behaviors feel authentic and sincere. This will happen naturally. The proposed interventions that we used in this chapter are a starting point and are meant to evolve and grow with your comfort level. This might take some practice, but it will be well worth it to expand your repertoire of potential responses to concerning or disruptive behaviors. You may find that your own words are more effective or more impactful than the words and phrases we have suggested in this book. The more you are a part of the interventions, the more meaningful they may be to your students. As we know, students need repetition, so please be patient as you try out new ways to respond to them.

CHAPTER 12

Aggression, Bullying, Fighting, Out-of-Control Temper

"Anger is an acid that can do more damage to the vessel in which it is stored than anything onto which it is poured."
—Mark Twain

How to Use This Chapter

1. As you prepare to read this chapter, choose one child from your class on whom you wish to focus. Selecting one child at a time allows for a more concentrated exploration of the material and how it relates to each child uniquely. **As a guide, we will use "Melody," a second grader who often teases her classmates when they do not do what she wants.**

2. Read the paragraphs from the following headings to begin the process: *Format and Theme* and *Common Forms of the Behavior*.

3. Choose one behavior that the selected child is exhibiting. Selecting one behavior at a time allows for a more concentrated exploration of the material centering on how the child communicates using this specific behavior. **Melody's behavior of teasing peers when she gets upset with them.**

4. Read the paragraphs from the following headings to learn more about the general category that this behavior falls within from a more holistic perspective: *Manifest Communication* and *Latent Communication*.

5. Read the paragraphs from the heading *Responses and Affirmations* as background to how we structured the proposed responses and the expectation that you will ultimately personalize the responses provided in this chapter.

6. Turn to the page that contains the behavior in question. There you will find the number of the behavior and its name. **We select Behavior (6) Teasing Peers.**

7. On that page, below the number and name, you will find all the possible latent communication prompts for that behavior, ranging from (1) to (4). From these prompts, choose the prompt that most closely reminds you of how this child

exhibits this behavior. Your choice may not fit one prompt exactly. If your sense is that multiple prompts could fit, choose the closest one to begin the process. You can return to the other prompts later. You will notice that each prompt corresponds with a child communication Persona (i.e., Troubling, Testing, Worrying, Hiding). **For Melody, we choose "persistent and willful; seemingly inflammatory and challenging (see Troubling Child)."**

8. After choosing a latent communication prompt, use the child communication Persona and read the corresponding Core Feelings, Core Wish, Core Question. This information describes the underlying meaning of the behavior and creates an empathic guide for you to keep in mind when responding to the child's behavior.

9. On the following page(s), you will find responses and affirmations for the number and name of the behavior in question. **We select Responses for: Behavior (1) Teasing Peers** section **The Troubling Child**. Find and read the responses and affirmations for the behavior in question that corresponds with the child communication Persona.

10. **Try the responses and affirmations with Melody and determine how they feel to you.**

Theme and Format

Each of these behavior chapters in this section of the book should be considered with the following format in mind. In this chapter, we will focus on children who **fight with others, display aggression, bully others, and/or exhibit out-of-control tempers**. That said, the title of this chapter is an umbrella descriptor, and these behaviors comprise a theme or group of communications. We observe these manifest communications as thematic, as there are many permutations within a category of behavior.

Common Forms of This Behavior

- Arguing with peers/teachers
- Bullying peers
- Feeling irate with peers/teachers
- Getting into physical altercations with peers/teachers (hitting, biting, pushing, kicking, etc.)
- Self-harming (persistent nail-biting, cutting oneself, hitting head, running into walls, pulling one's hair, playing with scissors, etc.)
- Teasing peers
- Throwing temper tantrums

Manifest Communication

Anger is an emotion that makes many of us feel uncomfortable. Whether we are feeling it ourselves or responding to another's, anger has an energy that typically affects both emotional and physical boundaries more than any other emotion. Anger can be explosive, fiery, or rageful and the child behaviors related to these expressions are powerful, with an intensity that can repel and attract.

As we will see in the next section, the reasons for this anger are many and varied and the complexity around their underlying dynamics requires close examination. That said, the behavior/communications—the activities generated by anger—are themselves fairly straightforward to identify (albeit often hard to manage). Children argue, bully, defy, disparage, discriminate, fight, harm, menace, tease and yell. They can engage in any and all of these behaviors with observable patterns—quiet or loud, subtle or obvious, direct or indirect.

The passion associated with these behaviors, especially in schools, where concerns of injury and liability are heightened, has led to discourse around anger that can be confusing and unclear. This is especially so when many schools have an administrative policy of zero tolerance. Therefore, we think it is important to clearly define two of the more high-profile ideas in this arena. The concepts of aggression and bullying are ones that we worry are often used indiscriminately and, occasionally, incorrectly.

Aggression is "a forceful action or procedure especially when intended to dominate or master" (Merriam-Webster Dictionary, 2020). It can be as small as a look (micro) and as big as a movement (macro). By this definition, it is not simply boisterous activity that unintentionally can result in injury or harm. There is a purposefulness to aggression that we must differentiate from other types of "injurious" or "hurtful" behavior that may occur as a typical aspect of child development (during relationship building, boundary testing, etc.). Global patterned-based forms of aggression have recognizable names such as: discrimination, prejudice, and oppression.

The other term that we would like to define is bullying. As a subset of aggression, we want to differentiate this behavior from typical peer conflict such as, criticism, teasing, or general roughhousing. Bullying, as a behavior/communication, centers on a pattern of one child's use of dominance to intentionally diminish and/or control another child. It is important to highlight that bullying is far more complex than simply big versus small, strong versus weak, or tough versus meek. It has to do with vulnerability and power; and we will discuss this dynamic further in the next section (Bronfenbrenner, 1979; Craig, 1998; Swearer & Hymel, 2015).

In assessing or calibrating the intensity of any type of aggression, it is helpful to use a continuum from severe to mild. The continuum takes into account the frequency, impact on others, intentionality, and level of remorsefulness (see Figure 12.1).

Using the child Personas of the Troubling child, the Testing child, the Worrying child, and the Hiding child, we will explore specific teacher responses for each type of communication pattern (see Table 12.1). For more detailed information about background for each Persona and the reasoning behind the most productive teacher response configurations, please refer back to their respective chapters.

Chapter 12. Aggression, Bullying, Fighting, Out-of-Control Temper   199

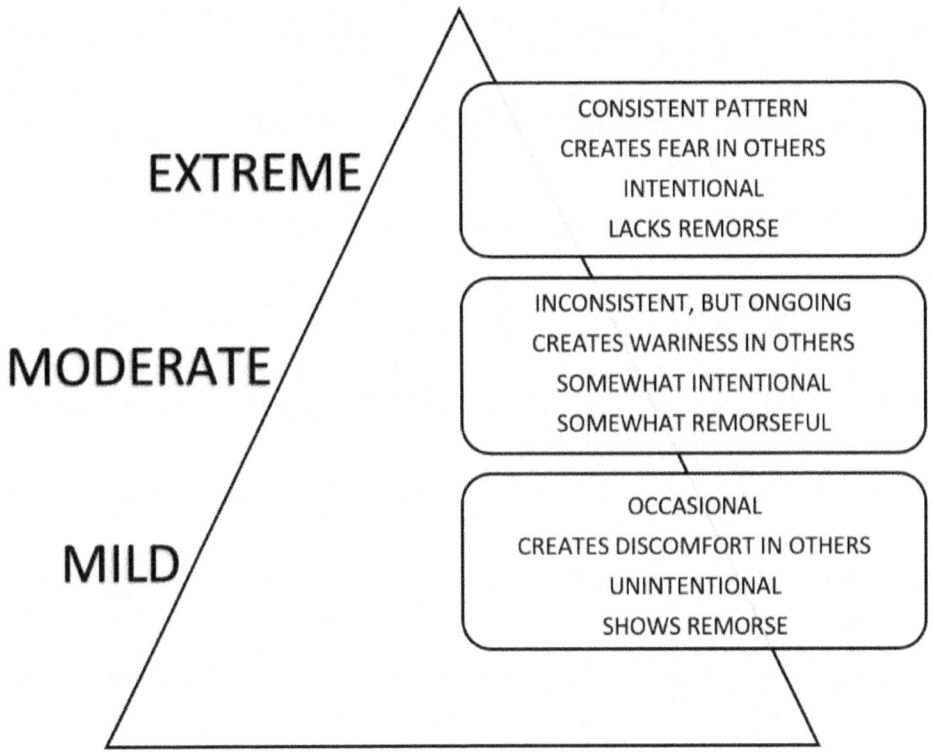

Figure 12.1: Levels of Aggressiveness

**Table 12.1:
Behavior Frequency by Persona**

	Persona			
Behavior	Troubling Child Loud & Over Reactive	Testing Child Loud & Under Reactive	Worrying Child Quiet & Over Reactive	Hiding Child Quiet & Under Reactive
Arguing with peers/teachers	X	X	X	X
Bullying peers	X			
Feeling irate with peers/teachers	X		X	X
Getting into physical altercations with peers/teachers (hitting, biting, pushing, kicking, etc.)	X		X	X
Self-harming	X	X	X	X
Teasing peers	X	X		
Throwing temper tantrums	X		X	X

The absence of an "X" indicates that this Persona does not typically engage in this type of behavior/communication.

Latent Communication

This process is not an exact science and should be conducted more as trial and error. We would like you to take your best professional guess as to your answers to the following inquiries and evaluations. If you find that, after working through the latent communication material and identifying a set of responses, they do not work as you hoped, you can always revise and try again. Just remember, children integrate learning following repetition, so do not give up too soon.

Responses and Affirmations

Children do not learn the first time we teach them a new concept or a task. We say this in order to manage our expectations about how quickly or completely these new interventions will change or extinguish any given behavior.

Let's keep in mind the following factors. First, the development of these behaviors has typically occurred over an extended period of time. Based on the ages of the children we address in this book, any behavior grew over at least two years and up to eight. As much as we would wish it, a behavior that has been developing over a lengthy period of time cannot change "overnight." Actually, rapid change is often poorly integrated by children and cannot be sustained. Second, children integrate responses at different rates based on a variety of factors, including temperament, environment, learning styles, family involvement/support, etc. We have addressed these earlier in the book. Last, we are constructing foundations from which to grow, one brick at a time, foundations that these children will be able to build on and rely on for years to come. To this end, we want you to know that each of your responses is remembered and cataloged by these children for future use—even if it does not outwardly appear to have been during your time with the child. This relates to the corrective emotional experience we wrote about earlier in this book. Your interactions become part of the child's long-term memory, exchanges that are saved for future use.

That said, we want us to have some benchmarks for our expectations. First, we believe that one month is a sufficient timeframe for some level of change in a behavior, given that a specific teacher response is maintained with consistency and repetition. Second, as we cannot factor in changes that are occurring in real time within these children and with their families, the one-month benchmark may need to be altered accordingly. Third, the one-month duration allows for these challenged children to test us. They will imagine that what we are doing cannot be sustained, that it is too good to last. Our consistency and repetition in responding to the underlying message ultimately quiet their negative thoughts. It is then when the child's expectations of the people around them begin to change to an inner message that is more hopeful and positive. This hopefulness alters their communications and behaviors and can become a more embedded part of their future interpersonal relationships.

Behavior (1)
Arguing with peers/teachers

If you find the child's disagreement, debating and/or negotiating *seems* for the most part to be:

1. persistent and willful; seemingly inflammatory and challenging (see Troubling Child)
2. persistently mischievous; mildly vexing, pushing limits/boundaries (see Testing Child)
3. sudden and volatile; possibly upsetting and tense for others (see Worrying Child)
4. sudden and seemingly arbitrary; possibly odd and/or confusing to others (see Hiding Child)

- **The Troubling Child**

    Core Feeling: The more frequent the child's arguing is, the greater the **sadness/anger** is being experienced by the child.

    Core Wish: Communicates unconscious wish to be **contained** and **supported** as a way of decreasing sense of **danger** and **rejection**.

    Core Question: Limit-testing question—I am being triggered by events because this moment in class feels overwhelming; can you accept me and handle me?

    Responses: **Structural & Less Emotional** (see Responses section)

- **The Testing Child**

    Core Feeling: The more frequent the child's arguing is, the greater the **sadness/anger** is being experienced by the child.

    Core Wish: Communicates unconscious wish to be **contained** and **validated** as a way of increasing sense of **security** and decreasing sense of **abandonment**.

    Core Question: Limit-testing question—I am feeling bad about myself and need to show this by creating a distraction; do you care about me enough to stop me?

    Responses: **Structural & More Emotional** (see Responses section)

- **The Worrying Child**

Core Feeling:	The more frequent the child's arguing is, the greater the **fear/anger** is being experienced by the child.
Core Wish:	Communicates unconscious wish to be **noticed** and **supported** as a way of decreasing sense of **danger** and **abandonment**.
Core Question:	Limit-testing question—I am being triggered by events and this is an expression of how afraid I am; do you care enough to protect me?
Responses:	**Verbal & Less Emotional** (see Responses section)

- **The Hiding Child**

Core Feeling:	The more frequent the child's arguing is, the greater the **fear/anger** is being experienced by the child.
Core Wish:	Communicates unconscious wish to be **noticed** and **validated** as a way of increasing sense of **security** and decreasing sense of **rejection**.
Core Question:	Limit-testing question—My behavior is a diversion from just how uncomfortable I feel right now; can you accept the way I am and contain me?
Responses:	**Verbal & More Emotional** (see Responses section)

Responses for: Behavior (1) Arguing with peers/teachers

The Troubling Child

- *Structural*:
    - ◊ Clear and calm voice (supportive).
    - ◊ Before class: Check in. Hold eye contact. "I'm with you. Let's keep working on this."
    - ◊ During class: Hand on shoulder; down on knee at eye level. Hold eye contact. Use the Less Emotional responses below.
    - ◊ After class: Check in. Hold eye contact. Reiterate response themes (boundaries, self-care). Track progress with chart.
- *Less Emotional*:
    - ◊ *Self-Care and Boundaries*: "I want you to try to hold on to your arguments. You are more in charge when you don't push my ideas away."
    - ◊ *Self-Care*: "Wait, take a deep breath and let it out very slowly when you feel like telling me I'm wrong."
    - ◊ *Boundaries*: "I want you to think to yourself, 'I have a choice to agree or not agree with someone.'"

Chapter 12. Aggression, Bullying, Fighting, Out-of-Control Temper

- ◊ *Self-Care and Boundaries*: "I want you to think about the way we eat our meals. We eat healthy food first and then sugary stuff. Even if it doesn't seem fair, we follow this pattern because it's better for us. We can argue, when we don't think something is fair. Sometimes, things can feel fairer if we understand someone's reasons first."
- *Affirmation*:
    - ◊ "Controlling your arguments before they leave your mouth takes great strength."
    - ◊ "Anyone can see what a huge effort you are making to not argue."

The Testing Child

- *Structural*:
    - ◊ Clear and crisp voice (supportive).
    - ◊ Before class: Check in. Hold eye contact. "I'm with you. Let's keep working on this."
    - ◊ During class: Hand on shoulder; down on knee at eye level. Hold eye contact. Use More Emotional responses below.
    - ◊ After class: Check in. Hold eye contact. Reiterate response themes (boundaries, self-awareness). Track progress with chart.
- *More Emotional*:
    - ◊ *Self-Awareness and Boundaries*: "It saddens me when you argue with what I say, because I feel like it pushes us apart."
    - ◊ *Self-Awareness*: "When you argue with what I say, I think you feel bad."
    - ◊ *Self-Awareness and Boundaries*: "Sometimes upset thoughts just feel like they need to come out of our mouths. This can make us feel worse. I want you to ask for my help to keep control of your arguing."
    - ◊ *Self-Awareness*: "Try to take a deep breath and let it out very slowly; and say to yourself, 'I will be okay,' before you let your argument out into the classroom."
    - ◊ *Self-Awareness and Boundaries*: "I want you to understand that my reasons for what we do together is important. Try to raise your hand if you feel like arguing and I will come over."
- *Affirmation*:
    - ◊ "I am proud of you for trying so hard to not arguing."
    - ◊ "You took good care of yourself by not arguing."

The Worrying Child

- *Verbal*:
    - ◊ Clear and calm voice (quiet).
    - ◊ Before class: Check in and talk about previous day. Occasional eye contact. "I want to check in with you to see how our talk felt for you. We can do this each day."
    - ◊ During class: Occasional eye contact. Maintain distance (two feet at

least). No physical contact. Use sound or words to get attention (Less Emotional responses below).
- ◊ After class: Occasional eye contact. Reiterate response themes (connection, self-care).
- **Less Emotional**:
  - ◊ *Self-Care*: "Take a deep breath and let it out very slowly when you want to argue with someone in the classroom. The argument can wait until you feel calmer."
  - ◊ *Self-Care and Connection*: "When we suddenly have a big thought, it can help us feel safer if we try and slow down a little. When you feel like arguing with someone, try to come over and see me first."
  - ◊ *Self-Care and Connection*: "Sometimes hearing your arguments helps me understand you better."
  - ◊ *Self-Care and Connection*: "When you argue, it makes me think about your safety. I would like to ask you about what you are thinking."
- **Affirmation**:
  - ◊ "Being in control of your need to argue takes strength."
  - ◊ "You are brave to try to control your need to argue in the classroom."

The Hiding Child

- **Verbal**:
  - ◊ Clear and calm voice (quiet).
  - ◊ Before class: Check in and talk about previous day. Occasional eye contact. "I want to check in with you to see if you remember our talk. We will do this each day."
  - ◊ During class: Occasional eye contact. Maintain distance (two feet at least). No physical contact. Use sound or words to get attention (More Emotional responses below).
  - ◊ After class: Occasional eye contact. Reiterate response themes (connection, self-awareness).
- **More Emotional**:
  - ◊ *Self-Awareness and Connection*: "When arguing with someone becomes very important to you, I think you have big feelings. Please try raising your hand if you feel like arguing. I can help with that."
  - ◊ *Self-Awareness*: "It looks like you just can't wait when you feel like you need to disagree with someone. It's important for you to know that waiting is a way to be strong."
  - ◊ *Connection*: "Look at my face. I am worried that you cannot keep yourself from arguing."
  - ◊ *Self-Awareness and Connection*: "Try to you to think to yourself, 'I can control my need to argue. My need to argue is like water coming out of a faucet. I can try to turn the faucet off for a moment.'"
- **Affirmation**:
  - ◊ "I see you using your thoughts to try and control your need to argue."

◊ "I am impressed how you are deciding to keep control of your arguing."

Behavior (2)
Bullying peers

If you find the child's oppressive provocation of others *seems* for the most part:

1. persistent and willful; seemingly inflammatory and challenging (see Troubling Child)

- **The Troubling Child**

Core Feeling:	The more frequent the child's bullying is, the greater the **sadness/anger** is being experienced by the child.
Core Wish:	Communicates unconscious wish to be **contained** and **supported** as a way of decreasing sense of **danger** and **rejection**.
Core Question:	Limit-testing question—I am being triggered by events because this moment in class feels overwhelming; can you accept me and handle me?
Responses:	**Structural & Less Emotional** (see Responses section)

Responses for: Behavior (2) Bullying peers

The Troubling Child

- ***Structural***:
    ◊ Clear and calm voice (supportive).
    ◊ Before class: Check in. Hold eye contact. "I'm with you. Let's keep working on this."
    ◊ During class: Hand on shoulder; down on knee at eye level. Hold eye contact. Use the Less Emotional responses below.
    ◊ After class: Check in. Hold eye contact. Reiterate response themes (boundaries, self-care). Track progress with chart.
- ***Less Emotional***:
    ◊ *Self-Care and Boundaries*: "I want you to stop making your classmate feel afraid. You are more in charge when you do not use cruel words and actions to push your classmates away."
    ◊ *Self-Care*: "Wait, take a deep breath and let it out very slowly when you feel like being cruel to a classmate and making them scared."
    ◊ *Boundaries*: "I want you to think to yourself, 'I have a choice to be cruel or not to be cruel to my classmate.'"

◊ *Self-Care and Boundaries*: "I want you to imagine that there is a big cat chasing a tiny mouse. The cat sees the mouse running away. In this story, the cat thinks about how the mouse might feel about being chased. The cat realizes that the mouse feels afraid and alone. The cat knows that feeling afraid and alone feels terrible because sometimes he gets chased by the dog and feels the same way. The cat decides to stop chasing the mouse."
- *Affirmation*:
  ◊ "Controlling your actions when you want to be cruel to someone takes great strength."
  ◊ "Anyone can see what a huge effort are making to not be cruel to your classmate."

Behavior (3)
Feeling irate with peers/teachers

If you find the child's intense emotions of outrage *seem* for the most part:

1. persistent and willful; seemingly inflammatory and challenging (see Troubling Child)

2. sudden and volatile; possibly upsetting and tense for others (see Worrying Child)

3. sudden and seemingly arbitrary; possibly odd and/or confusing to others (see Hiding Child)

- **The Troubling Child**

Core Feeling:	The more frequently the child expresses this irate stance, the greater the **sadness/anger** is being experienced by the child.
Core Wish:	Communicates unconscious wish to be **contained** and **supported** as a way of decreasing sense of **danger** and **rejection**.
Core Question:	Limit-testing question—I am being triggered by events because this moment in class feels overwhelming; can you accept me and handle me?
Responses:	**Structural & Less Emotional** (see Responses section)

- **The Worrying Child**

Core Feeling:	The more frequently the child expresses this irate stance, the greater the **fear/anger** is being experienced by the child.
Core Wish:	Communicates unconscious wish to be **noticed** and **supported** as a way of decreasing sense of **danger** and **abandonment**.

Core Question:	Limit-testing question—I am being triggered by events and this is an expression of how afraid I am; do you care enough to protect me?
Responses:	**Verbal & Less Emotional** (see Responses section)

- **The Hiding Child**

Core Feeling:	The more frequently the child expresses this irate stance, the greater the **fear/anger** is being experienced by the child.
Core Wish:	Communicates unconscious wish to be **noticed** and **validated** as a way of increasing sense of **security** and decreasing sense of **rejection**.
Core Question:	Limit-testing question—My behavior is a diversion from just how uncomfortable I feel right now; can you accept the way I am and contain me?
Responses:	**Verbal & More Emotional** (see Responses section)

Responses for: Behavior (3) Feeling irate with peers/teachers

The Troubling Child

- ***Structural*:**
    - ◊ Clear and calm voice (supportive).
    - ◊ Before class: Check in. Hold eye contact. "I'm with you. Let's keep working on this."
    - ◊ During class: Hand on shoulder; down on knee at eye level. Hold eye contact. Use the Less Emotional responses below.
    - ◊ After class: Check in. Hold eye contact. Reiterate response themes (boundaries, self-care). Track progress with chart.
- ***Less Emotional*:**
    - ◊ *Self-Care and Boundaries*: "I want you to try to hold on to your angry feelings. You are more in charge when you don't push people away with your angry feelings."
    - ◊ *Self-Care*: "Wait, take a deep breath and let it out very slowly when you feel yourself getting angry."
    - ◊ *Boundaries*: "I want you to think to yourself, 'I have a choice to be mad or to not be mad.'"
    - ◊ *Self-Care and Boundaries*: "I want you to think about the doctor giving you a shot. Shots are medicine and doctor give us shots to keep us healthy. It does not seem fair, because shots hurt, and pain is bad. We can very be angry, when we don't think something is fair. Sometimes, things can feel fairer if we understand someone's reasons first."
- ***Affirmation*:**

- ◊ "Controlling your angry feelings takes great strength."
- ◊ "Anyone can see what a huge effort you are making to control your angry feelings."

The Worrying Child

- **Verbal**:
    - ◊ Clear and calm voice (quiet).
    - ◊ Before class: Check in and talk about previous day. Occasional eye contact. "I want to check in with you to see how our talk felt for you. We can do this each day."
    - ◊ During class: Occasional eye contact. Maintain distance (two feet at least). No physical contact. Use sound or words to get attention (Less Emotional responses below).
    - ◊ After class: Occasional eye contact. Reiterate response themes (connection, self-care).
- **Less Emotional**:
    - ◊ *Self-Care*: "Take a deep breath and let it out very slowly when you are feeling angry with someone in the classroom. The angry feelings can wait until you feel calmer."
    - ◊ *Self-Care and Connection*: "When we suddenly have a big feeling, it can help us feel safer if we try and slow down a little. When you feel very angry with someone, try to come over and see me first."
    - ◊ *Connection*: "Sometimes knowing what is making you angry helps me understand you better."
    - ◊ *Self-Care and Connection*: "When you are very angry, it makes me think about your safety. I would like to ask you about what you are thinking when you get angry."
- **Affirmation**:
    - ◊ "Being in control of your feelings takes strength."
    - ◊ "You are brave to try to control your angry feelings in the classroom."

The Hiding Child

- **Verbal**:
    - ◊ Clear and calm voice (quiet).
    - ◊ Before class: Check in and talk about previous day. Occasional eye contact. "I want to check in with you to see if you remember our talk. We will do this each day."
    - ◊ During class: Occasional eye contact. Maintain distance (two feet at least). No physical contact. Use sound or words to get attention (More Emotional responses below).
    - ◊ After class: Occasional eye contact. Reiterate response themes (connection, self-awareness).

- *More Emotional*:
    ◊ *Self-Awareness and Connection*: "When you suddenly feel very angry at someone in a very strong way, I think you are having big feelings. I am worried about you. I want you to try raising your hand if you start to feel very angry. I can help with that."
    ◊ *Self-Awareness*: "It looks like your angry feelings just start to heat up when you feel something is wrong. It's important for you to know controlling your angry feelings is a way to be strong."
    ◊ *Connection*: "Look at my face. I am worried that you cannot keep yourself from becoming very angry."
    ◊ *Self-Awareness and Connection*: "Try to think to yourself, 'I am so upset that things are not going my way, but I can try to control my angry feelings when they bubble up. My angry feelings are like boiling water in a pot. I can try to turn the heat down or ask for someone to help me turn the heat down.'"
- *Affirmation*:
    ◊ "I see you using your thoughts to try and control your angry feelings."
    ◊ "I am impressed how you are deciding to keep control of your anger."

Behavior (4)
Getting into physical altercations with peers/ teachers (hitting, biting, pushing, kicking, etc.)

If you find the child's physical aggression *seems* for the most part:

1. persistent and willful; seemingly inflammatory and challenging (see Troubling Child)

2. sudden and volatile; possibly upsetting and alarming for others (see Worrying Child)

3. sudden and seemingly arbitrary; possibly odd and/or confusing to others (see Hiding Child)

- **The Troubling Child**

    Core Feeling: The more frequent the child's behavior is, the greater the **sadness/anger** is being experienced by the child.

    Core Wish: Communicates unconscious wish to be **contained** and **supported** as a way of decreasing sense of **danger** and **rejection**.

    Core Question: Limit-testing question—I am being triggered by events because this moment in class feels overwhelming; can you accept me and handle me?

    Responses: **Structural & Less Emotional** (see Responses section)

- **The Worrying Child**

Core Feeling:	The more frequent the child's behavior is, the greater the **fear/anger** is being experienced by the child.
Core Wish:	Communicates unconscious wish to be **noticed** and **supported** as a way of decreasing sense of **danger** and **abandonment**.
Core Question:	Limit-testing question—I am being triggered by events and this is an expression of how afraid I am; do you care enough to protect me?
Responses:	**Verbal & Less Emotional** (see Responses section)

- **The Hiding Child**

Core Feeling:	The more frequent the child's behavior is, the greater the **fear/anger** is being experienced by the child.
Core Wish:	Communicates unconscious wish to be **noticed** and **validated** as a way of increasing sense of **security** and decreasing sense of **rejection**.
Core Question:	Limit-testing question—My behavior is a diversion from just how uncomfortable I feel right now; can you accept the way I am and contain me?
Responses:	**Verbal & More Emotional** (see Responses section)

Responses for: Behavior (4) Getting into physical altercations with peers/teachers

The Troubling Child

- *Structural*:
    - ◊ Clear and calm voice (supportive).
    - ◊ Before class: Check in. Hold eye contact. "I'm with you. Let's keep working on this."
    - ◊ During class: Hand on shoulder; down on knee at eye level. Hold eye contact. Use the Less Emotional responses below.
    - ◊ After class: Check in. Hold eye contact. Reiterate response themes (boundaries, self-care). Track progress with chart.
- *Less Emotional*:
    - ◊ *Self-Care and Boundaries*: "Try to control your body when your anger makes you want to hit someone. You are more in charge when you don't push people away by hitting them with your body."
    - ◊ *Self-Care*: "Wait, take a deep breath and let it out very slowly when you think about hitting someone."

Chapter 12. Aggression, Bullying, Fighting, Out-of-Control Temper

◊ *Boundaries*: "I want you to think to yourself, 'I have a choice to hit someone or to not hit them.'"
◊ *Self-Care and Boundaries*: "I want you to imagine a pot of water on a stove. When you turn up the heat under the pot, the water heats up and starts to boil. We need to be careful because if boiling becomes too much, burning water can pop over the edge of the pot and could hurt someone. Before this happens, we have to be able to turn the heat down to stay safe."

- *Affirmation*:
    ◊ "Controlling your body when it gets angry takes great strength."
    ◊ "Anyone can see what a huge effort you are making to control your angry body."

The Worrying Child

- *Verbal*:
    ◊ Clear and calm voice (quiet).
    ◊ Before class: Check in and talk about previous day. Occasional eye contact. "I want to check in with you to see how our talk felt for you. We can do this each day."
    ◊ During class: Occasional eye contact. Maintain distance (two feet at least). No physical contact. Use sound or words to get attention (Less Emotional responses below).
    ◊ After class: Occasional eye contact. Reiterate response themes (connection, self-care).
- *Less Emotional*:
    ◊ *Self-Care*: "Take a deep breath and let it out very slowly when you are feeling angry with people and want to hit them. The angry feelings can wait until you feel calmer and safer."
    ◊ *Self-Care and Connection*: "When we suddenly have a big, angry feeling that makes our body want to hit someone, we are safer if we try and slow down a little. Try to come over and see me first."
    ◊ *Self-Care and Connection*: "Knowing when you may be thinking about hurting someone else, helps me understand you better. Try to come over and see me first."
    ◊ *Self-Care and Connection*: "When you have an angry body, it makes me think about your safety. To help with safety, I would like to ask you about what you are thinking when you get angry like this."
- *Affirmation*:
    ◊ "Being in control of your angry body takes strength."
    ◊ "You are brave to try to control your angry body in the classroom."

The Hiding Child

- *Verbal*:
    ◊ Clear and calm voice (quiet).

◊ Before class: Check in and talk about previous day. Occasional eye contact. "I want to check in with you to see if you remember our talk. We will do this each day."
◊ During class: Occasional eye contact. Maintain distance (two feet at least). No physical contact. Use sound or words to get attention (More Emotional responses below).
◊ After class: Occasional eye contact. Reiterate response themes (connection, self-awareness).

- *More Emotional*:
    ◊ *Self-Awareness and Connection*: "When you suddenly feel angry at people and want to hit them, I think you are having big feelings and I am worried about you. I want you to try raising your hand when you start to feel your body wanting to hit. I can help with that."
    ◊ *Self-Awareness*: "It looks like your angry body just starts to heat up sometimes, and has a hard time staying in control. It's important for you to know controlling your angry body is a way to be strong and safe."
    ◊ *Self-Awareness and Connection*: "Look at my face. I am worried that you cannot keep yourself from using your angry body to hit someone."
    ◊ *Self-Awareness and Connection*: "Try to think to yourself, 'I can try to control my angry body when it starts to heat up. My angry feelings are like a boiling water in a pot. When I need to, I can get help to turn the heat down before I use my angry body to hit someone.'"
- *Affirmation*:
    ◊ "I see you using your thoughts to try and control your angry body."
    ◊ "I am impressed how you are deciding to keep control of your anger body."

Behavior (5)
Self-harming (persistent nail-biting, cutting oneself, hitting head, running into walls, pulling one's hair, playing with scissors, etc.)

If you find the child's self-harming behaviors **seem** for the most part:

1. persistent and willful; seemingly inflammatory and challenging (see Troubling Child)

2. persistently noticeable; mildly concerning, pushing limits/boundaries (see Testing Child)

3. sudden and volatile; typically upsetting and disconcerting for others (see Worrying Child)

4. sudden and seemingly arbitrary; possibly odd and/or confusing to others (see Hiding Child)

Chapter 12. Aggression, Bullying, Fighting, Out-of-Control Temper

- **The Troubling Child**

  - *Core Feeling*: The more frequent and/or acute the child's self-harming is, the greater the **sadness/anger** is being experienced by the child.
  - *Core Wish*: Communicates unconscious wish to be **contained** and **supported** as a way of decreasing sense of **danger** and **rejection**.
  - *Core Question*: Limit-testing question—I am being triggered by events because this moment in class feels overwhelming; can you accept me and protect me?
  - *Responses*: **Structural & Less Emotional** (see Responses section)

- **The Testing Child**

  - *Core Feeling*: The more frequent and/or acute the child's self-harming is, the greater the **sadness/anger** is being experienced by the child.
  - *Core Wish*: Communicates unconscious wish to be **contained** and **validated** as a way of increasing sense of **security** and decreasing sense of **abandonment**.
  - *Core Question*: Limit-testing question—I am feeling bad about myself and need to show this by creating a distraction; do you care about me enough to stop me?
  - *Responses*: **Structural & More Emotional** (see Responses section)

- **The Worrying Child**

  - *Core Feeling*: The more frequent and/or acute the child's self-harming is, the greater the **fear/anger** is being experienced by the child.
  - *Core Wish*: Communicates unconscious wish to be **noticed** and **supported** as a way of decreasing sense of **danger** and **abandonment**.
  - *Core Question*: Limit-testing question—I am being triggered by events and this is an expression of how afraid I am; do you care enough to protect me?
  - *Responses*: **Verbal & Less Emotional** (see Responses section)

- **The Hiding Child**

  - *Core Feeling*: The more frequent and/or acute the child's self-harming is, the greater the **fear/anger** is being experienced by the child.
  - *Core Wish*: Communicates unconscious wish to be **noticed** and **validated** as a way of increasing sense of **security** and decreasing sense of **rejection**.

Core Question: Limit-testing question—My behavior is a diversion from just how uncomfortable I feel right now; can you accept the way I am and protect me?

Responses: **Verbal & More Emotional** (see Responses section)

Responses for: Behavior (5) Self-harming

The Troubling Child

- *Structural*:
    - ◊ Clear and calm voice (supportive).
    - ◊ Before class: Check in. Hold eye contact. "I'm with you. Let's keep working on this."
    - ◊ During class: Hand on shoulder; down on knee at eye level. Hold eye contact. Use the Less Emotional responses below.
    - ◊ After class: Check in. Hold eye contact. Reiterate response themes (boundaries, self-care). Track progress with chart.
- *Less Emotional*:
    - ◊ *Self-Care and Boundaries*: "Try to control your body when your anger makes you want to hurt yourself. You are more in charge when you keep yourself safe and don't push people away who care."
    - ◊ *Self-Care*: "Wait, take a deep breath and let it out very slowly when you think about hurting yourself."
    - ◊ *Boundaries*: "I want you to think to yourself, 'I have a choice to keep myself safe or not.'"
    - ◊ *Self-Care and Boundaries*: "I want you to imagine a pot of water on a stove. When you turn up the heat under the pot, the water heats up and starts to boil. We need to be careful because if boiling becomes too much, burning water can pop over the edge of the pot and we can get burned badly. Before this happens, we have to be able to turn the heat down to stay safe."
- *Affirmation*:
    - ◊ "Keeping yourself safe when you get upset takes great strength."
    - ◊ "Anyone can see what a huge effort you are making keep yourself safe."

The Testing Child

- *Structural*:
    - ◊ Clear and crisp voice (supportive).
    - ◊ Before class: Check in. Hold eye contact. "I'm with you. Let's keep working on this."
    - ◊ During class: Hand on shoulder; down on knee at eye level. Hold eye contact. Use More Emotional responses below.

Chapter 12. Aggression, Bullying, Fighting, Out-of-Control Temper

◊ After class: Check in. Hold eye contact. Reiterate response themes (boundaries, self-awareness). Track progress with chart.
- **More Emotional:**
    ◊ *Self-Awareness and Boundaries*: "It saddens me when I see you hurting yourself, because I feel like it pushes us apart."
    ◊ *Self-Awareness*: "When you don't keep yourself safe, I think you feel bad."
    ◊ *Self-Awareness and Boundaries*: "Sometimes we feel like we need to do something with our upset feelings. This can make us feel worse. I want you to ask for help if you are having trouble keeping yourself safe."
    ◊ *Self-Awareness*: "Try to take a deep breath and let it out very slowly; and say to yourself, 'I will be okay,' before you do something that could hurt you."
    ◊ *Self-Awareness and Boundaries*: "I want you to understand that my reasons for wanting you to be safe are important. Try to notice if you feel like hurting yourself and let me know. I will come over."
- **Affirmation:**
    ◊ "I am proud of you for trying so hard to keep yourself safe."
    ◊ "You took good care of yourself not doing anything that hurts you."

The Worrying Child

- **Verbal:**
    ◊ Clear and calm voice (quiet).
    ◊ Before class: Check in and talk about previous day. Occasional eye contact. "I want to check in with you to see how our talk felt for you. We can do this each day."
    ◊ During class: Occasional eye contact. Maintain distance (two feet at least). No physical contact. Use sound or words to get attention (Less Emotional responses below).
    ◊ After class: Occasional eye contact. Reiterate response themes (connection, self-care).
- **Less Emotional:**
    ◊ *Self-Care*: "Take a deep breath and let it out very slowly when you are feeling unsafe or like you want to hurt yourself. Try to make the hurting thoughts wait until you feel calmer."
    ◊ *Self-Care and Connection*: "When we suddenly have a big, angry feeling that makes our body want to hurt our self, we are safer if we try and slow down a little. Try to come over and see me first if you are having these thoughts."
    ◊ *Self-Care and Connection*: "Knowing when someone I care about might be thinking about hurting themselves, helps me protect them better."
    ◊ *Self-Care and Connection*: "When you have danger thoughts, it makes me think about your safety. To help with your safety, I would like to ask you about what exactly you are thinking when you feel this way."

- *Affirmation*:
  - ◊ "Being in control of your angry and unsafe thoughts takes strength."
  - ◊ "You are brave to try to control your angry and unsafe thoughts in the classroom."

The Hiding Child

- *Verbal*:
  - ◊ Clear and calm voice (quiet).
  - ◊ Before class: Check in and talk about previous day. Occasional eye contact. "I want to check in with you to see if you remember our talk. We will do this each day."
  - ◊ During class: Occasional eye contact. Maintain distance (two feet at least). No physical contact. Use sound or words to get attention (More Emotional responses below).
  - ◊ After class: Occasional eye contact. Reiterate response themes (connection, self-awareness).
- *More Emotional*:
  - ◊ *Self-Awareness and Connection*: "When you suddenly feel angry and want to hurt yourself, I think you have big feelings. Try raising your hand when you start to feel these unsafe feelings. I can help with them."
  - ◊ *Self-Awareness*: "It looks like your unsafe thoughts just start to heat up sometimes, and you have a hard time staying in control of them. It's important for you to know controlling your unsafe thoughts is a way to be strong and safe."
  - ◊ *Self-Awareness and Connection*: "Look at my face. I am worried that you cannot keep yourself safe."
  - ◊ *Self-Awareness and Connection*: "Try to think to yourself, 'I can try to control my unsafe thoughts when they start to heat up. My unsafe thoughts are like a boiling water in a pot. When I need it, I can get help to turn the heat down before I use my anger to hurt myself.'"
- *Affirmation*:
  - ◊ "I see you using your thoughts to try and control your unsafe feelings."
  - ◊ "I am impressed how you are deciding to keep control of your anger and safety."

Behavior (6)
Teasing peers

If you find the child's playful, yet unkind, provocation of others **seems** for the most part:

1. persistent and willful; seemingly inflammatory and challenging (see Troubling Child)

2. persistently mischievous; mildly vexing, pushing limits/boundaries (see Testing Child)

- **The Troubling Child**

    Core Feeling: The more frequent the child's teasing of others is, the greater the **sadness/anger** is being experienced by the child.

    Core Wish: Communicates unconscious wish to be **contained** and **supported** as a way of decreasing sense of **danger** and **rejection**.

    Core Question: Limit-testing question—I am being triggered by events because this moment in class feels overwhelming; can you accept me and handle me?

    Responses: **Structural & Less Emotional** (see Responses section)

- **The Testing Child**

    Core Feeling: The more frequent the child's teasing of others is, the greater the **sadness/anger** is being experienced by the child.

    Core Wish: Communicates unconscious wish to be **contained** and **validated** as a way of increasing sense of **security** and decreasing sense of **abandonment**.

    Core Question: Limit-testing question—I am feeling bad about myself and need to show this by creating a distraction; do you care about me enough to stop me?

    Responses: **Structural & More Emotional** (see Responses section)

Responses for: Behavior (6) Teasing peers

The Troubling Child

- ***Structural:***
    - ◊ Clear and calm voice (supportive).
    - ◊ Before class: Check in. Hold eye contact. "I'm with you. Let's keep working on this."
    - ◊ During class: Hand on shoulder; down on knee at eye level. Hold eye contact. Use the Less Emotional responses below.
    - ◊ After class: Check in. Hold eye contact. Reiterate response themes (boundaries, self-care). Track progress with chart.
- ***Less Emotional:***
    - ◊ *Self-Care and Boundaries*: "I want you to try to stop making your classmates feel sad. You are more in charge when you do not use unkind words and actions to push your classmates away."

- ◊ *Self-Care*: "Wait, take a deep breath and let it out very slowly when you feel like being unkind."
- ◊ *Boundaries*: "I want you to think to yourself, 'I have a choice to be unkind or not to my classmate.'"
- ◊ *Self-Care and Boundaries*: "I want you to imagine that there is a turtle trying to climb a hill, but he keeps falling down. The other animals see the turtle falling down and they laugh at him. In this story, the animals realize that the turtle feels sad and not smart when he falls down and is laughed at. The animals know that feeling sad and not smart feels terrible because sometimes they feel the same way. The animals decide to stop laughing at the turtle."
- **Affirmation**:
  - ◊ "Controlling your actions when you want to be unkind to someone takes great strength."
  - ◊ "Anyone can see what a huge effort are making to not be unkind to your classmate."

The Testing Child

- **Structural**:
  - ◊ Clear and crisp voice (supportive).
  - ◊ Before class: Check in. Hold eye contact. "I'm with you. Let's keep working on this."
  - ◊ During class: Hand on shoulder; down on knee at eye level. Hold eye contact. Use More Emotional responses below.
  - ◊ After class: Check in. Hold eye contact. Reiterate response themes (boundaries, self-awareness). Track progress with chart.
- **More Emotional**:
  - ◊ *Self-Awareness and Boundaries*: "I am sad when you make other people feel sad, because I feel like it pushes us apart."
  - ◊ *Self-Awareness*: "When you make other people feel sad, I think you feel bad."
  - ◊ *Self-Awareness and Boundaries*: "Sometimes unkind thoughts just feel like they need to come out of our mouths. This can make us feel worse. I want you to ask for my help to keep control of unkind thoughts."
  - ◊ *Self-Awareness and Boundaries*: "Try to take a deep breath and let it out very slowly; and say to yourself, 'I will be okay,' before you let your unkind words out into the classroom. Try to raise your hand if you feel like saying something unkind and I will come over."
- **Affirmation**:
  - ◊ "I am proud of you for trying so hard to not say unkind words to others."
  - ◊ "You took good care of yourself by not saying unkind words to anyone."

Behavior (7)
Throwing temper tantrums

If you find the child's intense physical expression of a loss of control *seems* for the most part:

1. persistent and willful; seemingly inflammatory and challenging (see Troubling Child)
2. sudden and volatile; possibly upsetting and tense for others (see Worrying Child)
3. sudden and seemingly arbitrary; possibly odd and/or confusing to others (see Hiding Child)

- **The Troubling Child**

Core Feeling:	The more frequently the child reaches the level of temper tantrum, the greater the **sadness/anger** is being experienced by the child.
Core Wish:	Communicates unconscious wish to be **contained** and **supported** as a way of decreasing sense of **danger** and **rejection**.
Core Question:	Limit-testing question—I am being triggered by events because this moment in class feels overwhelming; can you accept me and handle me?
Responses:	**Structural & Less Emotional** (see Responses section)

- **The Worrying Child**

Core Feeling:	The more frequently the child reaches the level of temper tantrum, the greater the **fear/anger** is being experienced by the child.
Core Wish:	Communicates unconscious wish to be **noticed** and **supported** as a way of decreasing sense of **danger** and **abandonment**.
Core Question:	Limit-testing question—I am being triggered by events and this is an expression of how afraid I am; do you care enough to protect me?
Responses:	**Verbal & Less Emotional** (see Responses section)

- **The Hiding Child**

Core Feeling:	The more frequently the child reaches the level of temper tantrum, the greater the **fear/anger** is being experienced by the child.

Core Wish: Communicates unconscious wish to be **noticed** and **validated** as a way of increasing sense of **security** and decreasing sense of **rejection**.

Core Question: Limit-testing question—My behavior is a diversion from just how uncomfortable I feel right now; can you accept the way I am and contain me?

Responses: **Verbal & More Emotional** (see Responses section)

Responses for: Behavior (7) Throwing temper tantrums

The Troubling Child

- ***Structural***:
    - ◊ Clear and calm voice (supportive).
    - ◊ Before class: Check in. Hold eye contact. "I'm with you. Let's keep working on this."
    - ◊ During class: Hand on shoulder; down on knee at eye level. Hold eye contact. Use the Less Emotional responses below.
    - ◊ After class: Check in. Hold eye contact. Reiterate response themes (boundaries, self-care). Track progress with chart.
- ***Less Emotional***:
    - ◊ *Self-Care and Boundaries*: "I want you to try to hold on to your body's super angry feelings. You are more in charge when you don't push people away with your angry feelings."
    - ◊ *Self-Care*: "Wait, take a deep breath and let it out very slowly when you feel your body getting angry."
    - ◊ *Boundaries*: "I want you to think to yourself, 'I have a choice for my body to be very mad or not be.'"
    - ◊ *Self-Care and Boundaries*: "I want you to think about the doctor giving you a shot. It does not seem fair, because shots really hurt and maybe we do not want them. We can very be angry, when we have to do something we do not want to do. Sometimes it can help for someone to explain why a shot is important, even though it hurts, or someone to sit with us when we feel the shot is not fair but have to do it anyway."
- ***Affirmation***:
    - ◊ "Controlling your angry feelings takes great strength."
    - ◊ "Anyone can see what a huge effort you are making to control your angry feelings."

The Worrying Child

- ***Verbal***:
    - ◊ Clear and calm voice (quiet).
    - ◊ Before class: Check in and talk about previous day. Occasional eye

contact. "I want to check in with you to see how our talk felt for you. We can do this each day."
- ◊ During class: Occasional eye contact. Maintain distance (two feet at least). No physical contact. Use sound or words to get attention (Less Emotional responses below).
- ◊ After class: Occasional eye contact. Reiterate response themes (connection, self-care).

- **Less Emotional**:
    - ◊ *Self-Care*: "Take a deep breath and let it out very slowly when your emotions and body feel out of control. Everything can wait until you feel calmer."
    - ◊ *Self-Care and Connection*: "When we suddenly have a big angry feeling, it can help us feel safer if we try and slow down a little. When you feel very angry, try to come over and see me. I am safe."
    - ◊ *Connection*: "Sometimes knowing what is making you angry helps me understand you better."
    - ◊ *Self-Care and Connection*: "When you and your body are very angry, it makes me think about your safety. To help with safety, I would like to ask you what you are thinking when you get angry like this."
- **Affirmation**:
    - ◊ "Being in control of your feelings takes strength."
    - ◊ "You are brave to try to control your angry feelings in the classroom."

The Hiding Child

- **Verbal**:
    - ◊ Clear and calm voice (quiet).
    - ◊ Before class: Check in and talk about previous day. Occasional eye contact. "I want to check in with you to see if you remember our talk. We will do this each day."
    - ◊ During class: Occasional eye contact. Maintain distance (two feet at least). No physical contact. Use sound or words to get attention (More Emotional responses below).
    - ◊ After class: Occasional eye contact. Reiterate response themes (connection, self-awareness).
- **More Emotional**:
    - ◊ *Self-Awareness and Connection*: "When you and your body suddenly feel very angry in a very strong way, I think you are having big feelings and I am worried about you. I want you to try raising your hand if you realize you are starting to feel this way. I can help with that."
    - ◊ *Self-Awareness*: "It looks like your very angry feelings can just start to heat up sometimes when you don't feel like you have a choice. It's important for you to know controlling your angry feelings is a way to be strong."
    - ◊ *Connection*: "Look at my face. I am worried that you cannot keep yourself from becoming very angry when you don't get to choose."

◊ *Self-Awareness and Connection*: "Try to you to think to yourself, 'It is not fair that I don't get to choose this time, but I can try to control my angry feelings when they bubble up. My angry feelings are like boiling water in a pot. I can try to turn the heat down or ask for someone to help me turn the heat down.'"
- **Affirmation**:
    ◊ "I see you using your thoughts to try and control your very angry feelings."
    ◊ "I am impressed how you are deciding to keep control of your big anger."

Your Evolving Responses

As you have read, there are different motivations for your students' behaviors depending on their latent communication patterns. This demonstrates that your responses cannot be "one size fits all" in nature. While we have provided specific words for you to follow, we intend this chapter and the others like it to be a framework for your responses, not a script. You certainly can use our suggested language as you experiment with the interventions we have described. Overtime, it will be more helpful for you to find your own words to communicate with your students. As you continue to try these techniques, using your own communication style will make the responses to your students' behaviors feel authentic and sincere. This will happen naturally. The proposed interventions that we used in this chapter are a starting point and are meant to evolve and grow with your comfort level. This might take some practice, but it will be well worth it to expand your repertoire of potential responses to concerning or disruptive behaviors. You may find that your own words are more effective or more impactful than the words and phrases we have suggested in this book. The more you are a part of the interventions, the more meaningful they may be to your students. As we know, students need repetition, so please be patient as you try out new ways to respond to them.

Chapter 13

"Hyperactivity"

"Water is like a child, it always wants to be in motion."—Viraj J. Mahajan

How to Use This Chapter

1. As you prepare to read this chapter, choose one child from your class on whom you wish to focus. Selecting one child at a time allows for a more concentrated exploration of the material and how it relates to each child uniquely. **As a guide, we will use "Melody," a second grader who regularly gets out of her seat and wanders around the room.**

2. Read the paragraphs from the following headings to begin the process: *Format and Theme* and *Common Forms of the Behavior*.

3. Choose one behavior that the selected child is exhibiting. Selecting one behavior at a time allows for a more concentrated exploration of the material centering on how the child communicates using this specific behavior. **Melody's behavior of getting up from her seat excessively.**

4. Read the paragraphs from the following headings to learn more about the general category that this behavior falls within from a more holistic perspective: *Manifest Communication* and *Latent Communication*.

5. Read the paragraphs from the heading *Responses and Affirmations* as background to how we structured the proposed responses and the expectation that you will ultimately personalize the responses provided in this chapter.

6. Turn to the page that contains the behavior in question. There you will find the number of the behavior and its name. **We select Behavior (4) Getting up from seat excessively.**

7. On that page, below the number and name, you will find all the possible latent communication prompts for that behavior, ranging from (1) to (4). From these prompts, choose the prompt that most closely reminds you of how this child exhibits this behavior. Your choice may not fit one prompt exactly. If your sense is that multiple prompts could fit, choose the closest one to begin the process. You can return to the other prompts later. You will notice that each prompt corresponds with a child communication Persona (i.e., Troubling, Testing,

Worrying, Hiding). **For Melody, we choose "peculiar; possibly odd and/or confusing to others (see Hiding Child)."**

8. After choosing a latent communication prompt, use the child communication Persona and read the corresponding Core Feelings, Core Wish, Core Question. This information describes the underlying meaning of the behavior and creates an empathic guide for you to keep in mind when responding to the child's behavior.

9. On the following page(s), you will find responses and affirmations for the number and name of the behavior in question. **We select Responses for: *Behavior (4) Getting up from seat excessively* section The Hiding Child**. Find and read the responses and affirmations for the behavior in question that corresponds with the child communication Persona.

10. **Try the responses and affirmations with Melody and determine how they feel to you.**

Theme and Format

Each of the following behavior chapters in this section of the book should be considered with the following format in mind. In this chapter, we will focus on the **"hyperactivity"** that we see in the classroom and try to understand it more deeply. That said, the title of this chapter is an umbrella descriptor, and these behaviors comprise a theme or group of communications. We observe these manifest communications as thematic, as there are many permutations within a category of behavior.

Common Forms of This Behavior

- Excessive talking or verbalizing
- Fidgeting and/or moving body around excessively
- Frenetically moving from one activity to another (prior to achievement)
- Getting up from seat excessively

Manifest Communication

Children are kinetic. They move in the womb; they move in the crib; they move in the stroller. They roll over and sit up; they crawl and stand. Eventually, they cruise, toddle, and walk. This developmental growth is normative, and unless there is a medical, neurological or physiological that alters this progression, all children move through it. All these activities use energy.

Hyperactivity is the accelerated, excessive, or exaggerated form of this kinetic presentation—it is the overabundance of energy discharge. Energy discharge is what fuels active play and sports activities during recess. It is the recognition that children

Chapter 13. "Hyperactivity"

need to "burn-off" energy that is a key component in the foundation of recess. In our time, the word "hyperactivity" comes with a great deal of stigma and emotion connected to it. It is a medicalized term related to a neurological disorder that comes with a diagnosis and the all-too-frequent recommendation for psychotropic medication. The pressures related to this concept and its expressions affect children, teachers, parents, pediatricians, and mental health professionals, and impact them all in different yet very significant ways. It is because of this weighty prominence that we want to be cautious about how we describe this behavior (Salomonsson, 2017).

There are two central elements of this behavior/communication—form and intensity. Let's begin with form, which exists on a continuum from stationary partial-body energy discharge to dynamic full-body energy discharge. By energy discharge, we are referring to how the energy necessary for a child's kinetic activity gets used and dispelled by that child ("burned-off"). It is a practice that is unique to each and every child (see Figure 13.1). Partial-body energy discharge includes leg bouncing, fidgeting with an object, chatting, and looking around. Full-body energy discharge includes standing, rolling, walking around, squirming, bouncing in one's seat, and running.

The second element is intensity of the energy discharge. We calibrate intensity by categorizing it into three forms: extreme, moderate and mild for either stationary partial body energy discharge or dynamic full body energy discharge. Extreme intensity of energy discharge is the most disruptive to the student and the class as a whole. Moderate intensity of energy discharge sometimes disrupts the class but not always. Finally, mild intensity of energy discharge is the least disruptive, though the child's behavior is noticeable to the teacher and her peers (see Figure 13.2).

As we focus more on responses later in this chapter, it will be important to acknowledge that, at times, our expectations rework these levels of intensity of energy discharge; and that, based on the environment's demands for containment and structure (or lack thereof), we may alter our view of a child's intensity. For example, energy discharge (i.e., running) on the playground would be viewed as mild intensity, while that identical energy discharge in the classroom would be viewed as extreme intensity. Cross-referencing our responses with those that address the

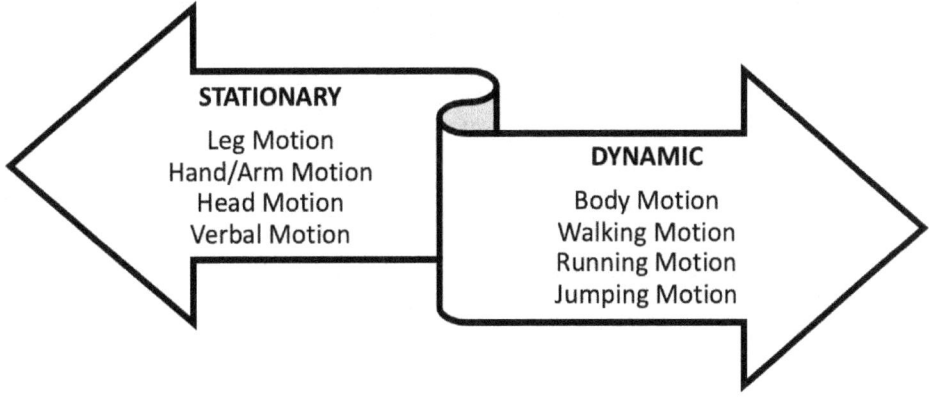

Figure 13.1: Forms of Energy Discharge

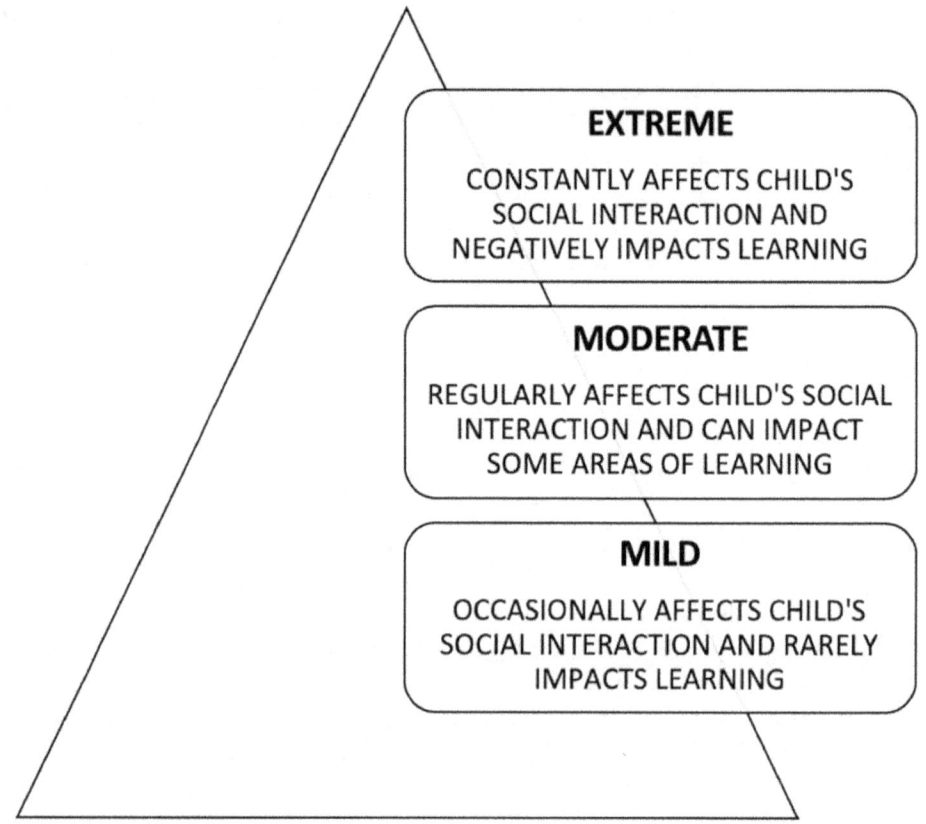

Figure 13.2: Intensity of Energy Discharge

behaviors/communications related to impulsivity (see Chapters 9, 10, 11, 12 and 14) will be a useful process to properly address this fluid aspect of energy discharge.

Using the child Personas of the Troubling child, the Testing child, the Worrying child, and the Hiding child, we will explore specific teacher responses for each type of communication pattern (see Table 13.1). For more detailed information about background for each Persona and the reasoning behind the most productive teacher response configurations, please refer back to their respective chapters.

Table 13.1: Behavior Frequency by Persona

	Persona			
Behavior	Troubling Child Loud & Over Reactive	Testing Child Loud & Under Reactive	Worrying Child Quiet & Over Reactive	Hiding Child Quiet & Under Reactive
Excessive talking or verbalizing	X	X	X	X
Fidgeting and/or moving body around excessively	X	X	X	X

	Persona			
Behavior	Troubling Child Loud & Over Reactive	Testing Child Loud & Under Reactive	Worrying Child Quiet & Over Reactive	Hiding Child Quiet & Under Reactive
Frenetically moving from one activity to another (prior to achievement)	X	X	X	X
Getting up from seat excessively	X	X	X	X

Latent Communication

This process is not an exact science and should be conducted more as trial and error. We would like you to take your best professional guess as to your answers to the following inquiries and evaluations. If you find that, after working through the latent communication material and identifying a set of responses, they do not work as you hoped, you can always revise and try again. Just remember, children integrate learning following repetition, so do not give up too soon.

Responses and Affirmations

Children do not learn the first time we teach them a new concept or a task. We say this in order to manage our expectations about how quickly or completely these new interventions will change or extinguish any given behavior.

Let's keep in mind the following factors. First, the development of these behaviors has typically occurred over an extended period of time. Based on the ages of the children we address in this book, any behavior grew over at least two years and up to eight. As much as we would wish it, a behavior that has been developing over a lengthy period of time cannot change "overnight." Actually, rapid change is often poorly integrated by children and cannot be sustained. Second, children integrate responses at different rates based on a variety of factors, including temperament, environment, learning styles, family involvement/support, etc. We have addressed these earlier in the book. Last, we are constructing foundations from which to grow, one brick at a time, foundations that these children will be able to build on and rely on for years to come. To this end, we want you to know that each of your responses is remembered and cataloged by these children for future use—even if it does not outwardly appear to have been during your time with the child. This relates to the corrective emotional experience we wrote about earlier in this book. Your interactions become part of the child's long-term memory, exchanges that are saved for future use.

That said, we want us to have some benchmarks for our expectations. First, we believe that one month is a sufficient timeframe for some level of change in a behavior, given that a specific teacher response is maintained with consistency and repetition. Second, as we cannot factor in changes that are occurring in real time within these children and with their families, the one-month benchmark may need to be altered accordingly. Third, the one-month duration allows for these challenged children to test us. They will imagine that what we are doing cannot be sustained, that it is too good to last. Our consistency and repetition in responding to the underlying message ultimately quiet their negative thoughts. It is then when the child's expectations of the people around them begin to change to an inner message that is more hopeful and positive. This hopefulness alters their communications and behaviors and can become a more embedded part of their future interpersonal relationships.

Behavior (1)
Excessive talking or verbalizing

If you find the child's excessive chattiness, crosstalk, or verbalizations **seem** for the most part to be:

1. willful; seemingly inflammatory and challenging (see Troubling Child)
2. mischievous; mildly vexing, pushing limits/boundaries (see Testing Child)
3. unsettling; possibly upsetting and tense for others (see Worrying Child)
4. peculiar; possibly unusual and/or confusing to others (see Hiding Child)

- **The Troubling Child**

    Core Feeling: The more frequent the child's talking or noise making is, the greater the **sadness/anger** is being experienced by the child.

    Core Wish: Communicates unconscious wish to be **contained** and **supported** as a way of decreasing sense of **danger** and **rejection**.

    Core Question: Limit-testing question—I am being triggered by events because this moment in class feels overwhelming; can you accept me and handle me?

    Responses: **Structural & Less Emotional** (see Responses section)

- **The Testing Child**

    Core Feeling: The more frequent the child's talking or noise making is, the greater the **sadness/anger** is being experienced by the child.

    Core Wish: Communicates unconscious wish to be **contained** and **validated** as a way of increasing sense of **security** and decreasing sense of **abandonment**.

Core Question: Limit-testing question—I am feeling bad about myself and need to show this by creating a distraction; do you care about me enough to stop me?

Responses: **Structural & More Emotional** (see Responses section)

- **The Worrying Child**

Core Feeling: The more frequent the child's talking or noise making is, the greater the **fear/anger** is being experienced by the child.

Core Wish: Communicates unconscious wish to be **noticed** and **supported** as a way of decreasing sense of **danger** and **abandonment**.

Core Question: Limit-testing question—I am being triggered by events and this is an expression of how afraid I am; do you care enough to protect me?

Responses: **Verbal & Less Emotional** (see Responses section)

- **The Hiding Child**

Core Feeling: The more frequent the child's talking or noise making is, the greater the **fear/anger** is being experienced by the child.

Core Wish: Communicates unconscious wish to be **noticed** and **validated** as a way of increasing sense of **security** and decreasing sense of **rejection**.

Core Question: Limit-testing question—My behavior is a diversion from just how uncomfortable I feel right now; can you accept the way I am and contain me?

Responses: **Verbal & More Emotional** (see Responses section)

Responses for: Behavior (1) Excessive talking or verbalizing

The Troubling Child

- *Structural*:
    ◊ Clear and calm voice (supportive).
    ◊ Before class: Check in. Hold eye contact. "I'm with you. Let's keep working on this."
    ◊ During class: Hand on shoulder; down on knee at eye level. Hold eye contact. Use the Less Emotional responses below.
    ◊ After class: Check in. Hold eye contact. Reiterate response themes (boundaries, self-care). Track progress with chart.
- *Less Emotional*:
    ◊ *Self-Care and Boundaries*: "I want you to try to hold on to your talking to

neighbors (or noise making) during class. You are more in charge when you don't push people away by talking (or noise making)."
- ◊ *Self-Care*: "Wait, take a deep breath and let it out very slowly when you feel like talking to a classmate (or making a noise)."
- ◊ *Self-Care and Boundaries*: "Think to yourself, 'I have a choice to talk or not talk with someone during class time.'"
- ◊ *Self-Care and Boundaries*: "Think about us building a dam together across a stream and trying to stop all the water from flowing. If we can do it, it can feel great when we see that we have stopped the water in the stream completely. Controlling your talking is the same. It's like a victory."

- *Affirmation*:
  - ◊ "Controlling your talking to classmates during class time takes great strength."
  - ◊ "Anyone can see what a huge effort you are making to not make noises during class."

The Testing Child

- *Structural*:
  - ◊ Clear and crisp voice (supportive).
  - ◊ Before class: Check in. Hold eye contact. "I'm with you. Let's keep working on this."
  - ◊ During class: Hand on shoulder; down on knee at eye level. Hold eye contact. Use More Emotional responses below.
  - ◊ After class: Check in. Hold eye contact. Reiterate response themes (boundaries, self-awareness). Track progress with chart.
- *More Emotional*:
  - ◊ *Self-Awareness and Boundaries*: "It saddens me when you talk to your neighbors (or make noises) during class, because I feel like it pushes us apart."
  - ◊ *Self-Awareness*: "When you talk to your neighbors (or make noises) during class, I think you feel bad."
  - ◊ *Self-Awareness and Boundaries*: "Sometimes bad thoughts just feel like popping out of us. They are like balloons that blow up too big. We have to ask for help to let some air out before it pops because this makes us feel worse."
  - ◊ *Self-Awareness*: "Try to take a deep breath and let it out very slowly; and say to yourself, 'I will be okay,' before you begin your talking to classmates (or noises making) during the classroom."
- *Affirmation*:
  - ◊ "I am proud of you for trying so hard to not talk to classmates (or making noises)."
  - ◊ "You took good care of yourself by trying to not talk to classmates (or making noises)."

The Worrying Child

- **Verbal**:
    - ◊ Clear and calm voice (quiet).
    - ◊ Before class: Check in and talk about previous day. Occasional eye contact. "I want to check in with you to see how our talk felt for you. We can do this each day."
    - ◊ During class: Occasional eye contact. Maintain distance (two feet at least). No physical contact. Use sound or words to get attention (Less Emotional responses below).
    - ◊ After class: Occasional eye contact. Reiterate response themes (connection, self-care).
- **Less Emotional**:
    - ◊ *Self-Care*: "Take a deep breath and let it out very slowly when you feel the need to talk to a neighbor (or to make noises) in the classroom. What you want to say can wait until you feel calmer."
    - ◊ *Self-Care and Connection*: "When we suddenly have a big thought, it can help us feel safer if we try and slow down and stay near a person we trust. When you feel the need to talk to a neighbor (or to make noises) during class time, try to come over to me first."
    - ◊ *Self-Care and Connection*: "When you are talking (or making noises) during class, it makes me think about your safety. I would like to ask you about what you are thinking."
- **Affirmation**:
    - ◊ "Being in control of your need to talk (or make noises) takes strength."
    - ◊ "You are brave to try to control your need to talk (or make noises) in the classroom."

The Hiding Child

- **Verbal**:
    - ◊ Clear and calm voice (quiet).
    - ◊ Before class: Check in and talk about previous day. Occasional eye contact. "I want to check in with you to see if you remember our talk. We will do this each day."
    - ◊ During class: Occasional eye contact. Maintain distance (two feet at least). No physical contact. Use sound or words to get attention (More Emotional responses below).
    - ◊ After class: Occasional eye contact. Reiterate response themes (connection, self-awareness).
- **More Emotional**:
    - ◊ *Self-Awareness and Connection*: "When you start to talk to yourself (or making sounds) during class time, I think you are having big feelings, and I am worried. I want you to try raising your hand if you are feeling like doing these things during class time. I can help with that."

◊ *Self-Awareness and Connection*: "A way to be strong is to think about your classmates who are trying to learn."
◊ *Connection*: "Look at my face. I am worried that you can't keep from talking (or making sounds)."
◊ *Self-Awareness and Connection*: "Think to yourself, 'I can control my talking (or my sounds). My need to talk (or make sounds) is like water coming out of a faucet. I can turn the faucet off when I want to.'"

- **Affirmation**:
    ◊ "I see you using your thoughts to try and control your need to talk (or to make sounds)."
    ◊ "I am impressed how you are deciding to keep control of your talk (of your sounds)."

Behavior (2)
Fidgeting and/or moving body around excessively

If you find the child's persistent movements including with his/her hands or feet, or with his head, or with his legs or arms *seem* for the most part:

1. willful; seemingly inflammatory and challenging (see Troubling Child)
2. mischievous; mildly vexing, pushing limits/boundaries (see Testing Child)
3. unsettling; possibly upsetting and tense for others (see Worrying Child)
4. peculiar; possibly unusual and/or confusing to others (see Hiding Child)

- **The Troubling Child**

    Core Feeling: The more intense the child's fidgeting is, the greater the **sadness/anger** is being experienced by the child.

    Core Wish: Communicates unconscious wish to be **contained** and **supported** as a way of decreasing sense of **danger** and **rejection**.

    Core Question: Limit-testing question—I am being triggered by events because this moment in class feels overwhelming; can you accept me and handle me?

    Responses: **Structural & Less Emotional** (see Responses section)

- **The Testing Child**

    Core Feeling: The more intense the child's fidgeting is, the greater the **sadness/anger** is being experienced by the child.

    Core Wish: Communicates unconscious wish to be **contained** and **validated** as a way of increasing sense of **security** and decreasing sense of **abandonment**.

Core Question: Limit-testing question—I am feeling bad about myself and need to show this by creating a distraction; do you care about me enough to stop me?

Responses: **Structural & More Emotional** (see Responses section)

- **The Worrying Child**

Core Feeling: The more intense the child's fidgeting is, the greater the **fear/ anger** is being experienced by the child.

Core Wish: Communicates unconscious wish to be **noticed** and **supported** as a way of decreasing sense of **danger** and **abandonment**.

Core Question: Limit-testing question—I am being triggered by events and this is an expression of how afraid I am; do you care enough to protect me?

Responses: **Verbal & Less Emotional** (see Responses section)

- **The Hiding Child**

Core Feeling: The more intense the child's fidgeting is, the greater the **fear/ anger** is being experienced by the child.

Core Wish: Communicates unconscious wish to be **noticed** and **validated** as a way of increasing sense of **security** and decreasing sense of **rejection**.

Core Question: Limit-testing question—My behavior is a diversion from just how uncomfortable I feel right now; can you accept the way I am and contain me?

Responses: **Verbal & More Emotional** (see Responses section)

Responses for: Behavior (2) Fidgeting and/or moving body around excessively

The Troubling Child

- ***Structural***:
    ◊ Clear and calm voice (supportive).
    ◊ Before class: Check in. Hold eye contact. "I'm with you. Let's keep working on this."
    ◊ During class: Hand on shoulder; down on knee at eye level. Hold eye contact. Use the Less Emotional responses below.
    ◊ After class: Check in. Hold eye contact. Reiterate response themes (boundaries, self-care). Track progress with chart.
- ***Less Emotional***:

- ◊ *Self-Care and Boundaries*: "I want you to try to stop (*description of movement*) during class. You are more in charge when you don't push people away by (*description of movement*) during class."
- ◊ *Self-Care*: "Take a deep breath and let it out very slowly when you feel like (*description of movement*)."
- ◊ *Boundaries*: "Think to yourself, 'I have a choice to (*description of movement*) or not during class.'"
- ◊ *Self-Care and Boundaries*: "Think about building a dam together across a stream and trying to stop all the water from flowing. If we can do it, it can feel great when we see that we have stopped the water in the stream completely. Controlling your (*description of movement*) by yourself, with my help, is the same. It's like a victory."

- *Affirmation*:
  - ◊ "Controlling your (*description of movement*) during class time takes great strength."
  - ◊ "Anyone can see what a huge effort you are making to not (*description of movement*)."

The Testing Child

- *Structural*:
  - ◊ Clear and crisp voice (supportive).
  - ◊ Before class: Check in. Hold eye contact. "I'm with you. Let's keep working on this."
  - ◊ During class: Hand on shoulder; down on knee at eye level. Hold eye contact. Use More Emotional responses below.
  - ◊ After class: Check in. Hold eye contact. Reiterate response themes (boundaries, self-awareness). Track progress with chart.
- *More Emotional*:
  - ◊ *Self-Awareness and Boundaries*: "It saddens me when you move around during class, because I feel like it pushes us apart."
  - ◊ *Self-Awareness*: "When you (*description of movement*) during class, I think you feel bad."
  - ◊ *Self-Awareness and Boundaries*: "Sometimes having bad thoughts is like having a cut that is healing and itches. The itch bothers us, and we really want to scratch it, but if we scratch, it could bleed. When it is really itchy, we have to ask for someone to help us."
  - ◊ *Self-Awareness*: "Try to take a deep breath and let it out very slowly; and say to yourself, 'I will be okay, I can get help' before you begin your (*description of movement*) during class."
- *Affirmation*:
  - ◊ "I am proud of you for trying so hard to not (*description of movement*) during class."
  - ◊ "You took good care of yourself by trying to not (*description of movement*) during class."

The Worrying Child

- **Verbal**:
    - ◊ Clear and calm voice (quiet).
    - ◊ Before class: Check in and talk about previous day. Occasional eye contact. "I want to check in with you to see how our talk felt for you. We can do this each day."
    - ◊ During class: Occasional eye contact. Maintain distance (two feet at least). No physical contact. Use sound or words to get attention (Less Emotional responses below).
    - ◊ After class: Occasional eye contact. Reiterate response themes (connection, self-care).
- **Less Emotional**:
    - ◊ *Self-Care*: "Take a deep breath and let it out very slowly when you start to feel the need to (*description of movement*). Needing to (*description of movement*) can wait until you feel calmer."
    - ◊ *Self-Care and Connection*: "When we suddenly have a big thought, it can help us feel safer if we try and slow down and stay near a person we trust. When you feel the need to (*description of movement*), come over and see me first."
    - ◊ *Self-Care and Connection*: "When you are (*description of movement*) during class, it makes me think about your safety. I would like to ask you about what you are thinking."
- **Affirmation**:
    - ◊ "Being in control of your need to (*description of movement*) takes strength."
    - ◊ "You are brave to try to control your need to (*description of movement*) in the class."

The Hiding Child

- **Verbal**:
    - ◊ Clear and calm voice (quiet).
    - ◊ Before class: Check in and talk about previous day. Occasional eye contact. "I want to check in with you to see if you remember our talk. We will do this each day."
    - ◊ During class: Occasional eye contact. Maintain distance (two feet at least). No physical contact. Use sound or words to get attention (More Emotional responses below).
    - ◊ After class: Occasional eye contact. Reiterate response themes (connection, self-awareness).
- **More Emotional**:
    - ◊ *Self-Awareness and Connection*: "When you start to (*description of movement*) during class time, I think you have big feelings, and I am worried. I want you to raise your hand if you are feeling like (*description of movement*) during class time. I can help with that."

◊ *Self-Awareness*: "A way to be strong is to think about when you feel like (*description of movement*)."
◊ *Connection*: "Look at my face. I am worried that you can't keep from (*description of movement*)."
◊ *Self-Awareness*: "Think to yourself, 'I can control (*description of movement*). My need to (*description of movement*) is like water coming out of a faucet. I can turn the faucet off if I want to.'"

- **Affirmation**:
  ◊ "I see you using your thoughts to control your need to (*description of movement*)."
  ◊ "I am impressed how you are deciding to keep control of the (*description of movement*)."

Behavior (3)
Frenetically moving from one activity to another (prior to achievement)

If you find the child's frenetic movement from one activity to another *seems* for the most part:

1. willful; seemingly inflammatory and challenging (see Troubling Child)
2. mischievous; mildly vexing, pushing limits/boundaries (see Testing Child)
3. unsettling; possibly upsetting and tense for others (see Worrying Child)
4. peculiar; possibly odd and/or confusing to others (see Hiding Child)

- **The Troubling Child**

    Core Feeling: The more frenetic the child's behavior is, the greater the **sadness/anger** is being experienced by the child.

    Core Wish: Communicates unconscious wish to be **contained** and **supported** as a way of decreasing sense of **danger** and **rejection**.

    Core Question: Limit-testing question—I am being triggered by events because this moment in class feels overwhelming; can you accept me and handle me?

    Responses: **Structural & Less Emotional** (see Responses section)

- **The Testing Child**

    Core Feeling: The more frenetic the child's behavior is, the greater the **sadness/anger** is being experienced by the child.

Core Wish:	Communicates unconscious wish to be **contained** and **validated** as a way of increasing sense of **security** and decreasing sense of **abandonment**.
Core Question:	Limit-testing question—I am feeling bad about myself and need to show this by creating a distraction; do you care about me enough to stop me?
Responses:	**Structural & More Emotional** (see Responses section)

- **The Worrying Child**

Core Feeling:	The more frenetic the child's behavior is, the greater the **fear/anger** is being experienced by the child.
Core Wish:	Communicates unconscious wish to be **noticed** and **supported** as a way of decreasing sense of **danger** and **abandonment**.
Core Question:	Limit-testing question—I am being triggered by events and this is an expression of how afraid I am; do you care enough to protect me?
Responses:	**Verbal & Less Emotional** (see Responses section)

- **The Hiding Child**

Core Feeling:	The more frenetic the child's behavior is, the greater the **fear/anger** is being experienced by the child.
Core Wish:	Communicates unconscious wish to be **noticed** and **validated** as a way of increasing sense of **security** and decreasing sense of **rejection**.
Core Question:	Limit-testing question—My behavior is a diversion from just how uncomfortable I feel right now; can you accept the way I am and contain me?
Responses:	**Verbal & More Emotional** (see Responses section)

Responses for: Behavior (3) Frenetically moving from one activity to another

The Troubling Child

- *Structural*:
    ◊ Clear and calm voice (supportive).
    ◊ Before class: Check in. Hold eye contact. "I'm with you. Let's keep working on this."
    ◊ During class: Hand on shoulder; down on knee at eye level. Hold eye contact. Use the Less Emotional responses below.

- ◊ After class: Check in. Hold eye contact. Reiterate response themes (boundaries, self-care). Track progress with chart.
- ◊ **Less Emotional**:
- ◊ *Self-Care and Boundaries*: "I want you to try to stay in one activity until you complete it. You are more in charge when you don't push people away by changing your activities so often during a class."
- ◊ *Self-Care*: "Take a deep breath and let it out very slowly when you feel like switching activities."
- ◊ *Boundaries*: "Think to yourself, 'I can make a choice to switch activities or to stay with one activity.'"
- ◊ *Self-Care and Boundaries*: "There is a very long race called a marathon. Lots of people run it and everyone tries to finish. Some people run slow, some fast. Some people take breaks and rest, some get help from others. Staying with an activity is the same as running a long race. What matters is that we keep trying, either on our own or with help. Trying is how we win."

- *Affirmation*:
  - ◊ "Staying with an activity when we want to stop takes great strength."
  - ◊ "Anyone can see what a huge effort you are making to stay with that activity."

The Testing Child

- *Structural*:
  - ◊ Clear and crisp voice (supportive).
  - ◊ Before class: Check in. Hold eye contact. "I'm with you. Let's keep working on this."
  - ◊ During class: Hand on shoulder; down on knee at eye level. Hold eye contact. Use More Emotional responses below.
  - ◊ After class: Check in. Hold eye contact. Reiterate response themes (boundaries, self-awareness). Track progress with chart.
- *More Emotional*:
  - ◊ *Self-Awareness and Boundaries*: "It saddens me when you keep switching activities, because I feel like it pushes us apart."
  - ◊ *Self-Awareness*: "When you keep switching activities, I think you feel bad."
  - ◊ *Self-Awareness and Boundaries*: "Sometimes when we play hide and go seek, we find a great hiding place, and no one can find us. If we are alone for a long time, we start to get worried. Is the game over? Will they ever find me? Staying with an activity is like waiting to be found in hide and seek. Even though it is part of the game, it can be hard to do it alone. I know you can do it."
  - ◊ *Self-Awareness*: "Try to take a deep breath and let it out very slowly; and say to yourself, 'I will be okay, I can get help' before you start to switch an activity."

- *Affirmation*:
    - ◊ "I am proud of you for trying so hard to not keep switching activities."
    - ◊ "You took good care of yourself by staying with one activity today."

The Worrying Child

- *Verbal*:
    - ◊ Clear and calm voice (quiet).
    - ◊ Before class: Check in and talk about previous day. Occasional eye contact. "I want to check in with you to see how our talk felt for you. We can do this each day."
    - ◊ During class: Occasional eye contact. Maintain distance (two feet at least). No physical contact. Use sound or words to get attention (Less Emotional responses below).
    - ◊ After class: Occasional eye contact. Reiterate response themes (connection, self-care).
- *Less Emotional*:
    - ◊ *Self-Care*: "Take a deep breath and let it out very slowly if you suddenly want to switch to another activity. Just wait for a moment. Moving can wait until you feel calmer."
    - ◊ *Self-Care and Connection*: "When we suddenly have a big thought, it can help us feel safer if we try and slow down and stay near a person we trust. When you feel like you want to keep changing activities, come over and see me."
    - ◊ *Self-Care and Connection*: "When you keep switching your activities, it makes me think about your safety. I would like to ask you about what you are thinking."
- *Affirmation*:
    - ◊ "Staying with an activity when we want to stop takes great strength."
    - ◊ "You are brave when you try to stay with an activity that you want to leave."

The Hiding Child

- *Verbal*:
    - ◊ Clear and calm voice (quiet).
    - ◊ Before class: Check in and talk about previous day. Occasional eye contact. "I want to check in with you to see if you remember our talk. We will do this each day."
    - ◊ During class: Occasional eye contact. Maintain distance (two feet at least). No physical contact. Use sound or words to get attention (More Emotional responses below).
    - ◊ After class: Occasional eye contact. Reiterate response themes (connection, self-awareness).

- *More Emotional*:
    - ◊ *Self-Awareness and Connection*: "When I see you switching quickly between activities, I think you are having big feelings, and I am worried. I want you to try raising your hand if you are feeling like switching between activities. I can help with that."
    - ◊ *Self-Awareness and Connection*: "A way you can be strong is to stay longer at each activity, before you switch."
    - ◊ *Connection*: "Look at my face. I am worried that you keep moving from one activity to another."
    - ◊ *Self-Awareness and Connection*: "Think to yourself, 'I can stay at this activity. When I move from one activity to another, I am like a fast rolling ball. But I can pick it up and hold it in one place if I want.'"
- *Affirmation*:
    - ◊ "I see you using your thoughts to control yourself from switching activities too quickly."
    - ◊ "I am impressed how you are deciding to stay a one activity for a longer time."

Behavior (4)
Getting up from seat excessively

If you find the child's persistent getting up from his/her seat *seems* for the most part:

1. willful; seemingly inflammatory and challenging (see Troubling Child)
2. mischievous; mildly vexing, pushing limits/boundaries (see Testing Child)
3. unsettling; possibly upsetting and tense for others (see Worrying Child)
4. peculiar; possibly odd and/or confusing to others (see Hiding Child)

- **The Troubling Child**

Core Feeling:	The more frequently the child leaves his/her seat, the greater the **sadness/anger** is being experienced by the child.
Core Wish:	Communicates unconscious wish to be **contained** and **supported** as a way of decreasing sense of **danger** and **rejection**.
Core Question:	Limit-testing question—I am being triggered by events because this moment in class feels overwhelming; can you accept me and handle me?
Responses:	**Structural & Less Emotional** (see Responses section)

The Testing Child

Core Feeling:	The more frequently the child leaves his/her seat, the greater the **sadness/anger** is being experienced by the child.
Core Wish:	Communicates unconscious wish to be **contained** and **validated** as a way of increasing sense of **security** and decreasing sense of **abandonment**.
Core Question:	Limit-testing question—I am feeling bad about myself and need to show this by creating a distraction; do you care about me enough to stop me?
Responses:	**Structural & More Emotional** (see Responses section)

- **The Worrying Child**

Core Feeling:	The more frequently the child leaves his/her seat, the greater the **fear/anger** is being experienced by the child.
Core Wish:	Communicates unconscious wish to be **noticed** and **supported** as a way of decreasing sense of **danger** and **abandonment**.
Core Question:	Limit-testing question—I am being triggered by events and this is an expression of how afraid I am; do you care enough to protect me?
Responses:	**Verbal & Less Emotional** (see Responses section)

- **The Hiding Child**

Core Feeling:	The more frequently the child leaves his/her seat, the greater the **fear/anger** is being experienced by the child.
Core Wish:	Communicates unconscious wish to be **noticed** and **validated** as a way of increasing sense of **security** and decreasing sense of **rejection**.
Core Question:	Limit-testing question—My behavior is a diversion from just how uncomfortable I feel right now; can you accept the way I am and contain me?
Responses:	**Verbal & More Emotional** (see Responses section)

Responses for: Behavior (4) Getting up from seat excessively

The Troubling Child

- ***Structural*:**
    ◊ Clear and calm voice (supportive).

◊ Before class: Check in. Hold eye contact. "I'm with you. Let's keep working on this."
◊ During class: Hand on shoulder; down on knee at eye level. Hold eye contact. Use the Less Emotional responses below.
◊ After class: Check in. Hold eye contact. Reiterate response themes (boundaries, self-care). Track progress with chart.

- **Less Emotional**:
    ◊ *Self-Care and Boundaries*: "I want you to try to stay in your seat during class. You are more in charge when you don't push me away by getting out of your seat during class."
    ◊ *Self-Care*: "Take a deep breath and let it out very slowly when you feel like getting out of your seat."
    ◊ *Boundaries*: "Think to yourself, 'I have a choice to get up out of my seat or not during class.'"
    ◊ *Self-Care and Boundaries*: "Think about building a dam together across a stream and trying to stop all the water from flowing. If we can do it, it can feel great when we see that we have stopped the water in the stream completely. Staying in our seat by yourself, or even with my help, is the same. It's like a victory. It can feel really good when you succeed."
- **Affirmation**:
    ◊ "Staying in your seat during class time takes great strength."
    ◊ "Anyone can see what a huge effort you are making to stay in your seat."

The Testing Child

- **Structural**:
    ◊ Clear and crisp voice (supportive).
    ◊ Before class: Check in. Hold eye contact. "I'm with you. Let's keep working on this."
    ◊ During class: Hand on shoulder; down on knee at eye level. Hold eye contact. Use More Emotional responses below.
    ◊ After class: Check in. Hold eye contact. Reiterate response themes (boundaries, self-awareness). Track progress with chart.
- **More Emotional**:
    ◊ *Self-Awareness and Boundaries*: "It saddens me when leave your seat during class, because I feel like it pushes us apart."
    ◊ *Self-Awareness*: "When you get up out of your seat during class, I think you feel bad."
    ◊ *Self-Awareness and Boundaries*: "Sometimes when we play hide and go seek, we find a great hiding place, and no one can find us. If we are alone for a long time, we start to get worried. Is the game over? Will they ever find me? Staying with an activity is like waiting to be found in hide and seek. Even though it is part of the game, it can be hard to do it alone. I know you can do it."
    ◊ *Self-Awareness*: "Try to take a deep breath and let it out very slowly; and

say to yourself, 'I will be okay, I can get help when I am having a hard time staying in my seat.'"
- *Affirmation*:
    ◊ "I am proud of you for trying so hard to stay in your seat during class."
    ◊ "You took good care of yourself by trying to stay in your seat during class."

The Worrying Child

- *Verbal*:
    ◊ Clear and calm voice (quiet).
    ◊ Before class: Check in anj274d talk about previous day. Occasional eye contact. "I want to check in with you to see how our talk felt for you. We can do this each day."
    ◊ During class: Occasional eye contact. Maintain distance (two feet at least). No physical contact. Use sound or words to get attention (Less Emotional responses below).
    ◊ After class: Occasional eye contact. Reiterate response themes (connection, self-care).
- *Less Emotional*:
    ◊ *Self-Care*: "Take a deep breath and let it out very slowly when you start to feel like getting out of your seat. Just wait for a moment. Leaving your seat can wait until you feel calmer."
    ◊ *Self-Care and Connection*: "When we suddenly have a big thought, it can help us feel safer if we try and slow down and stay near a person we trust. When you feel like leaving your seat, wait, try to raise your hand first and I will come over. If I don't see you, then you can come over to me."
    ◊ *Self-Care and Connection*: "When you leave your seat during class, it makes me think about your safety. I would like to ask you about what you are thinking when that happens."
- *Affirmation*:
    ◊ "Staying in your seat when you really want to get up takes strength."
    ◊ "You are being brave when you try to stay in your seat when you really want to get up."

The Hiding Child

- *Verbal*:
    ◊ Clear and calm voice (quiet).
    ◊ Before class: Check in and talk about previous day. Occasional eye contact. "I want to check in with you to see if you remember our talk. We will do this each day."
    ◊ During class: Occasional eye contact. Maintain distance (two feet at least). No physical contact. Use sound or words to get attention (More Emotional responses below).

- ◊ After class: Occasional eye contact. Reiterate response themes (connection, self-awareness).
- *More Emotional*:
    - ◊ *Self-Awareness and Connection*: "When you leave your seat during class time a lot, I think you are having big feelings, and I am worried. I want you to raise your hand, first, if you are feeling like getting out of your seat. I can help with that."
    - ◊ *Self-Awareness and Connection*: "A way to be strong is to think about getting out of your seat before you do it."
    - ◊ *Connection*: "Look at my face. I am worried that you keep getting out of your seat during class."
    - ◊ *Self-Awareness and Connection*: "Think to yourself, 'I can control my body and stay seated. Leaving my seat is like water leaving a faucet. I can stop the water, and my body, by turning the faucet off if I want.'"
- *Affirmation*:
    - ◊ "I see you using your thoughts to try to stay in your seat."
    - ◊ "I am impressed how you are deciding to keep control of your body and stay seated."

Your Evolving Responses

As you have read, there are different motivations for your students' behaviors depending on their latent communication patterns. This demonstrates that your responses cannot be "one size fits all" in nature. While we have provided specific words for you to follow, we intend this chapter and the others like it to be a framework for your responses, not a script. You certainly can use our suggested language as you experiment with the interventions we have described. Overtime, it will be more helpful for you to find your own words to communicate with your students. As you continue to try these techniques, using your own communication style will make the responses to your students' behaviors feel authentic and sincere. This will happen naturally. The proposed interventions that we used in this chapter are a starting point and are meant to evolve and grow with your comfort level. This might take some practice, but it will be well worth it to expand your repertoire of potential responses to concerning or disruptive behaviors. You may find that your own words are more effective or more impactful than the words and phrases we have suggested in this book. The more you are a part of the interventions, the more meaningful they may be to your students. As we know, students need repetition, so please be patient as you try out new ways to respond to them.

Chapter 14

Difficulty Observing Personal Space and Other Boundary Problems

"Out of limitations comes creativity."—Debbie Allen

How to Use This Chapter

1. As you prepare to read this chapter, choose one child from your class on whom you wish to focus. Selecting one child at a time allows for a more concentrated exploration of the material and how it relates to each child uniquely. **As a guide, we will use "Melody," a second grader who lies to teachers and her classmates.**

2. Read the paragraphs from the following headings to begin the process: *Format and Theme* and *Common Forms of the Behavior*.

3. Choose one behavior that the selected child is exhibiting. Selecting one behavior at a time allows for a more concentrated exploration of the material centering on how the child communicates using this specific behavior. **Melody's behavior of lying.**

4. Read the paragraphs from the following headings to learn more about the general category that this behavior falls within from a more holistic perspective: *Manifest Communication* and *Latent Communication*.

5. Read the paragraphs from the heading *Responses and Affirmations* as background to how we structured the proposed responses and the expectation that you will ultimately personalize the responses provided in this chapter.

6. Turn to the page that contains the behavior in question. There you will find the number of the behavior and its name. We select **Behavior (3) Lying**.

7. On that page, below the number and name, you will find all the possible latent communication prompts for that behavior, ranging from (1) to (4). From these prompts, choose the prompt that most closely reminds you of how this child exhibits this behavior. Your choice may not fit one prompt exactly. If your sense is that multiple prompts could fit, choose the closest one to begin the process. You can return to the other prompts later. You will notice that each prompt corresponds with a child communication Persona (i.e., Troubling, Testing,

Worrying, Hiding). **For Melody, we choose "occasional and reactive; possibly upsetting and disturbing for others (see Worrying Child)."**

8. After choosing a latent communication prompt, use the child communication Persona and read the corresponding Core Feelings, Core Wish, Core Question. This information describes the underlying meaning of the behavior and creates an empathic guide for you to keep in mind when responding to the child's behavior.

9. On the following page(s), you will find responses and affirmations for the number and name of the behavior in question. **We select Responses for: Behavior (3) Lying** section **The Worrying Child**. Find and read the responses and affirmations for the behavior in question that corresponds with the child communication Persona.

10. **Try the responses and affirmations with Melody and determine how they feel to you.**

Theme and Format

Each of the following behavior chapters in this section of the book should be considered with the following format in mind. In this chapter, we will focus on children who display difficulty **observing personal space or display other boundary problems**. That said, the title of this chapter is an umbrella descriptor, and these behaviors comprise a theme or group of communications. We observe these manifest communications as thematic, as there are many permutations within a category of behavior.

Common Forms of This Behavior

- Altering another child's work without asking
- Exhibiting distress during and/or after a caregiver's departure
- Lying
- Not waiting for one's turn
- Sharing too much personal information
- Stealing
- Touching and/or displaying genitals in public
- Touching another person's body without asking

Manifest Communication

In child development, a boundary is a demarcation between (1) where the child begins and ends as an individual person and (2) where a child perceives that another person begins and ends. In this way, it is similar to an invisible barrier of separation. Called "separation and individuation" in the child development literature, the creation of this barrier is a natural and typical part of how children grow and mature (Mahler, et al., 1975). The "how" of navigating boundaries, and the related personal space, is part of the push and pull of a child's evolving character over each developmental stage. The jargon we typically use daily when talking about boundary maintenance is limits, limit setting and limit testing. All refer to this same process.

As children play with their boundaries, we can see the results in real time. We can observe these results in three main areas: the physical, the cognitive, and the symbolic. Each of these areas speak a slightly different language. Physical boundaries focus on the body and the ways children interacts with the concrete aspects of their environment. Cognitive boundaries center on thoughts and feelings and the interplay between the children's' and those of individuals around them. Finally, symbolic boundaries deal with the abstract and the intangible spaces between the child and others. All communicate information about the child. We will examine the meanings further in the next section of this chapter, but first, let us detail these categories.

Table 14.1:
Potential Problems with Boundary Maintenance

Boundaries	Sub-Group	Examples
Physical	Body	Touching another's face without consent Hugging/Kissing without asking Hitting/Biting/Pushing Pulling hair Playing physically too rough Touching genitals (self or others) Displaying genitals
	Physical Creations	Tearing up other's drawings Knocking down other's block constructions Stealing
	Environment	Leaving room without permission Touching items that one is not allowed to touch Not staying in line Not sharing Talking loudly in a quiet space Having discomfort with loud noise, bright lights, intense odors
Cognitive	Thoughts	Struggling with constructive criticism Needing to get own way Not following directions Not wanting anyone to help Not responding when time to go/time's up Lying
	Feelings	Having a tantrum Experiencing irritability when tired/hungry Demanding attention Demanding affection

Boundaries	Sub-Group	Examples
Symbolic	Personal space	Close-up talking (in someone's face) Climbing on someone when going around is possible Not making eye contact Experiencing distress when in crowds
	Separation	Struggling with goodbyes Experiencing distress when alone

Weiner, Gallo-Silver, & Lucas, 2020

The complication with boundary-related behaviors/communications is that many of the "potentially problematic" presentations are ubiquitous within our everyday experiences and may be considered normative to a point. Taking what does not belong, grabbing, not waiting one's turn, or demanding a hug are all behaviors we see nearly every day in school. In addition, they are behaviors/communications that do not typically phase us. In order to identify the tipping point at which a child's boundary presentation becomes one of concern, we must examine these behaviors through the prism of safety. It is when we sense that the child is being unsafe that we begin to respond with more urgency.

For our purposes, there are two ways one may use to measure a child's lack of boundary safety—its focus and degree (see Figure 14.1). In terms of focus, there are two distinct vectors of boundary intrusions:

- Intrusions that are unsafe to the self (the child, him, her, or themself) and
- Intrusions that are unsafe to others (classmates, teachers, or objects in the environment).

In terms of degree, we can break this down into boundary intrusions that are severe, moderate, and mild:

- Severe—a consistent pattern of boundary intrusion, several forms of boundary intrusion, across multiple settings
- Moderate—an intermittent pattern of boundary intrusion, occasionally repeated forms of boundary intrusion, several recurring settings
- Mild—No actual pattern of boundary intrusion, an individual form of boundary intrusion, in one selected setting

Using these concepts and measurements, we can provide two characterizations of a child's impulsivity safety, one for each nature.

Using the child Personas of the Troubling child, the Testing child, the Worrying child, and the Hiding child, we will explore specific teacher responses for each type of communication pattern (see Table 14.2). For more detailed information about background for each Persona and the reasoning behind the most productive teacher response configurations, please refer back to their respective chapters.

Chapter 14. Personal Space and Boundary Problems

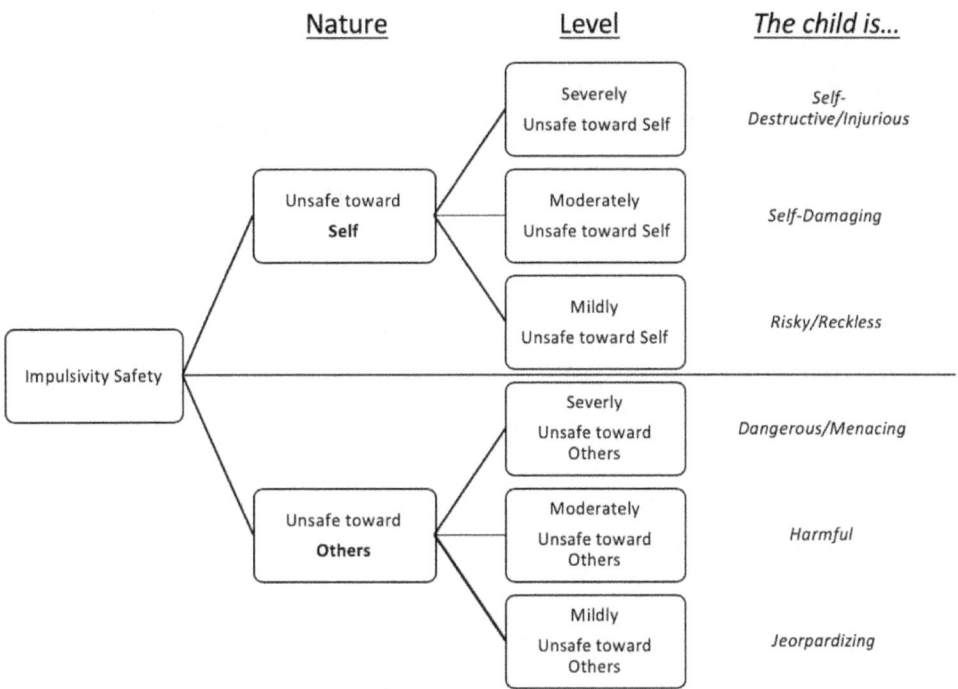

Figure 14.1: Lack of Boundary Safety and Descriptors

Table 14.2:
Behavior Frequency by Persona

	Persona			
Behavior	Troubling Child Loud & Over Reactive	Testing Child Loud & Under Reactive	Worrying Child Quiet & Over Reactive	Hiding Child Quiet & Under Reactive
Altering another child's work without asking	X	X		
Exhibiting distress during and/or after a caregiver's departure		X	X	X
Lying	X	X	X	X
Not waiting for one's turn	X	X	X	X
Sharing too much personal information	X		X	
Stealing	X			X
Touching and/or displaying genitals in public			X	X
Touching another person's body without asking	X	X		

The absence of an "X" indicates that this Persona does not typically engage in this type of behavior/communication.

Latent Communication

This process is not an exact science and should be conducted more as trial and error. We would like you to take your best professional guess as to your answers to the following inquiries and evaluations. If you find that, after working through the latent communication material and identifying a set of responses, they do not work as you hoped, you can always revise and try again. Just remember, children integrate learning following repetition, so do not give up too soon.

Responses and Affirmations

Children do not learn the first time we teach them a new concept or a task. We say this in order to manage our expectations about how quickly or completely these new interventions will change or extinguish any given behavior.

Let's keep in mind the following factors. First, the development of these behaviors has typically occurred over an extended period of time. Based on the ages of the children we address in this book, any behavior grew over at least two years and up to eight. As much as we would wish it, a behavior that has been developing over a lengthy period of time cannot change "overnight." Actually, rapid change is often poorly integrated by children and cannot be sustained. Second, children integrate responses at different rates based on a variety of factors, including temperament, environment, learning styles, family involvement/support, etc. We have addressed these earlier in the book. Last, we are constructing foundations from which to grow, one brick at a time, foundations that these children will be able to build on and rely on for years to come. To this end, we want you to know that each of your responses is remembered and cataloged by these children for future use—even if it does not outwardly appear to have been during your time with the child. This relates to the corrective emotional experience we wrote about earlier in this book. Your interactions become part of the child's long-term memory, exchanges that are saved for future use.

That said, we want us to have some benchmarks for our expectations. First, we believe that one month is a sufficient timeframe for some level of change in a behavior, given that a specific teacher response is maintained with consistency and repetition. Second, as we cannot factor in changes that are occurring in real time within these children and with their families, the one-month benchmark may need to be altered accordingly. Third, the one-month duration allows for these challenged children to test us. They will imagine that what we are doing cannot be sustained, that it is too good to last. Our consistency and repetition in responding to the underlying message ultimately quiet their negative thoughts. It is then when the child's expectations of the people around them begin to change to an inner message that is more hopeful and positive. This hopefulness alters their communications and behaviors and can become a more embedded part of their future interpersonal relationships.

Behavior (1)
Altering another child's work without asking

If you find the alteration of another child's work without permission (ranging from modifying slightly to spoiling irrevocably) *seems* for the most part to be:

1. persistent and willful; seemingly inflammatory and challenging (see Troubling Child)
2. persistently mischievous; mildly vexing, pushing limits/boundaries (see Testing Child)

- **The Troubling Child**

    Core Feeling: The more frequent and/or extensive the child's alteration is, the greater the **sadness/anger** is being experienced by the child.

    Core Wish: Communicates unconscious wish to be **contained** and **supported** as a way of decreasing sense of **danger** and **rejection**.

    Core Question: Limit-testing question—I am being triggered by events because this moment in class feels overwhelming; can you accept me and handle me?

    Responses: **Structural & Less Emotional** (see Responses section)

- **The Testing Child**

    Core Feeling: The more frequent and/or extensive the child's alterations are, the greater the **sadness/anger** is being experienced by the child.

    Core Wish: Communicates unconscious wish to be **contained** and **validated** as a way of increasing sense of **security** and decreasing sense of **abandonment**.

    Core Question: Limit-testing question—I am feeling bad about myself and need to show this by creating a distraction; do you care about me enough to stop me?

    Responses: **Structural & More Emotional** (see Responses section)

Responses for: Behavior (1) Altering another child's work without asking

The Troubling Child

- *Structural*:
    ◊ Clear and calm voice (supportive).

- Before class: Check in. Hold eye contact. "I'm with you. Let's keep working on this."
- During class: Hand on shoulder; down on knee at eye level. Hold eye contact. Use the Less Emotional responses below.
- After class: Check in. Hold eye contact. Reiterate response themes (boundaries, self-care). Track progress with chart.

- **Less Emotional**:
  - *Self-Care and Boundaries*: "I want you to ask permission before you do anything to your classmates' work. You are safer when you ask before you touch."
  - *Self-Care*: "Wait, take a deep breath and let it out very slowly when you want to touch someone's work."
  - *Boundaries*: "Think to yourself, 'I can make a choice to touch their work without asking or not.'"
  - *Self-Care and Boundaries*: "I want you to think about being in a museum. The artwork on the walls looks exciting with its colors and textures. So exciting that we often want to touch it and see what it might feel like. The problem is that the artists are not there to give permission and so the museums have a rule for all the art. 'Look, but don't touch.' Classroom art is the same."
- **Affirmation**:
  - "Controlling your wish to touch a classmate's work without asking takes great strength."
  - "Anyone can see what a huge effort you make to leave your classmate's work alone."

The Testing Child

- **Structural**:
  - Clear and crisp voice (supportive).
  - Before class: Check in. Hold eye contact. "I'm with you. Let's keep working on this."
  - During class: Hand on shoulder; down on knee at eye level. Hold eye contact. Use More Emotional responses below.
  - After class: Check in. Hold eye contact. Reiterate response themes (boundaries, self-awareness). Track progress with chart.
- **More Emotional**:
  - *Self-Awareness and Boundaries*: "It saddens me when you touch your classmate's work without asking, because I feel like it pushes you away from your classmates and pushes us apart."
  - *Self-Awareness*: "When you touch your classmate's work without asking, I think you are feeling bad."
  - *Self-Awareness and Boundaries*: "Sometimes bad thoughts like these just feel like they need to push our body around and make us do things that are not safe. I really want you to ask for help to keep your body doing safe things."

◊ *Boundaries*: "Try to take a deep breath and let it out very slowly; and say to yourself, 'I will be okay,' before you touch your classmate's work."
- **Affirmation**:
  ◊ "I am proud of you for trying to not touch your classmate's work without asking."
  ◊ "You took good care of yourself by not touching your classmate's work without asking."

Behavior (2)
Exhibiting distress during and/or after a caregiver's departure

If you find the child's distress after a caregiver's departure *seems* for the most part:

    1. incessant; mildly vexing, pushing limits/boundaries (see Testing Child)
    2. volatile; possibly upsetting and disconcerting for others (see Worrying Child)
    3. inaccessible; possibly odd and/or confusing to others (see Hiding Child)

- **The Testing Child**

Core Feeling:	The more frequent and/or the child's distress is, the greater the **sadness/anger** is being experienced by the child.
Core Wish:	Communicates unconscious wish to be **contained** and **validated** as a way of increasing sense of **security** and decreasing sense of **abandonment**.
Core Question:	Limit-testing question—I am feeling bad about myself and need to show this by creating a distraction; do you care about me enough to stop me?
Responses:	**Structural & More Emotional** (see Responses section)

- **The Worrying Child**

Core Feeling:	The more frequent and/or acute the child's distress is, the greater the **fear/anger** is being experienced by the child.
Core Wish:	Communicates unconscious wish to be **noticed** and **supported** as a way of decreasing sense of **danger** and **abandonment**.
Core Question:	Limit-testing question—I am being triggered by events and this is an expression of how afraid I am; do you care enough to protect me?
Responses:	**Verbal & Less Emotional** (see Responses section)

- **The Hiding Child**

Core Feeling:	The more frequent and/or acute the child's distress is, the greater the **fear/anger** is being experienced by the child.
Core Wish:	Communicates unconscious wish to be **noticed** and **validated** as a way of increasing sense of **security** and decreasing sense of **rejection**.
Core Question:	Limit-testing question—My behavior is a diversion from just how uncomfortable I feel right now; can you accept the way I am and contain me?
Responses:	**Verbal & More Emotional** (see Responses section)

Responses for: Behavior (2) Exhibiting distress during and/or after a caregiver's departure

The Testing Child

- *Structural*:
    - ◊ Clear and crisp voice (supportive).
    - ◊ Before class: Check in. Hold eye contact. "I'm with you. Let's keep working on this."
    - ◊ During class: Hand on shoulder; down on knee at eye level. Hold eye contact. Use More Emotional responses below.
    - ◊ After class: Check in. Hold eye contact. Reiterate response themes (boundaries, self-awareness). Track progress with chart.
- *More Emotional*:
    - ◊ *Self-Awareness and Boundaries*: "It saddens me when you get very upset when your (caregiver) leaves. I am here and will not leave you alone because I do not want you to feel far away from me."
    - ◊ *Self-Awareness*: "When get very upset when your (caregiver) leaves, I think you are feeling bad and sad."
    - ◊ *Self-Awareness and Boundaries*: "Sometimes bad and sad thoughts just feel like popping out of us. They are like balloons that blow up too big. I can help if we have to ask for help to let some air out very slowly before it pops. When a balloon pops, the loud noise can feel scary."
    - ◊ *Boundaries*: "Try to take a deep breath and let it out very slowly; and say to yourself, 'I will be okay,' even if I feel sad that my (caregiver) had to go."
- *Affirmation*:
    - ◊ "I am proud of you for showing me your feelings and letting me stay with you."
    - ◊ "You took good care of yourself by showing me your feelings when (your caregiver) has to go."

The Worrying Child

- **Verbal**:
    ◊ Clear and calm voice (quiet).
    ◊ Before class: Check in and talk about previous day. Occasional eye contact. "I want to check in with you to see how our talk felt for you. We can do this each day."
    ◊ During class: Occasional eye contact. Maintain distance (two feet at least). No physical contact. Use sound or words to get attention (Less Emotional responses below).
    ◊ After class: Occasional eye contact. Reiterate response themes (connection, self-care).
- **Less Emotional**:
    ◊ *Self-Care*: "Take a deep breath and let it out very slowly when your emotions feel sad and mad that your (caregiver) has to leave. Everything can wait until you feel calmer."
    ◊ *Self-Care and Connection*: "When we have big sad and mad feelings, it can help us feel safer if we try and slow down a little. When you feel sad and mad, try to come over and see me. I am safe."
    ◊ *Self-Care and Connection*: "Sometimes talking about what is upsetting you helps me understand you better."
    ◊ *Self-Care and Connection*: "When you have big sad and mad feelings, it makes me think about your safety. To help with safety, I would like to ask you what you are thinking when you (caregiver) goes."
- **Affirmation**:
    ◊ "Letting me help you shows that you are a very strong kid."
    ◊ "You are brave to try to let me help you feel safer after your (caregiver) has to go."

The Hiding Child

- **Verbal**:
    ◊ Clear and calm voice (quiet).
    ◊ Before class: Check in and talk about previous day. Occasional eye contact. "I want to check in with you to see if you remember our talk. We will do this each day."
    ◊ During class: Occasional eye contact. Maintain distance (two feet at least). No physical contact. Use sound or words to get attention (More Emotional responses below).
    ◊ After class: Occasional eye contact. Reiterate response themes (connection, self-awareness).
- **More Emotional**:
    ◊ *Self-Awareness and Connection*: "When your (caregiver) has to go and you are very upset, I think you have big feelings. When (he/she/they) starts to leave, let's you and I stand together. I can help with that."

- *Self-Awareness*: "It looks like your very upset feelings can just start to heat up sometimes when your (caregiver) starts to leave. It's important for you to know controlling your upset feelings is a way to be strong."
- *Connection*: "Look at my face. I am here and I am worried that you cannot keep yourself from becoming so upset when your (caregiver) has to leave."
- *Self-Awareness and Connection*: "Try to you to think to yourself, 'I know it is not fair that I don't get to go with my (caregiver) when (he/she/they) has to go, but I can try to control my upset feelings with my teacher's help. My upset feelings are like boiling water in a pot. I can try to turn the heat down or ask for someone to help me turn the heat down.'"

- **Affirmation:**
  - "I see you using your thoughts to try and control your upset feelings about your (caregiver) leaving."
  - "I am impressed how you are deciding to keep control of your upset feelings about your (caregiver) leaving."

Behavior (3)
Lying

If you find the child's need to control a narrative by altering the facts *seems* for the most part:

1. persistent and willful; seemingly inflammatory and challenging (see Troubling Child)
2. persistently mischievous; mildly vexing, pushing limits/boundaries (see Testing Child)
3. occasional and reactive; possibly upsetting and disturbing for others (see Worrying Child)
4. occasional and seemingly arbitrary; possibly odd and/or confusing to others (see Hiding Child)

- **The Troubling Child**

  Core Feeling: The more frequent and/or egregious the child's lying is, the greater the **sadness/anger** is being experienced by the child.

  Core Wish: Communicates unconscious wish to be **contained** and **supported** as a way of decreasing sense of **danger** and **rejection**.

  Core Question: Limit-testing question—I am being triggered by events because this moment in class feels overwhelming; can you accept me and handle me?

  Responses: **Structural & Less Emotional** (see Responses section)

- **The Testing Child**

  Core Feeling: The more frequent and/or egregious the child's lying is, the greater the **sadness/anger** is being experienced by the child.

  Core Wish: Communicates unconscious wish to be **contained** and **validated** as a way of increasing sense of **security** and decreasing sense of **abandonment**.

  Core Question: Limit-testing question—I am feeling bad about myself and need to show this by creating a distraction; do you care about me enough to stop me?

  Responses: **Structural & More Emotional** (see Responses section)

- **The Worrying Child**

  Core Feeling: The more frequent and/or egregious the child's lying is, the greater the **fear/anger** is being experienced by the child.

  Core Wish: The more frequent and/or egregious the child's lying is, the greater the **fear/anger** is being experienced by the child.

  Core Question: Limit-testing question—I am being triggered by events and this is an expression of how afraid I am; do you care enough to protect me?

  Responses: **Verbal & Less Emotional** (see Responses section)

- **The Hiding Child**

  Core Feeling: The more frequent and/or egregious the child's lying is, the greater the **fear/anger** is being experienced by the child.

  Core Wish: Communicates unconscious wish to be **noticed** and **validated** as a way of increasing sense of **security** and decreasing sense of **rejection**.

  Core Question: Limit-testing question—My behavior is a diversion from just how uncomfortable I feel right now; can you accept the way I am and contain me?

  Responses: **Verbal & More Emotional** (see Responses section)

Responses for: Behavior (3) Lying

The Troubling Child

- ***Structural*:**
    - ◊ Clear and calm voice (supportive).
    - ◊ Before class: Check in. Hold eye contact. "I'm with you. Let's keep working on this."

- ◊ During class: Hand on shoulder; down on knee at eye level. Hold eye contact. Use the Less Emotional responses below.
- ◊ After class: Check in. Hold eye contact. Reiterate response themes (boundaries, self-care). Track progress with chart.
- **Less Emotional:**
    - ◊ *Self-Care and Boundaries*: "I want you to try to tell the truth. You are safer when you tell the truth."
    - ◊ *Self-Care*: "Wait, take a deep breath and let it out very slowly when you want to lie to someone."
    - ◊ *Boundaries*: "I want you to think to yourself, 'I can make a choice to lie or tell the truth and be safe.'"
    - ◊ *Self-Care and Boundaries*: "I want you to think about us building a dam together across a stream and trying to stop all the water from flowing. If we can do it, it can feel really good when we see that we have stopped the water in the stream completely. Controlling whether you lie or not is the same. When you tell the truth, it's like a victory."
- **Affirmation:**
    - ◊ "Telling the truth takes great strength."
    - ◊ "Anyone can see what a huge effort you make to tell the truth."

The Testing Child

- **Structural:**
    - ◊ Clear and crisp voice (supportive).
    - ◊ Before class: Check in. Hold eye contact. "I'm with you. Let's keep working on this."
    - ◊ During class: Hand on shoulder; down on knee at eye level. Hold eye contact. Use More Emotional responses below.
    - ◊ After class: Check in. Hold eye contact. Reiterate response themes (boundaries, self-awareness). Track progress with chart.
- **More Emotional:**
    - ◊ *Self-Awareness and Boundaries*: "It saddens me when you do not tell the truth, because I feel like it pushes us apart."
    - ◊ *Self-Awareness*: "When you do not tell the truth, I think you feel bad and alone."
    - ◊ *Self-Awareness and Boundaries*: "Sometimes lies and other bad thoughts just feel like they need to push out of our mouths and makes us less safe. Sometimes, we have to ask for help to keep ourselves safe by telling the truth."
    - ◊ *Boundaries*: "Try to take a deep breath and let it out very slowly; and say to yourself, 'I will be okay,' before you decide to lie to me or someone else."
    - ◊ *Self-Awareness and Boundaries*: "Telling the truth to me is important. If you are worried about telling the truth, try to say to me 'I feel bad' before telling me a lie. I will help you with the truth."

- *Affirmation*:
    - ◊ "I am proud of you for trying so hard to tell the truth."
    - ◊ "You took good care of yourself by telling the truth."

The Worrying Child

- *Verbal*:
    - ◊ Clear and calm voice (quiet).
    - ◊ Before class: Check in and talk about previous day. Occasional eye contact. "I want to check in with you to see how our talk felt for you. We can do this each day."
    - ◊ During class: Occasional eye contact. Maintain distance (two feet at least). No physical contact. Use sound or words to get attention (Less Emotional responses below).
    - ◊ After class: Occasional eye contact. Reiterate response themes (connection, self-care).
- *Less Emotional*:
    - ◊ *Self-Care*: "Take a deep breath and let it out very slowly when you feel like you need to lie to someone. The lie can wait."
    - ◊ *Self-Care and Connection*: "It can help us feel safer if we tell the truth. When you feel like you need to lie, try to say to me 'I feel worried' before telling the lie. I will help you feel safe with the truth."
    - ◊ *Self-Care and Connection*: "When you lie, it makes me think about your safety. I would like to ask you about what you are thinking."
- *Affirmation*:
    - ◊ "Telling the truth takes strength."
    - ◊ "You show a lot of bravery when you tell the truth."

The Hiding Child

- *Verbal*:
    - ◊ Clear and calm voice (quiet).
    - ◊ Before class: Check in and talk about previous day. Occasional eye contact. "I want to check in with you to see if you remember our talk. We will do this each day."
    - ◊ During class: Occasional eye contact. Maintain distance (two feet at least). No physical contact. Use sound or words to get attention (More Emotional responses below).
    - ◊ After class: Occasional eye contact. Reiterate response themes (connection, self-awareness).
- *More Emotional*:
    - ◊ *Self-Awareness and Connection*: "When telling a lie becomes very important to you, I think you have big feelings, and I am worried. Tell me that you are having trouble telling the truth. I can help with that."
    - ◊ *Self-Awareness and Connection*: "It looks like it's just so hard for you to

keep the lie from coming out. I want you to remember, telling the truth is a way to be strong."
- ◊ *Connection*: "Look at my face. I am worried that you are having difficulty telling the truth."
- ◊ *Self-Awareness*: "Try to you to think to yourself, 'I can control the lies leaving my mouth. They are like water coming out of a faucet. I can decide between the cold truth or the hot lie.'"

- **Affirmation**:
  - ◊ "I see you using your thought to control whether you tell the truth or the lie."
  - ◊ "I am impressed how you decided to tell the truth."

Behavior (4)
Not waiting for one's turn

If you find the child's behavior of not waiting for his/her turn **seems** for the most part:

1. persistently willful; seemingly inflammatory and challenging (see Troubling Child)

2. persistent, yet playful; mildly vexing, pushing limits and boundaries (see Testing Child)

3. sudden and restless; possibly upsetting and stressful for you (see Worrying Child)

4. sudden and seemingly arbitrary; possibly odd and/or confusing to you (see Hiding Child)

- **The Troubling Child**

Core Feeling:	The more frequent the child's behavior is, the greater the **sadness/anger** is being experienced by the child.
Core Wish:	Communicates unconscious wish to be **contained** and **supported** as a way of decreasing sense of **danger** and **rejection**.
Core Question:	Limit-testing question—I am being triggered by events because this moment in class feels overwhelming; can you accept me and handle me?
Responses:	**Structural & Less Emotional** (see Responses section)

- **The Testing Child**

Core Feeling:	The more frequent the child's behavior is, the greater the **sadness/anger** is being experienced by the child.

Core Wish:	Communicates unconscious wish to be **contained** and **validated** as a way of increasing sense of **security** and decreasing sense of **abandonment**.
Core Question:	Limit-testing question—I am feeling bad about myself and need to show this by creating a distraction; do you care about me enough to stop me?
Responses:	**Structural & More Emotional** (see Responses section)

- **The Worrying Child**

Core Feeling:	The more frequent the child's behavior is, the greater the **fear/anger** is being experienced by the child.
Core Wish:	Communicates unconscious wish to be **noticed** and **supported** as a way of decreasing sense of **danger** and **abandonment**.
Core Question:	Limit-testing question—I am being triggered by events and this is an expression of how afraid I am; do you care enough to protect me?
Responses:	**Verbal & Less Emotional** (see Responses section)

- **The Hiding Child**

Core Feeling:	The more frequent the child's behavior is, the greater the **fear/anger** is being experienced by the child.
Core Wish:	Communicates unconscious wish to be **noticed** and **validated** as a way of increasing sense of **security** and decreasing sense of **rejection**.
Core Question:	Limit-testing question—My behavior is a diversion from just how uncomfortable I feel right now; can you accept the way I am and contain me?
Responses:	**Verbal & More Emotional** (see Responses section)

Responses for: Behavior (4) Not waiting for one's turn

The Troubling Child

- ***Structural:***
    - ◊ Clear and calm voice (supportive).
    - ◊ Before class: Check in. Hold eye contact. "I'm with you. Let's keep working on this."
    - ◊ During class: Hand on shoulder; down on knee at eye level. Hold eye contact. Use the Less Emotional responses below.
    - ◊ After class: Check in. Hold eye contact. Reiterate response themes (boundaries, self-care). Track progress with chart.

- *Less Emotional*:
  - ◊ *Self-Care and Boundaries*: "I want you to try wait your turn. You are safer when you wait your turn."
  - ◊ *Self-Care*: "Wait, take a deep breath and let it out very slowly, if you feel you can't wait for your turn."
  - ◊ *Boundaries*: "I want you to think to yourself, 'I can make a choice to skip over my classmates turn or to wait for my turn and be safe.'"
  - ◊ *Self-Care and Boundaries*: "Waiting for your turn is like saving a piece of candy for after lunch. It's difficult and it may even feel unfair, but sometimes we just have to do it and then maybe we get to have more dessert later because we waited. It can be like a victory if we can do it."
- *Affirmation*:
  - ◊ "Controlling your choice to wait or not takes great strength."
  - ◊ "Anyone can see what a huge effort you make not skip anyone else's turn."

The Testing Child

- *Structural*:
  - ◊ Clear and crisp voice (supportive).
  - ◊ Before class: Check in. Hold eye contact. "I'm with you. Let's keep working on this."
  - ◊ During class: Hand on shoulder; down on knee at eye level. Hold eye contact. Use More Emotional responses below.
  - ◊ After class: Check in. Hold eye contact. Reiterate response themes (boundaries, self-awareness). Track progress with chart.
- *More Emotional*:
  - ◊ *Self-Awareness and Boundaries*: "It saddens me when you cannot wait for your turn, because I feel like it pushes us apart."
  - ◊ *Self-Awareness*: "When you cannot wait for your turn, I think you feel bad and alone."
  - ◊ *Self-Awareness and Boundaries*: "Sometimes the bad thoughts just feel like they need to push our body and words around in ways that are not safe. I want you to let me help you keep yourself in a safe place."
  - ◊ *Boundaries*: "Try to take a deep breath and let it out very slowly; and repeat to yourself, 'I will be okay,' I can wait my turn,' when you feel that you are having trouble waiting."
  - ◊ *Self-Awareness and Boundaries*: "Waiting your turn is important to me. Try to raise your hand if you feel like you cannot wait, and I will come over."
- *Affirmation*:
  - ◊ "I am proud of you for trying so hard to wait for your turn."
  - ◊ "You took good care of yourself by waiting for your turn."

The Worrying Child

- **Verbal**:
    - ◊ Clear and calm voice (quiet).
    - ◊ Before class: Check in and talk about previous day. Occasional eye contact. "I want to check in with you to see how our talk felt for you. We can do this each day."
    - ◊ During class: Occasional eye contact. Maintain distance (two feet at least). No physical contact. Use sound or words to get attention (Less Emotional responses below).
    - ◊ After class: Occasional eye contact. Reiterate response themes (connection, self-care).
- **Less Emotional**:
    - ◊ *Self-Care*: "Take a deep breath and let it out very slowly when you are having difficulty waiting your turn. Your body and words can stay still and quiet for a moment."
    - ◊ *Self-Care and Connection*: "It can help us feel safer if we try and slow down a little. When you are having trouble waiting for you turn, try to come over and see me first. We can wait together."
    - ◊ *Connection*: "Sometimes your difficulty waiting makes me want to know what you are thinking about."
    - ◊ *Self-Care and Connection*: "When you are having difficulty waiting for your turn, it makes me think about your safety. I would like to ask you about what you are thinking."
- **Affirmation**:
    - ◊ "Waiting for your turn takes strength."
    - ◊ "You are brave to wait for your turn when you really do not want to."

The Hiding Child

- **Verbal**:
    - ◊ Clear and calm voice (quiet).
    - ◊ Before class: Check in and talk about previous day. Occasional eye contact. "I want to check in with you to see if you remember our talk. We will do this each day."
    - ◊ During class: Occasional eye contact. Maintain distance (two feet at least). No physical contact. Use sound or words to get attention (More Emotional responses below).
    - ◊ After class: Occasional eye contact. Reiterate response themes (connection, self-awareness).
- **More Emotional**:
    - ◊ *Self-Awareness and Connection*: "When you have trouble waiting for your turn, I think you have big feelings, and I am worried. Try to raise your hand if you want to take a turn. I can help with that."
    - ◊ *Self-Awareness*: "It looks like you just can't wait for your turn when you have big feelings. Waiting is a way to be strong."

- ◊ *Connection*: "Look at my face. I am concerned that you are having difficulty waiting for you turn."
- ◊ *Self-Awareness*: "Try to you to think to yourself, 'I can control my body and words. They are like water coming out of a faucet. I can turn the faucet off for a moment and wait for my moment.'"
- *Affirmation*:
  - ◊ "I see you using your thoughts to control your ability to wait for you turn."
  - ◊ "I am impressed how you decide to wait for your turn instead of taking someone else's."

Behavior (5)
Sharing too much personal information

If you find the child's need to control a situation by sharing personal information *seems* for the most part:

1. persistent and willful; seemingly inflammatory and challenging (see Troubling Child)

2. occasional and reactive; possibly upsetting and disturbing for others (see Worrying Child)

- **The Troubling Child**

Core Feeling:	The more frequent and/or personal the child's sharing is, the greater the **sadness/anger** is being experienced by the child.
Core Wish:	Communicates unconscious wish to be **contained** and **supported** as a way of decreasing sense of **danger** and **rejection**.
Core Question:	Limit-testing question—I am being triggered by events because this moment in class feels overwhelming; can you accept me and handle me?
Responses:	**Structural & Less Emotional** (see Responses section)

- **The Worrying Child**

Core Feeling:	The more frequent and/or personal the child's sharing is, the greater the **fear/anger** is being experienced by the child.
Core Wish:	Communicates unconscious wish to be **noticed** and **supported** as a way of decreasing sense of **danger** and **abandonment**.
Core Question:	Limit-testing question—I am being triggered by events and this is an expression of how afraid I am; do you care enough to protect me?
Responses:	**Verbal & Less Emotional** (see Responses section)

Responses for: Behavior (5) Sharing too much personal information

The Troubling Child

- **Structural**:
    - ◊ Clear and calm voice (supportive).
    - ◊ Before class: Check in. Hold eye contact. "I'm with you. Let's keep working on this."
    - ◊ During class: Hand on shoulder; down on knee at eye level. Hold eye contact. Use the Less Emotional responses below.
    - ◊ After class: Check in. Hold eye contact. Reiterate response themes (boundaries, self-care). Track progress with chart.
- **Less Emotional**:
    - ◊ *Self-Care and Boundaries*: "I want you to try to keep stories about you more private. Your safety is important. It is safer to keep your stories close to you and only share it with people who you trust."
    - ◊ *Self-Care*: "When you think about sharing stories about yourself with just anyone, take a deep breath, let it out very slowly; and say to yourself 'It's okay, I can wait to share it with my teacher.'"
    - ◊ *Self-Care and Boundaries*: "I want you to think…. I can keep stories about me private. It makes me safer and braver."
    - ◊ *Self-Care and Boundaries*: "If you share your personal stories with just anyone, you cannot decide who they will tell. The people who have the job to keep you safe need your help to keep your private stories safe too. You are stronger when you think about who to share with."
- **Affirmation**:
    - ◊ "You are strong when you think about sharing your personal information first."
    - ◊ "Anyone can see what huge effort you made to think first and share stuff second."

The Worrying Child

- **Verbal**:
    - ◊ Clear and calm voice (quiet).
    - ◊ Before class: Check in and talk about previous day. Occasional eye contact. "I want to check in with you to see how our talk felt for you. We can do this each day."
    - ◊ During class: Occasional eye contact. Maintain distance (two feet at least). No physical contact. Use sound or words to get attention (Less Emotional responses below).
    - ◊ After class: Occasional eye contact. Reiterate response themes (connection, self-care).
- **Less Emotional**:
    - ◊ *Self-Care*: "Take a deep breath and let it out very slowly when you start

to think about sharing stories about yourself with just anyone. Your private stories can wait for a moment."
- ◊ *Self-Care and Connection*: "It can help us feel safer if we try and slow down a little. When you start to think about sharing stuff about yourself, try to come over and see me first. We can think together."
- ◊ *Self-Care and Connection*: "When you really want to share private stuff about yourself with another person, it makes me think about your safety. When you want to do this, I would like to ask you about what you are thinking."

- **Affirmation**:
  - ◊ "Making a decision whether or not to sharing personal stuff about you takes strength."
  - ◊ "You are brave to thinking about whether to share private stuff about your or not."

Behavior (6)
Stealing

If you find the child's stealing behavior *seems*, for the most part:

1. persistent and willful; seemingly inflammatory and challenging (see Troubling Child)

2. seemingly arbitrary; possibly odd and/or confusing to you (see Hiding Child)

- **The Troubling Child**

Core Feeling:	The more frequent the child's stealing is, the greater the **sadness/anger** is being experienced by the child.
Core Wish:	Communicates unconscious wish to be **contained** and **supported** as a way of decreasing sense of **danger** and **rejection**.
Core Question:	Limit-testing question—I am being triggered by events because this moment in class feels overwhelming; can you accept me and handle me?
Responses:	**Structural & Less Emotional** (see Responses section)

- **The Hiding Child**

Core Feeling:	The more frequent the child's stealing is, the greater the **fear/anger** is being experienced by the child.

Core Wish: Communicates unconscious wish to be **noticed** and **validated** as a way of increasing sense of **security** and decreasing sense of **rejection**.

Core Question: Limit-testing question—My behavior is a diversion from just how uncomfortable I feel right now; can you accept the way I am and contain me?

Responses: **Verbal & More Emotional** (see Responses section)

Responses for: Behavior (6) Stealing

The Troubling Child

- *Structural*:
    - ◊ Clear and calm voice (supportive).
    - ◊ Before class: Check in. Hold eye contact. "I'm with you. Let's keep working on this."
    - ◊ During class: Hand on shoulder; down on knee at eye level. Hold eye contact. Use the Less Emotional responses below.
    - ◊ After class: Check in. Hold eye contact. Reiterate response themes (boundaries, self-care). Track progress with chart.
- *Less Emotional*:
    - ◊ *Self-Care and Boundaries*: "I want you to try to ask permission to take something that does not belong to you before you take it without asking. You are safer when you ask before you touch."
    - ◊ *Self-Care*: "Wait, take a deep breath and let it out very slowly when you want to take something that does not belong to you."
    - ◊ *Boundaries*: "Think to yourself, 'I have a choice to take something that does not belong to me or not.'"
    - ◊ *Self-Care and Boundaries*: "I want you to think about being in a toy store. The toys are so fun that we often want them now so we can play. The problem is that the toys belong to the store until they are paid for and we do not have permission to just take them. It's the same for everything, even for you. Stuff that belongs to you is yours until you agree to give it to someone."
- *Affirmation*:
    - ◊ "Controlling your wish to take something without asking work takes great strength."
    - ◊ "Anyone can see what a huge effort you make to make sure you ask before taking."

The Hiding Child

- *Verbal*:
    - ◊ Clear and calm voice (quiet).

- Before class: Check in and talk about previous day. Occasional eye contact. "I want to check in with you to see if you remember our talk. We will do this each day."
- During class: Occasional eye contact. Maintain distance (two feet at least). No physical contact. Use sound or words to get attention (More Emotional responses below).
- After class: Occasional eye contact. Reiterate response themes (connection, self-awareness).

- **More Emotional:**
  - *Self-Awareness and Connection*: "When you want to take something that does not belong to you, I think you are having feelings, and I am worried. Before you do it, come and see me. I can help with that."
  - *Self-Awareness and Connection*: "Look at my face. I am worried that you are not asking permission to take something that does not belong to you. You can be stronger by asking for permission first."
  - *Self-Awareness*: "Try to think to yourself, 'I can control my body and thoughts. Taking a persons' stuff without asking is like blowing out someone's birthday candle. It is something important that belongs to them and we have to ask if we want to help.'"

- **Affirmation:**
  - "I see you using your thought to control your wish to take someone else's things."
  - "I am impressed how you decide to ask permission before you take a person's things."

Behavior (7)
Touching and/or displaying genitals in public

If you find the child's touching and/or displaying genitals in public ***seems*** for the most part:

1. occasional and reactive; possibly upsetting and disturbing for others (see Worrying Child)
2. seemingly arbitrary; possibly odd and/or confusing to others (see Hiding Child)

- **The Worrying Child**

  Core Feeling: The more frequent the child's behavior is, the greater the **fear/anger** is being experienced by the child.

  Core Wish: Communicates unconscious wish to be **noticed** and **supported** as a way of decreasing sense of **danger** and **abandonment**.

Chapter 14. Personal Space and Boundary Problems   269

Core Question: Limit-testing question—I am being triggered by events and this is an expression of how afraid I am; do you care enough to protect me?

Responses: **Verbal & Less Emotional** (see Responses section)

- **The Hiding Child**

Core Feeling: The more frequent the child's behavior is, the greater the **fear/anger** is being experienced by the child.

Core Wish: Communicates unconscious wish to be **noticed** and **validated** as a way of increasing sense of **security** and decreasing sense of **rejection**.

Core Question: Limit-testing question—My behavior is a diversion from just how uncomfortable I feel right now; can you accept the way I am and contain me?

Responses: **Verbal & More Emotional** (see Responses section)

Responses for: Behavior (7) Touching and/or displaying genitals in public

The Worrying Child

- ***Verbal*:**
    - ◊ Clear and calm voice (quiet).
    - ◊ Before class: Check in and talk about previous day. Occasional eye contact. "I want to check in with you to see how our talk felt for you. We can do this each day."
    - ◊ During class: Occasional eye contact. Maintain distance (two feet at least). No physical contact. Use sound or words to get attention (Less Emotional responses below).
    - ◊ After class: Occasional eye contact. Reiterate response themes (connection, self-care).
- ***Less Emotional*:**
    - ◊ *Self-Care and Connection*: "This might be embarrassing to talk about. You are safe. I want you to take a deep breath and let it out very slowly when you start to think about touching/showing your private parts in the class. Before you do it, come and see me. If not, I will quietly come talk to you."
    - ◊ *Self-Care and Connection*: "It can help us feel safer if we come up with a plan. When you start to think about touching/showing your privates, come over and see me first. We can find something else for you to do. You are strong and brave when you keep your privates to yourself."
    - ◊ *Self-Care and Connection*: "When you really want to touch/show your

privates, it makes me think about your safety. When you want to do this, I would like to ask you about what you are thinking."
- *Affirmation*:
    ◊ "Making a safe choice to not touch/show your privates in class takes strength."
    ◊ "You are brave when you choose to not touch/show your privates in class."

The Hiding Child

- *Verbal*:
    ◊ Clear and calm voice (quiet).
    ◊ Before class: Check in and talk about previous day. Occasional eye contact. "I want to check in with you to see if you remember our talk. We will do this each day."
    ◊ During class: Occasional eye contact. Maintain distance (two feet at least). No physical contact. Use sound or words to get attention (More Emotional responses below).
    ◊ After class: Occasional eye contact. Reiterate response themes (connection, self-awareness).
- *More Emotional*:
    ◊ *Self-Awareness and Connection*: "This might be embarrassing to talk about. When you touch/show your privates in class, I think you are having big feelings, and I am worried. I want your privates to be private."
    ◊ *Self-Awareness and Connection*: "Look at my face. I am worried when you touch/show your privates in class. I want you to be safe and strong. You can be strong by remembering that your privates are private."
    ◊ *Self-Awareness and Connection*: "Try to you to think to yourself, 'I can control myself. Touching/Showing my privates in class is like crossing a street without looking. I am safer if I think and wait to see if it is safe.'"
- *Affirmation*:
    ◊ "I see you using your strong thoughts to control the need to touch your privates in class."
    ◊ "I am impressed how you stay strong and decide to not touch your privates in class."

Behavior (8)
Touching another person's body without asking

If you find the child's physical contact (ranging from hugging or kissing to grabbing or shoving) ***seems*** for the most part:

1. persistent and willful; seemingly inflammatory and challenging (see Troubling Child)

2. persistent, yet playful; mildly vexing, pushing limits and boundaries (see Testing Child)

3. sudden and volatile; possibly upsetting and alarming to others (see Worrying Child)

- **The Troubling Child**

    Core Feeling: The more frequent and/or acute the child's physical contact of another is, the greater the **sadness/anger** is being experienced by the child.

    Core Wish: Communicates unconscious wish to be **contained** and **supported** as a way of decreasing sense of **danger** and **rejection**.

    Core Question: Limit-testing question—I am being triggered by events because this moment in class feels overwhelming; can you accept me and handle me?

    Responses: **Structural & Less Emotional** (see Responses section)

- **The Testing Child**

    Core Feeling: The more frequent and/or acute the child's physical contact of another is, the greater the **sadness/anger** is being experienced by the child.

    Core Wish: Communicates unconscious wish to be **contained** and **validated** as a way of increasing sense of **security** and decreasing sense of **abandonment**.

    Core Question: Limit-testing question—I am feeling bad about myself and need to show this by creating a distraction; do you care about me enough to stop me?

    Responses: **Structural & More Emotional** (see Responses section)

- **The Worrying Child**

    Core Feeling: The more frequent and/or acute the child's physical contact of another is, the greater the **fear/anger** is being experienced by the child.

    Core Wish: Communicates unconscious wish to be **noticed** and **supported** as a way of decreasing sense of **danger** and **abandonment**.

    Core Question: Limit-testing question—I am being triggered by events and this is an expression of how afraid I am; do you care enough to protect me?

    Responses: **Verbal & Less Emotional** (see Responses section)

Responses for: Behavior (8) Touching another person's body without asking

The Troubling Child

- **Structural**:
    - ◊ Clear and calm voice (supportive).
    - ◊ Before class: Check in. Hold eye contact. "I'm with you. Let's keep working on this."
    - ◊ During class: Hand on shoulder; down on knee at eye level. Hold eye contact. Use the Less Emotional responses below.
    - ◊ After class: Check in. Hold eye contact. Reiterate response themes (boundaries, self-care). Track progress with chart.
- **Less Emotional**:
    - ◊ *Self-Care and Boundaries*: "I want you to ask permission to touch someone instead of touching them without asking. You are safer when you ask before you touch."
    - ◊ *Self-Care*: "Wait, take a deep breath and let it out very slowly when you feel you want touch someone."
    - ◊ *Boundaries*: "Think to yourself, 'I have a choice to touch this person without asking or not.'"
    - ◊ *Self-Care and Boundaries*: "I want you to think about being in a museum. The artwork on the walls looks exciting with its colors and textures. So exciting that we often want to touch it and see what it might feel like. The problem is that the artists are not there to give permission and so the museums has a rule for all the art. 'Look. Don't touch.' People's bodies are the same."
- **Affirmation**:
    - ◊ "Controlling your wish to touch a classmate without asking takes great strength."
    - ◊ "Anyone can see what a huge effort you make to leave your classmate's work alone."

The Testing Child

- **Structural**:
    - ◊ Clear and crisp voice (supportive).
    - ◊ Before class: Check in. Hold eye contact. "I'm with you. Let's keep working on this."
    - ◊ During class: Hand on shoulder; down on knee at eye level. Hold eye contact. Use More Emotional responses below.
    - ◊ After class: Check in. Hold eye contact. Reiterate response themes (boundaries, self-awareness). Track progress with chart.
- **More Emotional**:
    - ◊ *Self-Awareness and Boundaries*: "It worries me when you touch someone

without asking, because I feel like it pushes you away from your classmates and pushes us apart."
- ◊ *Self-Awareness*: "When you touch someone without asking, I think you are feeling bad."
- ◊ *Self-Awareness and Boundaries*: "Sometimes bad thoughts like these just feel like they need to push our body around and make us do things that are not safe. I really want you to ask for help to keep your body doing safe things."
- ◊ *Boundaries*: "Try to take a deep breath and let it out very slowly; and say to yourself, 'I will be okay,' before you touch someone without asking."

- *Affirmation*:
  - ◊ "I am proud of you for trying to not touch someone without asking."
  - ◊ "You took good care of yourself by not touching anyone without asking."

The Worrying Child

- *Verbal*:
  - ◊ Clear and calm voice (quiet).
  - ◊ Before class: Check in and talk about previous day. Occasional eye contact. "I want to check in with you to see how our talk felt for you. We can do this each day."
  - ◊ During class: Occasional eye contact. Maintain distance (two feet at least). No physical contact. Use sound or words to get attention (Less Emotional responses below).
  - ◊ After class: Occasional eye contact. Reiterate response themes (connection, self-care).

- *Less Emotional*:
  - ◊ *Self-Care*: "Take a deep breath and let it out very slowly if you suddenly feel like you want to touch another person's body without asking. You are safer when you ask before you touch."
  - ◊ *Self-Care and Connection*: "It can help us feel safer if we try and slow down a little. When you start to think about touching someone, try to come over and see me first. We can think together about what is safe."
  - ◊ *Self-Care and Connection*: "When you really want to touch another person without permission, it makes me think about your safety. When you want to do this, I would like to ask you about what you are thinking."

- *Affirmation*:
  - ◊ "Making a safe decision to not touch a person without permission takes strength."
  - ◊ "You are brave to think about whether to touch a person without permission."

Your Evolving Responses

As you have read, there are different motivations for your students' behaviors depending on their latent communication patterns. This demonstrates that your responses cannot be "one size fits all" in nature. While we have provided specific words for you to follow, we intend this chapter and the others like it to be a framework for your responses, not a script. You certainly can use our suggested language as you experiment with the interventions we have described. Overtime, it will be more helpful for you to find your own words to communicate with your students. As you continue to try these techniques, using your own communication style will make the responses to your students' behaviors feel authentic and sincere. This will happen naturally. The proposed interventions that we used in this chapter are a starting point and are meant to evolve and grow with your comfort level. This might take some practice, but it will be well worth it to expand your repertoire of potential responses to concerning or disruptive behaviors. You may find that your own words are more effective or more impactful than the words and phrases we have suggested in this book. The more you are a part of the interventions, the more meaningful they may be to your students. As we know, students need repetition, so please be patient as you try out new ways to respond to them.

Chapter 15

Not Speaking

"Sometimes not speaking says more that all the words in the world."
—Colleen Hoover

How to Use This Chapter

1. As you prepare to read this chapter, choose one child from your class on whom you wish to focus. Selecting one child at a time allows for a more concentrated exploration of the material and how it relates to each child uniquely. **As a guide, we will use "Melody," a second grader who does not speak to her classmates when working in groups.**

2. Read the paragraphs from the following headings to begin the process: *Format and Theme* and *Common Forms of the Behavior*.

3. Choose one behavior that the selected child is exhibiting. Selecting one behavior at a time allows for a more concentrated exploration of the material centering on how the child communicates using this specific behavior. **Melody's behavior of not speaking with peers during group work.**

4. Read the paragraphs from the following headings to learn more about the general category that this behavior falls within from a more holistic perspective: *Manifest Communication* and *Latent Communication*.

5. Read the paragraphs from the heading *Responses and Affirmations* as background to how we structured the proposed responses and the expectation that you will ultimately personalize the responses provided in this chapter.

6. Turn to the page that contains the behavior in question. There you will find the number of the behavior and its name. **We select Behavior (3) Not speaking with peers during group work.**

7. On that page, below the number and name, you will find all the possible latent communication prompts for that behavior, ranging from (1) to (4). From these prompts, choose the prompt that most closely reminds you of how this child exhibits this behavior. Your choice may not fit one prompt exactly. If your sense is that multiple prompts could fit, choose the closest one to begin the process. You can return to the other prompts later. You will notice that each prompt

corresponds with a child communication Persona (i.e., Troubling, Testing, Worrying, Hiding). **For Melody, we choose "out-of-place and/or disconnected; possibly odd and/or confusing to others (see Hiding Child)."**

8. After choosing a latent communication prompt, use the child communication Persona and read the corresponding Core Feelings, Core Wish, Core Question. This information describes the underlying meaning of the behavior and creates an empathic guide for you to keep in mind when responding to the child's behavior.

9. On the following page(s), you will find responses and affirmations for the number and name of the behavior in question. **We select Responses for: Behavior (3) Not speaking with peers during group work** section **The Hiding Child**. Find and read the responses and affirmations for the behavior in question that corresponds with the child communication Persona.

10. **Try the responses and affirmations with Melody and determine how they feel to you.**

Theme and Format

Each of these behavior chapters in this section of the book should be considered with the following format in mind. In this chapter, we will focus on children who **do not speak, speak only when spoken to, have very little expressive language functions, or speak so quietly as to be very difficult to hear**. That said, the title of this chapter is an umbrella descriptor, and these behaviors comprise a theme or group of communications. We observe these manifest communications as thematic, as there are many permutations within a category of behavior.

Common Forms of This Behavior

- Mumbling and/or whispering
- Not speaking to peers during play
- Not speaking with peers during group work
- Only speaking when spoken to
- Responding to teacher's question with minimal reply
- Responding with non-verbal communication frequently (when words are known)
- Responding with sounds frequently (when words are known)

Manifest Communication

It is important to acknowledge that a dearth of speaking may require a professional assessment for a child to determine any physiological, neurological, or developmental issues that are preventing or affecting speech. Ruling out these causes is a critical step in addressing any child's needs in the areas of speech development. While this is happening, or if a parent chooses to not follow a professional assessment path, there are ways for us to respond to a child who communicates in this way.

Selective Mutism is a diagnosis (sometimes called Elective Mutism) that centers on a child's absence of speech in social settings (American Psychiatric Association, 2013). The reason we use the word "Selective" is that these children have the ability to speak, but there is a process at work in which they are "selecting" where and/or when they will use this verbal skill. To this end, it becomes critical to observe this behavior/communication carefully, because the subtleties of Selective Mutism can be highly nuanced and are instrumental in our responses. The "silence" must be heard (Camposano, 2011).

While silence is often considered "blissful," children who do not seem to be able to respond to our questions or do not vocalize the way other children in their peer group/cohort do, can feel confuse and upset us. We want to feel helpful and useful as teachers, to assist children in the journey and forward motion of learning. Because words and word development are such an integral part of that process, when they are not present, we may feel lost as to how to proceed.

With a lack of words, it is these children's non-verbal communication that can take and hold our attention and focus. The manifest demonstrations often augment and supplement the message. So, what are the possible expressions that we may look to for information? Let's think about them in terms of our senses: sight, smell, touch, and hearing. Children communicate within each of these forms.

Table 15.1:
Forms of Non-Verbal Communication

Aspects of the child teachers are able to…	Sub-categories	Examples
See	Eye Contact	None, Darting, Eyes Closed, Looking off into the distance
	Apparel Choices	Bright, Dull, Tight, Loose Fitting
	Body Posture	Open, Closed
	Grooming	Unkempt, Doll-Like
Smell	Hygiene	Clean, Dirty
	Body Odor	
Touch	Proximity	Close, Far
	Boundary Maintenance	Aware, Unaware
Hear	Inorganic sounds	Banging, Clapping
	Organic sounds	Grunts, Sighs, Tongue clicks, Humming

Using the child Personas of the Troubling child, the Testing child, the Worrying child, and the Hiding child, we will explore specific teacher responses for each type of communication pattern (see Table 15.2.). For more detailed information about background for each Persona and the reasoning behind the most productive teacher response configurations, please refer back to their respective chapters.

Table 15.2:
Behavior Frequency by Persona

Behavior	Persona			
	Troubling Child Loud & Over Reactive	Testing Child Loud & Under Reactive	Worrying Child Quiet & Over Reactive	Hiding Child Quiet & Under Reactive
Mumbling or whispering			X	X
Not speaking to peers during play			X	X
Not speaking with peers during group work	X		X	X
Only speaking when spoken to			X	X
Responding to teacher's question with minimal reply	X		X	X
Responding with non-verbal communication frequently (when words are known)	X		X	X
Responding with sounds frequently (when words are known)	X			X

The absence of an "X" indicates that this Persona does not typically engage in this type of behavior/communication.

Latent Communication

This process is not an exact science and should be conducted more as trial and error. We would like you to take your best professional guess as to your answers to the following inquiries and evaluations. If you find that, after working through the latent communication material and identifying a set of responses, they do not work as you hoped, you can always revise and try again. Just remember, children integrate learning following repetition, so do not give up too soon.

Responses and Affirmations

Children do not learn the first time we teach them a new concept or a task. We say this in order to manage our expectations about how quickly or completely these new interventions will change or extinguish any given behavior.

Let's keep in mind the following factors. First, the development of these behaviors has typically occurred over an extended period of time. Based on the ages of the children we address in this book, any behavior grew over at least two years and up to eight. As much as we would wish it, a behavior that has been developing over a lengthy period of time cannot change "overnight." Actually, rapid change is often poorly integrated by children and cannot be sustained. Second, children integrate responses at different rates based on a variety of factors, including temperament, environment, learning styles, family involvement/support, etc. We have addressed these earlier in the book. Last, we are constructing foundations from which to grow, one brick at a time, foundations that these children will be able to build on and rely on for years to come. To this end, we want you to know that each of your responses is remembered and cataloged by these children for future use—even if it does not outwardly appear to have been during your time with the child. This relates to the corrective emotional experience we wrote about earlier in this book. Your interactions become part of the child's long-term memory, exchanges that are saved for future use.

That said, we want us to have some benchmarks for our expectations. First, we believe that one month is a sufficient timeframe for some level of change in a behavior, given that a specific teacher response is maintained with consistency and repetition. Second, as we cannot factor in changes that are occurring in real time within these children and with their families, the one-month benchmark may need to be altered accordingly. Third, the one-month duration allows for these challenged children to test us. They will imagine that what we are doing cannot be sustained, that it is too good to last. Our consistency and repetition in responding to the underlying message ultimately quiet their negative thoughts. It is then when the child's expectations of the people around them begin to change to an inner message that is more hopeful and positive. This hopefulness alters their communications and behaviors and can become a more embedded part of their future interpersonal relationships.

Behavior (1)
Mumbling and/or whispering

If you find the child's mumbling/whispering *seems* for the most part to be:

1. cautious and/or somewhat fearful; possibly upsetting and stressful for others (see Worrying Child)

2. out-of-place and/or disconnected; possibly odd and/or confusing to others (see Hiding Child)

- **The Worrying Child**

    Core Feeling: The more frequent the child's whispering and/or mumbling is, the greater the **fear/anger** is being experienced by the child.

Core Wish:	Communicates unconscious wish to be **noticed** and **supported** as a way of decreasing sense of **danger** and **abandonment**.
Core Question:	Limit-testing question—I am being triggered by events and this is an expression of how afraid I am; do you care enough to protect me?
Responses:	**Verbal & Less Emotional** (see Responses section)

- **The Hiding Child**

Core Feeling:	The more frequent the child's whispering and/or mumbling is, the greater the **fear/anger** is being experienced by the child.
Core Wish:	Communicates unconscious wish to be **noticed** and **validated** as a way of increasing sense of **security** and decreasing sense of **rejection**.
Core Question:	Limit-testing question—My behavior is a diversion from just how uncomfortable I feel right now; can you accept the way I am and contain me?
Responses:	**Verbal & More Emotional** (see Responses section)

Responses for: Behavior (1) Mumbling and/or whispering

The Worrying Child

- ***Verbal*:**
    - ◊ Clear and calm voice (quiet).
    - ◊ Before class: Check in and talk about previous day. Occasional eye contact. "I want to check in with you to see how our talk felt for you. We can do this each day."
    - ◊ During class: Occasional eye contact. Maintain distance (two feet at least). No physical contact. Use sound or words to get attention (Less Emotional responses below).
    - ◊ After class: Occasional eye contact. Reiterate response themes (connection, self-care).
- ***Less Emotional*:**
    - ◊ *Self-Care and Connection*: "Mumbling/Whispering is a way of being very careful about what you want to say. Can we try other ways?"
    - ◊ *Self-Care and Connection*: "If I notice you are mumbling/whispering, I will come over and say your name and quietly remind you that you are safe … your words are very important for others to hear."
    - ◊ *Self-Care and Connection*: "Do you want to come up with a code word that is just between you and me that means, 'I notice you are mumbling/

whispering?' This is a way of us working as a team and a way to make sure you feel safer."
- *Affirmation*:
    ◊ "I can see how you are trying to take care of yourself by being careful with your words."
    ◊ "You are very strong when you try to let other people hear your words."

The Hiding Child

- *Verbal*:
    ◊ Clear and calm voice (quiet).
    ◊ Before class: Check in and talk about previous day. Occasional eye contact. "I want to check in with you to see if you remember our talk. We will do this each day."
    ◊ During class: Occasional eye contact. Maintain distance (two feet at least). No physical contact. Use sound or words to get attention (More Emotional responses below).
    ◊ After class: Occasional eye contact. Reiterate response themes (connection, self-awareness).
- *More Emotional*:
    ◊ *Self-Awareness and Connection*: "Mumbling/Whispering is a way of being very careful about what you want to say. I think you are being careful, because something is making you have big feelings. That worries me and I can help with that."
    ◊ *Self-Awareness and Connection*: "Look at my face. I am worried that you are mumbling/whispering and that I might not be able to hear something important you need to share."
    ◊ *Self-Awareness and Connection*: "Think about the volume control on a television. When the sound is too loud, it can hurt our ears. When the sound is too low, we cannot hear what is happening. When you are mumbling/whispering, I think the volume of your television is on very low. Can we try together to turn the volume up a little."
- *Affirmation*:
    ◊ "I think you are being strong when you turn up your volume a little bit."
    ◊ "I am impressed when you decide to turn up your volume a little bit."

Behavior (2)
Not speaking to peers during play

If you find the child's lack of speaking *seems* for the most part:

1. cautious and/or somewhat fearful; possibly upsetting and stressful for others (see Worrying Child)

2. out-of-place and/or disconnected; possibly odd and/or confusing to others (see Hiding Child)

- **The Worrying Child**

    Core Feeling: The more prevalent the child's lack of speaking during peer play is, the greater the **fear/anger** is being experienced by the child.

    Core Wish: Communicates unconscious wish to be **noticed** and **supported** as a way of decreasing sense of **danger** and **abandonment**.

    Core Question: Limit-testing question—I am being triggered by events and this is an expression of how afraid I am; do you care enough to protect me?

    Responses: **Verbal & Less Emotional** (see Responses section)

- **The Hiding Child**

    Core Feeling: The more prevalent the child's lack of speaking during peer play is, the greater the **fear/anger** is being experienced by the child.

    Core Wish: Communicates unconscious wish to be **noticed** and **validated** as a way of increasing sense of **security** and decreasing sense of **rejection**.

    Core Question: Limit-testing question—My behavior is a diversion from just how uncomfortable I feel right now; can you accept the way I am and contain me?

    Responses: **Verbal & More Emotional** (see Responses section)

Responses for: Behavior (2) Not speaking to peers during play

The Worrying Child

- **Verbal**:
    - ◊ Clear and calm voice (quiet).
    - ◊ Before class: Check in and talk about previous day. Occasional eye contact. "I want to check in with you to see how our talk felt for you. We can do this each day."
    - ◊ During class: Occasional eye contact. Maintain distance (two feet at least). No physical contact. Use sound or words to get attention (Less Emotional responses below).
    - ◊ After class: Occasional eye contact. Reiterate response themes (connection, self-care).

- *Less Emotional*:
    - *Self-Care and Connection*: "Not speaking to your classmates is a way of being careful about what you want to say. Can we try other ways?"
    - *Self-Care and Connection*: "If I notice you are not speaking to classmates, I will come over and say your name and quietly remind you that you are safe … your words are very important for others to hear."
    - *Self-Care and Connection*: "Do you want to come up with a code word that is just between you and me that means, 'I notice you are not speaking to your classmates? This is a way of us working as a team and a way to make sure you feel safer."
- *Affirmation*:
    - "I can see how you are trying to take care of yourself by being careful with your words."
    - "You are very strong when you try to let other people hear your words."

The Hiding Child

- *Verbal*:
    - Clear and calm voice (quiet).
    - Before class: Check in and talk about previous day. Occasional eye contact. "I want to check in with you to see if you remember our talk. We will do this each day."
    - During class: Occasional eye contact. Maintain distance (two feet at least). No physical contact. Use sound or words to get attention (More Emotional responses below).
    - After class: Occasional eye contact. Reiterate response themes (connection, self-awareness).
    - *More Emotional*:
    - *Self-Awareness and Connection*: "Not speaking to your classmates is a way of being very careful about what you want to say. I think you are being careful, because something is making you have big feelings. That worries me and I can help with that."
    - *Self-Awareness and Connection*: "Look at my face. I am worried that you are not speaking to your classmates and that that they will not be able to know about important ideas that you are having."
    - *Self-Awareness and Connection*: "Think about the volume control on a television. When the sound is too loud, it can hurt our ears. When the sound is off, we cannot hear what is happening. When you are not speaking with your classmates, I think the volume of your television is off. Can we try together to turn the volume up a little, so everyone can know what is happening?"
- *Affirmation*:
    - "I think you are being strong when you turn up the volume of your speaking a little bit."
    - "I am impressed when you decide to turn up the volume of your speaking a little bit."

Behavior (3)
Not speaking with peers during group work

If you find the child's lack of speaking with peers during group work *seems* for the most part:

    1. willful; seemingly inflammatory and challenging (see Troubling Child)
    2. cautious and/or somewhat fearful; possibly upsetting and stressful for others (see Worrying Child)
    3. out-of-place and/or disconnected; possibly odd and/or confusing to others (see Hiding Child)

- **The Troubling Child**

    Core Feeling: The more prevalent the child's lack of speaking with peers is, the greater the **sadness/anger** is being experienced by the child.

    Core Wish: Communicates unconscious wish to be **contained** and **supported** as a way of decreasing sense of **danger** and **rejection**.

    Core Question: Limit-testing question—I am being triggered by events because this discussion feels overwhelming; can you accept me and handle me?

    Responses: **Structural & Less Emotional** (see Responses section)

- **The Worrying Child**

    Core Feeling: The more prevalent the child's lack of speaking with peers is, the greater the **fear/anger** is being experienced by the child.

    Core Wish: Communicates unconscious wish to be **noticed** and **supported** as a way of decreasing sense of **danger** and **abandonment**.

    Core Question: Limit-testing question—I am being triggered by events and this is an expression of how afraid I am; do you care enough to protect me?

    Responses: **Verbal & Less Emotional** (see Responses section)

- **The Hiding Child**

    Core Feeling: The more prevalent the child's lack of speaking with peers is, the greater the **fear/anger** is being experienced by the child.

    Core Wish: Communicates unconscious wish to be **noticed** and **validated** as a way of increasing sense of **security** and decreasing sense of **rejection**.

Core Question: Limit-testing question—My question is a diversion from just how uncomfortable I feel right now; can you accept the way I am and contain me?

Responses: **Verbal & More Emotional** (see Responses section)

Responses for: Behavior (3) Not speaking with peers during group work

The Troubling Child

- *Structural*:
    - ◊ Clear and calm voice (supportive).
    - ◊ Before class: Check in. Hold eye contact. "I'm with you. Let's keep working on this."
    - ◊ During class: Hand on shoulder; down on knee at eye level. Hold eye contact. Use the Less Emotional responses below.
    - ◊ After class: Check in. Hold eye contact. Reiterate response themes (boundaries, self-care). Track progress with chart.
- *More Emotional*:
    - ◊ *Boundaries*: "I want you to try to speak to your classmates when you are working with them?"
    - ◊ *Self-Care and Boundaries*: "When you don't want to speak to your classmates, take a deep breath and say, 'It's okay, I can try to speak to them this time.' I will remind you that you can do it."
    - ◊ *Self-Care*: "Speaking to the other kids does not mean that you have to agree with them or with me."
    - ◊ *Self-Care and Boundaries*: "I want to imagine a glass that you can drink out of. The glass can be filled up with water so we can have a drink. Not speaking is like pouring your thoughts in the glass until it fills up and spills over of the top. If you share your thoughts, it makes more room for more thoughts in your glass so there is no spilling out."
- *Affirmation*:
    - ◊ "I can see how hard you are working, when you try to speak to your classmates."
    - ◊ "Anyone can see the effort you make to speak to your classmates."

The Worrying Child

- *Verbal*:
    - ◊ Clear and calm voice (quiet).
    - ◊ Before class: Check in and talk about previous day. Occasional eye contact. "I want to check in with you to see how our talk felt for you. We can do this each day."
    - ◊ During class: Occasional eye contact. Maintain distance (two feet at

least). No physical contact. Use sound or words to get attention (Less Emotional responses below).
	◊ After class: Occasional eye contact. Reiterate response themes (connection, self-care).
- *Less Emotional*:
	◊ *Self-Care and Connection*: "Not speaking to your classmates is a way of being careful about what you want to say. Can we try other ways?"
	◊ *Self-Care and Connection*: "If I notice you are not speaking to classmates, I will come over and say your name and quietly remind you that you are safe … your words are very important for others to hear."
	◊ *Self-Care and Connection*: "Do you want to come up with a code word that is just between you and me that means, 'I notice you are not speaking to your classmates? This is a way of us working as a team and a way to make sure you feel safer."
- *Affirmation*:
	◊ "I can see how you are trying to take care of yourself by being careful with your words."
	◊ "You are very strong when you try to let other people hear your words."

The Hiding Child

- *Verbal*:
	◊ Clear and calm voice (quiet).
	◊ Before class: Check in and talk about previous day. Occasional eye contact. "I want to check in with you to see if you remember our talk. We will do this each day."
	◊ During class: Occasional eye contact. Maintain distance (two feet at least). No physical contact. Use sound or words to get attention (More Emotional responses below).
	◊ After class: Occasional eye contact. Reiterate response themes (connection, self-awareness).
- *More Emotional*:
	◊ *Self-Awareness and Connection*: "Not speaking to your classmates is a way of being very careful about what you want to say. I think you are being careful, because something is making you have big feelings. That worries me and I can help with that."
	◊ *Self-Awareness and Connection*: "Look at my face. I am worried that you are not speaking to your classmates and that that they will not be able to know about important ideas that you are having."
	◊ *Self-Awareness and Connection*: "Think about the volume control on a television. When the sound is too loud, it can hurt our ears. When the sound is off, we cannot hear what is happening. When you are not speaking with your classmates, I think the volume of your television is off. Can we try together to turn the volume up a little, so everyone can know what is happening."

- *Affirmation*:
    - ◊ "I think you are being strong when you turn on your speaking a little bit."
    - ◊ "I am impressed when you decide to turn on your speaking a little bit."

Behavior (4)
Only speaking when spoken to

If you find the child's lack of spontaneous speech *seems* for the most part:

1. cautious and/or somewhat fearful; possibly upsetting and stressful for others (see Worrying Child)
2. out-of-place and/or disconnected; possibly odd and/or confusing to others (see Hiding Child)

- **The Worrying Child**

Core Feeling:	The more frequent the child's lack of spontaneous speech is, the greater the **fear/anger** is being experienced by the child.
Core Wish:	Communicates unconscious wish to be **noticed** and **supported** as a way of decreasing sense of **danger** and **abandonment**.
Core Question:	Limit-testing question—I am being triggered by events and this is an expression of how afraid I am; do you care enough to protect me?
Responses:	**Verbal & Less Emotional** (see Responses section)

- **The Hiding Child**

Core Feeling:	The more frequent the child's lack of spontaneous speech is, the greater the **fear/anger** is being experienced by the child.
Core Wish:	Communicates unconscious wish to be **noticed** and **validated** as a way of increasing sense of **security** and decreasing sense of **rejection**.
Core Question:	Limit-testing question—My behavior is a diversion from just how uncomfortable I feel right now; can you accept the way I am and contain me?
Responses:	**Verbal & More Emotional** (see Responses section)

Responses for: Behavior (4) Only speaking when spoken to

The Worrying Child

- *Verbal*:
    - ◊ Clear and calm voice (quiet).

- Before class: Check in and talk about previous day. Occasional eye contact. "I want to check in with you to see how our talk felt for you. We can do this each day."
- During class: Occasional eye contact. Maintain distance (two feet at least). No physical contact. Use sound or words to get attention (Less Emotional responses below).
- After class: Occasional eye contact. Reiterate response themes (connection, self-care).

- **Less Emotional**:
  - *Self-Care and Connection*: "Not sharing your words or your ideas is a way of being careful. Can we try other ways?"
  - *Self-Care and Connection*: "If I notice you are not sharing your words or your ideas, I will come over and say your name and quietly remind you that you are safe … your words and ideas are very important for others to hear."
  - *Self-Care and Connection*: "Do you want to come up with a code word that is just between you and me that means, 'I notice you are not sharing your words and ideas? This is a way of us working as a team and a way to make sure you feel safer so you can share."

- **Affirmation**:
  - "I can see how you are trying to take care of yourself by being careful with your words."
  - "You are very strong when you try to let other people hear your words."

The Hiding Child

- **Verbal**:
  - Clear and calm voice (quiet).
  - Before class: Check in and talk about previous day. Occasional eye contact. "I want to check in with you to see if you remember our talk. We will do this each day."
  - During class: Occasional eye contact. Maintain distance (two feet at least). No physical contact. Use sound or words to get attention (More Emotional responses below).
  - After class: Occasional eye contact. Reiterate response themes (connection, self-awareness).

- **More Emotional**:
  - *Self-Awareness and Connection*: "Not sharing your words or your ideas is a way of being very careful about what you want to say. I think you are being careful because something is making you have big feelings. That worries me and I can help with that."
  - *Self-Awareness and Connection*: "Look at my face. I am worried that you are not sharing your words or your ideas and that I will not be able to know about important thoughts that you are having."
  - *Self-Awareness and Connection*: "Think about the volume control on a

television. When the sound is too loud, it can hurt our ears. When the sound is off, we cannot hear what is happening at all. When you are not sharing your words or your ideas, I think the volume of your television is off. Can we try together to turn the volume up a little, so I can know what is happening with you?"

- *Affirmation*:
    ◊ "I think you are being strong when you turn on your speaking a little bit."
    ◊ "I am impressed when you decide to turn on your speaking a little bit."

Behavior (5)
Responding to teacher's question with minimal reply

If you find the child's minimal response pattern ***seems*** for the most part:

1. willful; seemingly inflammatory and challenging (see Troubling Child)
2. cautious and/or somewhat fearful; possibly upsetting and stressful for others (see Worrying Child)
3. out-of-place and/or disconnected; possibly odd and/or confusing to others (see Hiding Child)

- **The Troubling Child**

Core Feeling:	The more prevalent the minimal response pattern is, the greater the **sadness/anger** is being experienced by the child.
Core Wish:	Communicates unconscious wish to be **contained** and **supported** as a way of decreasing sense of **danger** and **rejection**.
Core Question:	Limit-testing question—I am being triggered by events because this moment in class feels overwhelming; can you accept me and handle me?
Responses:	**Structural & Less Emotional** (see Responses section)

- **The Worrying Child**

Core Feeling:	The more prevalent the minimal response pattern is, the greater the **fear/anger** is being experienced by the child.
Core Wish:	Communicates unconscious wish to be **noticed** and **supported** as a way of decreasing sense of **danger** and **abandonment**.
Core Question:	Limit-testing question—I am being triggered by events and this is an expression of how afraid I am; do you care enough to protect me?
Responses:	**Verbal & Less Emotional** (see Responses section)

- **The Hiding Child**

    Core Feeling: The more prevalent the minimal response pattern is, the greater the **fear/anger** is being experienced by the child.

    Core Wish: Communicates unconscious wish to be **noticed** and **validated** as a way of increasing sense of **security** and decreasing sense of **rejection**.

    Core Question: Limit-testing question—My behavior is a diversion from just how uncomfortable I feel right now; can you accept the way I am and contain me?

    Responses: **Verbal & More Emotional** (see Responses section)

Responses for: Behavior (5) Responding to teacher's question with minimal reply

The Troubling Child

- *Structural*:
    ◊ Clear and calm voice (supportive).
    ◊ Before class: Check in. Hold eye contact. "I'm with you. Let's keep working on this."
    ◊ During class: Hand on shoulder; down on knee at eye level. Hold eye contact. Use the Less Emotional responses below.
    ◊ After class: Check in. Hold eye contact. Reiterate response themes (boundaries, self-care). Track progress with chart.
- *More Emotional*:
    ◊ *Self-Care and Boundaries*: "I want you to try to share more with me when we speak. I think you have a lot to say."
    ◊ *Self-Care and Boundaries*: "When you don't feel like giving me full answers, take a deep breath and say, 'It's okay, I can try to say a bit more to the teacher.' I will remind you that you can do it."
    ◊ *Self-Care and Boundaries*: "Saying a bit more does not mean that you have to share everything with me. You can always keep some for yourself."
    ◊ *Self-Care and Boundaries*: "Think about being in room by yourself. The door can be closed or open. When you do not want to talk to someone, you close the door. Not talking to me is like closing the door in the room. I will not come into your room without asking. I want you to try to open your door and share a little bit more with me when we speak. Just a little."
- *Affirmation*:
    ◊ "I can see how hard you are working to share more with me when we speak."
    ◊ "I can see how strong you are being when you share more with me when we speak."

The Worrying Child

- **Verbal:**
  - ◊ Clear and calm voice (quiet).
  - ◊ Before class: Check in and talk about previous day. Occasional eye contact. "I want to check in with you to see how our talk felt for you. We can do this each day."
  - ◊ During class: Occasional eye contact. Maintain distance (two feet at least). No physical contact. Use sound or words to get attention (Less Emotional responses below).
  - ◊ After class: Occasional eye contact. Reiterate response themes (connection, self-care).
- **Less Emotional:**
  - ◊ *Self-Care and Connection*: "Only sharing a little with me is a way of being very careful about what you want to say. Can we try other ways of being careful?"
  - ◊ *Self-Care and Connection*: "If I notice you are only sharing a little bit, I will come over and say your name and quietly remind you that you are safe … your ideas are very important for me to listen to."
  - ◊ *Self-Care and Connection*: "Do you want to come up with a code word that is just between you and me that means, 'I notice you are only sharing a little bit?' This is a way of us working as a team and a way to make sure you feel safer."
- **Affirmation:**
  - ◊ "I can see how you are trying to take care of yourself by being careful with your words."
  - ◊ "You are very strong when you try to let me hear more of your words and ideas."

The Hiding Child

- **Verbal:**
  - ◊ Clear and calm voice (quiet).
  - ◊ Before class: Check in and talk about previous day. Occasional eye contact. "I want to check in with you to see if you remember our talk. We will do this each day."
  - ◊ During class: Occasional eye contact. Maintain distance (two feet at least). No physical contact. Use sound or words to get attention (More Emotional responses below).
  - ◊ After class: Occasional eye contact. Reiterate response themes (connection, self-awareness).
- **More Emotional:**
  - ◊ *Self-Awareness and Connection*: "Sharing only a small amount of your words and ideas is a way of being very careful about what you want to say. I think you are being careful, because something is making you have big feelings. That worries me and I can help with that."

◊ *Self-Awareness and Connection*: "Look at my face. I am worried that you are sharing only a small amount of your words and ideas and that I might not be able to learn something important you need to share."
◊ *Self-Awareness and Connection*: "Think about the volume control on a television. When the sound is too loud, it can hurt our ears. When the sound is too low, we cannot hear what is happening. When you share only a small amount of your words and ideas, I think the volume of your television is on very low. Can we try together to turn the volume up a little."

- *Affirmation*:
  ◊ "I think you are being strong when your turn up the amount you are sharing with me."
  ◊ "I am impressed when you decide to turn up the amount you are sharing with me."

Behavior (6)
Responding with non-verbal communication frequently (when words are known)

If you find the child's non-verbal communicating *seems* for the most part:

1. willful; seemingly inflammatory and challenging (see Troubling Child)
2. cautious and/or somewhat fearful; possibly upsetting and stressful for others (see Worrying Child)
3. out-of-place and/or disconnected; possibly odd and/or confusing to others (see Hiding Child)

- **The Troubling Child**

  Core Feeling: The more prevalent the child's non-verbal communicating is, the greater the **sadness/anger** is being experienced by the child.

  Core Wish: Communicates unconscious wish to be **contained** and **supported** as a way of decreasing sense of **danger** and **rejection**.

  Core Question: Limit-testing question—I am being triggered by events because this discussion feels overwhelming; can you accept me and handle me?

  Responses: **Structural & Less Emotional** (see Responses section)

- **The Worrying Child**

  Core Feeling: The more prevalent the child's non-verbal communicating is, the greater the **fear/anger** is being experienced by the child.

Core Wish: Communicates unconscious wish to be **noticed** and **supported** as a way of decreasing sense of **danger** and **abandonment**.

Core Question: Limit-testing question—I am being triggered by events and this is an expression of how afraid I am; do you care enough to protect me?

Responses: **Verbal & Less Emotional** (see Responses section)

- **The Hiding Child**

Core Feeling: The more prevalent the child's non-verbal communicating is, the greater the **fear/anger** is being experienced by the child.

Core Wish: Communicates unconscious wish to be **noticed** and **validated** as a way of increasing sense of **security** and decreasing sense of **rejection**.

Core Question: Limit-testing question—My behavior is a diversion from just how uncomfortable I feel right now; can you accept the way I am and contain me?

Responses: **Verbal & More Emotional** (see Responses section)

Responses for: Behavior (6) Responding with non-verbal communication frequently

The Troubling Child

- *Structural*:
    - ◊ Clear and calm voice (supportive).
    - ◊ Before class: Check in. Hold eye contact. "I'm with you. Let's keep working on this."
    - ◊ During class: Hand on shoulder; down on knee at eye level. Hold eye contact. Use the Less Emotional responses below.
    - ◊ After class: Check in. Hold eye contact. Reiterate response themes (boundaries, self-care). Track progress with chart.
- *More Emotional*:
    - ◊ *Self-Care and Boundaries*: "I want you to share your words when you speak. I think you have a lot to say."
    - ◊ *Self-Care and Boundaries*: "When you don't feel like giving other people your words, take a deep breath and say, 'It's okay, I can try using my words with people.' I will remind you that you can do it."
    - ◊ *Self-Care and Boundaries*: "Using words does not mean that you have to share everything. You can always keep some for yourself."
    - ◊ *Self-Care and Boundaries*: "Think about being in room by yourself. The

door can be closed or open. When you do not want to talk to someone, you close the door. Not talking is like closing the door in the room. In this class, you can decide when your door is open or closed. I want you to try to open your door and speak a bit more with me and your classmates. Just a little."

- *Affirmation*:
    - ◊ "I can see how hard you are working to use your words with people."
    - ◊ "I can see how strong you are being when you use your words with people."

The Worrying Child

- *Verbal*:
    - ◊ Clear and calm voice (quiet).
    - ◊ Before class: Check in and talk about previous day. Occasional eye contact. "I want to check in with you to see how our talk felt for you. We can do this each day."
    - ◊ During class: Occasional eye contact. Maintain distance (two feet at least). No physical contact. Use sound or words to get attention (Less Emotional responses below).
    - ◊ After class: Occasional eye contact. Reiterate response themes (connection, self-care).
- *Less Emotional*:
    - ◊ *Self-Care and Connection*: "Not using your words is a way of being very careful about what you want to say. Can we try other ways of being careful?"
    - ◊ *Self-Care and Connection*: "If I notice you are not using words to speak, I will come over and say your name and quietly remind you that you are safe … your ideas are very important for people to hear."
    - ◊ *Self-Care and Connection*: "Do you want to come up with a code word that is just between you and me that means, 'I notice you are you are not using your words to speak?' This is a way of us working as a team and a way to make sure you feel safer."
- *Affirmation*:
    - ◊ "I can see how you are trying to take care of yourself by being careful with your words."
    - ◊ "You are very strong when you try to let people hear your words and ideas."

The Hiding Child

- *Verbal*:
    - ◊ Clear and calm voice (quiet).
    - ◊ Before class: Check in and talk about previous day. Occasional eye contact. "I want to check in with you to see if you remember our talk. We will do this each day."

- ◊ During class: Occasional eye contact. Maintain distance (two feet at least). No physical contact. Use sound or words to get attention (More Emotional responses below).
- ◊ After class: Occasional eye contact. Reiterate response themes (connection, self-awareness).
- **More Emotional:**
  - ◊ *Self-Awareness and Connection*: "Not using your words is a way of being very careful about what you want to say. I think you are being careful, because something is making you have big feelings. That worries me and I can help with that."
  - ◊ *Self-Awareness and Connection*: "Look at my face. I am worried that you are not using your words and that people might not be able to learn something important you need to share."
  - ◊ *Self-Awareness and Connection*: "Think about the volume control on a television. When the sound is too loud, it can hurt our ears. When there is no sound, we cannot hear what is happening and we can only guess. When you do not use your words to share your ideas, I think the sound on your television is not on. Can we try together to turn the volume up a little?"
- **Affirmation:**
  - ◊ "I think you are being strong when you turn up the sound and share your words with people."
  - ◊ "I am impressed when you decide to turn up the sound and share your words with others."

Behavior (7)
Responding with sounds frequently (when words are known)

If you find the child's making of sounds *seems* for the most part:

1. persistent and willful; seemingly inflammatory and challenging (see Troubling Child)

2. out-of-place and/or disconnected; possibly odd and/or confusing to others (see Hiding Child)

- **The Troubling Child**

Core Feeling:	The more frequent the child's response pattern is, the greater the **sadness/anger** is being experienced by the child.
Core Wish:	Communicates unconscious wish to be **contained** and **supported** as a way of decreasing sense of **danger** and **rejection**.

Core Question: Limit-testing question—I am being triggered by events because this moment in class feels overwhelming; can you accept me and handle me?

Responses: **Structural & Less Emotional** (see Responses section)

- **The Hiding Child**

Core Feeling: The more frequent the child's response pattern is, the greater the **fear/anger** is being experienced by the child.

Core Wish: Communicates unconscious wish to be **noticed** and **validated** as a way of increasing sense of **security** and decreasing sense of **rejection**.

Core Question: Limit-testing question—My behavior is a diversion from just how uncomfortable I feel right now; can you accept the way I am and contain me?

Responses: **Verbal & More Emotional** (see Responses section)

Responses for: Behavior (7) Responding with sounds frequently

The Troubling Child

- *Structural*:
    - ◊ Clear and calm voice (supportive).
    - ◊ Before class: Check in. Hold eye contact. "I'm with you. Let's keep working on this."
    - ◊ During class: Hand on shoulder; down on knee at eye level. Hold eye contact. Use the Less Emotional responses below.
    - ◊ After class: Check in. Hold eye contact. Reiterate response themes (boundaries, self-care). Track progress with chart.
- *More Emotional*:
    - ◊ *Self-Care and Boundaries*: "I want you to share your words when you speak. I think you have a lot to say."
    - ◊ *Self-Care and Boundaries*: "When you want to give other people your sounds, take a deep breath and say, 'It's okay, I can try using my words with people.' I will remind you that you can do it."
    - ◊ *Self-Care and Boundaries*: "Think about being in room by yourself. The door can be closed or open. When you do not want to talk to someone, you close the door. Not using words keeping the door closed in your room. No one will come into the room without asking. I want you to try to open your door and share your words with me and your classmates. Just a few."
- *Affirmation*:
    - ◊ "I can see how hard you are working to use your words with people."
    - ◊ "I can see how strong you are being when you use your words with people."

The Hiding Child

- *Verbal*:
  - ◊ Clear and calm voice (quiet).
  - ◊ Before class: Check in and talk about previous day. Occasional eye contact. "I want to check in with you to see if you remember our talk. We will do this each day."
  - ◊ During class: Occasional eye contact. Maintain distance (two feet at least). No physical contact. Use sound or words to get attention (More Emotional responses below).
  - ◊ After class: Occasional eye contact. Reiterate response themes (connection, self-awareness).
- *More Emotional*:
  - ◊ *Self-Awareness and Connection*: "Using your sounds is a way of being very careful about what you want to say. I think you are being careful, because something is making you have big feelings. That worries me and I can help with that."
  - ◊ *Self-Awareness and Connection*: "Look at my face. I am worried that you are not using your words and that people might not be able to learn something important you need to share."
  - ◊ *Self-Awareness and Connection*: "I want you to think about covering your ears. When you cover your ears, you cannot hear very well, and you don't know exactly what people are saying. When we use our words instead of our sounds, it's like taking our hands off our ears. We can understand each other better. I want you to use your words, so people can understand."
- *Affirmation*:
  - ◊ "I think you are being strong when you choose to your words with people."
  - ◊ "I am impressed when you decide to share your words with others."

Your Evolving Responses

As you have read, there are different motivations for your students' behaviors depending on their latent communication patterns. This demonstrates that your responses cannot be "one size fits all" in nature. While we have provided specific words for you to follow, we intend this chapter and the others like it to be a framework for your responses, not a script. You certainly can use our suggested language as you experiment with the interventions we have described. Overtime, it will be more helpful for you to find your own words to communicate with your students. As you continue to try these techniques, using your own communication style will make the responses to your students' behaviors feel authentic and sincere. This will happen naturally. The proposed interventions that we used in this chapter are a starting point and are meant to evolve and grow with your comfort level. This might take some practice, but it will be well worth it to expand your repertoire of potential responses to concerning or disruptive behaviors. You may find that your own words are more effective or more impactful than the words and phrases we have suggested in this book. The more you are a part of the interventions, the more meaningful they may be to your students. As we know, students need repetition, so please be patient as you try out new ways to respond to them.

CHAPTER 16

Toileting Accidents and Toilet-Related Issues

"You can lead a toddler to the potty, but you can't make him pee."
—Anonymous

How to Use This Chapter

1. As you prepare to read this chapter, choose one child from your class on whom you wish to focus. Selecting one child at a time allows for a more concentrated exploration of the material and how it relates to each child uniquely. **As a guide, we will use "Melody," a second grader who asks to use the toilet excessively.**

2. Read the paragraphs from the following headings to begin the process: *Format and Theme* and *Common Forms of the Behavior*.

3. Choose one behavior that the selected child is exhibiting. Selecting one behavior at a time allows for a more concentrated exploration of the material centering on how the child communicates using this specific behavior. **Melody's behavior of demonstrating excessive need to use the toilet.**

4. Read the paragraphs from the following headings to learn more about the general category that this behavior falls within from a more holistic perspective: *Manifest Communication* and *Latent Communication*.

5. Read the paragraphs from the heading *Responses and Affirmations* as background to how we structured the proposed responses and the expectation that you will ultimately personalize the responses provided in this chapter.

6. Turn to the page that contains the behavior in question. There you will find the number of the behavior and its name. **We select Behavior (*1*) *Demonstrating excessive need to use the toilet.***

7. On that page, below the number and name, you will find all the possible latent communication prompts for that behavior, ranging from (1) to (4). From these prompts, choose the prompt that most closely reminds you of how this child exhibits this behavior. Your choice may not fit one prompt exactly. If your sense is that multiple prompts could fit, choose the closest one to begin the process.

You can return to the other prompts later. You will notice that each prompt corresponds with a child communication Persona (i.e., Troubling, Testing, Worrying, Hiding). **For Melody, we choose "persistently mischievous; mildly vexing, pushing limits/boundaries (see Testing Child)."**

8. After choosing a latent communication prompt, use the child communication Persona and read the corresponding Core Feelings, Core Wish, Core Question. This information describes the underlying meaning of the behavior and creates an empathic guide for you to keep in mind when responding to the child's behavior.

9. On the following page(s), you will find responses and affirmations for the number and name of the behavior in question. **We select Responses for:** *Behavior (1) Demonstrating excessive need to use the toilet* section *The Testing Child*. Find and read the responses and affirmations for the behavior in question that corresponds with the child communication Persona.

10. **Try the responses and affirmations with Melody and determine how they feel to you.**

Theme and Format

Each of the following behavior chapters in this section of the book should be considered with the following format in mind. In this chapter, we will focus on **toileting accidents and toilet-related issues** as behaviors we see in the classroom and as communications that we try to understand. That said, the title of this chapter is an umbrella descriptor, and these behaviors comprise a theme or group of communications. We observe these manifest communications as thematic, as there are many permutations within a category of behavior.

Common Forms of This Behavior

- Demonstrating excessive need to use the toilet
- Exhibiting an unwillingness to use the toilet when needed
- Urinating/Defecating "accidentally" in a place other than the toilet
- Urinating/Defecating "on purpose" in a place other than the toilet
- Using toilet paper excessively (wiping)

Manifest Communication

It is important to acknowledge that difficulties with toileting such as those listed above may require a professional assessment for a child to determine any environment, physiological, neurological, or developmental issues that are preventing typical developmental progress. Ruling out these causes—such as urinary infections, intestinal parasites, viruses, irritable bowel syndrome, Colitis, Krone's disease, underdeveloped sphincter muscles, Diabetes Type 1, and any sexual abuse or physical

Chapter 16. Toileting Accidents and Toilet-Related Issues

abuse-related issues—is a critical step in addressing any child's needs in the areas of toileting development. If you are concerned, we recommend coordinating with your administration. While discussions regarding further assessment are happening or have concluded with a decision to no further assessment, there are ways for us to respond to these intense child communications within the class setting.

Toilet training is one of those developmental milestones that everyone has an opinion about. What method does one choose to accomplish toilet training? Does one use rewards or consequences? Does one have to have a child toilet trained before he or she goes to school? These questions seem to come with a notable level of tension. We believe that the debates around these issues are due in large part to the fact that this process feels so central to an "appropriate" trajectory of incorporation into society. It is like a rite of passage for a young child and frees their caregivers from dealing with dirty diapers and pull-ups.

From a teacher point of view, it is also one of those activities that plays a critical role in a student's life (as all children need to go to bathroom during the school day). There are rules governing appropriate bathroom use, timing, and social interaction. Not following these classroom norms causes disruption and the need for extra attention.

Yet, as important as it is, we have very little insight into the intimate machinations that establish the toileting behaviors that we can see each day from our students. For most of the children, this lack of knowledge does not matter, but for those children who exhibit behaviors that set them outside the typical, responding without understanding becomes a challenge.

The children who struggle with toileting issues can exhibit a whole range of behaviors. It is helpful to see these behaviors on a continuum that stretches from the "outward" to the "inward." By outward, we are speaking of communications around toileting that are overt and obvious. These may include excessive wiping, peeing on the floor, continuously having one's hand down one's pants—behaviors that are observable. On the other end of the continuum are toileting communications that are more covert, hidden, and obscured. These can include toileting accidents of any kind that remain confined to a child's underwear and that are typically noticed by an odor or by some non-verbal discomfort displayed by the child.

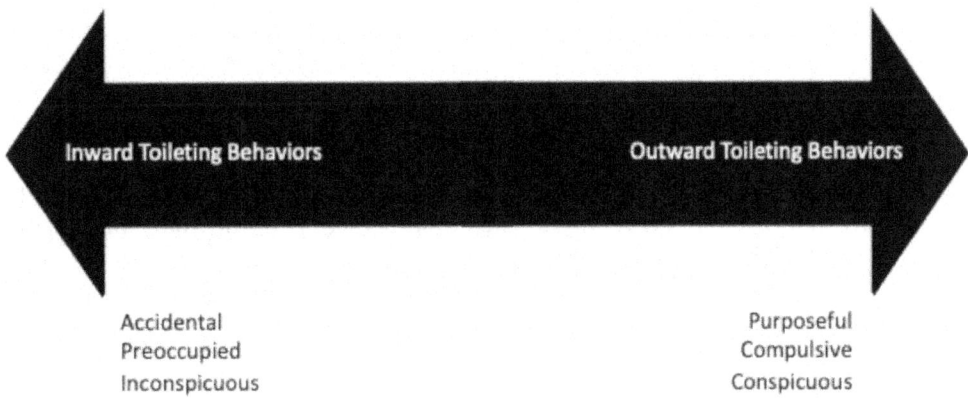

Figure 16.1: Nature of Problematic Toileting Behavior

Using the child Personas of the Troubling Child, the Testing Child, the Worrying Child, and the Hiding Child, we will explore specific teacher responses for each type of communication pattern (see Table 16.1). For more detailed information about background for each Persona and the reasoning behind the most productive teacher response configurations, please refer back to their respective chapters.

**Table 16.1:
Behavior Frequency by Persona**

Behavior	Troubling Child Loud & Over Reactive	Testing Child Loud & Under Reactive	Worrying Child Quiet & Over Reactive	Hiding Child Quiet & Under Reactive
Demonstrating excessive need to use the toilet	X	X	X	X
Exhibiting an unwillingness to use the toilet when needed			X	X
Urinating/Defecating "accidentally" in place other than the toilet			X	X
Urinating/Defecating "on purpose" in place other than toilet	X			X
Using toilet paper excessively (wiping)			X	

The absence of an "X" indicates that this Persona does not typically engage in this type of behavior/communication.

Latent Communication

This process is not an exact science and should be conducted more as trial and error. We would like you to take your best professional guess as to your answers to the following inquiries and evaluations. If you find that, after working through the latent communication material and identifying a set of responses, they do not work as you hoped, you can always revise and try again. Just remember, children integrate learning following repetition, so do not give up too soon.

Responses and Affirmations

Children do not learn the first time we teach them a new concept or a task. We say this in order to manage our expectations about how quickly or completely these new interventions will change or extinguish any given behavior.

Let's keep in mind the following factors. First, the development of these behaviors has typically occurred over an extended period of time. Based on the ages of the children we address in this book, any behavior grew over at least two years and up to eight. As much as we would wish it, a behavior that has been developing over a lengthy period of time cannot change "overnight." Actually, rapid change is often poorly integrated by children and cannot be sustained. Second, children integrate responses at different rates based on a variety of factors, including temperament, environment, learning styles, family involvement/support, etc. We have addressed these earlier in the book. Last, we are constructing foundations from which to grow, one brick at a time, foundations that these children will be able to build on and rely on for years to come. To this end, we want you to know that each of your responses is remembered and cataloged by these children for future use—even if it does not outwardly appear to have been during your time with the child. This relates to the corrective emotional experience we wrote about earlier in this book. Your interactions become part of the child's long-term memory, exchanges that are saved for future use.

That said, we want us to have some benchmarks for our expectations. First, we believe that one month is a sufficient timeframe for some level of change in a behavior, given that a specific teacher response is maintained with consistency and repetition. Second, as we cannot factor in changes that are occurring in real time within these children and with their families, the one-month benchmark may need to be altered accordingly. Third, the one-month duration allows for these challenged children to test us. They will imagine that what we are doing cannot be sustained, that it is too good to last. Our consistency and repetition in responding to the underlying message ultimately quiet their negative thoughts. It is then when the child's expectations of the people around them begin to change to an inner message that is more hopeful and positive. This hopefulness alters their communications and behaviors and can become a more embedded part of their future interpersonal relationships.

Behavior (1)
Demonstrating excessive need to use the toilet

If you find the child's excessive need to use the toilet ***seems*** for the most part to be:

1. persistently willful; seemingly inflammatory and challenging (see Troubling Child)

2. persistently mischievous; mildly vexing, pushing limits/boundaries (see Testing Child)

3. anxious and/or troubled; possibly upsetting and tense for others (see Worrying Child)

4. disconnected and/or arbitrary; possibly odd and/or confusing to others (see Hiding Child)

- **The Troubling Child**

    Core Feeling: The more frequent the child's "need" to use the toilet is, the greater the **sadness/anger** is being experienced by the child.

    Core Wish: Communicates unconscious wish to be **contained** and **supported** as a way of decreasing sense of **danger** and **rejection**.

    Core Question: Limit-testing question—I am being triggered by events because this moment in class feels overwhelming; can you accept me and handle me?

    Responses: **Structural & Less Emotional** (see Responses section)

- **The Testing Child**

    Core Feeling: The more frequent the child's "need" to use the toilet is, the greater the **sadness/anger** is being experienced by the child.

    Core Wish: Communicates unconscious wish to be **contained** and **validated** as a way of increasing sense of **security** and decreasing sense of **abandonment**.

    Core Question: Limit-testing question—I am feeling bad about myself and need to show this by creating a distraction; do you care about me enough to stop me?

    Responses: **Structural & More Emotional** (see Responses section)

- **The Worrying Child**

    Core Feeling: The more frequent the child's "need" to use the toilet is, the greater the **fear/anger** is being experienced by the child.

    Core Wish: Communicates unconscious wish to be **noticed** and **supported** as a way of decreasing sense of **danger** and **abandonment**.

    Core Question: Limit-testing question—I am being triggered by events and this is an expression of how afraid I am; do you care enough to protect me?

    Responses: **Verbal & Less Emotional** (see Responses section)

- **The Hiding Child**

    Core Feeling: The more frequent the child's "need" to use the toilet is, the greater the **fear/anger** is being experienced by the child.

Core Wish: Communicates unconscious wish to be **noticed** and **validated** as a way of increasing sense of **security** and decreasing sense of **rejection**.

Core Question: Limit-testing question—My behavior is a diversion from just how uncomfortable I feel right now; can you accept the way I am and contain me?

Responses: **Verbal & More Emotional** (see Responses section)

Responses for: Behavior (1) Demonstrating excessive need to use the toilet

The Troubling Child

- *Structural*:
    - ◊ Clear and calm voice (supportive).
    - ◊ Before class: Check in. Hold eye contact. "I'm with you. Let's keep working on this."
    - ◊ During class: Hand on shoulder; down on knee at eye level. Hold eye contact. Use the Less Emotional responses below.
    - ◊ After class: Check in. Hold eye contact. Reiterate response themes (boundaries, self-care). Track progress with chart.
- *Less Emotional*:
    - ◊ *Self-Care and Boundaries*: "I want you to try to stop going to the bathroom so often during class. You are more in charge when you don't push people away by leaving for the bathroom during class."
    - ◊ *Self-Care*: "Take a deep breath and let it out very slowly when you feel like you need to use the toilet."
    - ◊ *Boundaries*: "Think to yourself, 'I have a choice to use the toilet or not during class.'"
    - ◊ *Self-Care and Boundaries*: "Think about us building a dam together across a stream and trying to stop all the water from flowing. If we can do it, it can feel great when we see that we have stopped the water in the stream completely. Controlling your need to use the toilet by yourself, or even with my help, is the same. It's like a victory."
- *Affirmation*:
    - ◊ "Controlling your need to use the toilet during class time takes great strength."
    - ◊ "It is clear what a huge effort you make to not need to leave for the bathroom."

The Testing Child

- *Structural*:
    - ◊ Clear and crisp voice (supportive).

- Before class: Check in. Hold eye contact. "I'm with you. Let's keep working on this."
- During class: Hand on shoulder; down on knee at eye level. Hold eye contact. Use More Emotional responses below.
- After class: Check in. Hold eye contact. Reiterate response themes (boundaries, self-awareness). Track progress with chart.

- **More Emotional:**
  - *Self-Awareness and Boundaries*: "It saddens me when you ask so often to use the toilet, because I feel like it pushes us apart."
  - *Self-Awareness*: "When you need to use the toilet a lot during class, I think you feel bad."
  - *Self-Awareness and Boundaries*: "Sometimes having bad thoughts is like having a cut that is healing and itches. The itch bothers us, and we really want to scratch it, but we need to leave it alone. If we scratch, it could bleed. When it is really itchy, we have to ask for someone to help us."
  - *Self-Awareness*: "Try to take a deep breath and let it out very slowly; and say to yourself, 'I will be okay, I can get help' before you begin your requests to use the bathroom during class."
- **Affirmation:**
  - "I am proud of you for trying so hard to not use the bathroom so often during class."
  - "You took good care of yourself by trying to not use the bathroom so often during class."

The Worrying Child

- **Verbal:**
  - Clear and calm voice (quiet).
  - Before class: Check in and talk about previous day. Occasional eye contact. "I want to check in with you to see how our talk felt for you. We can do this each day."
  - During class: Occasional eye contact. Maintain distance (two feet at least). No physical contact. Use sound or words to get attention (Less Emotional responses below).
  - After class: Occasional eye contact. Reiterate response themes (connection, self-care).
- **Less Emotional:**
  - *Self-Care*: "Take a deep breath and let it out very slowly when you start to need to use the toilet during class. It is safe and powerful to help your body to wait until you feel calmer."
  - *Self-Care and Connection*: "When we suddenly have an uncomfortable thought, it can help us feel safer if we try and slow down and stay near a person we trust. When you feel the need to use the toilet, try to come over and see me first, and we will slowly figure out how to help you."
  - *Self-Care and Connection*: "When you are needing to use the toilet so

often during class, it makes me think about your safety. I would like to ask you about what you are thinking when this is going on."
- *Affirmation*:
    ◊ "Being in control of your need to use the toilet takes strength."
    ◊ "You are brave to try to control your need to use the toilet during class time."

The Hiding Child

- *Verbal*:
    ◊ Clear and calm voice (quiet).
    ◊ Before class: Check in and talk about previous day. Occasional eye contact. "I want to check in with you to see if you remember our talk. We will do this each day."
    ◊ During class: Occasional eye contact. Maintain distance (two feet at least). No physical contact. Use sound or words to get attention (More Emotional responses below).
    ◊ After class: Occasional eye contact. Reiterate response themes (connection, self-awareness).
- *More Emotional*:
    ◊ *Self-Awareness and Connection*: "When you need to use the toilet so often during class time, I think you have big feelings, and I am worried. I want you to try raising your hand if you need to use the toilet during class time. I can help with figuring out what to do next."
    ◊ *Self-Awareness and Connection*: "A way to be strong is to ask yourself, 'do I need to use the toilet now, or can it wait?'"
    ◊ *Connection*: "Look at my face. I am worried that you can't keep from needing to use the toilet."
    ◊ *Self-Awareness and Connection*: "Think to yourself, 'I can control my body. My need to use the toilet is like water coming out of a faucet. I can turn the faucet off if I want to.'"
- *Affirmation*:
    ◊ "I see you using your thoughts to control your choice to use the toilet so much in class."
    ◊ "I am impressed how you are deciding to keep control of your body."

Behavior (2)
Exhibiting an unwillingness to use the toilet when needed

If you find the child's reluctance to use the toilet when needed *seems* for the most part:

1. anxious and/or troubled; possibly upsetting and tense for others (see Worrying Child)

2. disconnected and/or arbitrary; possibly odd and/or confusing to others (see Hiding Child)

- **The Worrying Child**

    Core Feeling: The more frequent and/or urgent the child's unwillingness to use the toilet is, the greater the **fear/anger** is being experienced by the child.

    Core Wish: Communicates unconscious wish to be **noticed** and **supported** as a way of decreasing sense of **danger** and **abandonment**.

    Core Question: Limit-testing question—I am being triggered by events and this is an expression of how afraid I am; do you care enough to protect me?

    Responses: **Verbal & Less Emotional** (see Responses section)

- **The Hiding Child**

    Core Feeling: The more frequent and/or urgent the child's unwillingness to use the toilet is, the greater the **fear/anger** is being experienced by the child.

    Core Wish: Communicates unconscious wish to be **noticed** and **validated** as a way of increasing sense of **security** and decreasing sense of **rejection**.

    Core Question: Limit-testing question—My behavior is a diversion from just how uncomfortable I feel right now; can you accept the way I am and contain me?

    Responses: **Verbal & More Emotional** (see Responses section)

Responses for: Behavior (2) Exhibiting an unwillingness to use the toilet when needed

The Worrying Child

- ***Verbal:***
    - ◊ Clear and calm voice (quiet).
    - ◊ Before class: Check in and talk about previous day. Occasional eye contact. "I want to check in with you to see how our talk felt for you. We can do this each day."
    - ◊ During class: Occasional eye contact. Maintain distance (two feet at least). No physical contact. Use sound or words to get attention (Less Emotional responses below).
    - ◊ After class: Occasional eye contact. Reiterate response themes (connection, self-care).

- *Less Emotional*:
    - *Self-Care*: "Take a deep breath and let it out very slowly when you start to get uncomfortable about using the toilet during school. It is safe and powerful to help your body to feel better."
    - *Self-Care and Connection*: "When we suddenly have an uncomfortable thought, it can help us feel safer if we try and slow down and stay near a person we trust. When you feel the need to use the toilet, try to come over and see me first, and we will slowly figure out how to help you."
    - *Self-Care and Connection*: "When you don't want to use the toilet during school, it makes me think about your safety. I would like to ask you about what you are thinking about when this is going on."
- *Affirmation*:
    - "Being in control of how your body uses the toilet takes strength."
    - "You are brave to try to use the toilet during school."

The Hiding Child

- *Verbal*:
    - Clear and calm voice (quiet).
    - Before class: Check in and talk about previous day. Occasional eye contact. "I want to check in with you to see if you remember our talk. We will do this each day."
    - During class: Occasional eye contact. Maintain distance (two feet at least). No physical contact. Use sound or words to get attention (More Emotional responses below).
    - After class: Occasional eye contact. Reiterate response themes (connection, self-awareness).
- *More Emotional*:
    - *Self-Awareness and Connection*: "When you refuse to use the toilet during school even when you have to, I think you have big feelings, and I am worried. I want you to tell me when you need to use the toilet. Raise your hand and I will come over; then we can figure out together what to do next."
    - *Self-Awareness*: "A way to be strong is to tell yourself, 'I do need to use the toilet now, I will be okay.'"
    - *Connection*: "Look at my face. I am worried that you won't use the toilet even if your body needs to."
    - *Self-Awareness and Connection*: "Think to yourself, 'I can control my body. My need to use the toilet is like water coming out of a faucet. I can turn the faucet on when it is time to let the water out.'"
- *Affirmation*:
    - "I see you using your thoughts to make the choice to use the toilet when you need to."
    - "I am impressed how you are deciding to help your body feel better."

Behavior (3)
Urinating/Defecating "accidentally" in place other than the toilet

If you find the child's conduct related to his/her toileting accidents *seems* for the most part:

1. anxious and/or troubled; possibly upsetting and tense for others (see Worrying Child)

2. disconnected and/or arbitrary; possibly odd and/or confusing to others (see Hiding Child)

- **The Worrying Child**

    Core Feeling: The more frequent the child's toileting accidents are, the greater the **fear/anger** is being experienced by the child.

    Core Wish: Communicates unconscious wish to be **noticed** and **supported** as a way of decreasing sense of **danger** and **abandonment**.

    Core Question: Limit-testing question—I am being triggered by events and this is an expression of how afraid I am; do you care enough to protect me?

    Responses: **Verbal & Less Emotional** (see Responses section)

- **The Hiding Child**

    Core Feeling: The more frequent the child's toileting accidents are, the greater the **fear/anger** is being experienced by the child.

    Core Wish: Communicates unconscious wish to be **noticed** and **validated** as a way of increasing sense of **security** and decreasing sense of **rejection**.

    Core Question: Limit-testing question—My behavior is a diversion from just how uncomfortable I feel right now; can you accept the way I am and contain me?

    Responses: **Verbal & More Emotional** (see Responses section)

Responses for: Behavior (3) Urinating/Defecating "accidentally" in place other than the toilet

The Worrying Child

- ***Verbal:***
    ◊ Clear and calm voice (quiet).

Chapter 16. Toileting Accidents and Toilet-Related Issues

- ◊ Before class: Check in and talk about previous day. Occasional eye contact. "I want to check in with you to see how our talk felt for you. We can do this each day."
- ◊ During class: Occasional eye contact. Maintain distance (two feet at least). No physical contact. Use sound or words to get attention (Less Emotional responses below).
- ◊ After class: Occasional eye contact. Reiterate response themes (connection, self-care).

- **Less Emotional:**
  - ◊ *Self-Care and Connection*: "Crumple a piece of paper and squeeze it tightly when you get that uncomfortable 'I have to use the toilet' feeling. The squeezing feeling helps your body feel safe and powerful."
  - ◊ *Self-Care and Connection*: "When we suddenly have that 'I have to use the toilet' feeling, it can help us feel safer if you quickly find a person we trust. When you feel the need to use the toilet, try to come over and see me quickly, and we will figure out how to help you."
  - ◊ *Self-Care and Connection*: "When you have 'accidents,' it makes me think about your safety. I would like to ask you about what you are thinking about when this happens."

- **Affirmation:**
  - ◊ "Helping your body get to the toilet in time takes strength."
  - ◊ "You are brave when you do your best to get the toilet in time."

The Hiding Child

- **Verbal:**
  - ◊ Clear and calm voice (quiet).
  - ◊ Before class: Check in and talk about previous day. Occasional eye contact. "I want to check in with you to see if you remember our talk. We will do this each day."
  - ◊ During class: Occasional eye contact. Maintain distance (two feet at least). No physical contact. Use sound or words to get attention (More Emotional responses below).
  - ◊ After class: Occasional eye contact. Reiterate response themes (connection, self-awareness).

- **More Emotional:**
  - ◊ *Self-Awareness and Connection*: "When you have toileting 'accidents,' I think you have big feelings, and I am worried. I want you to tell me when you to get that 'I have to use the toilet' feeling. Raise your hand and I will come over; then we can figure out together what to do next."
  - ◊ *Self-Awareness*: "A way to be strong is to tell yourself, 'I do need to use the toilet now, I will be okay."
  - ◊ *Connection*: "Look at my face. I am worried that you won't use the toilet even if your body needs to."
  - ◊ *Self-Awareness and Connection*: "Think to yourself, 'I can control my

body. My need to use the toilet is like a faucet. I can wait to turn the faucet on until it is the right time.'"
- **Affirmation:**
  - ◊ "I see you using your thoughts to make the choice to get to the toilet when you need to."
  - ◊ "I am impressed how you are deciding to help your body by getting to the toilet."

Behavior (4)
Urinating/Defecating "on purpose" in place other than the toilet

If you find the child's conduct related to his/her toileting *seems*, for the most part:

1. persistently willful; seemingly inflammatory and challenging (see Troubling Child)

2. disconnected and/or arbitrary; possibly odd and/or confusing to others (see Hiding Child)

- **The Troubling Child**

  Core Feeling: The more frequent and/or flagrant the child's toileting behavior is, the greater the **sadness/anger** is being experienced by the child.

  Core Wish: Communicates unconscious wish to be **contained** and **supported** as a way of decreasing sense of **danger** and **rejection**.

  Core Question: Limit-testing question—I am being triggered by events because this moment in class feels overwhelming; can you accept me and handle me?

  Responses: **Structural & Less Emotional** (see Responses section)

- **The Hiding Child**

  Core Feeling: The more frequent and/or flagrant the child's toileting behavior is, the greater the **fear/anger** is being experienced by the child.

  Core Wish: Communicates unconscious wish to be **noticed** and **validated** as a way of increasing sense of **security** and decreasing sense of **rejection**.

Core Question: Limit-testing question—My behavior is a diversion from just how uncomfortable I feel right now; can you accept the way I am and contain me?

Responses: **Verbal & More Emotional** (see Responses section)

Responses for: Behavior (4) Urinating/Defecating "on purpose" in place other than the toilet

The Troubling Child

- *Structural*:
  ◊ Clear and calm voice (supportive).
  ◊ Before class: Check in. Hold eye contact. "I'm with you. Let's keep working on this."
  ◊ During class: Hand on shoulder; down on knee at eye level. Hold eye contact. Use the Less Emotional responses below.
  ◊ After class: Check in. Hold eye contact. Reiterate response themes (boundaries, self-care). Track progress with chart.
- *Less Emotional*:
  ◊ *Self-Care and Boundaries*: "I want you to stop going to the bathroom in places outside the toilet. You are more in charge when you don't push people away by doing that. This is very important."
  ◊ *Self-Care and Boundaries*: "Crumple a piece of paper and squeeze it tightly if you want to use the bathroom outside the toilet."
  ◊ *Boundaries*: "Think to yourself, 'I can make the strong choice to go inside the toilet. I have control.'"
  ◊ *Self-Care and Boundaries*: "Think about us building a dam together across a stream and trying to stop all the water from flowing. If we can do it, it can feel great. Making sure you use the toilet when you go to the bathroom is the same. It's a victory."
- *Affirmation*:
  ◊ "Controlling where you go to the bathroom takes great strength."
  ◊ "Anyone can see what a huge effort you are making to go to the bathroom in the toilet."

The Hiding Child

- *Verbal*:
  ◊ Clear and calm voice (quiet).
  ◊ Before class: Check in and talk about previous day. Occasional eye contact. "I want to check in with you to see if you remember our talk. We will do this each day."
  ◊ During class: Occasional eye contact. Maintain distance (two feet at

least). No physical contact. Use sound or words to get attention (More Emotional responses below).
◊ After class: Occasional eye contact. Reiterate response themes (connection, self-awareness).
- **More Emotional**:
  ◊ *Self-Awareness and Connection*: "When you go to the bathroom outside of the toilet, I think are having big feelings, and I am worried. I want you to raise your hand if you suddenly want to go to the bathroom in a place that is not the toilet. It is important. Then, I can help with what to do next."
  ◊ *Self-Awareness*: "A way to be strong is to say yourself, 'Using the bathroom happens in the bathroom.'"
  ◊ *Connection*: "Look at my face. I am worried that you are going to the bathroom outside of the toilet."
  ◊ *Self-Awareness and Connection*: "Think to yourself, 'I can control my body. My need to use the toilet is like a faucet. I can wait to turn the faucet on until it is the right time.'"
- *Affirmation*:
  ◊ "Controlling where you go to the bathroom takes great strength."
  ◊ "It is clear what a huge effort you are making to go to the bathroom in the toilet."

Behavior (5)
Using toilet paper excessively (wiping)

If you find the child's compulsive use of toilet paper to clean himself/herself *seems*, for the most part:

1. anxious and/or troubled; possibly upsetting and tense for others (see Worrying Child)

- **The Worrying Child**

Core Feeling:	The more frequent the child's "need" to use the toilet is, the greater the **fear/anger** is being experienced by the child.
Core Wish:	Communicates unconscious wish to be **noticed** and **supported** as a way of decreasing sense of **danger** and **abandonment**.
Core Question:	Limit-testing question—I am being triggered by events and this is an expression of how afraid I am; do you care enough to protect me?
Responses:	**Verbal & Less Emotional** (see Responses section)

Chapter 16. Toileting Accidents and Toilet-Related Issues

Responses for: Behavior (5) Using toilet paper excessively (wiping)

The Worrying Child

- *Verbal*:
    - ◊ Clear and calm voice (quiet).
    - ◊ Before class: Check in and talk about previous day. Occasional eye contact. "I want to check in with you to see how our talk felt for you. We can do this each day."
    - ◊ During class: Occasional eye contact. Maintain distance (two feet at least). No physical contact. Use sound or words to get attention (Less Emotional responses below).
    - ◊ After class: Occasional eye contact. Reiterate response themes (connection, self-care).
- *Less Emotional*:
    - ◊ *Self-Care*: "Take a deep breath and let it out very slowly when you start to need to use a lot of toilet paper to clean yourself. It is safe and powerful to help your body to wait until you feel calmer."
    - ◊ *Self-Care and Connection*: "When we suddenly have an uncomfortable thought, it can help us feel safer if we try and slow down and find a person we trust. When you need to use a lot of toilet paper to clean yourself, you can let me know, and we will slowly figure out how to help you. We can come up with a code, so when you need my help, it stays private."
    - ◊ *Self-Care and Connection*: "When you are needing to use a lot of toilet paper, it makes me think about your safety. I would like to ask you about what you are thinking when this is going on."
- *Affirmation*:
    - ◊ "Using just the safe amount of toilet paper when we clean ourselves takes strength."
    - ◊ "You are brave to try to use just the safe amount of toilet paper to clean yourself."

Your Evolving Responses

As you have read, there are different motivations for your students' behaviors depending on their latent communication patterns. This demonstrates that your responses cannot be "one size fits all" in nature. While we have provided specific words for you to follow, we intend this chapter and the others like it to be a framework for your responses, not a script. You certainly can use our suggested language as you experiment with the interventions we have described. Overtime, it will be more helpful for you to find your own words to communicate with your students. As you continue to try these techniques, using your own communication style will make the responses to your students' behaviors feel authentic and sincere. This will happen naturally. The proposed interventions that we used in this chapter are a starting point and are meant to evolve and grow with your comfort level. This might take some practice, but it will be well worth it to expand your repertoire of potential responses to concerning or disruptive behaviors. You may find that your own words are more effective or more impactful than the words and phrases we have suggested in this book. The more you are a part of the interventions, the more meaningful they may be to your students. As we know, students need repetition, so please be patient as you try out new ways to respond to them.

Chapter 17

Upsetting Artwork, Writings, and Play

"The artist is not a special kind of person; rather each person is a special kind of artist."

—Ananda Coomaraswamy

How to Use This Chapter

1. As you prepare to read this chapter, choose one child from your class on whom you wish to focus. Selecting one child at a time allows for a more concentrated exploration of the material and how it relates to each child uniquely. **As a guide, we will use "Melody," a second grader who has created drawings with sexual content.**

2. Read the paragraphs from the following headings to begin the process: *Format and Theme* and *Common Forms of the Behavior.*

3. Choose one behavior that the selected child is exhibiting. Selecting one behavior at a time allows for a more concentrated exploration of the material centering on how the child communicates using this specific behavior. **Melody's behavior of creating artwork that includes sexual content.**

4. Read the paragraphs from the following headings to learn more about the general category that this behavior falls within from a more holistic perspective: *Manifest Communication* and *Latent Communication.*

5. Read the paragraphs from the heading *Responses and Affirmations* as background to how we structured the proposed responses and the expectation that you will ultimately personalize the responses provided in this chapter.

6. Turn to the page that contains the behavior in question. There you will find the number of the behavior and its name. **We select Behavior (4) Creating artwork that includes sexual content.**

7. On that page, below the number and name, you will find all the possible latent communication prompts for that behavior, ranging from (1) to (4). From these prompts, choose the prompt that most closely reminds you of how this child exhibits this behavior. Your choice may not fit one prompt exactly. If your sense is that multiple prompts could fit, choose the closest one to begin the process.

You can return to the other prompts later. You will notice that each prompt corresponds with a child communication Persona (i.e., Troubling, Testing, Worrying, Hiding). **For Melody, we choose "anxious and/or troubled; possibly upsetting and tense for others (see Worrying Child)."**

8. After choosing a latent communication prompt, use the child communication Persona and read the corresponding Core Feelings, Core Wish, Core Question. This information describes the underlying meaning of the behavior and creates an empathic guide for you to keep in mind when responding to the child's behavior.

9. On the following page(s), you will find responses and affirmations for the number and name of the behavior in question. **We select Responses for:** *Behavior (4) Creating artwork that includes sexual content* section **The Worrying Child.** Find and read the responses and affirmations for the behavior in question that corresponds with the child communication Persona.

10. **Try the responses and affirmations with Melody and determine how they feel to you.**

Theme and Format

Each of the behavior chapters in this section of the book should be considered with the following format in mind. In this chapter, we will focus on children who create **upsetting artwork, writing, and play**. The word "upsetting" is an all-encompassing idea that includes any content or process that feels simultaneously out-of-place and unsettling and compels us to take a closer look. That said, the title of this chapter is an umbrella descriptor, and these behaviors comprise a theme or group of communications. We observe these manifest communications as thematic, as there are many permutations within a category of behavior.

Common Forms of This Behavior

- Creating artwork that appears overly regressed
- Generating play that appears overly regressed
- Generating writing that includes appears overly regressed
- Creating artwork that includes sexual content
- Generating play that includes sexual content
- Generating writing that includes sexual content
- Creating artwork that includes violence (self or others)
- Generating play that includes violence (self or others)
- Generating writing that includes violence (self or others)

Manifest Communication

For these communications/behaviors, we recommend always coordinating with your administration. It is important to acknowledge that the meaning behind the behaviors such as those listed above may require a professional assessment for a child, in order to determine any environmental, psychological, neurological, or developmental issues that are driving the creation and/or generation of graphic and provocative material. Ruling out possible etiological causes that require outside-school intervention—such as maltreatment (sexual abuse, physical abuse, emotional abuse, neglect), traumatic experience (domestic violence, divorce, death in the family, substance abuse in the family), mental health issues (psychosis, depression), or medical health issues (brain trauma), among others—is a critical step in addressing any child who is communicating through the use of regressed and/or alarming imagery/activity. This may entail involving parents, medical professionals, mental health professionals, child protective services, or even law enforcement, at times. That said, while discussions regarding further assessment are happening, there are ways for us to respond to these intense child communications within the class setting.

As a default, we expect young children to be innocent and naïve. It is our wish as loving caregivers that they are to be sheltered from harm and all things unpleasant. And so, it is provocative to see behaviors and communications from these children that are contrary to this fantasy. The word "upsetting," from the title of this chapter, is a mild description of the disquiet that we may experience when children create, from their imagination, images of a different life than we expected them to know—dangerous, scary, menacing, sexual, overwhelming, confusing, and/or dark.

All creating that comes from the mind of a child conveys information about that child. Before we explore the potential meanings in the following sections, we want to provide an organizational system for collecting and collating these creations. First, we define creations in a broad sense that includes all forms of expression:

- 2-dimensional artwork
- 3-dimentional artwork
- Comments made
- Eating
- Imaginary play
- Questions asked
- Structured play
- Writing

Second, the attributes of these creations can be examined using a "who, what, when, where, and how" process of inquiry and data collection. How are children understanding and conveying their experiences? The material that we consider "upsetting" gets under our skin and gives us pause. It stands out, attracting our notice and often creating an increased level of distress in us. A methodical (and calm, if we can) noticing of the details that define these behaviors/communications becomes critical (see Table 17.1). The process of cataloguing the details of a child's disturbing creations helps to focus us and hold back from speculating about its meaning until we have more information.

Table 17.1:
Types of Creative Expressions and Attributes

Type of Expression	Attributes
2-dimensional artwork (drawings, painting, etc.)	people, subject matter, actions, color scheme, choice of material, density of stroke
3-dimensional artwork (sculpture, collage)	form, subject matter, choice of material, density of material
Comments made (to self or others)	subject matter, form of the question, level of urgency, relative connectedness to material being discussed
Eating	type of food and/or non-food materials, variety of food, style of eating
Imaginary play	people, subject matter, relational dynamics and conduct (who is in charge, level of urgency)
Questions asked	subject matter, form of the question, urgency, relative connectedness to material being discussed
Structured play (board games, etc.)	choice of game, relational dynamics and conduct (winning, losing, rule adherence)
Writing	subject matter, people, actions, and storyline

Weiner, Gallo-Silver, & Lucas, 2020

In addition to trying to remain calm, an important aspect of engagement regarding these types of communications is the language we use to discuss what can sometimes be graphic or provocative material. The word "age-appropriate" means that a description (of an idea, an environment, or a dynamic) is geared to the developmental age of a child. Remember that developmental age and biological age can be different. Maintaining an age-appropriateness in our back and forth with children is a way of managing their anxiety by not introducing notions that they are not prepared to hear or integrate. Do you use the word privates, genitals, or penis/vagina? Do you refer to someone being mean, being dangerous, or being violent? Do you describe something as scary, frightening, or disturbing?

For early childhood students, we recommend erring on the side of choosing an earlier stage of development as a default and then moving to a more sophisticated description, if appropriate. For example, this acknowledges the fact that some parents use the actual terms for genitals, while others do not. Using euphemisms is not overly cautious parenting, however; it is a choice that we should honor. For our interventions we will use the following language for the different communication content:

Regressed content

- "big" for developmentally age-matching artwork, activity, and writing
- "little" for developmentally regressed artwork, activity, and writing (Kris, 1975)

Sexual content

- "privates" and "private areas" for genital artwork, activity, and writing
- "grown-up touching" for sexual act artwork, activity, and writing

Violent content

- "danger" and "dangerous" for violent artwork, activity, and writing
- "safe" "safer" for non-violent artwork, activity, and writing

In addition, we must always check as we go whether or not the children are understanding the meaning of our words. Does that make sense? When I say "privates" or "grown-up touching," what do you think I am talking about? Clarifying the meaning of words with the children and modifying them with more details or less, if necessary, is a way of showing empathy.

Using the child Personas of the Troubling child, the Testing child, the Worrying child, and the Hiding child, we will explore specific teacher responses for each type of communication pattern (see Table 17.2). For more detailed information about background for each Persona and the reasoning behind the most productive teacher response configurations, please refer back to their respective chapters.

Table 17.2:
Behavior Frequency by Persona

	Persona			
Behavior	*Troubling Child Loud & Over Reactive*	*Testing Child Loud & Under Reactive*	*Worrying Child Quiet & Over Reactive*	*Hiding Child Quiet & Under Reactive*
Creating artwork that appears overly regressed	X	X	X	X
Generating play that appears overly regressed	X	X	X	X
Generating writing that appears overly regressed	X	X	X	X
Creating artwork that includes sexual content	X	X	X	X
Generating play that includes sexual content	X	X	X	X
Generating writing that includes sexual content	X	X	X	X
Creating artwork that includes violence (self or others)	X	X	X	X
Generating play that includes violence (self or others)	X	X	X	X

	Persona			
Behavior	Troubling Child Loud & Over Reactive	Testing Child Loud & Under Reactive	Worrying Child Quiet & Over Reactive	Hiding Child Quiet & Under Reactive
Generating writing that includes violence (self or others)	X	X	X	X

Latent Communication

This process is not an exact science and should be conducted more as trial and error. We would like you to take your best professional guess as to your answers to the following inquiries and evaluations. If you find that, after working through the latent communication material and identifying a set of responses, they do not work as you hoped, you can always revise and try again. Just remember, children integrate learning following repetition, so do not give up too soon.

Responses and Affirmations

Children do not learn the first time we teach them a new concept or a task. We say this in order to manage our expectations about how quickly or completely these new interventions will change or extinguish any given behavior.

Let's keep in mind the following factors. First, the development of these behaviors has typically occurred over an extended period of time. Based on the ages of the children we address in this book, any behavior grew over at least two years and up to eight. As much as we would wish it, a behavior that has been developing over a lengthy period of time cannot change "overnight." Actually, rapid change is often poorly integrated by children and cannot be sustained. Second, children integrate responses at different rates based on a variety of factors, including temperament, environment, learning styles, family involvement/support, etc. We have addressed these earlier in the book. Last, we are constructing foundations from which to grow, one brick at a time, foundations that these children will be able to build on and rely on for years to come. To this end, we want you to know that each of your responses is remembered and cataloged by these children for future use—even if it does not outwardly appear to have been during your time with the child. This relates to the corrective emotional experience we wrote about earlier in this book. Your interactions become part of the child's long-term memory, exchanges that are saved for future use.

That said, we want us to have some benchmarks for our expectations. First, we believe that one month is a sufficient timeframe for some level of change in a behavior, given that a specific teacher response is maintained with consistency and repetition. Second, as we cannot factor in changes that are occurring in real time within these children and with their families, the one-month benchmark may need to be altered accordingly. Third, the one-month duration allows for these challenged children to test us. They will imagine that what we are doing cannot be sustained, that it is too good to last. Our consistency and repetition in responding to the underlying message ultimately quiet their negative thoughts. It is then when the child's expectations of the people around them begin to change to an inner message that is more hopeful and positive. This hopefulness alters their communications and behaviors and can become a more embedded part of their future interpersonal relationships.

Behavior (1)
Creating artwork that appears overly regressed

If you find the child's overly regressed artwork *seems* for the most part:

1. willful; seemingly inflammatory and challenging (see Troubling Child)
2. mischievous; mildly vexing, pushing limits/boundaries (see Testing Child)
3. anxious and/or troubled; possibly upsetting and tense for others (see Worrying Child)
4. disconnected and/or arbitrary; possibly odd and/or confusing to others (see Hiding Child)

- **The Troubling Child**

Core Feeling:	The more ubiquitous the child's overly regressed artwork is, the greater the **sadness/anger** is being experienced by the child.
Core Wish:	Communicates unconscious wish to be **contained** and **supported** as a way of decreasing sense of **danger** and **rejection**.
Core Question:	Limit-testing question—I am being triggered by events because this moment in class feels overwhelming; can you accept me and handle me?
Responses:	**Structural & Less Emotional** (see Responses section)

- **The Testing Child**

Core Feeling:	The more ubiquitous the child's overly regressed artwork is, the greater the **sadness/anger** is being experienced by the child.
Core Wish:	Communicates unconscious wish to be **contained** and **validated** as a way of increasing sense of **security** and decreasing sense of **abandonment**.

Core Question:	Limit-testing question—I am feeling bad about myself and need to show this by creating a distraction; do you care about me enough to stop me?
Responses:	**Structural & More Emotional** (see Responses section)

- ## The Worrying Child

Core Feeling:	The more ubiquitous the child's overly regressed artwork is, the greater the **fear/anger** is being experienced by the child.
Core Wish:	Communicates unconscious wish to be **noticed** and **supported** as a way of decreasing sense of **danger** and **abandonment**.
Core Question:	Limit-testing question—I am being triggered by events and this is an expression of how afraid I am; do you care enough to protect me?
Responses:	**Verbal & Less Emotional** (see Responses section)

- ## The Hiding Child

Core Feeling:	The more ubiquitous the child's overly regressed artwork is, the greater the **fear/anger** is being experienced by the child.
Core Wish:	Communicates unconscious wish to be **noticed** and **validated** as a way of increasing sense of **security** and decreasing sense of **rejection**.
Core Question:	Limit-testing question—My behavior is a diversion from just how uncomfortable I feel right now; can you accept the way I am and contain me?
Responses:	**Verbal & More Emotional** (see Responses section)

Responses for: Behavior (1) Creating artwork that appears overly regressed

The Troubling Child

- *Structural*:
    - ◊ Clear and calm voice (supportive).
    - ◊ Before class: Check in. Hold eye contact. "I'm with you. Let's keep working on this."
    - ◊ During class: Hand on shoulder; down on knee at eye level. Hold eye contact. Use the Less Emotional responses below.
    - ◊ After class: Check in. Hold eye contact. Reiterate response themes (boundaries, self-care). Track progress with chart.

- *Less Emotional*:
    - *Self-Care and Boundaries*: "When you make (*types of artwork*) that seems little for you, you are saying something about your safety. It can be important to share more about what you are thinking."
    - *Self-Care and Boundaries*: "I want you to make (*types of artwork*) that are big like you. You are more in charge when you don't push people away by making (*types of artwork*) that seem little for you."
    - *Boundaries*: "Think to yourself, 'I have a choice. I can choose to make a (*type of artwork*) that is big like me. I am big and strong, and I can make a (*type of artwork*) that is big like me.'"
    - *Self-Care and Boundaries*: "Think about having a birthday and imagine, we get to choose a gift. We can choose an (*age-appropriate toy*) or we can choose a (*baby toy*). Sometimes it's fun to remember our baby toys. For now, let's choose the gift is that big like us. Making a big kid (*type of artwork*) is like choosing a big kid toy for our birthday. It fits us better."
- *Affirmation*:
    - "Making (*types of artwork*) that is big like you takes great strength."
    - "Anyone can see your big effort to make (*types of artwork*) that are big like you are."

The Testing Child

- *Structural*:
    - Clear and crisp voice (supportive).
    - Before class: Check in. Hold eye contact. "I'm with you. Let's keep working on this."
    - During class: Hand on shoulder; down on knee at eye level. Hold eye contact. Use More Emotional responses below.
    - After class: Check in. Hold eye contact. Reiterate response themes (boundaries, self-awareness). Track progress with chart.
- *More Emotional*:
    - *Self-Awareness and Boundaries*: "When you make (*types of artwork*) that seems little for you, I think you are feeling bad, and I am worried. I would like you to share what you are thinking."
    - *Self-Awareness and Boundaries*: "It saddens me when you make (*types of artwork*) that seems little for you, because I feel it pushes us apart."
    - *Self-Awareness*: "When you make (*types of artwork*) that seems little for you, I think you feel bad."
    - *Self-Awareness and Boundaries*: "Sometimes having bad thoughts is like having to get a shot at the doctor. It can feel scary. It can make us afraid and small. When we are afraid, we can ask for someone to be with us. That can help us feel big. Let's make your (*types of artwork*) big together."
    - *Self-Awareness and Boundaries*: "If I see that your (*types of artwork*) seem too little for you, I will say to you, 'I am with you. Let's make your (*type of artwork*) big like you are by adding big kid ideas.'"

- *Affirmation*:
    - ◊ "I am proud of you for trying so hard to make (*types of artwork*) that are big like you are."
    - ◊ "You took good care of yourself by making (*types of artwork*) that are big like you are."

The Worrying Child

- *Verbal*:
    - ◊ Clear and calm voice (quiet).
    - ◊ Before class: Check in and talk about previous day. Occasional eye contact. "I want to check in with you to see how our talk felt for you. We can do this each day."
    - ◊ During class: Occasional eye contact. Maintain distance (two feet at least). No physical contact. Use sound or words to get attention (Less Emotional responses below).
    - ◊ After class: Occasional eye contact. Reiterate response themes (connection, self-care).
- *Less Emotional*:
    - ◊ *Self-Care and Connection*: "When you make (*types of artwork*) that seems little for you, it makes me think about your safety. I would like to ask you about what you are thinking when this is going on."
    - ◊ *Self-Care*: "When you make a (*type of artwork*), take a deep breath and let it out very slowly. It is safer to wait until you feel calmer so you can make a (*type of artwork*) that is big like you are."
    - ◊ *Self-Care and Connection*: "When we make a (*type of artwork*) and we have an uncomfortable thought, it can make us feel little. We can feel safe if we slow down and stay near a person we trust. When you feel safe, we can slowly figure out how to make a (*type of artwork*) that is big like you."
- *Affirmation*:
    - ◊ "Making your (*types of artwork*) big like the big kid you are takes strength."
    - ◊ "You are brave to try to make your (*types of artwork*) big like you are."

The Hiding Child

- *Verbal*:
    - ◊ Clear and calm voice (quiet).
    - ◊ Before class: Check in and talk about previous day. Occasional eye contact. "I want to check in with you to see if you remember our talk. We will do this each day."
    - ◊ During class: Occasional eye contact. Maintain distance (two feet at least). No physical contact. Use sound or words to get attention (More Emotional responses below).
    - ◊ After class: Occasional eye contact. Reiterate response themes (connection, self-awareness).

- *More Emotional*:
  - ◊ *Self-Awareness and Connection*: "When you make (*types of artwork*) that seems little for you, I think you are having big feelings. I am worried and want to know more."
  - ◊ *Self-Awareness and Connection*: "If I see that your (*types of artwork*) seem too little for you, I will say to you, 'You can choose to make your (*types of artwork*) big.' I can help with that."
  - ◊ *Self-Awareness*: "Be big and strong. Say to yourself, 'I am big. My (*types of artwork*) can be big too.'"
  - ◊ *Self-Awareness and Connection*: "Look at my face. I am worried that you are making (*types of artwork*) that seems little for you. You are in charge of your (*types of artwork*). I want them to be big like you."
- *Affirmation*:
  - ◊ "I see you using your thoughts to make your (*types of artwork*) big like you are."
  - ◊ "I am impressed how you are deciding to make your (*types of artwork*) big like you are."

Behavior (2)
Generating play that appears overly regressed

If you find that the child's creation of and engagement in overly regressed play *seem* for the most part:

1. willful; seemingly inflammatory and challenging (see Troubling Child)
2. mischievous; mildly vexing, pushing limits/boundaries (see Testing Child)
3. anxious and/or troubled; possibly upsetting and tense for others (see Worrying Child)
4. disconnected and/or arbitrary; possibly odd and/or confusing to others (see Hiding Child)

- **The Troubling Child**

Core Feeling:	The more ubiquitous the child's overly regressed play is, the greater the **sadness/anger** is being experienced by the child.
Core Wish:	Communicates unconscious wish to be **contained** and **supported** as a way of decreasing sense of **danger** and **rejection**.
Core Question:	Limit-testing question—I am being triggered by events because this moment in class feels overwhelming; can you accept me and handle me?
Responses:	**Structural & Less Emotional** (see Responses section)

- **The Testing Child**

Core Feeling:	The more ubiquitous the child's overly regressed play is, the greater the **sadness/anger** is being experienced by the child.
Core Wish:	Communicates unconscious wish to be **contained** and **validated** as a way of increasing sense of **security** and decreasing sense of **abandonment**.
Core Question:	Limit-testing question—I am feeling bad about myself and need to show this by creating a distraction; do you care about me enough to stop me?
Responses:	**Structural & More Emotional** (see Responses section)

- **The Worrying Child**

Core Feeling:	The more ubiquitous the child's overly regressed play is, the greater the **fear/anger** is being experienced by the child.
Core Wish:	Communicates unconscious wish to be **noticed** and **supported** as a way of decreasing sense of **danger** and **abandonment**.
Core Question:	Limit-testing question—I am being triggered by events and this is an expression of how afraid I am; do you care enough to protect me?
Responses:	**Verbal & Less Emotional** (see Responses section)

- **The Hiding Child**

Core Feeling:	The more ubiquitous the child's overly regressed play is, the greater the **fear/anger** is being experienced by the child.
Core Wish:	Communicates unconscious wish to be **noticed** and **validated** as a way of increasing sense of **security** and decreasing sense of **rejection**.
Core Question:	Limit-testing question—My behavior is a diversion from just how uncomfortable I feel right now; can you accept the way I am and contain me?
Responses:	**Verbal & More Emotional** (see Responses section)

Responses for: Behavior (2) Generating play that appears overly regressed

The Troubling Child

- ***Structural*:**
  - ◊ Clear and calm voice (supportive).

Chapter 17. Upsetting Artwork, Writings, and Play

◊ Before class: Check in. Hold eye contact. "I'm with you. Let's keep working on this."
◊ During class: Hand on shoulder; down on knee at eye level. Hold eye contact. Use the Less Emotional responses below.
◊ After class: Check in. Hold eye contact. Reiterate response themes (boundaries, self-care). Track progress with chart.

- **Less Emotional:**
    ◊ *Self-Care and Boundaries*: "When you play in a way that seems little for you, you are saying something about your safety. It can be important to share more about what you are thinking."
    ◊ *Self-Care and Boundaries*: "I want you to play in a way that is big like you. You are more in charge when you don't push people away by playing in a way that seems too little for you."
    ◊ *Boundaries*: "Think to yourself, 'I have a choice. I can choose to play in a way that is big like me. I am big and strong, and I can play in a way that is big like me.'"
    ◊ *Self-Care and Boundaries*: "Think about having a birthday and imagine, we get to choose a gift. We can choose an (*age-appropriate toy*) or we can choose a (*baby toy*). Sometimes it's fun to remember our baby toys. For now, let's choose the gift that is big like us. Playing in way that a big kid does is like choosing a big kid toy for our birthday. It fits us better."

- **Affirmation:**
    ◊ "Playing in a way that fits our age takes great strength."
    ◊ "Anyone can see your big effort to play in a way that is big like you are."

The Testing Child

- **Structural:**
    ◊ Clear and crisp voice (supportive).
    ◊ Before class: Check in. Hold eye contact. "I'm with you. Let's keep working on this."
    ◊ During class: Hand on shoulder; down on knee at eye level. Hold eye contact. Use More Emotional responses below.
    ◊ After class: Check in. Hold eye contact. Reiterate response themes (boundaries, self-awareness). Track progress with chart.

- **More Emotional:**
    ◊ *Self-Awareness and Boundaries*: "When you play in a way that seems little for you, I think you are feeling bad, and I am worried. I would like you to share what you are thinking."
    ◊ *Self-Awareness and Boundaries*: "It saddens me when you are playing in a way that seems little for you, because I feel it pushes us apart."
    ◊ *Self-Awareness*: "When you are playing in a way that seems little for you, I think you feel bad."
    ◊ *Self-Awareness and Boundaries*: "Sometimes having bad thoughts is like having to get a shot at the doctor. It can feel scary. It can make us

afraid and small. When we are afraid, we can ask for someone to be with us. That can help us feel big. Let's make the way you are playing big together."
- ◊ *Self-Awareness and Boundaries*: "If I see that the way you are playing seems little for you, I will say to you, 'I am with you. Let's make the way you are playing big like you are by adding big kid ideas.'"
- *Affirmation*:
    - ◊ "I am proud of you for trying so hard to play in a way that is big like you are."
    - ◊ "You took good care of yourself by playing in a way that is big like you are."

The Worrying Child

- *Verbal*:
    - ◊ Clear and calm voice (quiet).
    - ◊ Before class: Check in and talk about previous day. Occasional eye contact. "I want to check in with you to see how our talk felt for you. We can do this each day."
    - ◊ During class: Occasional eye contact. Maintain distance (two feet at least). No physical contact. Use sound or words to get attention (Less Emotional responses below).
    - ◊ After class: Occasional eye contact. Reiterate response themes (connection, self-care).
- *Less Emotional*:
    - ◊ *Self-Care and Connection*: "When you play in a way that seems little for you, it makes me think about your safety. I would like to ask you about what you are thinking when this is going on."
    - ◊ *Self-Care*: "When you start to play, take a deep breath and let it out very slowly. It is safer to wait until you feel calmer so you can play in a way that is big like you are."
    - ◊ *Self-Care and Connection*: "When we are playing and we suddenly have an uncomfortable thought, it can make us feel little. We can feel safe if we try and slow down and stay near a person we trust. When you feel safe, then we can slowly figure out how to play in a way that is big like you."
- *Affirmation*:
    - ◊ "Playing big like the big kid you are takes strength."
    - ◊ "You are brave to try to play big like the big you are."

The Hiding Child

- *Verbal*:
    - ◊ Clear and calm voice (quiet).
    - ◊ Before class: Check in and talk about previous day. Occasional eye

contact. "I want to check in with you to see if you remember our talk. We will do this each day."
  - ◊ During class: Occasional eye contact. Maintain distance (two feet at least). No physical contact. Use sound or words to get attention (More Emotional responses below).
  - ◊ After class: Occasional eye contact. Reiterate response themes (connection, self-awareness).
- **More Emotional:**
  - ◊ *Self-Awareness and Connection*: "When you play in a way that seems little for you, I think you are having big feelings. I am worried and want to know more."
  - ◊ *Self-Awareness and Connection*: "If I see that you are playing in a way that seems too little for you, I will say to you, 'You can choose to play in a way that is big like you are.' I can help with that."
  - ◊ *Self-Awareness*: "Be big and strong. Say to yourself, 'I am big. I can play big like a big kid.'"
  - ◊ *Self-Awareness and Connection*: "Look at my face. I am worried that you are playing in a way that seems little for you. You are in charge of how you are playing. I want your playing to be big like you."
- *Affirmation*:
  - ◊ "I see you using your thoughts to play like the big kid you are."
  - ◊ "I am impressed how you are deciding to play like the big kid you are."

Behavior (3)
Generating writing that appears overly regressed

If you find the child's overly regressed artwork *seems* for the most part:

1. willful; seemingly inflammatory and challenging (see Troubling Child)
2. mischievous; mildly vexing, pushing limits/boundaries (see Testing Child)
3. anxious and/or troubled; possibly upsetting and tense for others (see Worrying Child)
4. disconnected and/or arbitrary; possibly odd and/or confusing to others (see Hiding Child)

- **The Troubling Child**

    Core Feeling: The more ubiquitous the child's overly regressed artwork is, the greater the **sadness/anger** is being experienced by the child.

    Core Wish: Communicates unconscious wish to be **contained** and **supported** as a way of decreasing sense of **danger** and **rejection**.

Core Question: Limit-testing question—I am being triggered by events because this moment in class feels overwhelming; can you accept me and handle me?

Responses: **Structural & Less Emotional** (see Responses section)

- **The Testing Child**

Core Feeling: The more ubiquitous the child's overly regressed artwork is, the greater the **sadness/anger** is being experienced by the child.

Core Wish: Communicates unconscious wish to be **contained** and **validated** as a way of increasing sense of **security** and decreasing sense of **abandonment**.

Core Question: Limit-testing question—I am feeling bad about myself and need to show this by creating a distraction; do you care about me enough to stop me?

Responses: **Structural & More Emotional** (see Responses section)

- **The Worrying Child**

Core Feeling: The more ubiquitous the child's overly regressed artwork is, the greater the **fear/anger** is being experienced by the child.

Core Wish: Communicates unconscious wish to be **noticed** and **supported** as a way of decreasing sense of **danger** and **abandonment**.

Core Question: Limit-testing question—I am being triggered by events and this is an expression of how afraid I am; do you care enough to protect me?

Responses: **Verbal & Less Emotional** (see Responses section)

- **The Hiding Child**

Core Feeling: The more ubiquitous the child's overly regressed artwork is, the greater the **fear/anger** is being experienced by the child.

Core Wish: Communicates unconscious wish to be **noticed** and **validated** as a way of increasing sense of **security** and decreasing sense of **rejection**.

Core Question: Limit-testing question—My behavior is a diversion from just how uncomfortable I feel right now; can you accept the way I am and contain me?

Responses: **Verbal & More Emotional** (see Responses section)

Responses for: Behavior (3) Generating writing that appears overly regressed

The Troubling Child

- *Structural*:
    - ◊ Clear and calm voice (supportive).
    - ◊ Before class: Check in. Hold eye contact. "I'm with you. Let's keep working on this."
    - ◊ During class: Hand on shoulder; down on knee at eye level. Hold eye contact. Use the Less Emotional responses below.
    - ◊ After class: Check in. Hold eye contact. Reiterate response themes (boundaries, self-care). Track progress with chart.
- *Less Emotional*:
    - ◊ *Self-Care and Boundaries*: "When you write in a way that seems little for you, you are saying something about your safety. It can be important to share more about what you are thinking."
    - ◊ *Self-Care and Boundaries*: "I want you to write in a way that is big like you. You are more in charge when you don't push people away by writing in a way that seems too little for you."
    - ◊ *Boundaries*: "Think to yourself, 'I have a choice. I can choose to write in a way that is big like me. I am big and strong, and I can write in a way that is big like me.'"
    - ◊ *Self-Care and Boundaries*: "Think about having a birthday and imagine, we get to choose a gift. We can choose an (*age-appropriate toy*) or we can choose a (*baby toy*). Sometimes it's fun to remember our baby toys. For now, let's choose the gift that is big like us. Writing in way that a big kid does is like choosing a big kid toy for our birthday. It fits us better."
- *Affirmation*:
    - ◊ "Writing in a way that is big like you takes great strength."
    - ◊ "Anyone can see your big effort to write in a way that is big like you are."

The Testing Child

- *Structural*:
    - ◊ Clear and crisp voice (supportive).
    - ◊ Before class: Check in. Hold eye contact. "I'm with you. Let's keep working on this."
    - ◊ During class: Hand on shoulder; down on knee at eye level. Hold eye contact. Use More Emotional responses below.
    - ◊ After class: Check in. Hold eye contact. Reiterate response themes (boundaries, self-awareness). Track progress with chart.
- *More Emotional*:
    - ◊ *Self-Awareness and Boundaries*: "When you write in a way that seems

little for you, I think you are feeling bad, and I am worried. I would like you to share what you are thinking."
- ◊ *Self-Awareness and Boundaries*: "It saddens me when you write in a way seems little for you, because I feel it pushes us apart."
- ◊ *Self-Awareness*: "When you write in a way that seems little for you, I think you feel bad."
- ◊ *Self-Awareness and Boundaries*: "Sometimes having bad thoughts is like having to get a shot at the doctor. It can feel scary. It can make us afraid and small. When we are afraid, we can ask for someone to be with us. That can help us feel big. Let's make the way you write be big together."
- ◊ *Self-Awareness and Boundaries*: "If I see that the way you are writing seems little for you, I will say to you, 'I am with you. Let's make the way you write be big like you are by adding big kid ideas.'"

- *Affirmation*:
  - ◊ "I am proud of you for trying so hard to write in a way that is big like you are."
  - ◊ "You took good care of yourself by writing in a way that is big like you are."

The Worrying Child

- *Verbal*:
  - ◊ Clear and calm voice (quiet).
  - ◊ Before class: Check in and talk about previous day. Occasional eye contact. "I want to check in with you to see how our talk felt for you. We can do this each day."
  - ◊ During class: Occasional eye contact. Maintain distance (two feet at least). No physical contact. Use sound or words to get attention (Less Emotional responses below).
  - ◊ After class: Occasional eye contact. Reiterate response themes (connection, self-care).
- *Less Emotional*:
  - ◊ *Self-Care and Connection*: "When you write in a way that seems little for you, it makes me think about your safety. I would like to ask you about what you are thinking when this is going on."
  - ◊ *Self-Care*: "When you start to write, take a deep breath and let it out very slowly. It is safer to wait until you feel calmer so you can write in a way that is big like you are."
  - ◊ *Self-Care and Connection*: "When we are writing and we suddenly have an uncomfortable thought, it can make us feel little. We can feel safe if we try and slow down and stay near a person we trust. When you feel safe, then we can slowly figure out how to write in a way that is big like you."
- *Affirmation*:
  - ◊ "Making your writing big like the big kid you are takes strength."
  - ◊ "You are brave to try to write like the big kid you are."

The Hiding Child

- **Verbal:**
    ◊ Clear and calm voice (quiet).
    ◊ Before class: Check in and talk about previous day. Occasional eye contact. "I want to check in with you to see if you remember our talk. We will do this each day."
    ◊ During class: Occasional eye contact. Maintain distance (two feet at least). No physical contact. Use sound or words to get attention (More Emotional responses below).
    ◊ After class: Occasional eye contact. Reiterate response themes (connection, self-awareness).
- **More Emotional:**
    ◊ *Self-Awareness and Connection*: "When you write in a way that seems little for you, I think you are having big feelings. I am worried and want to know more."
    ◊ *Self-Awareness and Connection*: "If I see that you are writing in a way that seems too little for you, I will say to you, 'You can choose to write in a way that is big like you are.' I can help with that."
    ◊ *Self-Awareness*: "Be big and strong. Say to yourself, 'I am big. I can write big like a big kid.'"
    ◊ *Self-Awareness and Connection*: "Look at my face. I am worried that you are writing in a way that seems little for you. You are in charge of how you write. I want your writing to be big like you."
- **Affirmation:**
    ◊ "I see you using your thoughts to write like the big kid you are."
    ◊ "I am impressed how you are deciding to write like the big kid you are."

Behavior (4)
Creating artwork that includes sexual content

If you find the child's creation of artwork with sexual content *seems*, for the most part:

1. willful; seemingly inflammatory and challenging (see Troubling Child)
2. mischievous; mildly vexing, pushing limits/boundaries (see Testing Child)
3. anxious and/or troubled; possibly upsetting and tense for others (see Worrying Child)
4. disconnected and/or arbitrary; possibly odd and/or confusing to others (see Hiding Child)

- **The Troubling Child**

  Core Feeling: The more frequent and/or detailed the child's sexual-content artwork is, the greater the **sadness/anger** is being experienced by the child.

  Core Wish: Communicates unconscious wish to be **contained** and **supported** as a way of decreasing sense of **danger** and **rejection**.

  Core Question: Limit-testing question—I am being triggered by events because this moment in class feels overwhelming; can you accept me and handle me?

  Responses: **Structural & Less Emotional** (see Responses section)

- **The Testing Child**

  Core Feeling: The more frequent and/or detailed the child's sexual-content artwork is, the greater the **sadness/anger** is being experienced by the child.

  Core Wish: Communicates unconscious wish to be **contained** and **validated** as a way of increasing sense of **security** and decreasing sense of **abandonment**.

  Core Question: Limit-testing question—I am feeling bad about myself and need to show this by creating a distraction; do you care about me enough to stop me?

  Responses: **Structural & More Emotional** (see Responses section)

- **The Worrying Child**

  Core Feeling: The more frequent and/or detailed the child's sexual-content artwork is, the greater the **fear/anger** is being experienced by the child.

  Core Wish: Communicates unconscious wish to be **noticed** and **supported** as a way of decreasing sense of **danger** and **abandonment**.

  Core Question: Limit-testing question—I am being triggered by events and this is an expression of how afraid I am; do you care enough to protect me?

  Responses: **Verbal & Less Emotional** (see Responses section)

- **The Hiding Child**

  Core Feeling: The more frequent and/or detailed the child's sexual-content artwork is, the greater the **fear/anger** is being experienced by the child.

Core Wish: Communicates unconscious wish to be **noticed** and **validated** as a way of increasing sense of **security** and decreasing sense of **rejection**.

Core Question: Limit-testing question—My behavior is a diversion from just how uncomfortable I feel right now; can you accept the way I am and contain me?

Responses: **Verbal & More Emotional** (see Responses section)

Responses for: Behavior (4) Creating artwork that includes sexual content

The Troubling Child

- *Structural*:
    - ◊ Clear and calm voice (supportive).
    - ◊ Before class: Check in. Hold eye contact. "I'm with you. Let's keep working on this."
    - ◊ During class: Hand on shoulder; down on knee at eye level. Hold eye contact. Use the Less Emotional responses below.
    - ◊ After class: Check in. Hold eye contact. Reiterate response themes (boundaries, self-care). Track progress with chart.
- *Less Emotional*:
    - ◊ *Self-Care and Boundaries*: "When you make (*types of artwork*) with (*sexual content*), you are saying something about your safety. It can be important to share more about what you are thinking."
    - ◊ *Self-Care and Boundaries*: "I don't want you to make (*types of artwork*) with (*sexual content*). You can be in charge more if you don't push people away by making (*types of artwork*) with (*sexual content*)."
    - ◊ *Boundaries*: "Think to yourself, 'I have a choice. I can choose to make a (*type of artwork*) with no (*sexual content*). I am strong. I can make a (*type of artwork*) with no (*sexual content*).'"
    - ◊ *Self-Care and Boundaries*: "Think about seeing a pot cooking on a stove. We get to choose if we go near the pot or not. The pot might be hot and might burn us. We might worry, is it dangerous to touch it? Let's stay away from the hot pot. Making a (*type of artwork*) with no (*sexual content*) is like staying away from the hot pot. It will not burn us if we do not go near it."
- *Affirmation*:
    - ◊ "Making (*types of artwork*) with no (*sexual content*) takes great strength."
    - ◊ "Anyone can see your big effort to make (*types of artwork*) with no (*sexual content*)."

The Testing Child

- *Structural*:
    - ◊ Clear and crisp voice (supportive).

- Before class: Check in. Hold eye contact. "I'm with you. Let's keep working on this."
- During class: Hand on shoulder; down on knee at eye level. Hold eye contact. Use More Emotional responses below.
- After class: Check in. Hold eye contact. Reiterate response themes (boundaries, self-awareness). Track progress with chart.

- **More Emotional**:
    - *Self-Awareness and Boundaries*: "When you make (*types of artwork*) with (*sexual content*), I think you are feeling bad, and I am worried. I would like you to share what you are thinking."
    - *Self-Awareness and Boundaries*: "It saddens me when you make (*types of artwork*) that has (*sexual content*) in them, because I feel it pushes us apart."
    - *Self-Awareness*: "When you make a (*type of artwork*) that with (*sexual content*) in it, I think you feel bad."
    - *Self-Awareness and Boundaries*: "Sometimes having bad thoughts is like having a bad dream. We can feel lonely. It can make us upset. When we are upset and lonely, asking for someone to be with us can help. Let's work together. We can make (*types of artwork*) with no (*sexual content*)."
    - *Self-Awareness and Boundaries*: "If I see that your (*type of artwork*) has (*sexual content*) in it, I will say to you, 'I am with you. Let's make your (type of artwork) have no (*sexual content*). Let's make it feel safe.'"
- **Affirmation**:
    - "I am proud of you for making (*types of artwork*) that does not use (*sexual content*)."
    - "You took good care of yourself by making (*types of artwork*) with no (*sexual content*)."

The Worrying Child

- **Verbal**:
    - Clear and calm voice (quiet).
    - Before class: Check in and talk about previous day. Occasional eye contact. "I want to check in with you to see how our talk felt for you. We can do this each day."
    - During class: Occasional eye contact. Maintain distance (two feet at least). No physical contact. Use sound or words to get attention (Less Emotional responses below).
    - After class: Occasional eye contact. Reiterate response themes (connection, self-care).
- **Less Emotional**:
    - *Self-Care and Connection*: "When you make (*types of artwork*) that uses (*sexual content*) in them, it makes me think about your safety. I would like to ask you, what you are thinking when you make them."
    - *Self-Care*: "When you make a (*type of artwork*), take a deep breath and

let it out very slowly. It is safer to wait until you feel calmer so you can make a (*type of artwork*) with no (*sexual content*)."
- ◊ *Self-Care and Connection*: "When we are making a (*type of artwork*) with (*sexual content*), we can have scared or mad thoughts. These can make us feel upset. We can feel safe if we slow down and stay near a person we trust. When you feel safe, we can slowly figure out how to make a (*type of artwork*) that does not use (*sexual content*) and seems not so upsetting."
- **Affirmation**:
    - ◊ "Making your (*types of artwork*) without using (*sexual content*) takes strength."
    - ◊ "You are brave to try to make your (*types of artwork*) without using (*sexual content*)."

The Hiding Child

- **Verbal**:
    - ◊ Clear and calm voice (quiet).
    - ◊ Before class: Check in and talk about previous day. Occasional eye contact. "I want to check in with you to see if you remember our talk. We will do this each day."
    - ◊ During class: Occasional eye contact. Maintain distance (two feet at least). No physical contact. Use sound or words to get attention (More Emotional responses below).
    - ◊ After class: Occasional eye contact. Reiterate response themes (connection, self-awareness).
- **More Emotional**:
    - ◊ *Self-Awareness and Connection*: "When you make (*types of artwork*) that use (*sexual content*) in them, I think you are having big feelings. I am worried and I want to know more."
    - ◊ *Self-Awareness and Connection*: "If I see that you are making a (*types of artwork*) that uses (*sexual content*) in it, I will say to you, 'You can choose to make your (*types of artwork*) with (*sexual content*) or not.' I can help with that and with making a safe choice."
    - ◊ *Self-Awareness*: "Be safe and strong. Say to yourself, 'I am safe. My (*types of artwork*) can be safe too.'"
    - ◊ *Self-Awareness and Connection*: "Look at my face. I'm worried that you are making (*types of artwork*) with (*sexual content*). That's not safe. You are in charge of your (*types of artwork*). I want them safe."
- **Affirmation**:
    - ◊ "I see you using your thoughts to make (*types of artwork*) with no (*sexual content*)."
    - ◊ "I am impressed with your choice to make (*types of artwork*) with no (*sexual content*)."

Behavior (5)
Generating play that includes sexual content

If you find that the child's creation of and engagement in play with sexual content *seem* for the most part:

1. willful; seemingly inflammatory and challenging (see Troubling Child)
2. mischievous; mildly vexing, pushing limits/boundaries (see Testing Child)
3. anxious and/or troubled; possibly upsetting and tense for others (see Worrying Child)
4. disconnected and/or arbitrary; possibly odd and/or confusing to others (see Hiding Child)

- **The Troubling Child**

Core Feeling:	The more frequent and/or detailed the child's sexual-content play is, the greater the **sadness/anger** is being experienced by the child.
Core Wish:	Communicates unconscious wish to be **contained** and **supported** as a way of decreasing sense of **danger** and **rejection**.
Core Question:	Limit-testing question—I am being triggered by events because this moment in class feels overwhelming; can you accept me and handle me?
Responses:	**Structural & Less Emotional** (see Responses section)

- **The Testing Child**

Core Feeling:	The more frequent and/or detailed the child's sexual-content play is, the greater the **sadness/anger** is being experienced by the child.
Core Wish:	Communicates unconscious wish to be **contained** and **validated** as a way of increasing sense of **security** and decreasing sense of **abandonment**.
Core Question:	Limit-testing question—I am feeling bad about myself and need to show this by creating a distraction; do you care about me enough to stop me?
Responses:	**Structural & More Emotional** (see Responses section)

- **The Worrying Child**

Core Feeling:	The more frequent and/or detailed the child's sexual-content play is, the greater the **fear/anger** is being experienced by the child.

Core Wish: Communicates unconscious wish to be **noticed** and **supported** as a way of decreasing sense of **danger** and **abandonment**.

Core Question: Limit-testing question—I am being triggered by events and this is an expression of how afraid I am; do you care enough to protect me?

Responses: **Verbal & Less Emotional** (see Responses section)

- **The Hiding Child**

Core Feeling: The more frequent and/or detailed the child's sexual-content play is, the greater the **fear/anger** is being experienced by the child.

Core Wish: Communicates unconscious wish to be **noticed** and **validated** as a way of increasing sense of **security** and decreasing sense of **rejection**.

Core Question: Limit-testing question—My behavior is a diversion from just how uncomfortable I feel right now; can you accept the way I am and contain me?

Responses: **Verbal & More Emotional** (see Responses section)

Responses for: Behavior (5) Generating play that includes sexual content

The Troubling Child

- *Structural*:
  ◊ Clear and calm voice (supportive).
  ◊ Before class: Check in. Hold eye contact. "I'm with you. Let's keep working on this."
  ◊ During class: Hand on shoulder; down on knee at eye level. Hold eye contact. Use the Less Emotional responses below.
  ◊ After class: Check in. Hold eye contact. Reiterate response themes (boundaries, self-care). Track progress with chart.
- *Less Emotional*:
  ◊ *Self-Care and Boundaries*: "When you play in a way that uses (*sexual content*), you are saying something about your safety. It can be important to share more about what you are thinking."
  ◊ *Self-Care and Boundaries*: "I don't want you to play in a way that uses (*sexual content*). You can be in charge more if you don't push people away by playing in a way that uses (*sexual content*)."
  ◊ *Boundaries*: "Think to yourself, 'I have a choice. I can choose to play in a way that does not use (*sexual content*). I am strong. I can play in a way that does not use (*sexual content*).'"

- *Self-Care and Boundaries*: "Think about seeing a pot cooking on a stove. We get to choose if we go near the pot or not. The pot might be hot and might burn us. We might worry, is it dangerous to touch it? Let's stay away from the hot pot. Playing in way that does not use (*sexual content*) is like staying away from the hot pot. It will not burn us if we do not go near it."
- *Affirmation*:
    - "Playing in a way that does not use (*sexual content*) takes great strength."
    - "Anyone can see your big effort to play in a way that does not use (*sexual content*)."

The Testing Child

- *Structural*:
    - Clear and crisp voice (supportive).
    - Before class: Check in. Hold eye contact. "I'm with you. Let's keep working on this."
    - During class: Hand on shoulder; down on knee at eye level. Hold eye contact. Use More Emotional responses below.
    - After class: Check in. Hold eye contact. Reiterate response themes (boundaries, self-awareness). Track progress with chart.
- *More Emotional*:
    - *Self-Awareness and Boundaries*: "When you play in a way that uses (*sexual content*), I think you are feeling bad, and I am worried. I would like you to share what you are thinking."
    - *Self-Awareness and Boundaries*: "It saddens me when you play in a way that uses (*sexual content*) in them, because I feel it pushes us apart."
    - *Self-Awareness*: "When you play in a way that uses (*sexual content*), I think you feel bad."
    - *Self-Awareness and Boundaries*: "Sometimes having bad thoughts is like having a bad dream. We can feel lonely. It can make us upset. When we are upset and lonely, asking for someone safe to be with us can help. Let's work together. We can figure out how to play without using (*sexual content*)."
    - *Self-Awareness and Boundaries*: "If I see that your play has (*sexual content*) in it, I will say to you, 'I am with you. Let's change the way you are playing to have no (*sexual content*). Let's make it feel safe.'"
- *Affirmation*:
    - "I am proud of you for playing in a way that does not use (*sexual content*)."
    - "You took good care of yourself by playing in a way that does not use (*sexual content*)."

The Worrying Child

- *Verbal*:
    - Clear and calm voice (quiet).

Chapter 17. Upsetting Artwork, Writings, and Play

- ◊ Before class: Check in and talk about previous day. Occasional eye contact. "I want to check in with you to see how our talk felt for you. We can do this each day."
- ◊ During class: Occasional eye contact. Maintain distance (two feet at least). No physical contact. Use sound or words to get attention (Less Emotional responses below).
- ◊ After class: Occasional eye contact. Reiterate response themes (connection, self-care).
- **Less Emotional:**
    - ◊ *Self-Care and Connection*: "When you play in a way that uses (*sexual content*), it makes me think about your safety. I would like to ask you, what you are thinking when you play that way."
    - ◊ *Self-Care*: "When you play, take a deep breath and let it out very slowly. It is safer to wait until you feel calmer so you can play in way that does not use (*sexual content*)."
    - ◊ *Self-Care and Connection*: "When we are playing in a way that uses (*sexual content*), we can have scared or mad thoughts. These can make us feel upset. We can feel safe if we slow down and stay near a person we trust. When you feel safe, we can slowly figure out how to play in a way that does not use (*sexual content*) and does not seem so upsetting."
- **Affirmation:**
    - ◊ "Playing in way that does not use (*sexual content*) takes strength."
    - ◊ "You are brave to try to play in a way that does not use (*sexual content*)."

The Hiding Child

- **Verbal:**
    - ◊ Clear and calm voice (quiet).
    - ◊ Before class: Check in and talk about previous day. Occasional eye contact. "I want to check in with you to see if you remember our talk. We will do this each day."
    - ◊ During class: Occasional eye contact. Maintain distance (two feet at least). No physical contact. Use sound or words to get attention (More Emotional responses below).
    - ◊ After class: Occasional eye contact. Reiterate response themes (connection, self-awareness).
- **More Emotional:**
    - ◊ *Self-Awareness and Connection*: "When you play in a way that uses (*sexual content*), I think you are having big feelings. I am worried and I want to know more."
    - ◊ *Self-Awareness and Connection*: "If I see that you are playing in a way that uses (*sexual content*), I will say to you, 'You can choose to play in a way that uses (*sexual content*) or not.' I can help you with that and with making a safe choice."

◊ *Self-Awareness*: "Be safe and strong. Say to yourself, 'I am safe. The way I play can be safe too.'"
◊ *Self-Awareness and Connection*: "Look at my face. I'm worried that you are playing in a way that uses (*sexual content*). That's not safe. You are in charge of the way you play. I want it to be safe."
- **Affirmation**:
    ◊ "I see you using your thoughts to play in a way that does not use (*sexual content*)."
    ◊ "I am impressed with your choice to play in a way that does not use (*sexual content*)."

Behavior (6)
Generating writing that includes sexual content

If you find the child's creation of writing with sexual content *seems* for the most part:

1. willful; seemingly inflammatory and challenging (see Troubling Child)
2. mischievous; mildly vexing, pushing limits/boundaries (see Testing Child)
3. anxious and/or troubled; possibly upsetting and tense for others (see Worrying Child)
4. disconnected and/or arbitrary; possibly odd and/or confusing to others (see Hiding Child)

- **The Troubling Child**

Core Feeling:	The more frequent and/or detailed the child's sexual-content writing is, the greater the **sadness/anger** is being experienced by the child.
Core Wish:	Communicates unconscious wish to be **contained** and **supported** as a way of decreasing sense of **danger** and **rejection**.
Core Question:	Limit-testing question—I am being triggered by events because this moment in class feels overwhelming; can you accept me and handle me?
Responses:	**Structural & Less Emotional** (see Responses section)

- The Testing Child

Core Feeling:	The more frequent and/or detailed the child's sexual-content writing is, the greater the **sadness/anger** is being experienced by the child.

Chapter 17. Upsetting Artwork, Writings, and Play

Core Wish: Communicates unconscious wish to be **contained** and **validated** as a way of increasing sense of **security** and decreasing sense of **abandonment**.

Core Question: Limit-testing question—I am feeling bad about myself and need to show this by creating a distraction; do you care about me enough to stop me?

Responses: **Structural & More Emotional** (see Responses section)

- The Worrying Child

    Core Feeling: The more frequent and/or detailed the child's sexual-content writing is, the greater the **fear/anger** is being experienced by the child.

    Core Wish: Communicates unconscious wish to be **noticed** and **supported** as a way of decreasing sense of **danger** and **abandonment**.

    Core Question: Limit-testing question—I am being triggered by events and this is an expression of how afraid I am; do you care enough to protect me?

    Responses: **Verbal & Less Emotional** (see Responses section)

- The Hiding Child

    Core Feeling: The more frequent and/or detailed the child's sexual-content writing is, the greater the **fear/anger** is being experienced by the child.

    Core Wish: Communicates unconscious wish to be **noticed** and **validated** as a way of increasing sense of **security** and decreasing sense of **rejection**.

    Core Question: Limit-testing question—My behavior is a diversion from just how uncomfortable I feel right now; can you accept the way I am and contain me?

    Responses: **Verbal & More Emotional** (see Responses section)

Responses for: Behavior (6) Generating writing that includes sexual content

The Troubling Child

- ***Structural:***
    - ◊ Clear and calm voice (supportive).
    - ◊ Before class: Check in. Hold eye contact. "I'm with you. Let's keep working on this."

◊ During class: Hand on shoulder; down on knee at eye level. Hold eye contact. Use the Less Emotional responses below.
◊ After class: Check in. Hold eye contact. Reiterate response themes (boundaries, self-care). Track progress with chart.

- *Less Emotional*:
    ◊ *Self-Care and Boundaries*: "When you create writing that uses (*sexual content*), you are saying something about your safety. It can be important to share more about what you are thinking."
    ◊ *Self-Care and Boundaries*: "I don't want you to create writing that uses (*sexual content*). You can be in charge more if you don't push people away by creating writing that uses (*sexual content*)."
    ◊ *Boundaries*: "Think to yourself, 'I have a choice. I can choose to create writing with no (*sexual content*). I am strong. I can create writing that does not use (*sexual content*).'"
    ◊ *Self-Care and Boundaries*: "Think about seeing a pot cooking on a stove. We get to choose if we go near the pot or not. The pot might be hot and might burn us. We might worry, is it dangerous to touch it? Let's stay away from the hot pot. Writing with no (*sexual content*) is like staying away from the hot pot. It will not burn us if we do not go near it."
- *Affirmation*:
    ◊ "Creating writing that does not use (*sexual content*) takes great strength."
    ◊ "Anyone can see your big effort to create writing that does not use (*sexual content*)."

The Testing Child

- *Structural*:
    ◊ Clear and crisp voice (supportive).
    ◊ Before class: Check in. Hold eye contact. "I'm with you. Let's keep working on this."
    ◊ During class: Hand on shoulder; down on knee at eye level. Hold eye contact. Use More Emotional responses below.
    ◊ After class: Check in. Hold eye contact. Reiterate response themes (boundaries, self-awareness). Track progress with chart.
- *More Emotional*:
    ◊ *Self-Awareness and Boundaries*: "When you create writing that uses (*sexual content*), I think you are feeling bad, and I am worried. I would like you to share what you are thinking."
    ◊ *Self-Awareness and Boundaries*: "It saddens me when you create writing that uses (*sexual content*), because I feel it pushes us apart."
    ◊ *Self-Awareness*: "When you create writing that uses (*sexual content*), I think you feel bad."
    ◊ *Self-Awareness and Boundaries*: "Sometimes having bad thoughts is like having a bad dream. We can feel lonely. It can make us upset. When we are upset and lonely, asking for someone safe to be with us can help.

Let's work together. We'll figure out how to write without using (*sexual content*)."
- ◊ *Self-Awareness and Boundaries*: "If I see that your writing has (*sexual content*) in it, I will say to you, 'I am with you. Let's change what you are writing to have no (*sexual content*). Let's make it feel safe.'"
- *Affirmation*:
  - ◊ "I am proud of you for creating writing that does not use (*sexual content*)."
  - ◊ "You took good care of yourself by creating writing that does not use (*sexual content*)."

The Worrying Child

- *Verbal*:
  - ◊ Clear and calm voice (quiet).
  - ◊ Before class: Check in and talk about previous day. Occasional eye contact. "I want to check in with you to see how our talk felt for you. We can do this each day."
  - ◊ During class: Occasional eye contact. Maintain distance (two feet at least). No physical contact. Use sound or words to get attention (Less Emotional responses below).
  - ◊ After class: Occasional eye contact. Reiterate response themes (connection, self-care).
- *Less Emotional*:
  - ◊ *Self-Care and Connection*: "When you create writing that uses (*sexual content*) in it, it makes me think about your safety. I would like to ask you what you are thinking when you create it."
  - ◊ *Self-Care*: "When you create writing, take a deep breath and let it out very slowly. It is safer to wait until you feel calmer so you can create writing with no (*sexual content*)."
  - ◊ *Self-Care and Connection*: "When we are creating writing with (*sexual content*), we can have scared or mad thoughts. These can make us feel upset. We can feel safe if we slow down and stay near a person we trust. When you feel safe, we can slowly figure out how to create writing that does not use (*sexual content*) and seems not so upsetting."
- *Affirmation*:
  - ◊ "Creating writing without using (*sexual content*) in it takes strength."
  - ◊ "You are brave to try to create your writing without using (*sexual content*) in it."

The Hiding Child

- *Verbal*:
  - ◊ Clear and calm voice (quiet).
  - ◊ Before class: Check in and talk about previous day. Occasional eye

contact. "I want to check in with you to see if you remember our talk. We will do this each day."
- ◊ During class: Occasional eye contact. Maintain distance (two feet at least). No physical contact. Use sound or words to get attention (More Emotional responses below).
- ◊ After class: Occasional eye contact. Reiterate response themes (connection, self-awareness).

- **More Emotional:**
  - ◊ *Self-Awareness and Connection*: "When you create writing that uses (*sexual content*) in it, I think you are having big feelings. I am worried and want to know more."
  - ◊ *Self-Awareness and Connection*: "If I see that you are creating writing that uses (*sexual content*) in it, I will say to you, 'You can choose to create your writing with (*sexual content*) or not.' I can help you with that and with making a safe choice."
  - ◊ *Self-Awareness*: "Be safe and strong. Say to yourself, 'I am safe. My writing can be safe too.'"
  - ◊ *Self-Awareness and Connection*: "Look at my face. I'm worried that you are creating writing with (*sexual content*) in it. That's not safe. You are in charge of your writing. I want it to be safe."

- **Affirmation:**
  - ◊ "I see you using your thoughts to create writing with no (*sexual content*) in it."
  - ◊ "I am impressed with your choice to create writing with no (*sexual content*) in it."

Behavior (7)
Creating artwork that includes violence (self or others)

If you find the child's creation of artwork with violent content **seems** for the most part:

1. willful; seemingly inflammatory and challenging (see Troubling Child)
2. mischievous; mildly vexing, pushing limits/boundaries (see Testing Child)
3. anxious and/or troubled; possibly upsetting and tense for others (see Worrying Child)
4. disconnected and/or arbitrary; possibly odd and/or confusing to others (see Hiding Child)

- **The Troubling Child**

  Core Feeling: The more frequent and/or detailed the child's violent-content artwork is, the greater the **sadness/anger** is being experienced by the child.

Core Wish: Communicates unconscious wish to be **contained** and **supported** as a way of decreasing sense of **danger** and **rejection**.

Core Question: Limit-testing question—I am being triggered by events because this moment in class feels overwhelming; can you accept me and handle me?

Responses: **Structural & Less Emotional** (see Responses section)

- **The Testing Child**

Core Feeling: The more frequent and/or detailed the child's violent-content artwork is, the greater the **sadness/anger** is being experienced by the child.

Core Wish: Communicates unconscious wish to be **contained** and **validated** as a way of increasing sense of **security** and decreasing sense of **abandonment**.

Core Question: Limit-testing question—I am feeling bad about myself and need to show this by creating a distraction; do you care about me enough to stop me?

Responses: **Structural & More Emotional** (see Responses section)

- **The Worrying Child**

Core Feeling: The more frequent and/or detailed the child's violent-content artwork is, the greater the **fear/anger** is being experienced by the child.

Core Wish: Communicates unconscious wish to be **noticed** and **supported** as a way of decreasing sense of **danger** and **abandonment**.

Core Question: Limit-testing question—I am being triggered by events and this is an expression of how afraid I am; do you care enough to protect me?

Responses: **Verbal & Less Emotional** (see Responses section)

- **The Hiding Child**

Core Feeling: The more frequent and/or detailed the child's violent-content artwork is, the greater the **fear/anger** is being experienced by the child.

Core Wish: Communicates unconscious wish to be **noticed** and **validated** as a way of increasing sense of **security** and decreasing sense of **rejection**.

Core Question: Limit-testing question—My behavior is a diversion from just how uncomfortable I feel right now; can you accept the way I am and contain me?

Responses: **Verbal & More Emotional** (see Responses section)

Responses for: Behavior (7) Creating artwork that includes violence (self or others)

The Troubling Child

- ***Structural*:**
  - ◊ Clear and calm voice (supportive).
  - ◊ Before class: Check in. Hold eye contact. "I'm with you. Let's keep working on this."
  - ◊ During class: Hand on shoulder; down on knee at eye level. Hold eye contact. Use the Less Emotional responses below.
  - ◊ After class: Check in. Hold eye contact. Reiterate response themes (boundaries, self-care). Track progress with chart.
- ***Less Emotional*:**
  - ◊ *Self-Care and Boundaries*: "When you make (*types of artwork*) with too much danger in it, you are saying something about your safety. It can be important to share more about what you are thinking."
  - ◊ *Self-Care and Boundaries*: "I want you to make (*types of artwork*) with less danger in them. You are more in charge when you don't push people away by making (*types of artwork*) with so much danger."
  - ◊ *Boundaries*: "Think to yourself, 'I have a choice. I can choose to make a (*type of artwork*) with less danger. I am strong and powerful, and I can make a (*type of artwork*) with less danger.'"
  - ◊ *Self-Care and Boundaries*: "Think about walking across a street. We get to choose if we cross dangerously or safely. We can look both ways or move without looking. Let's choose to cross safely. Making a (*type of artwork*) with less danger is like choosing to look before crossing. Less danger is more power."
- ***Affirmation*:**
  - ◊ "Making (*types of artwork*) with less danger takes great strength."
  - ◊ "Anyone can see your big effort to make (*types of artwork*) with less danger."

The Testing Child

- ***Structural*:**
  - ◊ Clear and crisp voice (supportive).
  - ◊ Before class: Check in. Hold eye contact. "I'm with you. Let's keep working on this."

◊ During class: Hand on shoulder; down on knee at eye level. Hold eye contact. Use More Emotional responses below.
◊ After class: Check in. Hold eye contact. Reiterate response themes (boundaries, self-awareness). Track progress with chart.
- *More Emotional*:
    ◊ *Self-Awareness and Boundaries*: "When you make (*types of artwork*) that have too much danger in them, I think you are feeling bad, and I am worried. I would like you to share what you are thinking."
    ◊ *Self-Awareness and Boundaries*: "It saddens me when you make (*types of artwork*) that have too much danger in them, because I feel it pushes us apart."
    ◊ *Self-Awareness*: "When you make a (*type of artwork*) that has too much danger in it, I think you feel bad."
    ◊ *Self-Awareness and Boundaries*: "Sometimes having bad thoughts is like having a bad dream. We can feel lonely. It can make us upset. When we are upset and lonely, asking for someone to be with us can help. Let's work together. We can make (*types of artwork*) with less danger in them."
    ◊ *Self-Awareness and Boundaries*: "If I see that your (*type of artwork*) has too much danger in it, I will say to you, 'I am with you. Let's make your (type of artwork) have less danger. Let's make it seem safer.'"
- *Affirmation*:
    ◊ "I am proud of you for trying to make (*types of artwork*) with less danger in them."
    ◊ "You took good care of yourself by making (*types of artwork*) with less danger in them."

The Worrying Child

- *Verbal*:
    ◊ Clear and calm voice (quiet).
    ◊ Before class: Check in and talk about previous day. Occasional eye contact. "I want to check in with you to see how our talk felt for you. We can do this each day."
    ◊ During class: Occasional eye contact. Maintain distance (two feet at least). No physical contact. Use sound or words to get attention (Less Emotional responses below).
    ◊ After class: Occasional eye contact. Reiterate response themes (connection, self-care).
- *Less Emotional*:
    ◊ *Self-Care and Connection*: "When you make (*types of artwork*) that have so much danger in them, it makes me think about your safety. I would like to ask you, what you are thinking when you make them."
    ◊ *Self-Care*: "When you make a (*type of artwork*), take a deep breath and let it out very slowly. It is safer to wait until you feel calmer so you can make a (*type of artwork*) that has less danger."

- *Self-Care and Connection*: "When we are making a (*type of artwork*) with danger, we can have scared or mad thoughts. These can make us feel upset. We can feel safe if we slow down and stay near a person we trust. When you feel safe, we can slowly figure out how to make a (*type of artwork*) that has less danger and seems not so upsetting."
- *Affirmation*:
  - "Making your (*types of artwork*) seem safer and not so dangerous takes strength."
  - "You are brave to try to make your (*types of artwork*) seem safer and not so dangerous."

The Hiding Child

- *Verbal*:
  - Clear and calm voice (quiet).
  - Before class: Check in and talk about previous day. Occasional eye contact. "I want to check in with you to see if you remember our talk. We will do this each day."
  - During class: Occasional eye contact. Maintain distance (two feet at least). No physical contact. Use sound or words to get attention (More Emotional responses below).
  - After class: Occasional eye contact. Reiterate response themes (connection, self-awareness).
- *More Emotional*:
  - *Self-Awareness and Connection*: "When you make (*types of artwork*) that have too much danger in them, I think you are having big feelings. I am worried and I want to know more."
  - *Self-Awareness and Connection*: "If I see that you are making a (*types of artwork*) that seems to have too much danger in it, I will say to you, 'You can choose to make your (*types of artwork*) with danger in them or not. I can help with that.'"
  - *Self-Awareness*: "Be safe and strong. Say to yourself, 'I am safe. My (*types of artwork*) can be safe too.'"
  - *Self-Awareness and Connection*: "Look at my face. I am worried that you are making (*types of artwork*) that seem to have too much danger. You are in charge of your (*types of artwork*). I want them to be safe."
- *Affirmation*:
  - "I see you using your thoughts to make your (*types of artwork*) have less danger."
  - "I am impressed how you are deciding to make your (*types of artwork*) seem safer."

Behavior (8)
Generating play that includes violence (self or others)

If you find that the child's creation of and engagement in play with violent content *seem* for the most part:

1. willful; seemingly inflammatory and challenging (see Troubling Child)
2. mischievous; mildly vexing, pushing limits/boundaries (see Testing Child)
3. anxious and/or troubled; possibly upsetting and tense for others (see Worrying Child)
4. disconnected and/or arbitrary; possibly odd and/or confusing to others (see Hiding Child)

- **The Troubling Child**

  Core Feeling: The more frequent and/or detailed the child's violent-content play is, the greater the **sadness/anger** is being experienced by the child.

  Core Wish: Communicates unconscious wish to be **contained** and **supported** as a way of decreasing sense of **danger** and **rejection**.

  Core Question: Limit-testing question—I am being triggered by events because this moment in class feels overwhelming; can you accept me and handle me?

  Responses: **Structural & Less Emotional** (see Responses section)

- **The Testing Child**

  Core Feeling: The more frequent and/or detailed the child's violent-content play is, the greater the **sadness/anger** is being experienced by the child.

  Core Wish: Communicates unconscious wish to be **contained** and **validated** as a way of increasing sense of **security** and decreasing sense of **abandonment**.

  Core Question: Limit-testing question—I am feeling bad about myself and need to show this by creating a distraction; do you care about me enough to stop me?

  Responses: **Structural & More Emotional** (see Responses section)

- **The Worrying Child**

  Core Feeling: The more frequent and/or detailed the child's violent-content play is, the greater the **fear/anger** is being experienced by the child.

  Core Wish: Communicates unconscious wish to be **noticed** and **supported** as a way of decreasing sense of **danger** and **abandonment**.

  Core Question: Limit-testing question—I am being triggered by events and this is an expression of how afraid I am; do you care enough to protect me?

  Responses: **Verbal & Less Emotional** (see Responses section)

- **The Hiding Child**

  Core Feeling: The more frequent and/or detailed the child's violent-content play is, the greater the **fear/anger** is being experienced by the child.

  Core Wish: Communicates unconscious wish to be **noticed** and **validated** as a way of increasing sense of **security** and decreasing sense of **rejection**.

  Core Question: Limit-testing question—My behavior is a diversion from just how uncomfortable I feel right now; can you accept the way I am and contain me?

  Responses: **Verbal & More Emotional** (see Responses section)

Responses for: Behavior (8) Generating play that includes violence (self or others)

The Troubling Child

- ***Structural***:
  - ◊ Clear and calm voice (supportive).
  - ◊ Before class: Check in. Hold eye contact. "I'm with you. Let's keep working on this."
  - ◊ During class: Hand on shoulder; down on knee at eye level. Hold eye contact. Use the Less Emotional responses below.
  - ◊ After class: Check in. Hold eye contact. Reiterate response themes (boundaries, self-care). Track progress with chart.
- ***Less Emotional***:
  - ◊ *Self-Care and Boundaries*: "When the way you play has too much danger in it, you are saying something about your safety. It can be important to share more about what you are thinking."

◊ *Self-Care and Boundaries*: "I want your playing to have less danger in it. You are more in charge when you don't push people away by having so much danger in your playing. I'm thinking about safety."
◊ *Boundaries*: "Think to yourself, 'I have a choice. I can choose to play with less danger in it. I am strong and powerful, and I am able to play with less danger in it.'"
◊ *Self-Care and Boundaries*: "Think about walking across a street. We get to choose if we cross dangerously or safely. We can look both ways or move without looking. Let's choose to cross safely. Playing with less danger is like choosing to look before crossing. Less danger is more power."
- *Affirmation*:
    ◊ "Putting less danger in your playing takes great strength."
    ◊ "Anyone can see your big effort you are making to put less danger in your playing."

The Testing Child

- *Structural*:
    ◊ Clear and crisp voice (supportive).
    ◊ Before class: Check in. Hold eye contact. "I'm with you. Let's keep working on this."
    ◊ During class: Hand on shoulder; down on knee at eye level. Hold eye contact. Use More Emotional responses below.
    ◊ After class: Check in. Hold eye contact. Reiterate response themes (boundaries, self-awareness). Track progress with chart.
- *More Emotional*:
    ◊ *Self-Awareness and Boundaries*: "When the way you play has too much danger in it, I think you are feeling bad, and I am worried. I would like you to share what you are thinking."
    ◊ *Self-Awareness and Boundaries*: "It saddens me when you play in a way that is dangerous to you or to your classmates, because I feel it pushes us apart."
    ◊ *Self-Awareness*: "When you play in a way that has danger in it, I think you feel bad."
    ◊ *Self-Awareness and Boundaries*: "Sometimes having bad thoughts is like having a bad dream. We can feel lonely. It can make us upset. When we are upset and lonely, asking for someone to be with us can help. Let's work together. We can figure out how to play in a way with less danger in it."
    ◊ *Self-Awareness and Boundaries*: "If I see you playing in a way that has too much danger in it, I will say to you, 'I am with you. Let's figure out a way to play that has less danger in it. Let's play safer.'"
- *Affirmation*:
    ◊ "I am proud of you for trying to play in a way that is less dangerous."

- ◊ "You took good care of yourself by playing in a way with less danger in it."

The Worrying Child

- **Verbal**:
    - ◊ Clear and calm voice (quiet).
    - ◊ Before class: Check in and talk about previous day. Occasional eye contact. "I want to check in with you to see how our talk felt for you. We can do this each day."
    - ◊ During class: Occasional eye contact. Maintain distance (two feet at least). No physical contact. Use sound or words to get attention (Less Emotional responses below).
    - ◊ After class: Occasional eye contact. Reiterate response themes (connection, self-care).
- **Less Emotional**:
    - ◊ *Self-Care and Connection*: "When you play in a way that has so much danger in it, it makes me think about your safety. I would like to ask you what you are thinking when you play this way."
    - ◊ *Self-Care*: "When you are playing in a dangerous way, take a deep breath and let it out very slowly. It is safer to wait until you feel calmer so you can play in a way that has less danger."
    - ◊ *Self-Care and Connection*: "When we are playing in a dangerous way, we can have scared or mad thoughts. These can make us feel upset. We can feel safe if we slow down and stay near a person we trust. When you feel safe, we can slowly figure out how to play in a way that has less danger and does not seem so upsetting."
- **Affirmation**:
    - ◊ "Playing in a way that seems safe and not so dangerous takes strength."
    - ◊ "You are brave to try to play in a way that seems safer and not so dangerous."

The Hiding Child

- **Verbal**:
    - ◊ Clear and calm voice (quiet).
    - ◊ Before class: Check in and talk about previous day. Occasional eye contact. "I want to check in with you to see if you remember our talk. We will do this each day."
    - ◊ During class: Occasional eye contact. Maintain distance (two feet at least). No physical contact. Use sound or words to get attention (More Emotional responses below).
    - ◊ After class: Occasional eye contact. Reiterate response themes (connection, self-awareness).
- **More Emotional**:

◊ *Self-Awareness and Connection*: "When you play in a way that has too much danger in it, I think you are having big feelings. I am worried and want to know more."
◊ *Self-Awareness and Connection*: "If I see that you are playing in a way that seems to have too much danger in it, I will say to you, 'You can choose to play in a dangerous way or not.' I can help with that."
◊ *Self-Awareness*: "Be safe and strong. Say to yourself, 'I am safe. The way I play can be safe too.'"
◊ *Self-Awareness and Connection*: "Look at my face. I am worried that you are playing in way that seems to have too much danger in it. You are in charge of how you play. I want it to be safe."
- *Affirmation*:
    ◊ "I see you using your thoughts to make the way you play have less danger."
    ◊ "I am impressed you are deciding to play in a way that seems safer."

Behavior (9)
Generating writing that includes violence (self or others)

If you find the child's creation of writing with violent content *seems* for the most part:

1. willful; seemingly inflammatory and challenging (see Troubling Child)
2. mischievous; mildly vexing, pushing limits/boundaries (see Testing Child)
3. anxious and/or troubled; possibly upsetting and tense for others (see Worrying Child)
4. disconnected and/or arbitrary; possibly odd and/or confusing to others (see Hiding Child)

- **The Troubling Child**

Core Feeling:	The more frequent and/or detailed the child's violent-content writing is, the greater the **sadness/anger** is being experienced by the child.
Core Wish:	Communicates unconscious wish to be **contained** and **supported** as a way of decreasing sense of **danger** and **rejection**.
Core Question:	Limit-testing question—I am being triggered by events because this moment in class feels overwhelming; can you accept me and handle me?
Responses:	**Structural & Less Emotional** (see Responses section)

- **The Testing Child**

Core Feeling:	The more frequent and/or detailed the child's violent-content writing is, the greater the **sadness/anger** is being experienced by the child.
Core Wish:	Communicates unconscious wish to be **contained** and **validated** as a way of increasing sense of **security** and decreasing sense of **abandonment**.
Core Question:	Limit-testing question—I am feeling bad about myself and need to show this by creating a distraction; do you care about me enough to stop me?
Responses:	**Structural & More Emotional** (see Responses section)

- **The Worrying Child**

Core Feeling:	The more frequent and/or detailed the child's violent-content writing is, the greater the **fear/anger** is being experienced by the child.
Core Wish:	Communicates unconscious wish to be **noticed** and **supported** as a way of decreasing sense of **danger** and **abandonment**.
Core Question:	Limit-testing question—I am being triggered by events and this is an expression of how afraid I am; do you care enough to protect me?
Responses:	**Verbal & Less Emotional** (see Responses section)

- **The Hiding Child**

Core Feeling:	The more frequent and/or detailed the child's violent-content writing is, the greater the **fear/anger** is being experienced by the child.
Core Wish:	Communicates unconscious wish to be **noticed** and **validated** as a way of increasing sense of **security** and decreasing sense of **rejection**.
Core Question:	Limit-testing question—My behavior is a diversion from just how uncomfortable I feel right now; can you accept the way I am and contain me?
Responses:	**Verbal & More Emotional** (see Responses section)

Responses for: Behavior (9) Generating writing that includes violence (self or others)

The Troubling Child

- ***Structural:***
  - ◊ Clear and calm voice (supportive).

Chapter 17. Upsetting Artwork, Writings, and Play 359

- ◊ Before class: Check in. Hold eye contact. "I'm with you. Let's keep working on this."
- ◊ During class: Hand on shoulder; down on knee at eye level. Hold eye contact. Use the Less Emotional responses below.
- ◊ After class: Check in. Hold eye contact. Reiterate response themes (boundaries, self-care). Track progress with chart.
- **Less Emotional**:
    - ◊ *Self-Care and Boundaries*: "When you create writing that has too much danger in it, you are saying something about your safety. It can be important to share more about what you are thinking."
    - ◊ *Self-Care and Boundaries*: "I want your writing to have less danger in it. You are more in charge when you don't push people away by putting so much danger in your writing. I'm thinking about safety."
    - ◊ *Boundaries*: "Think to yourself, 'I have a choice. I can choose to write with less danger in it. I am strong and powerful, and I am able to write with less danger in it.'"
    - ◊ *Self-Care and Boundaries*: "Think about walking across a street. We get to choose if we cross dangerously or safely. We can look both ways or move without looking. Let's choose to cross safely. Writing with less danger is like choosing to look before crossing. Less danger is more power."
- **Affirmation**:
    - ◊ "Putting less danger in your writing takes great strength."
    - ◊ "Anyone can see your big effort you are making to put less danger in your writing."

The Testing Child

- **Structural**:
    - ◊ Clear and crisp voice (supportive).
    - ◊ Before class: Check in. Hold eye contact. "I'm with you. Let's keep working on this."
    - ◊ During class: Hand on shoulder; down on knee at eye level. Hold eye contact. Use More Emotional responses below.
    - ◊ After class: Check in. Hold eye contact. Reiterate response themes (boundaries, self-awareness). Track progress with chart.
- **More Emotional**:
    - ◊ *Self-Awareness and Boundaries*: "When you create writing that has too much danger in it, I think you are feeling bad, and I am worried. I would like you to share what you are thinking."
    - ◊ *Self-Awareness and Boundaries*: "It saddens me when you write in way that has too much danger in it, because I feel it pushes us apart."
    - ◊ *Self-Awareness*: "When what you are writing and it has too much danger in it, I think you feel bad."
    - ◊ *Self-Awareness and Boundaries*: "Sometimes having bad thoughts is like

having a bad dream. It can make us feel lonely. It can make us upset. When we are upset and lonely, asking for someone to be with us can help. Let's work together. We can make your writing with less danger in it."
  - ◊ *Self-Awareness and Boundaries*: "If I see that your writing has too much danger in it, I will say to you, 'I am with you.'"
  - ◊ *Self-Awareness and Boundaries*: "Let's make your writing have less danger in it. Let's make it seem safer."
- **Affirmation**:
  - ◊ "I am proud of you for making what you are writing have less danger in it."
  - ◊ "You took good care of yourself by making what you are writing with less danger in it."

The Worrying Child

- **Verbal**:
  - ◊ Clear and calm voice (quiet).
  - ◊ Before class: Check in and talk about previous day. Occasional eye contact. "I want to check in with you to see how our talk felt for you. We can do this each day."
  - ◊ During class: Occasional eye contact. Maintain distance (two feet at least). No physical contact. Use sound or words to get attention (Less Emotional responses below).
  - ◊ After class: Occasional eye contact. Reiterate response themes (connection, self-care).
- **Less Emotional**:
  - ◊ *Self-Care and Connection*: "When you write in a way that has so much danger in it, it makes me think about your safety. I would like to ask you what you are thinking when your writing has danger in it."
  - ◊ *Self-Care*: "When you are writing with danger in it, take a deep breath and let it out very slowly. It is safer to wait until you feel calmer so you can write in a way that can have less danger."
  - ◊ *Self-Care and Connection*: "When we are writing in a way that has danger in it, we can have scared or mad thoughts. These can make us feel upset. We can feel safe if we slow down and stay near a person we trust. When you feel safe, we can slowly figure out how to write in a way that has less danger and seems not so upsetting."
- **Affirmation**:
  - ◊ "Writing in a way that seems safe and not so dangerous takes strength."
  - ◊ "You are brave to try to write in a way that seems safer and not so dangerous."

The Hiding Child

- **Verbal**:
  - ◊ Clear and calm voice (quiet).

- ◊ Before class: Check in and talk about previous day. Occasional eye contact. "I want to check in with you to see if you remember our talk. We will do this each day."
- ◊ During class: Occasional eye contact. Maintain distance (two feet at least). No physical contact. Use sound or words to get attention (More Emotional responses below).
- ◊ After class: Occasional eye contact. Reiterate response themes (connection, self-awareness).

- **More Emotional:**
  - ◊ *Self-Awareness and Connection*: "When you write in a way that has too much danger in it, I think you are having big feelings. I am worried and want to know more."
  - ◊ *Self-Awareness and Connection*: "If I see that you are writing in a way that seems to have too much danger in it, I will say to you, 'You can choose to write in a way that has danger in it or not.' I can help with that."
  - ◊ *Self-Awareness*: "Be safe and strong. Say to yourself, 'I am safe. My writing can be safe too.'"
  - ◊ *Self-Awareness and Connection*: "Look at my face. I am worried that you are writing in a way that seems to have too much danger in it. You are in charge of what you are writing. I want it to be safe."

- **Affirmation:**
  - ◊ "I see you using your thoughts to make the way you write have less danger in it."
  - ◊ "I am impressed how you are deciding to make the way you write seem safer."

Your Evolving Responses

As you have read, there are different motivations for your students' behaviors depending on their latent communication patterns. This demonstrates that your responses cannot be "one size fits all" in nature. While we have provided specific words for you to follow, we intend this chapter and the others like it to be a framework for your responses, not a script. You certainly can use our suggested language as you experiment with the interventions we have described. Overtime, it will be more helpful for you to find your own words to communicate with your students. As you continue to try these techniques, using your own communication style will make the responses to your students' behaviors feel authentic and sincere. This will happen naturally. The proposed interventions that we used in this chapter are a starting point and are meant to evolve and grow with your comfort level. This might take some practice, but it will be well worth it to expand your repertoire of potential responses to concerning or disruptive behaviors. You may find that your own words are more effective or more impactful than the words and phrases we have suggested in this book. The more you are a part of the interventions, the more meaningful they may be to your students. As we know, students need repetition, so please be patient as you try out new ways to respond to them.

Conclusion
Keeping Your Balance

Balance in Its Personal Form: Focusing Our Feelings

The stories of students returning to visit us years after having left our care are powerful and moving (even if they sometimes make us feel old). These visits speak to the long-term impact that teachers have on the children with whom they have connected. It is an impact borne out of hard work and relationship building. Teachers become teachers because they love helping children. We want to see our young charges learn, grow, mature, and become more than when we met them.

This dedication has two powerful poles. On the one end, there is a love for the connection that leads to learning and growth, and a commensurate passion for seeing a student "get it" and experience the light-bulb moment. On the other end, there is an aversion to any obstacles to this learning connection, and an equal yet opposite passion against seeing someone or something derail the learning process. Because of the existence of our fervent and visceral commitment (represented by the combination of both poles), we, as the authors of this book, acknowledge that the core feature of what we are asking of teachers may feel exasperatingly constraining.

We have presented a process in which, at the moment when teachers feel compelled to act, when their passion declares that a problem needs addressing now, we go the opposite way. We ask teachers to put on the brakes, to place on hold their professional instinct to address these imperatives—to wait, to slow down, and often to allow for a problematic behavior or communication to continue for a time. We acknowledge the external complications and internal pressure that this request may create for teachers. We ask this of teachers, not to stymie their instinct to help, nor to undermine their control within their classroom, but actually to enhance both.

Potential energy is stored energy. The energy of a stone in a sling shot as the rubber band holding it is drawn back. Kinetic energy is the energy of motion. The energy of the stone as it flies through the air after having been released. The relationship of potential energy to kinetic energy is such that the more potential energy is built up, the more powerful the kinetic energy will be upon its release. The more the rubber band on the sling shot is drawn back, the further, the faster and the more direct the stone will fly. However, there is an important balancing point between these two energies. Pull the rubber band too far back, and it will break; not enough, and the stone will go nowhere.

We want teachers to consider this model in achieving a balanced approach to their interventions with challenging students. Even though we may want, even need, to act on a problematic communication or behavior, it is best to wait if no emergency is at hand, and consider what is happening. In this way, potential energy can be thought of as our thinking and planning, while kinetic energy aligns with our acting and intervening. If we think and plan sufficiently, our interventions will fly true.

Fully recognizing the intensity of the feelings associated with difficult student behaviors and communications, we ask teachers to focus these forceful feelings into an organized cognitive process for creating useful, targeted, empathic interventions. We know from our knowledge of children that routines and procedures balance and contain powerful emotions. What is laid out in Chapter 8 are the steps, both abstract and concrete, that will begin the thinking and planning process. This process will take several weeks and will set a solid foundation for reworking our most challenging and provocative teacher-student interactions.

Balance in Its Process Form: Homeostasis

Homeostasis is the reactive effort of maintaining balance within all physiological processes or systems. It is often applied to the human body and all its sub-systems—the amount of water in the body (thirst to hydrate), the temperature of the body (shivering to warm), the nutrient level (craving to replenish), the contents in the blood (fever to fight infection), etc. Thirst, shivering, hunger and fever are all homeostatic responses of a body system that is out of balance. The response seeks to re-balance by altering the internal state of the body in specific, needed ways. Another word for balance is equilibrium, as a seesaw at rest with both seats equidistant from the ground (Rodolfo, 2000; Bailey, 1984; 1994; Benzinger, 1969).

This concept can also be used to understand the dynamics and workings of other systems—environments, societies, communities, and relationships. The entire discussion regarding climate change centers on the homeostatic reaction the planet is having to the pollutants that humans are introducing. The interactions between the parts of any system can be observed as they react and then, if possible, reach equilibrium again. This is homeostasis and it is useful for our work with challenging children in our classroom. For our purposes, we will be looking at four different systems. They are as follows:

- teacher, as individual
- child, as individual
- teacher-child relationship
- classroom environment

We can use homeostasis as the rationale that motivates us to focus on:

1. our own personal reactions to a challenging child
2. the manifest and latent communication of a child

3. a child's Persona
4. holistic responses from us to the child

When children have an "impact" on us, this is an indication that we, the child, our relationship with the child, and, most likely, the classroom, are all exhibiting some level of disequilibrium. The seesaw is moving.

To acknowledge this and then to examine the elements of these interrelated systems is to be able to respond to the needs of the whole environment. An accurate understanding of what is happening, and the resulting beneficial responses, can create a new balance in those systems, individually and collectively. Homeostasis is based on the theory that a functional system flourishes when it is in balance. The consternation, frustration, hopelessness, anger, sadness, worry, or anxiety that we feel when our classroom system is not flourishing is a loud message to try something new.

This book is that something new. Let us recast the steps that have been suggested within its pages:

1. Examining our own reactions—This is an aspect of self-care. Our reactions to a student are important not just because it can inform what the student needs, but also because it is an expression of our own needs. Feeling angry or sad about a student takes energy, it can be heavy and burdensome. Acknowledging these complex ideas and emotions about the children we work with, frees up room in our brain, allowing fresh air to circulate and light to penetrate the dark corners. The relief we can feel by releasing the thoughts we have about a challenging child is a good first step toward achieving a new balance.

2. Observing the levels of communication—This is an aspect of awareness. Knowing that we can look beneath every behavior and find information about a child is liberating. Being able to acquire new material about a child, even if it is speculative, can provide us with multiple avenues to travel down. The binary "control vs. no control" or "us vs. them" power struggle that is so familiar to teachers as an aspect of the adult-child relationship can be tempered and, at times, rendered moot by additional knowledge about a child's motivations. The empowerment we can feel through this understanding is another solid stop toward achieving a new balance.

3. Creating a framework using a child's Persona—This is an aspect of clarity. The uniqueness of each child can be a challenge in a full classroom, when some of those children require our increased attention. Being able to characterize complex children and constellations of their behaviors/communications into useful groupings creates a structure that consolidates our possible responses. This consolidation allows for a more useful expenditure of our teaching energy and time. The frenetic nature of helping an emotionally or developmentally complex child is contained using this Persona framework. The security we can feel through this enhanced structure is another important step toward achieving a new balance.

4. Responding with AURA using the whole self—This is an aspect of empathy. The process by which we create targeted responses to the children's internal dialogue establishes us as caring educators. We see them; they feel

heard by us. They experience a connection to us that allows for more than just teaching. It enables integration and movement that enhances their experience of relationships and humanity. This we can do for them, but also for ourselves. Being teachers who truly comprehend their children grows the teaching experience. We are not just disseminators of information but cultivators of people. The love they can feel through this holistic teaching format is the final step toward achieving a new balance.

To use these four steps is to engage ourselves, the children we teach, and our classrooms in a whole new way. A deeper way, a holistic way, an empathic way, and a self-aware way. These steps provide a level of control over the classroom environment and those within it. They are water for the thirsty person, vitamins for the anemic person, medicine for the ill person, and the clothing for the cold person. Knowing ourselves and the children, and how we relate to each other and all those around us is the mechanism to achieve a new balance.

Balance in Its Role Form: Teacher, AKA, the Shepherd

All teachers spend at least a part of their day trying to control their classrooms. This time is typically used to get the children to pay attention, to focus, to stop talking, to sit down, the list of interventions is wide-ranging. We think it is fair to say that the extent of distraction caused by the children's manifest communications cannot be understated. While we have spent the bulk of this book discussing the needs of individual children, the reality is that yours is a class of many children at one time. Creating empathic responses for one child is quite a bit of work. Creating them for multiple children whose underlying needs and latent communications have them all "moving" in different directions is exponentially more complex and time consuming. That we endeavoring to maintain a balance in ourselves and our classroom during this effort is crucial.

Shepherding is a skill that includes both a micro aspect (taking direct action) and a macro one (planning strategies and goals). Shepherds cannot expect to exert control over each distinct animal in a herd at all times. Trying such an approach is untenable with a large number of animals as it pulls the shepherd in too many directions. Shepherds intuit their herds' needs and connect with them, using all their senses. There is a breadth and a depth to the relationship and a skilled shepherd uses these to maintain a balance—the needs of the whole herd vs. needs of the one animal. Shepherd and sheep farmer Craig Rogers writes:

> "Shepherds, like the sheep themselves, learn quickly that the path to success depends not only on tending to the flock but caring for the individual. Providing clean water, ample forage, and shelter to an entire flock is essential to maintaining the health of the flock. But the success of the shepherd or shepherdess is in the compassion they have for each individual. This means being able to identify a sick or injured sheep or lamb within a flock of hundreds or thousands of sheep. The more concern the shepherd has for the individual who is in need of health care, supplemental food assistance, or individual attention, the healthier the flock and the more profitable the whole operation is" [Rogers, 2013].

Using the shepherding metaphor, we offer an approach that touches on maintaining balance in our classroom behavior control. It is one grounded in forethought and planning. Teachers as shepherds anticipate the inevitable complications and provide the essential, yet typical, classroom structures that a class needs in order to learn. Simultaneously, they scan for and try to predict the needs of those individual children who will require extra care and compassion. What we want to prevent is a teacher running from child to child to child, from injured sheep to lost sheep to sick sheep. It is too much, and it will most likely lead to exhaustion, resentment, or, worst of all, burn out.

The balance we want teachers to experience begins with thoughts only, not actions. It begins with how we prepare ourselves with a deeper understanding of the needs of our most complex children and how these children interact with the environment around them. This understanding empowers us with knowledge. We want to stress this point—if we can accurately recognize a child's communications, our ability to create successful responses will inevitably follow. Like the shepherd, she recognizes that she must look for the individual sheep who is struggling and reach out to him for the good of the flock. We want teachers to be in charge through the proactivity of preparation.

To this end, we identify some key concepts that frame this proactive version of balanced classroom behavior management. We developed four easy-to-remember guidelines for maintaining a balanced approach to addressing communications/behaviors. All four concepts begin with the letter "P." While these ideas can be useful in your classrooms any time, they are especially critical when you find that some of your students present with one of our four Personas:

- **Pacing**—Slow down when we discover a Persona child in our class
  At first it is hard to know how quickly or slowly children can absorb what project we want them to do and what it is we are trying to teach them, be it a concept such as sharing, a chore such as hand washing, or a fact. Finding the right pacing often means we need to move slowly, until we know the needs of our students as a group. By moving slowly, those students who are Troubling children, Testing children, Worrying children and Hiding children will reveal themselves by their manifest communications.
- **Patience**—Retain a perspective that working with a Persona child is a long process
  Children tend to become anxious when they sense an adult is becoming frustrated, angry, or exasperated with them. Patience is the key to keep children engaged. Patience is also the key to being able to sustain the amount of repetition children need in order for them to integrate and therefore remember what they have been taught. Expect that this is marathon not a sprint.
- **Positivity**—Maintain a stance of hope that can reach through a child's doubt
  Believing that the children will learn no matter the time frames sustains us as teachers and creates the most productive atmosphere in our classroom. This is equally true for our work trying to address the latent communications

of our Troubling, Testing, Worrying and Hiding children. We need to believe that these students will ultimately hear us, let us in, and keep their experience with us with them. Unconditional Positive Regard, Warm Acceptance.

- **Praise**—Find an empowering personal aspect for a child to build on

  Naturally, having stressed affirmations as part of our AURA paradigm, we believe praise is an essential need for children. Words are incredibly powerful, and sincere praise has considerable productive impact on children. We may be the only people who will take the time to re-characterize a child's difficulties into possible strengths. We are early childhood educators. We teach about the self.

Balance in Its Structural Form: Managing Unexpected Challenges

We all strive for competence that allows us to function well on a day to day basis. When we feel knowledgeable, we feel grounded and secure. The nature of a challenge is that it is often unexpected. It creates complex changes to a familiar and comfortable status quo. A challenge can undermine that very competence that we so highly value.

When a child is "acting up," and we do not know how to address the child's needs or manage our classroom at that moment, the lack of control we experience can be stressful. We are caught in the space between feeling insufficiently informed to manage the challenge and feeling knowledgeable enough to bring a complex classroom dynamic under control. Our reaction is one of significant consternation, and this consternation often stymies movement and fixes us in place, in a state of imbalance. When we are in a state of imbalance, it is very difficult to feel competent.

We are caught in the space between feeling insufficiently informed to manage the challenge and feeling knowledgeable enough to bring a complex classroom dynamic under control. Our reaction is one of significant consternation, and this consternation often stymies movement and fixes us in place, in a state of imbalance. When we are in a state of imbalance, it is very difficult to feel competent.

The key to managing a challenge is to have a preset plan that includes a structure to absorb the stress associated with losing control. When our classroom is in confusion during a situation that feels unfamiliar, finding a clear path out becomes overly demanding. The establishment of a set of steps to follow in the moment reduces the pressure to be in control when we do not feel in control. They are preset, and we can rely on them to stabilize us when we experience a loss of balance. They are a plan of action that puts us back in charge. We break down a challenge that feels too big and unclear into small digestible parts that are knowable:

1. Notice a challenging behavior
2. Remind myself that a behavior is a communication
3. Look at the manifest communication of the behavior
4. Try to identify the possible latent communication of the behavior

    - Try to identify the underlying feelings being communicated
    - Try to identify the underlying thoughts being communicated

5. Try to identify how the behavior/communication seems to us
6. Determine whether the child is Loud or Quiet
7. Determine whether the child is Over Reactive or Under Reactive
8. Identify the child's Persona (Troubling, Testing, Worrying, Hiding)
9. Determine and try various responses

- If Troubling, try Structural, Less Emotional Responses
- If Testing, try Structural, More Emotional Responses
- If Worrying, try Verbal, Less Emotional Responses
- If Hiding, try Verbal, More Emotional Responses

We all adhere to the idea that children thrive on structure. It gives them a sense of security, stemming from the consistency and routines that a solid structure provides. This structure around children is never more important than when they are going through changes, or when their environment is shifting around them. We provide them a level of steadiness, in the midst of flux. With this in mind, having a set of steps, a plan in place, for the inevitable eventuality that we could experience an "unsteadiness" in our classroom seems like good modeling. If it helps our children stay balanced, why shouldn't it work for us?

Final Thoughts

As early childhood educators, our job is to nurture the child's ability to learn while simultaneously participating in positive interpersonal relationships. This complementary structure is embedded in the social-emotional curricula included in all early childhood education. The integration and use of this construct stems in large part from our skills and dexterity as teachers to interact with a disparate student population as multi-faceted, developing individuals.

This is why we wrote this book, focusing on the notion that being an effective early-childhood educator has similarities to the profession of detective. We suggested this similarity in order to depict how young children often communicate in hidden and camouflaged ways. We always need to look beyond the obvious elements of the behaviors that often frustrate us and disrupt our classrooms. We always need to determine the meanings behind these behaviors as a way to strategize what to do about them. Understanding these behaviors enables us to respond in ways that demonstrate an empathy and willingness to help (invariably experienced as supportive and connecting) rather than a need and resolve to fix (often experienced as punishing and rejecting).

Being in the role of learner and explorer reminds us of the reason we love being teachers—to empower discovery of the unknown. As teachers/detectives, by solving each behavior mystery, we make a difference in the lives of the children we teach. We become purveyors of hope that the early childhood learning environment can be both educational and healing. That hope makes being an early childhood educator the very best job of all.

Appendix A
The Troubling Child Worksheet

> **Loud**—Feisty and externalizes thoughts and feelings; acts "out" as a way of striving for control
>
> **Over Reactive**—Overwhelmed by thoughts/feelings with extreme expression of these thoughts/feelings

Teacher's Role:

We tend to push these children away because of the scale of their disruption. Their behaviors can lead to their actual needs being missed. Troubling children are yearning to be contained by compassionate strength and desperate for the healthy release of pressure that this type of response can bring.

Child's Presentation:

- Impulsivity (lack of control over one's instinctual urges to act)
- Rule Breaking (the disregarding of guidelines set by one's environment)
- Elevated Physical Activity (the increase in one's body movement)
- Emotional Dysregulation (difficulty in managing one's expressive output)
- Difficulty with Boundaries (trouble accepting or working with the physical and emotional restrictions of other people and environments)

What Is Behind a Child's Behavior:

- *Core Feeling*: The more frequent the child's "need" to use the behavior, the greater the **sadness/anger** that is being experienced by the child.
- *Core Wish*: Communicates unconscious wish to be **contained** and **supported** as a way of decreasing sense of **danger** and **rejection**.
- *Core Question*: Limit-testing question–I am being triggered by events because this moment in class feels overwhelming; can you accept me and handle me?
- *Types of Responses Necessary*: Structural & Less Emotional

Teacher's Structural Responses:

- *Stance*: Clear and calm voice (sympathetic)
- *Before Class*: Check in. Hold eye contact. "I'm with you. Let's keep working on this."
- *During Class*: Hand on shoulder; down on knee at eye level. Hold eye contact. Use the Less Emotional responses below.
- *After Class*: Check in. Hold eye contact. Reiterate response themes (self-care, boundaries). Track progress with chart.

Teacher's Less Emotional Responses:

- *Self-Care Statement*: "I want you to try to stop (using the behavior) during class. You are more in charge when you don't push people away by (using the behavior) during class."
- *Boundaries Statement*: "Take a deep breath and let it out slowly when you feel like you need to (use the behavior)."
- *Boundaries Statement*: "Think to yourself, 'I have a choice to (use the behavior or not) during class.'"
- *Statement for Integrating Themes*: "Think about us building a dam together across a stream and trying to stop all the water from flowing. If we can do it, it can feel great when we see that we have stopped the water in the stream completely. Controlling your need to (use the behavior) by yourself, or even with my help, is the same. It's like a victory."

Teacher's Affirmations:

- "Controlling your need to (use the behavior) during class time takes great strength."
- "It is clear what a huge effort you make to not (use the behavior)."

Appendix B
The Testing Child Worksheet

> **Loud**—Feisty and externalizes thoughts and feelings; acts "out" as a way of striving for control
>
> **Under Reactive**—Disconnected by thoughts/feelings with little expression of these thoughts/feelings

Teacher's Role:

We tend to push away these children. Their needs may be overlooked because they typically drive us to annoyance and frustration. The same persistence that we experience in their behavior needs to be returned back to them in equal measure with empathy, thoughtfulness, and caring.

Child's Presentation:

- Rule Testing (the systematic pushing, but not breaking, of rules, boundaries and norms)
- Mischievous Activities (acting out displaying playfulness, yet disobedience toward authority figures)
- Clowning/Joking (verbally and/or non-verbally attempting to elicit laughter from other individuals)
- Verbally Active (trouble accepting or working with the restrictions related to talking)
- Not Listening or Following Directions (the emotional disconnecting from verbal and written messages and/or control coming from other individuals)

What Is Behind a Child's Behavior:

- *Core Feeling*: The more frequent the child's "need" to use the behavior, the greater the **sadness/anger** that is being experienced by the child.
- *Core Wish*: Communicates unconscious wish to be **contained** and

validated as a way of increasing sense of **security** and decreasing sense of **abandonment**.
- *Core Question*: Limit-testing question—I feel bad about myself and have the need to show this by using the behavior; do you care about me enough to redirect me?
- *Types of Responses Necessary*: Structural & More Emotional

Teacher's Structural Responses:

- *Stance*: Clear and calm voice (sympathetic).
- *Before Class*: Check in. Hold eye contact. "I'm with you. Let's keep working on this."
- *During Class*: Hand on shoulder; down on knee at eye level. Hold eye contact. Use More Emotional responses below.
- *After Cass*: Check in. Hold eye contact. Reiterate response themes (self-awareness, boundaries).

Teacher's More Emotional Responses:

- *Self-Awareness and Boundaries*: "It makes me sad when you keep (using the behavior), because I feel it pushes us apart."
- *Self-Awareness*: "When you (use the behavior), I think you feel bad."
- *Boundaries*: "Try to take a breath and say to yourself, 'I will be okay if (do not use the behavior).'"
- *Self-Awareness and Boundaries*: "(Not using the behavior) is important. When you (using the behavior), try to raise your hand and I will come over and be with you."

Teacher's Affirmations:

- "I am proud of you for trying so hard to (not use the behavior)."
- "You took good care of yourself by (not using the behavior)."

Appendix C
The Worrying Child Worksheet

> **Quiet**—Slow to warm and internalizes thoughts and feelings; acts "in" as a way of striving for control
>
> **Over Reactive**—Overwhelmed by thoughts/feelings with extreme expression of these thoughts/feelings

Teacher's Role:

There is an obviousness about these children's vulnerable presentation, that creates anxiety and gives the impression that, if they just received enough care, all would be "fixed." This is not the case. These children are powerful magnets for concern. Intervention for these children centers on empathy and safety.

Child's Presentation:

- Worrisome Artwork/Writing (violent, sexual, disturbing imagery, age-inappropriate relationships)
- Self-Criticism, Self-Dislike (comments indicating a lack of patience with or appreciation of self)
- Self-Harming Behavior (nail-biting, picking at scabs, clothes chewing, hitting oneself, inappropriate touching of oneself)
- Difficulty Connecting with Others (poor hygiene, destruction of others' work, inappropriate touching)
- Concerning Play (violent, sexual, disturbing content, age-inappropriate relationships)

What Is Behind a Child's Behavior:

- *Core Feeling*: The more frequent the child's "need" to use the behavior, the greater the **fear/anger** that is being experienced by the child.
- *Core Wish*: Communicates unconscious wish to be **noticed** and **supported** as a way of decreasing sense of **danger** and **abandonment**.

- *Core Question*: Limit-testing question—I am being triggered by events because this moment in class feels overwhelming; can you accept me and handle me?
- *Types of Responses Necessary*: Verbal & Less Emotional

Teacher's Verbal Responses:

- *Stance*: Clear and calm voice (quiet)
- *Before Class*: Check in and talk about previous day. Occasional eye contact. "I want to check in with you to see how our talk felt for you. We can do this each day."
- *During Class*: Occasional eye contact. Maintain distance (two feet at least). No physical contact. Use sound or words to get attention (Less Emotional responses below).
- *After Class*: Check-in. Reiterate response themes (self-care, connection).

Teacher's Less Emotional Responses:

- *Self-Care and Connection*: "If I notice you are (using the behavior), I will come over and say your name and calmly remind you that you are safe and that you are able to continue the work."
- *Self-Care*: "When you (do the behavior), take a deep breath and 'It's okay, I am okay, I can begin and do just a little at a time until I'm more comfortable.'"
- *Self-Care and Connection*: "Do you want to come up with a word that is just between you and me that means, 'I see you are (using the behavior)?' This is a way of us working as a team."
- *Self-Care and Connection*: "When you (do the behavior), it makes me think about your safety. To help with your safety, I would like to ask you about what you are thinking when (do the behavior)."

Teacher's Affirmations:

- "It is impressive to see you try (not doing the behavior)."
- "It takes a lot of courage to (not do the behavior)."

Appendix D

The Hiding Child Worksheet

> **Quiet**—Slow to warm and internalizes thoughts and feelings; acts "in" as a way of striving for control
>
> **Under Reactive**—Disconnected by thoughts/feelings with little expression of these thoughts/feelings

Teacher's Role:

These children instinctually hide—from others and even from themselves—and in their acts of hiding, it becomes very difficult to provide them care and education. They present as a diverse group who obscure their communications, and who require an increased sense control and security to in order to connect.

Child's Presentation:

- Preference for Parallel Play over Collaborative Play (not playing or reciprocating with others)
- Disconnectedness (daydreaming, talking/mumbling to self; distress in social situations)
- Non-responsiveness (not participating in group activities; not responding to questions/statements)
- Repetition and Rituals (hand flapping, rocking; humming; repeating vocalizations, "tic" like)
- Odd Reactions (spontaneously laughing; odd facial expressions, intruding into classmates' space, tantrums)

What Is Behind a Child's Behavior:

- *Core Feeling*: The more frequent and/or acute the child's self-harming is, the greater the **fear/anger** is being experienced by the child.
- *Core Wish*: Communicates unconscious wish to be **noticed** and **validated** as a way of increasing sense of **security** and decrease a sense of **rejection**.

- *Core Question*: Limit-testing question—My behavior is a diversion from just how uncomfortable I feel right now; can you accept the way I am and protect me?
- *Types of Responses Necessary*: Verbal & More Emotional

Teacher's Verbal Responses:

- *Stance*: Clear and calm voice (quiet)
- *Before Class*: Check in and talk about previous day. Occasional eye contact "I want to check in with you to see if you remember our talk. We will do this each day.."
- *During Class*: Occasional eye contact. Maintain distance (two feet at least). No physical contact. Use sound or words to get attention (More Emotional responses below).
- *After Class*: Check in. Occasional eye contact. Reiterate response themes (connection, self-awareness).

Teacher's More Emotional Responses:

- *Self-Awareness and Connection*: "When you (do the behavior), I think you have big feelings. Try raising your hand when you start to (think about or do the behavior). I can help with that."
- *Self-Awareness*: "When (you do the behavior), it looks like your big thoughts start to get bigger, and you have a hard time staying in control of them. It's important for you to know controlling your big thoughts is a way to be strong and safe."
- *Connection*: "Look at my face. I am worried when you (do the behavior)."
- *Self-Awareness and Connection*: "Try to think to yourself, 'I can try to control (the behavior) when it starts. The big thoughts I have (when I do the behavior) are like a boiling water in a pot. When I need to, I can get help to turn the heat down before I (do the behavior), or when I need to stop it.'"

Teacher's Affirmations:

- "I see you using your thoughts to try and control (doing the behavior)."
- "I am impressed how you are deciding to keep control of (doing the behavior)."

Appendix E
Self-Fulfilling Prophecies

The Troubling Child's Self-Fulfilling Prophecy

External Steps	Internal Steps
Children make false assumptions about themselves in the context of their current environment.	Because of their life experiences, Troubling children feel that they are always ignored, unloved, rejected and abandoned. These thoughts and feelings manifest as a belief that no one will listen to/hear them.
The child takes action to test the false assumption.	Convinced of these dynamics, this creates a great deal of consternation in Troubling children, and they try to enact a solution. They behave in a way that forces those around them to take notice.
Others react to the actions and misunderstand.	The demand for being noticed challenges teachers and classmates in its pervasiveness and intensity. They feel unable to listen to Troubling children because of the force of the behaviors and try to stop them by giving them consequences (teachers) or withdrawing (classmates).
The others' reactions/responses to the child's actions, confirm the false assumption for the child.	Based on the teacher's and classmates' reactions, Troubling children confirm to themselves that no one listens to/hears them (and maintains the feeling of being ignored, unloved, rejected, and abandoned).
The child takes more extreme actions.	Troubling children escalate, behaving more intensely and pervasively.

The Testing Child's Self-Fulfilling Prophecy

External Steps	Internal Steps
Children make a false assumption about themselves in the context of their current environment.	Because they feel ignored, unsupported, and abandoned, Testing children believe that no one cares about them. These feelings are too upsetting for them, Testing children do not let themselves think about this. They only think about the need to work hard to get people's attention.

External Steps	Internal Steps
The child takes action to test the false assumption.	Testing children make jokes, create mild disruptions, and generally act out in class. They present that they are worthy of attention and connection by presenting that they are "free-spirited" and are enjoyable to their peers.
Others react to their actions and misunderstand.	Even though the children laugh, Testing children feel only a brief moment of attention and connection. The teacher, who feels annoyed by their antics because of their disruptiveness and their rule breaking, gives them increasingly onerous consequences each time they act out.
The others' reactions/responses to the child's action, confirm the false assumption for the child.	Based on the teacher's reaction, Testing children feel negative attention and a reduced connection. This confirms to them that no one cares about them (and they continue to feel ignored, unsupported, and abandoned).
The child takes more extreme action.	Testing children try new and more disruptive ways to get the teacher's and class' attention and connection.

The Worrying Child's Self-Fulfilling Prophecy

External Steps	Internal Steps
Children make a false assumption about themselves in the context of their current environment.	Because of their life experiences, Worrying children believe that if they ask for help, there will be negative repercussions. This fear accompanies other feelings such as being ignored, unloved, rejected, hurt, and abandoned; and convinces them that they are alone.
A child takes action to test the false assumption.	Overwhelmed by these feelings, Worrying children cannot stop themselves from calling for help. However, because they are afraid of the consequences, they disguise their calls for help within indirect (upsetting and disquieting for us to witness) actions and behaviors.
Others react to their actions and misunderstand.	The disguised calls for help are often felt by their teachers and peers as distressing behavior that further isolates Worrying children. It provokes reactions—either too intense (come to me; let me rescue you) or too inadequate (stay away from me; you are making me uncomfortable)—that do not address their underlying issues.
The others' reactions/responses to the child's actions, confirm the false assumption for the child.	Based on the others' reaction, Worrying children confirm to themselves that they are alone and unable to be helped. The others' responses, along with the Worrying children's perception of their missteps, rejections, and abandonments, serve as proxies for those negative repercussions that they are so familiar with.

External Steps	Internal Steps
The child takes more extreme action.	Worrying children create more provocatively disguised communications to see if their teachers or peers will come to their aid and "get it right."

The Hiding Child's Self-Fulfilling Prophecy

External Steps	Internal Steps
Children make a false assumption about themselves in the context of their current environment.	Because of their life experiences, Hiding children feel that no one truly understands them, and this leaves them quite alone. While they may be upset with this, their own thoughts and feelings, in general, are difficult for them to process and can easily overwhelm them. Due to these reinforcing dynamics—their isolation, a lack of self-awareness, and their difficulty communicating, they think it is better to avoid being challenged by the demands of the outside world.
A child takes action to test the false assumption.	Hiding children try to control their world through disentanglement by (1) limiting their interactions with others and going unnoticed, when they can, or (2) protesting (passively or more vigorously) requests for engagement.
Others react to the action and misunderstand.	Behaving in this way, Hiding children seem odd and/or aloof to teachers (and classmates), as they struggle to understand exactly how to engage Hiding children in the work of school (and relationships). Attempts often miss the mark, leaving teachers (and classmates) confused, discouraged, or frustrated. To them, leaving Hiding children alone seems the easiest path.
The others' reactions/responses to the child's actions, confirm the false assumption for the child.	Based on the teacher's (and classmates') reaction, Hiding children confirm to themselves that no one understands them or really cares to try—and, for Hiding children, because of their discomfort with others and their difficulty understanding how they themselves feel, this result may feel "right" to them.
The child takes more extreme action.	Hiding children's solitary behaviors continue, and may even increase, deepening their isolation.

Bibliography

Ahnert, L., Milatz, A., Kappler, G., Schneiderwind, J., and Fischer, R. (2012). The impact of teacher-child relationships on child cognitive performance as explored by a priming paradigm. *Developmental Psychology.* 49.10.1037/a0031283.

Ainsworth, M.D.S., Blehar, M.C., Waters, E., and Wall, S. (2014). *Patterns of attachment (Classic edition): A psychological study of the strange situation.* Florence, KY: Guilford Press, Taylor & Frances Group.

Alexander, F., French, T.M., et al. (1946). *Psychoanalytic therapy: Principles and application.* New York: Ronald Press.

Alford, R. (1988). Naming and identity: A cross-cultural study of personal naming practices. New Haven, CT: HRAF-Human Relations Area Files, pp. viii–190.

Allport, G. (1937). *Personality: A psychological interpretation.* New York: Holt, Rinehart, & Winston.

Allport, G. (1954). *The nature of prejudice.* Cambridge, MA: Addison-Wellsley.

Allport, G. (1955). *Becoming: Basic considerations for a psychology of personality.* New Haven, CT: Yale University Press.

Allport, G. (1961). *Pattern and growth in personality.* New York: Holt, Rinehart & Winston.

American Psychiatric Association. (2013). *Diagnostic and statistical manual of mental disorders* (5th ed.). Washington, D.C.: Publisher.

American Psychological Association. (2020). State resources for early learning guidelines toolkit. Retrieved at https://www.apa.org/education/k12/states-early-learning.

Axline, V.M. (1981). *Play therapy: The groundbreaking book that has become a vital tool in the growth and development of children.* New York: Ballantine.

Bailey, K.D. (1984). Equilibrium, entropy and homeostasis: A multidisciplinary legacy. *Systems Research,* 1(1): 25–43.

Bailey, K.D. (1994). *Sociology and the new systems theory: Toward a theoretical synthesis.* Albany: State University of New York Press.

Bateson, P., and Gluckman, P. (2011). *Robustness, plasticity, development and evolution.* New York: Cambridge University Press.

Bellak, L. (1973). *Ego functions in schizophrenics, neurotics and normals* (Wiley Series on Personality Processes). Hoboken, NJ: Wiley.

Belsky, J. (1981). Early human experience: A family perspective. *Developmental Psychology,* 17(1): 3.

Benzinger, T.H. (1969). Heat regulation: Homeostasis of central temperature in man. *Physiological Reviews,* 49(4): 671–759.

Bibring, E. (1943). The conception of the repetition compulsion. *The Psychoanalytic Quarterly,* 12(4): 486–519. doi: 10.1080/21674086.1943.11925548.

Blumberg, MS (2005). *Basic instinct: The genesis of behavior.* New York: Basic.

Boeree, C.G. (2006). Personality theories. Psychology Department: Shippensburg University, Original E-Text-Site, http://www.ship.edu/%7Ecgboeree/perscontents.html accessed 12/2/16.

Bowlby, J. (1969). *Attachment and loss: Volume 1 attachment.* New York: Basic.

Bowlby, J. (1982). *The mind in conflict.* New York: International Universities Press.

Bronfenbrenner, U. (1979). *The ecology of human development.* Cambridge, MA: Harvard University Press.

Bronfenbrenner, U. (2004). *Making human beings human: Bioecological perspectives on human development.* SAGE Program on Applied Developmental Science, New York: SAGE.

Brumfield, B. (2012, December 18). Connecticut teachers were heroes in the face of death. *Cable News Network.* Retrieved from: https://www.cnn.com/2012/12/17/us/connecticut-shooting-teacher-heroism/index.html.

Camposano, L. (2011). Silent suffering: Children with selective mutism. *The Professional Counselor,* 1(1): 46–56. doi:10.15241/lc.1.1.46.

Cattell, R.B. (1946). *The description and measurement of personality.* Oxford, England: World Book Company.

Cattell, R.B. (1957). *Personality and motivation structure and measurement.* Oxford, England: World Book Company.

C8Sciences. (March 29, 2016). Fidgeting and ADHD: How movement aids learning. Retrieved from C8Sciences website: https://www.c8sciences.com/fidgeting-and-adhd-how-movement-aids-learning/.

Chess, S., and Thomas, A. (1990). 11 continuities

and discontinuities in temperament. In: LN Robins *Straight and devious pathways from childhood to adulthood*. New York: Cambridge University Press.

Chess, S., and Thomas, A. (1996). *Temperament: Theory and practice*. New York: Brunner/Mazel.

Craig, W.M. (1998). The relationship among bullying, victimization, depression, anxiety, and aggression in elementary school children. *Personality and Individual Differences*, 24, 123–130. http://dx.doi.org/10.1016/S0191–8869(97)00145–1.

Davies, C.T.M., White, M.J., and Young, K. (1983). Muscle function in children. *European Journal of Applied Physiology and Occupational Physiology*, 52(1): 111–114.

de Wilde, A., Koot, H.M., and van Lier, P. (2015). Developmental links between children's working memory and their social relations with teachers and peers in the early school years. *Journal of Abnormal Child Psychology*. doi: 10.1007/s10802-015-0053-4.

Ellenberger, H. (1970). *The discovery of the unconscious*. New York: Basic.

Erikson, E. (1950). *Childhood and society*. New York: W.W. Norton.

Erikson, E. (1968). *Identity, youth and crisis*. New York: W.W. Norton.

Everatt, J., Steffert, B., and Smythe, I. (March 1999). An eye for the unusual: Creative thinking in dyslexics. *Dyslexia*, 5(1): pp 28–46.

Eyerman, R. (2001). *Slavery and the formation of African-American identity*. Cambridge, UK: Cambridge University Press.

Fairbairn, W.R.D. (1954). *An object relations theory of personality*. New York: Basic.

Fairbairn, W.R.D., Scharf, D.E., and Fairbairn-Birtles, E. (Eds.) (1995). *Vol. I from instinct to self: Selected papers of W.R.D. Fairbairn. Clinical and theoretical papers* (Library of Object Relations) Lanham, MD: Jason Aronson.

Feliciano, L.C., and O'Connor, J. (2017, November 20). "We've got a runner...": Best practice strategies for preventing and reducing elopement behavior. *SCSD Behavior Matters*. Retrieved from: https://scsdbehaviormatters.weebly.com/blog/weve-got-a-runner-best-practice-strategies-for-preventing-and-reducing-elopement-behavior.

Felitti, V.J., Anda, R.F., Nordenberg, D., Williamson, D.F., Spitz, A.M., Edwards, V., Koss, M.P., and Marks, J.S. (1998). Relationship of childhood abuse and household dysfunction to many of the leading causes of death in adults: The adverse childhood experiences study. *American Journal of Preventive Medicine*, 14(4): 254–258.

Freud, A., and Burlingham, D. (1967). *The writings of Anna Freud: The ego and the mechanisms of defense, vol. 2*. New York: International Universities Press.

Freud, A., The Institute of Psychoanalysis. (1966). *The ego and the mechanisms of defense*. London: Routledge, https://doi.org/10.4324/9780429481550.

Freud, S. (1909). Analysis of a phobia in a five-year-old boy. *The Standard Edition of the Complete Psychological Works of Sigmund Freud*, [online] Volume X, pp. 1–150. Retrieved at: http://mrgregoryonline.com/Psystudies/Analysis-of-a-Phobia-in-a-Five-Year-Old-Boy.pdf.

Freud, S. (1914). Remembering, repeating and working-through (Further recommendations on the technique of psycho-analysis II). *The Standard Edition of the Complete Psychological Works of Sigmund Freud, Volume XII (1911–1913): The Case of Schreber, Papers on Technique and Other Works*, pp. 145–156.

Freud, S., and Strachey, James, Ed. (1990). *The ego and the id: Standard edition of the complete works of Sigmund Freud*. New York: W.W. Norton.

Gander, E.M. (2003). *On our minds: How evolutionary psychology is reshaping the nature versus nurture debate*. Baltimore, MD: Johns Hopkins University Press.

Gottlieb, G. (2007). Probabilistic epigenesist. *Developmental Science*, 10(1): 1–10.

Graff, G. (2014). The intergenerational trauma of slavery and its aftermath. *Journal of Psychohistory*, 41(3):181–197.

Gregory D. (2018). Commentary: The nature of unsymbolized thinking. *Frontiers in Psychology*, 9, 216. doi:10.3389/fpsyg.2018.00216.

Guerrero, L.K., DeVito, J.A., and Hecht, M.L. (2008). *The nonverbal communication reader: Classic and contemporary reading*. Long Grove, IL: Waveland Press.

Harlow, H.F. (1959). Love in infant monkeys. *Scientific American*, 200(6): 68–74. http://dx.doi.org/10.1038/scientificamerican, 695–68.

Hartanto, T.A., Krafft, C.E., Iosif, A.M., Schweitzer, J.B. (2015). A trial-by-trial analysis reveals more intense physical activity is associated with better cognitive control performance in attention-deficit/hyperactivity disorder. *Child Neuropsychology*; DOI: 10.1080/09297049.2015.1044511.

Hattie, J. (2009). *Visible learning: A synthesis of over 800 meta-analyses related to achievement*. London: Routledge.

Horney, K. (1945). *Our inner conflicts: A constructive theory of neurosis*. New York: W.W. Norton.

Horney, K. (1950). *Neurosis and human growth: The struggle toward self-realization*. New York: W.W. Norton.

Hurlburt R.T., and Heavey C. (2008). The phenomena of inner experience. *Conscious and Cognition*, 17, 798–810. doi:10.1016/j.concog.2007.12.006.

Jablonka, E., and Lamb, M. (2005). *Evolution in four dimensions: Genetic, epigenetic, behavioral and symbolic variation in the history of life* (Life and mind: Philosophical issues in biology and psychology). Cambridge, MA: A Bradford Book, MIT Press.

Janet, P. (1965) [1920/1929]. *The major symptoms of hysteria*. New York: Hafner. ISBN 978-1-4325-0431-1.

Kaufman, S.B., and Paul, E.S. (November 2014). Creativity and schizophrenia spectrum disorders across the arts and sciences. Retrieved from *Frontiers of Psychology* website: https://doi.org/10.3389/fpsyg.2014.01145.

Kingston, B., Regoli, B., and Hewitt, J.D. (2003). The theory of differential oppression: A developmental-ecological explanation of adolescent problem behavior. *Critical Criminology 11*, 237–260. https://doi.org/10.1023/B:CRIT.0000005812.05228.78.

Klein, M. (1932). *The psycho-analysis of children*. New York: W.W. Norton.

Klein, M., Heimann, P., and Money-Kyrle, R.E. (Eds.) (1955). *New directions in psychoanalysis: The significance of infant conflict in the pattern of adult behavior*. New York: Basic.

Kohut, H. (1971). *The analysis of self: A systemic approach to the psychoanalytic treatment of narcissistic personality disorder*. New York: International Universities Press.

Kris, E. (1975). *The selected papers of Ernest Kris*. New Haven, CT: Yale University Press.

Krumwiede, A. (2014). *Attachment theory according to John Bowlby and Mary Ainsworth: A seminar paper*. (English Language Version) Munich, Germany: GRIN Verlag Gmbh.

La Farge, L. (December 2014). How and why unconscious phantasy and transference are the defining features of psychoanalytic practice. *The International Journal of Psychoanalysis, 95*(6). 1265–1278. DOI: https://doi.org/10.1111/1745-8315.12292.

Landreth, G.L. (2012). *Play therapy: The art of relationships (3rd edition)*. New York: Routledge.

Lei, H., Cui, Y., and Chui, M.M. (2016). Affective teacher-student relationships and students' externalizing behavior problems: A meta analysis. *Frontier Psychology, 7*(1311). doi: 10.3389/fpsyg.2016.01311.

Lerner, R.M. (1982). Children and adolescents as producers of their own development. *Developmental Review, 2*(4): 342–370.

Lickliter, R. (2008). Developmental dynamics: The new view from the life sciences. In: A. Fogel. B. King, and Shanker, S. (Eds.), *Human development in the 21st century: Visionary policy ideas from systems scientists*. Cambridge University Press\.

Mahler, M., Pine, F., and Bergman, A. (1975). *The psychological birth of the human infant*. New York: Basic.

Maldonado-Carreno, C., and Votruba-Drzal, E. (March/April 2011). Teacher–child relationships and the development of academic and behavioral skills during elementary school: A within- and between-child analysis. *Child Development, 82*(2): 601–616.

Maslow, A. (1968). *Toward a psychology of being (2nd edition)*. Princeton, NJ: Van Nostrand Rheinhold.

Maslow, A. (1971). *The further reaches of human nature*. New York: Viking.

Maslow, A. (2013). *A theory of human motivation*. Eastford, CT: Martino Fine Books.

Maslow, A.H. (1943). A theory of human motivation. *Psychological Review, 50*(4): 370–396. https://doi.org/10.1037/h0054346.

May, R. (1953). *Man's search for himself*. New York: Norton.

May, R. (1967). *Psychology and human dilemma*. New York: Norton.

Mayor, T. (April 2, 2008). Asperger's and IT: Dark secret or open secret. Retrieved from *Computer World* website: computerworld.com/article/2536193/it-management-asperger-s-and-it-dark-secret-or-open-secret.html.

Meichenbaum, D. (1977). *Cognitive-behavior modification: An integrative approach*. New York: Plenum.

Merriam and webster dictionary, new edition, 2020. Springfield, MA: Merriam, and Webster Inc.

Merton, R. (1948). The Self-Fulfilling Prophecy. *The Antioch review (8)*2: 193–210.

Minuchin, S. (1974). *Families & family therapy*. Cambridge, MA: Harvard University Press.

Morgan, D.H.J. (2014). *Social theory and the family*. New York: Routledge.

National Association for the Education of Young Children. (2009). NAEYC standards for early childhood professional preparation. Available at: www.naeyc.org/sites/default/files/globally-shared/downloads/PDFs/resources/position-statements/2009%20Professional%20Prep%20stdsRevised%204_12.pdf.

National Association for the Education of Young Children. (2020). Available at: www.naeyc.org/our-work/families/10-naeyc-program-standards.

Neukrug, E.S. (2015). *The world of the counselor: An introduction to the counseling profession*, 5th Edition. Independence, KY: Brooks Cole, Cengage Learning.

Noble, K., Houston, S., Brito, N., Bartsch, H., Kan, E., Kuperman, J., Akshoomoff, N., Amaral, D., Bloss, C., Libiger, O., Schork, N., Murray, S., Casey, B., Chang, L., Ernst, T., Frazier, J., Gruen, J., Kennedy, D., and van zijl, P. (March 2015). Family income, parental education and brain structure in children and adolescents. *Nature Neuroscience, 18*(5). DOI: 10.1038/nn.3983.

Oyama, S. (2000). *The ontogeny of information: Developmental systems and evolution*. Durham, NC: Duke University Press.

Paley, V.G. (2004). *A child's work: The importance of fantasy play*. Chicago: University of Chicago Press.

Pennington, R., Strange, C., Stenhoff, D., Delano, M., and Ferguson, M. (2012). Leave the running shoes at home: Addressing elopement in the classroom. *Beyond Behavior, Spring 2012*, 3–7.

Piaget, J (2001) *The psychology of intelligence*. New York: Routledge.

Piaget, J., and Cook, M.T. (1952). *The origins of intelligence in children*. New York: International University Press.

Piaget, J, and Inhelder, B (1969) *The psychology of the child*. New York: Basic.

Quintana, S.M., and Segura-Herrera, T.A. (2003). Developmental transformations of self and identity in the context of oppression. *Self and Identity, 2*(4): 269–285.

Regoli, R., and Hewitt, J. (2001). *Differential oppression theory*. In: Bryant, C. (Ed.), Encyclopedia of criminology and deviant behavior, vol. 1. Philadelphia: Taylor & Francis, 131–133.

Ridley, M. (2003). *Nature versus nurture: Genes, experience, and what makes us human*. New York: HarperCollins.

Rodolfo, K. (2000, January 3). What is homeostasis? Retrieved from https://www.scientificamerican.com/article/what-is-homeostasis. Accessed on 12/8/2016.

Rogers, C. (1939). *The clinical treatment of the problem child*. Boston: Houghton Mifflin.

Rogers, C. (1995). *On becoming a person*. New York: Houghton Mifflin (Reprint 1961).

Rogers, C.R. (1951). *Client-centered therapy*. Boston: Houghton Mifflin.

Rudasill, K., Reio, T., Jr.; Stipanovic, N.; and Taylor, J.E. (2010). A longitudinal study of student–teacher relationship quality, difficult temperament, and risky behavior from childhood to early adolescence. *Educational Psychology Papers and Publications*, 120.

Saft, E.W., and Pianta, R.C. (2001). Teachers' perceptions of their relationships with students: Effects of child age, gender, and ethnicity of teachers, and children. School *Psychology quarterly*, 16(2): 125–141. https://doi.org/10.1521/scpq.16.2.125.18698.

Salomonsson, B. (2017, May 22). Interpreting the inner world of ADHD children: psychoanalytic perspectives. *International journal qualitive studies on health and well-being*, 12(sup1). doi: 10.1080/17482631.2017.1298269.

Sar, V., Middleton, W., and Dorahy, M. (2013). Individual, and societal oppression: Global perspectives on dissociative disorders. *Journal of trauma & dissociation*, 14(2): 121–126.

Saracho, O.N., and Spodek, B. (1995, January 1). Children's play, and early childhood education: Insights from history, and theory. *Journal of education*, 177(3): 129–148.

Satir, V.C. (1972) People making. Palo Alto: Science and Behavior Books.

Schore, A. (2012). *The science of the art of psychotherapy* (Norton series on interpersonal neurobiology). New York: W.W. Norton.

Siegel, L.S., and Mazabel, S. (2014). Basic cognitive processes and reading disabilities. In: Swanson, H.L., Harris, K.R., and Graham, S. (Eds.), Handbook of learning disabilities (p. 186–213). New York: Guilford.

Silberman, S. (2015). *Neurotribes: The legacy of autism and the future of neurodiversity*. New York: Penguin.

Solomon, J., and George, C. (Eds.). (2011). Disorganized attachment and caregiving. New York: Guilford.

Sonn, C.C., and Fisher, A.T. (2003). Identity and oppression: Differential responses to an in-between status. *American Journal of Community Psychology*, 31(1–2): 117–128.

Sotero, M. (2006). A conceptual model of historical trauma: Implications for public health practice and research. *Journal of Health Disparities Research and Practice*, 1(1): 93–10.

Spilt J.L., Hughes J.N., Wu J.Y., Kwok O.M. (2012a). Dynamics of teacher–student relationships: Stability and change across elementary school and the influence on children's academic success. *Child Development*, 83, 1180–1195. DOI: 10.1111/j.1467–8624.2012.01761.x.

Sroufe, L.A., Egland, B., Carlson, EA, and Collins, W.A. (2005). *The development of the person: The Minnesota study of risk and adaptation from birth to adulthood*. New York: Guilford.

Swearer, S.M., and Hymel, S. (2015). Understanding the psychology of bullying: Moving toward a social-ecological diathesis–stress model. *American Psychologist*, 70(4): 344–353. https://doi.org/10.1037/a0038929.

Szczerba, R. (2015). The best tech jobs for individuals with autism. *Forbes*. Retrieved from: https://www.forbes.com/sites/robertszczerba/2015/06/08/the-best-tech-jobs-for-individuals-withautism/#502ee9d4185d.

Tabery, J. (2014). *Beyond versus: The struggle to understand the interaction of nature and nurture*. Cambridge, MA: MIT Press.

Tang, Y.Y., Ma, Y., Wang, J., Fan, Y., Feng, S.; Lu, Q., Yu, Q., Sui, D., Rothbart, M.K., Fan, M., and Posner, M.I. (2007). Short-term meditation training improves attention and self-regulation. *Proceedings of the National Academy of Sciences*, 104(43): 17152–17156.

Taylor, M.L. (2004). *Remembering Esperanza*. Minneapolis: Fortress Press.

Taylor, S.E., Klein, L.C., Lewis, B.P., Gruenewald, T.L., Gurung, R.A., and Updegraff, J.A. (2000). Biobehavioral responses to stress in females: Tend-and-befriend, not fight-or-flight. *Psychological Review*, 107(3): 411.

Thicke, A., Loring, G., and Burton, A. (1979). "The facts of life" theme song.

Thomas, A., and Chess, S. (1956). An approach to the study of sources of individual differences in child behavior. *Journal of Clinical and Experimental Psychopathology*, 18(4): 347–357.

Thomas, A., and Chess, S. (1977). *Temperament and development*. New York: Brunner/Mazel.

Van Der Kolk, B. (2014). *The body keeps the score: Brain, mind, and body in the healing of trauma*. New York: Viking.

Warren, L. (2012, December 19). Family's tears as heroic teacher Vicki Soto, 27, is laid to rest five days after she died trying to save her student. *Daily Mail*. Retrieved from: https://www.dailymail.co.uk/news/article-2250682/Sandy-Hook-victims-Familys-tears-heroic-teacher-Vicki-Soto-27-laid-rest-days-died-trying-save-students.html.

Webb, N.B. (ed.) (2007) *Play therapy with child in crisis (3rd edition): Individual, group and family therapy*. Florence, KY: Guilford Press, Taylor & Frances Group.

Webb, N.B., and Terr, L.C. (2016) *Play therapy with adolescents and children in crisis*. Fourth Edition, New York: Guilford.

Wegscheider-Cruse, S. (1981). *Another chance: Hope and health for the alcoholic family*. New York: Science and Behavior Books.

Wei, X., Christiano, E.R., Yu, J.W., Blackorby J., Shattuck P., and Newman, L.A. (2014). Science, technology, engineering, and mathematics (STEM) participation among college students with autism spectrum disorder. *Autism Research and Treatment. 2014* (924182).

Weiner, M., and Gallo-Silver, L.P. (2015). *You and your child's psychotherapy: An essential guide for parents and caregivers*. New York: Oxford University Press.

West, M.J., and King, A.P. (1987). Settling nature and nurture into an ontogenetic niche. *Developmental Psychobiology, 20*(5): 549–562.

Winnicott, D.W. (1953). Transitional objects and transitional phenomena: A study of the first not me possession. *International Journal of Psychoanalysis, 34*: 89–97.

Winnicott, D.W. (1963). *Maturational process and facilitating environment*. Madison, CT: International Universities Press.

Winnicott, D.W. (1990). *Home is where we start from: Essays by a psychoanalyst*. New York: W.W. Norton.

Zimring, F.M. (2000) Empathic understanding grows the person. *Person-Centered Journal, 7*(2): 101–113.

Index

Numbers in ***bold italics*** indicate pages with illustrations

acknowledging 5, 41, 43, 44, 61, 70, 92, 97, 111, 365
acting in 49, 82
acting out 59, 69, 79, 82
activity level 21, 24, 43, ***46***
adaptability 23, ***45***
Adverse Childhood Experiences (ACEs) 88, ***89***, 90, 92
affirmation 42, 70
aggression 67, 76, 197–198
Ainsworth, Mary ***6***, ***25***, 31; *see also* attachment; Bowlby, John
anger 35, 38, 50–51, 74–76, 198
anxiety 21, 26, 33, 42, 49, 62, 73, 100, 320
artwork 5, 90, 97, 99, 318–319, ***320***, ***321***, 375; *see also* drawings
attachment ***6***, ***25***, 31, 59, 98–99
Attachment-Relatedness component 25–26
attention 20, 32, 49, 73, 75, ***131***, 366; seeking 29, 32, 56, 59–61, 66, 69, 71, 73–75, ***78***, 79, 84–85, 122, 124–125, 365
attention-deficit hyperactivity disorder (ADHD) 20, 24, 28, 58, 110
attunement 1, 2, 33, 99, 119
AURA (Acknowledging-Understanding-Responding-Affirming) 41, ***43***, 54, 70, 125, 127, 365, 368
autonomy 6, ***18***, 25, 77, 99
Autism Spectrum Disorder (ASD) 20, 29, 42, 110; *see also* neurodiversity
avoidance (avoidant) 23, ***32***, ***36***, 39, 50, 75, 105, ***111***

behavior as communication 7, 28–29; *see also* latent communication
behavior chart 39, 80, ***81***
Bio-Developmental component 17–19; *see also* Erikson, Erik
boundaries 19, 21, ***47***, 56, 67, 79, 90, 97, 99, 102, 106–107, ***109***
Bowlby, John ***6***, 25, 31; *see also* Ainsworth, Mary; attachment

brain 4, 6, 49, 110, 319
bullying 7, 197–***199***

caregiver 23, 32, 60, 82, 89, 93
cautious ***23***, 46, 71, 87, 91, 105
Chess, Stella 6, ***23***–24, 45–***47***; *see also* temperament; Thomas, Alexander
child protective services 57, 72, 86, 93, 95, 104, 319; *see also* mandatory reporting
clothing 20, 58, 87, 90, 97, 366
clowning 79, 182–184; *see also* silliness
cognitive component 19–21
communication 1, 3, 5–7, 20–21, 24–25; latent 30–31, 33–43, ***36***, ***37***, 44, 59–61, 64, 70, 72, 74–76, 81–84, 86, 88, 91–92, 99, 104, 106, 108–109, 128, 131, 133, 162, 185, 364, 366–368; levels 5, 7, 365; manifest 30–***32***, 33, 35, ***36***, 37–44, 54, 58–59, 61, 64, 70, 73–74, 76, 80–81, 83, 87, 89–90, 105, 107, 123, ***126***, ***127***, 131, 159–160, 183, 198, 224, 246, 276–277, 300, 319, 364, 366–368; non-verbal 5, 32, 35, 48, 64, 79, 99, 101, 119, 276, ***277***; *see also* behavior as communication
concentration 131
connection (with students) 5, 24–25, 33, 45, 65, 90, 97, 98, 113, 117–118, 363, 366
conscious mind 44–45, 49–52, 76, 82
corrective emotional experience 25, 60, 84, 133; *see also* Rogers, Carl
crying 23, 30, 33, 35

daydreaming 32, ***36***, 75, 107, 113, 131–132
decision tree 114–***115***
denial 75
depression 319
developmental skills areas 31–32, ***32***, ***33***, ***36***, ***37***
diagnosis 28, 40–42
disability 20, 89

discrimination 198
distortions 35, ***36***, ***37***, 98
distractibility 23, 45–***47***, 131–132
divorce 22, 30, 319
drawings 5, ***32***, ***36***, 48, 50–51, 86, 88, 91, 100, 114, ***247***, ***320***; *see also* artwork
dreams 35

eating 319–***320***
ego defenses 75, 90, 94; *see also* Freud, Anna; psychological defenses
elopement 160–***161***, ***162***; *see also* running away
empathy 3, 8, 26, 29–***32***, 33, 59, 62, 66, 71, 85, 99, 102, 109, 117, 119, 321, 365, 369
environmental component 21–23
erasing 90, 97, ***100***
Erikson, Erik ***6***, 17–***18***, 19, 24, 31, 63–64, 77, 90; *see also* biodevelopmental component
ethnicity 1
executive functioning 49
externality 45–***48***, 49–50, 59

Fairbairn, Ronald 17, 64, ***93***–94; *see also* introject
family dysfunction 16, 77
fantasies 35
fears 7, 35, 61
fighting 31, ***33***, ***37***, 196, 198
focus ***32***, ***36***, 46–***47***, 68–69, 72–73, 87, 92, 107, 110, ***131***–132
Freud, Anna 7, 75, 94; *see also* ego defenses; psychological defenses
Freud, Sigmund 5, ***7***, 17, 49, 62; *see also* Little Hans; repetition compulsion
frustration: in child 19, ***32***, ***36***, 38, 45, 48–49, ***96***, ***111***, 114; in teacher 28–29, 41, 62, 69, 71–74, 76, 80, 84, 119, ***123***, 125–***126***, 184, 365, 367, 369

good enough teaching 34, 42; *see also* Winnicott, D.W.
goodness of fit 24
guarded ***23***, 46, 107

Index

hair pulling 88, 90, 97, 195, *247*
hand flapping 107, 113; *see also* repetitive movements
Hewitt, John 7
hitting 30, *32*, *36*, 44, 97, 197
holding environment *6*, 26, 61, 67, 102; *see also* Winnicott, D.W.
homework 22–23, *32*, *36*, 48
hopelessness 91–92, 94–95, 102, 365
Horney, Karen 17, 64
humanistic model 4, 84
humor 74, 183
hyperactivity 7, 20, 24, 28, *32*–33, 36, 46, 58, 60, 67, 75, 110, 225

imaginary play *32*, *36*, 88, 319–*320*; concerning 90
impulsivity 20, 21, *33*, *37*, 45, 48–50, 58, 60–61, 67, 74, 107, *160*, 220, 248
intensity (level) 23, 45, *47*, 60, *63*, 66–67, 74–76, 78, 91, 92, 96, 101, 198, 225–*226*, 364
internality 46, *48*–50, 52
interpretations 35–*37*
introject 93–94; *see also* Fairbairn, Ronald

joking 72, 76, 79; *see also* clowning; silliness

Kohut, Heinz 17
Kris, Ernst 320; *see also* regression

latent communication *see* communication
less emotional responses (definition) *65*–66
limits (testing) 25, 50, 56, 60, 71, 85, 99, 160, 247
listening 3, 31, *32*, *36*, 38, 42, 67, 73–74, 79, *81*
Little Hans 5; *see also* Freud, Sigmund
locus of control 68, 80
loss 21–22, 26, 26, 74, 77, 82, 89, 368; of control 48, 67, 110
loud communication (definition) 49, 52

Mahler, Margaret *6*, 17, 25, 31; *see also* separation
maltreatment 88–90, 317
mandatory reporting 57, 72, 86, 93, 104; *see also* child protective services
manifest communication *see* communication
Maslow, Abraham *6*, 17, 21–*22*, 31, 59; *see also* hierarchy of needs
medical model 40
medication 28, 58, 111, 225
Merton, Robert *63*, *78*, *96*, *111*, *112*; *see also* self-fulfilling prophecy
mind-body connection *116*

mindfulness 107
Minuchin, Salvador 77; *see also* family dysfunction
mistrust *18*–19, 64, 67, 90, 98; *see also* Erikson, Erik
modeling 65, 70, 83–84, 112, 118, 369
mood 65
more emotional responses (definition) 65–66
mutism 7, 277

nail biting 90, 97, 197
name calling 57
National Association for the Education of Young Children (NAEYC) 1–*2*
nature vs. nurture 1, 16
neurodiversity 20, 110; *see also* Autism Spectrum Disorder
non-verbal communication *see* communication

observations 35
Oppositional Defiant Disorder (ODD) 28
oppression 16, 22, 89, 198
over reactive (definition) *51*–52

pacing 46, 67, 69, 100–101, 113, 115, 117, 160–*161*, 367
parallel play 112
parent(s) 2–*4*, 19, 21, 24–25, 30, 33, 39–41, 45, 58 66, 69, 75, 77, 80–84, 89, 93, 96, 102, 104, 107–108, 112, 119, 124, 225, 277, 319–320
passive aggressive 76, 79
persistence 23, 45, *47*, 71, 73
persona (definition) 52–*53*, 54
personal space 19–20, *32*, *36*, 97, 100, 106, 247–*248*
personality 23, 30, 58
personality component 23–24
physical abuse 319; *see also* maltreatment
Piaget, Jean 17, 49, 84
play 1, 5, *32*, *36*, 44, 82, 88, 90, 93, 97, 104–105, 107, 112, 116, 224, 276, 319–*320*
praise 42, 368
prejudice 198
projection 90, 92, 94
projective identification 94–95
psychological defenses 75, 90, 94; *see also* ego defenses; Freud, Anna
psychotherapy 1–2, 5–6, 21, 60, 101, 119

quiet communication (definition) 49, 52

race 1
re-enactment 77–83, 98
Regoli, Robert 7
regression 75; *see also* Kris, Ernst
relatedness 25, *47*

repetition compulsion 77, 98; *see also* Freud, Sigmund
repetitive movements 112–113
rescue fantasy 85, 102, 319
resistant *23*, *46*–47
risk-taking 36
Rogers, Carl 5, *7*, 60, 84; *see also* corrective emotional experience; humanistic model
roles 26, 77, 102, 301, 366, 369; in a dysfunctional family system 82
rules 21, 24, 49–51, 60, 74, 79, 81, 105, 116–117
running away 160; *see also* elopement

sadness 35, 39, 61, 74–75, 82, 85; in teacher 26
safety 3–*4*, 16, 23, *25*, 29, 36–37, 38, 61, 69–70, 90, 100, 102, *160*, 321
Satir, Virginia 77; *see also* family dysfunction
scab picking 90, 97
schema 84; *see also* Piaget, Jean
self-awareness 60, 66, 79, 82, 108–109, *111*–112, 114, 116–117, 127–128
self-disclosure 83, 91, *118*
self-fulfilling prophecy 62–*63*, 64–65, 74, *78*, *95*–96, *111*; *see also* Merton, Robert
sensory seeking 19–20, 23, 45–*47*, 107
separation *6*, *18*, 25–26, 31–*32*, *247*–*248*; *see also* Mahler, Margaret
separation anxiety 26
sexual abuse 300, 319
silliness 75, 78; *see also* clowning; joking
sleep 22, 39, *47*, 58
sports 21, 24, 224
structural responses (definition) *65*–66
symbolization 76, 82, 84, 99, 117; *see also* unsymbolized

talking excessively 224
teasing 74, 87, 197–198
temper tantrum 25, 58, 61, 247
temperament *6*, 17, *23*–24, 44–54; *see also* Chess, Stella
testing limits 25, 50, 56, 60, 71, 85, 160
Thomas, Alexander *6*, *23*–24, 45–*47*; *see also* Chess, Stella; temperament
toileting 33, 75, 88, 90, *301*
touching (inappropriate) 90, 97
transference 98
transitional space 87–88, 90–92, 102, 105–106, 114, *118*
trauma 16, 101–102
trust 3, 6, *18*–19, 25, 61, 63–64, 67, 90, 99, 117–118; *see also* Erikson, Erik

under reactive (definition) *51*–52
unsymbolized 76, 82, 84, 99, 117; *see also* symbolization

verbal responses (definition) *65*–66

violence 22, 87–88, 97, 318–321

Winnicott, D.W. *6*, 24, 26, 34, 61, 87, 102; *see also* good-enough teaching; holding environment
withdrawn (withdrawal) *23*, 25, 31, 45, *47*–48, 51, *63*
writing (concerning) 87, 320–321

www.ingramcontent.com/pod-product-compliance
Lightning Source LLC
Chambersburg PA
CBHW060334010526
44117CB00017B/2822